Keras to Kubernetes®

The Journey of a Machine Learning Model to Production

Dattaraj Jagdish Rao

WILEY

Keras to Kubernetes®: The Journey of a Machine Learning Model to Production

Published by
John Wiley & Sons, Inc.
10475 Crosspoint Boulevard
Indianapolis, IN 46256
`www.wiley.com`

ISBN: 978-1-119-56483-6
ISBN: 978-1-119-56487-4 (ebk)
ISBN: 978-1-119-56486-7 (ebk)

Manufactured in the United States of America

C10009311_040919

Library of Congress Control Number: 2019933735

To my late father Jagdish Rao, who taught me to love books and showed me the power of the written word.

Acknowledgments

The author would like to thank all his current and former colleagues at General Electric (GE), who have inspired and taught him so much over the years. Particularly his mentors – Ravi Salagame, Eric Haynes, Anthony Maiello, and Wesley Mukai. He would like to thank team members from several artificial intelligence projects who helped invigorate his interest in this field – Nidhi Naithani, Shruti Mittal, Ranjitha Kurup, S. Ritika, Nikhil Naphade, and Scott Nelson. Also, the excellent CTO team from GE Transportation – Aaron Mitti, Mark Kraeling, Shalinda Ranasinghe, Ninad Kulkarni, Anatoly Melamud, Ankoor Patel, Richard Baker, and Gokulnath Chidambaram. The author also thanks his friends from Goa Engineering college and Peoples High school.

The author would like to immensely thank his editor, Kezia Endsley, for all her patience and expertise. She was absolutely amazing helping structure the content of the book and making it more readable. Kezia's attention to detail was second to none and she was able to point out key issues that helped make the writing better. The author would like to thank his technical editor, Kunal Mittal, for sharing his wealth of knowledge to greatly improve content of the book. The author would like to thank Devon Lewis at Wiley for initiating this project and providing his valuable guidance. Also, the author would like to thank all the great folks at Wiley who helped get this book to market – particularly his production editor Athiyappan Lalith Kumar.

The author would like to thank his mom Ranjana for being his pillar of strength and his wonderful kids, Varada and Yug. Last but not least, the author thanks his wife Swati for being the source of inspiration for writing this book. She is the one who put the thought in his head and motivated him throughout completion of this work.

About the Author

Dattaraj Rao works as a principal architect at General Electric (GE) and is based in Bangalore, India. He is a Mechanical Engineer by education and spent the last 19 years at GE building software that monitors and controls industrial machines like gas turbines, compressors, and locomotives. He started his career at Global Research working on knowledge-based engineering for product design. Then he joined GE Power at Norfolk, VA as the lead for gas turbine condition monitoring software. He held several roles at GE Power, including Chief Software Architect for the remote monitoring and diagnostics business. Dattaraj moved back to India in 2013 and joined GE Transportation as innovation leader for programs on video analytics and prognostics.

Currently, Dattaraj leads the Analytics and Artificial Intelligence (AI) strategy for the transportation business. He is building Industrial IoT solutions that drive outcomes like predictive maintenance, machine vision, and digital twins. His team is building a state-of-the-art Machine Learning platform to address major data science concerns like data cleansing, preparation, model selection, hyper-parameter tuning, distributed training, and automated deployment. This platform based on Kubernetes will host the next generation industrial Internet solutions for transportation.

He has 11 patents filed through GE and is a certified GE Analytics Engineer. He holds a bachelor's degree in Mechanical Engineering from Goa Engineering College, India.

You can reach him at `dattarajrao@yahoo.com` or `linkedin.com/in/dattarajrao` or on Twitter `@DattarajR`.

About the Technical Editor

Kunal Mittal has worked in information technology for over 20 years and is an advisor and CTO consultant for multiple startups. He was most recently the CTO for a 2 billion dollar publicly traded company called MINDBODY. Kunal's passion is solving business problems with the effective use of technology and is known for building high performing and effective teams. His focus is driving product to achieve business outcomes while fostering an environment of innovation and agility in the delivery processes.

Kunal is a published author and technical reviewer of 40+ technical books on Cloud computing, service oriented architectures, Java, J2EE, and every major mobile platform.

Credits

Acquisitions Editor
Devon Lewis

Associate Publisher
Jim Minatel

Editorial Manager
Pete Gaughan

Production Manager
Katie Wisor

Project Editor
Kezia Endsley

Production Editor
Athiyappan Lalith Kumar

Technical Editor
Kunal Mittal

Copy Editor
Kim Cofer

Proofreader
Nancy Bell

Indexer
Johnna VanHoose Dinse

Cover Designer
Wiley

Cover Image
©nopparit/iStockphoto

Contents

Introduction

Welcome! This book introduces the topics of Machine Learning (ML) and Deep Learning (DL) from a practical perspective. I try to explain the basics of how these techniques work and the core algorithms involved. The main focus is on building real-world systems using these techniques. I see many ML and DL books cover the algorithms extensively but not always show a clear path to deploying these algorithms into production systems. Also, we often see a big gap in understanding around how these Artificial Intelligence (AI) systems can be scaled to handle large volume of data—also referred to as Big Data.

Today we have systems like Docker and Kubernetes that help us package our code and seamlessly deploy to large on-premise or Cloud systems. Kubernetes takes care of all the low-level infrastructure concerns like scaling, fail-over, load balancing, networking, storage, security, etc. I show how your ML and DL projects can take advantage of the rich features that Kubernetes provides. I focus on deployment of the ML and DL algorithms at scale and tips to handle large volumes of data.

I talk about many popular algorithms and show how you can build systems using them. I include code examples that are heavily commented so you can easily follow and possibly reproduce the examples. I use an example of a DL model to read images and classify logos of popular brands. Then this model is deployed on a distributed cluster so it can handle large volumes of client requests. This example shows you an end-to-end approach for building and deploying a DL model in production.

I also provide references to books and websites that cover details of items I do not cover fully in this book.

How This Book Is Organized

The first half of the book (Chapters 1–5) focuses on Machine Learning (ML) and Deep Learning (DL). I show examples of building ML models with code (in Python) and show examples of tools that automate this process. I also show an example of building an image classifier model using the Keras library and TensorFlow framework. This logo-classifier model is used to distinguish between the Coca-Cola and Pepsi logos in images.

In the second half of the book (Chapters 6–10), I talk about how these ML and DL models can actually be deployed in a production environment. We talk about some common concerns that data scientists have and how software developers can implement these models. I explain an example of deploying our earlier logo-classifier model at scale using Kubernetes.

Conventions Used

Italic terms indicate key concepts I want to draw attention to and which will be good to grasp.

`Underlined references` are references to other books or publications or external web links.

Code examples in Python will be shown as follows:

```
# This box carries code - mainly in Python
import tensorflow as tf
```

Results from code are shown as follows:

`Results from code are shown as a picture or in this font below the code box.`

Who Should Read This Book

This book is intended for software developers and data scientists. I talk about developing Machine Learning (ML) models, connecting these to application code, and deploying them as microservices packaged as Docker containers. Modern software systems are heavily driven by ML and I feel that data scientists and software developers can both benefit by knowing enough about each other's discipline.

Whether you are a beginner at software/data science or an expert in the field, I feel there will be something in this book for you. Although a programming background is best to understand the examples well, the code and examples are targeted to very general audience. The code presented is heavily commented as well, so it should be easy to follow. Although I have used Python and specific libraries—Scikit-Learn, and Keras—you should be able to find equivalent functions and convert the code to other languages and libraries like R, MATLAB, Java, SAS, C++, etc.

My effort is to provide as much theory as I can so you don't need to go through the code to understand the concepts. The code is very practical and helps you adapt the concepts to your data very easily. You are free (and encouraged) to copy the code and try the examples with your own datasets.

NOTE **All the code is available for free on my GitHub site listed here. This site also contains sample datasets and images we use in examples. Datasets are in comma-separated values (CSV) and are in the `data` folder.**

```
https://github.com/dattarajrao/keras2kubernetes
```

Tools You Will Need

My effort is to provide as much theory about the concepts as possible. The code is practical and commented to help you understand. Like most data scientists today, my preference is to use the Python programming language. You can install the latest version of Python from `https://www.python.org/`.

Using Python

A popular way to write Python code is using Jupyter Notebooks. It is a browser-based interface for running your Python code. You open a web page in a browser and write Python code that gets executed and you see the results right there on the same web page. It has an excellent user-friendly interface and shows you immediate results by executing individual code cells. The examples I present are also small blocks of code that you can quickly run separately in a Jupyter Notebook. This can be installed from `http://jupyter.org`.

The big advantage of Python is its rich set of libraries for solving different problems. We particularly use the Pandas library for loading and manipulating data to be used for building our ML models. We also use Scikit-Learn, which is a popular library that provides implementation for most of the ML techniques. These libraries are available from the following links:

```
https://pandas.pydata.org/
https://scikit-learn.org/
```

Using the Frameworks

Specifically, for Deep Learning, we use a framework for building our models. There are multiple frameworks available, but the one we use for examples is Google's TensorFlow. TensorFlow has a good Python interface we use to write Deep Learning code in Python. We use Keras, which is a high-level abstraction library that runs on top of TensorFlow. Keras comes packaged with TensorFlow. You can install TensorFlow for Python from `https://www.tensorflow.org`.

One disclaimer. TensorFlow, although production-ready, is under active development by Google. It releases new versions every two to three months, which is unprecedented for normal software development. But because of today's world of Agile development and continuous integration practices, Google is able to release huge functionalities in weeks rather than months. Hence the code I show for Deep Learning in Keras and TensorFlow may need updating to the latest version of the library. Usually this is pretty straightforward. The concepts I discuss will still be valid; you just may need to update the code periodically.

Setting Up a Notebook

If you don't want to set up your own Python environment, you can get a hosted notebook running entirely in the Cloud. That way all you need is a computer with an active Internet connection to run all the Python code. There are no libraries or frameworks to install. All this by using the magic of Cloud computing. Two popular choices here are Amazon's SageMaker and Google's Colaboratory. I particularly like Colaboratory for all the Machine Learning library support.

Let me show you how to set up a notebook using Google's Cloud-hosted programming environment, called *Colaboratory*. A special shout-out to our friends at Google, who made this hosted environment available for free to anyone with a Google account. To set up the environment, make sure you have a Google account (if not, you'll need to create one). Then open your web browser and go to `https://colab.research.google.com`.

Google Colaboratory is a free (as of writing this book) Jupyter environment that lets you create a notebook and easily experiment with Python code. This environment comes pre-packaged with the best data science and Machine Learning libraries like Pandas, Scikit-Learn, TensorFlow, and Keras.

The notebooks (work files) you create will be stored on your Google Drive account. Once you're logged in, open a new Python 3 notebook, as shown in Figure 1.

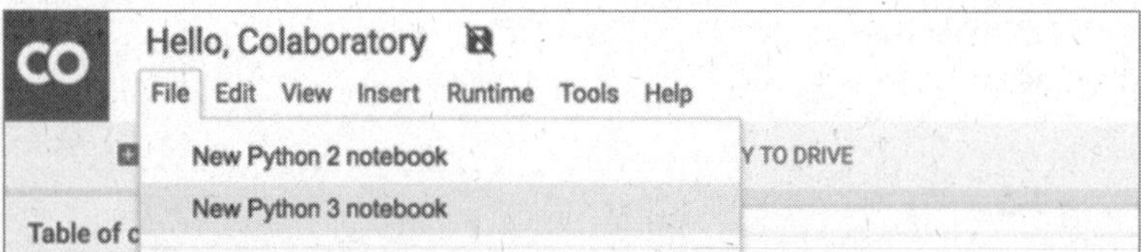

Figure 1: Opening a new notebook in Google Colaboratory

You will see a screen similar to the one in Figure 2, with your first Python 3 notebook called `Untitled1.pynb`. You can change the name to something relevant to you. Click Connect to connect to an environment and get started. This will commission a Cloud machine in the background and your code will run on that virtual machine. This is the beauty of working in a Cloud-hosted environment. You have all the processing, storage, and memory concerns handled by the Cloud and you can focus on your logic. This is an example of the Software-as-a-Service (SaaS) paradigm.

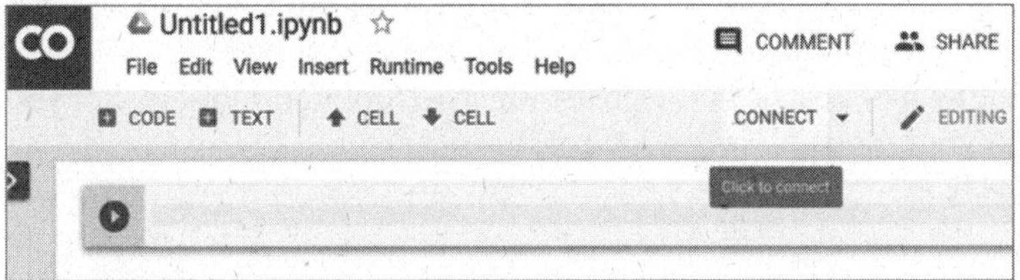

Figure 2: Click Connect to start the virtual machine

Once your notebook is connected to the Cloud runtime, you can add code cells and click the Play button on the slide to run your code. It's that simple. Once the code runs, you will see outputs popping up below the block. You can also add text blocks for informational material you want to include and format this text.

Figure 3 shows a simple example of a notebook with code snippets for checking the TensorFlow library and downloading a public dataset using the Pandas library. Remember that Python has a rich set of libraries that helps you load, process, and visualize data.

CO Simple Python Code

File Edit View Insert Runtime Tools Help

COMMENT SHARE

CODE TEXT CELL CELL ... BUSY EDITING

Simple Google Colaboratory Notebook example with Python code.

```
[1] import tensorflow as tf
    print(tf.__version__)

    1.10.1
```

Now we will open a simple CSV file and show its contents.

```
import pandas as pd
dataset = pd.read_csv('https://data.cityofchicago.org/api/views/pfsx-4n4m/rows.csv?accessType=DOWNLOAD')
dataset.head()
```

	ID	Traffic Volume Count Location Address	Street	Date of Count	Total Passing Vehicle Volume	Vehicle Volume By Each Direction of Traffic	Latitude	Longitude	Locati
0	2	1708 West	71st Street	03/09/2006	14600	East Bound: 6900 / West Bound: 7700	41.764877	-87.666635	(41.7648 -87.6666
1	3	1275 West	71st Street	02/28/2006	16500	East Bound: 7800 / West Bound: 8700	41.765008	-87.657067	(41.7650 -87.6570
2	5	920 West	71st Street	02/28/2006	18200	East Bound: 8800 / West Bound: 9400	41.765153	-87.647751	(41.7651 -87.6477
3	6	758 West	71st Street	02/28/2006	21600	East Bound: 10400 / West Bound: 11200	41.765204	-87.644371	(41.7652 -87.6443

Figure 3: Example of running code in a notebook

Finding a Dataset

Look at the second code block in Figure 3; it loads a CSV file from the Internet and shows the data in a data frame. This dataset shows traffic at different intersections in the city of Chicago. This dataset is maintained by the city.

Many such datasets are available for free, thanks to the amazing data science community. These datasets are cleansed and contain data in good format to be used for building models. These can be used to understand different ML algorithms and their effectiveness. You can find a comprehensive list at `https://catalog.data.gov/dataset?res_format=CSV`. You can search by typing **CSV** and clicking the CSV icon to download the dataset or copy the link.

Google also now has a dedicated website for searching for datasets that you can use to build your models. Have a look at this site at `https://toolbox.google.com/datasetsearch`.

Summary

We will now embark on a journey of building Machine Learning and Deep Learning models for real-world use cases. We will use the Python programming language and popular libraries for ML and DL, like Scikit-Learn, TensorFlow, and Keras. You could build an environment from scratch and try to work on the code provided in this book. Another option is to use a hosted notebook in Google's Colaboratory to run the code. There are many open datasets that are freely available for you to experiment with model building and testing. You can enhance your data science skills with these datasets. I show examples of the same. Let's get started!

CHAPTER

1

Big Data and Artificial Intelligence

Chapter 1 provides an overview of some of the hot trends in the industry around Big Data and Artificial Intelligence. We will see how the world is being transformed through digitization, leading to the Big Data phenomenon—both in the consumer and industrial spaces. We see data volumes increasing exponentially, from terabytes to exabytes to zettabytes. We see the processing power of computers increase in magnitudes of tens and hundreds. We will talk about software getting smarter with the application of Artificial Intelligence—whether it's IBM's Watson beating human champions at *Jeopardy!* or Facebook automatically tagging friends in your photos, or even Google's self-driving car. Finally, the chapter discusses the types of analytics and covers a simple example of building a system driven by analytics to deliver outcomes.

Data Is the New Oil and AI Is the New Electricity

We are living in the Internet age. Shopping on Amazon to booking cabs through Uber to binge-watching TV shows on Netflix—all these outcomes are enabled by the Internet. These outcomes involve huge volumes of data being constantly uploaded and downloaded from our computing devices to remote servers in the Cloud. The computing devices themselves are no longer restricted to personal computers, laptops, and mobile phones. Today, we have many more smart devices or "things" connected to the Internet, like TVs, air conditioners, washing machines, and more every day. These devices are powered with microprocessors just like in a computer and have communication interfaces to transfer data to the Cloud. These devices can upload their data to the Cloud using communication protocols like Wi-Fi, Bluetooth, and cellular. They can also download up-to-date content from remote servers, including the latest software updates.

The Internet of Things (IoT) is here to change our lives with outcomes that would easily fit in a science fiction novel from 10 years ago. We have fitness wristbands that suggest exercise routines based on our lifestyle, watches that monitor for heart irregularities, home electronics that listen to voice commands, and of course, the famous self-driving cars and trucks. These Internet-connected devices are smart enough to analyze complex data in the form of images, videos, and audio, understand their environments, predict expected results, and either take a recommended action or prescribe one to a human.

My Fitbit checks if I have not done enough exercise in a day and "asks" me politely to get up and start exercising. We have sensors that sense any absence of motion and shut off lights automatically if the room is empty. The Apple watch 4 has a basic EKG feature to measure your heart condition. Consumers of Tesla cars get new features delivered directly over the air through software updates. No need to visit the service shop. The modern IoT devices are not only connected but have the smarts to achieve some amazing outcomes, which were described only in science fiction novels just a few years back.

So great is the impact of this IoT revolution that we are now getting used to expecting such results. This technology is here to stay. The other day, my 4-year-old asked our Amazon Echo device, "Alexa, can you do my homework?" (See Figure 1.1.) The modern consumer is now expecting devices to provide these new outcomes. Anything less is becoming unacceptable!

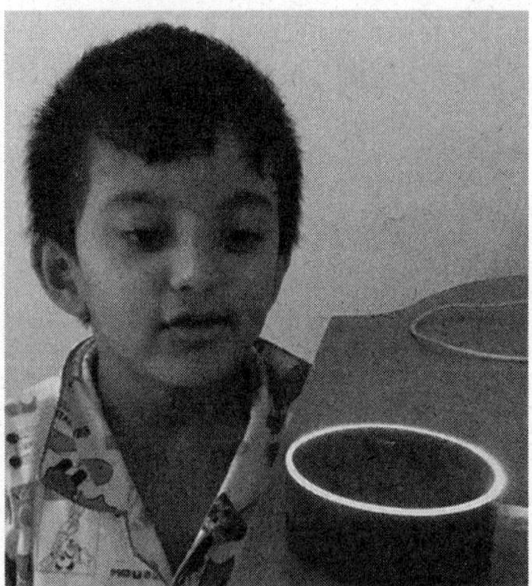

Figure 1.1: Alexa, can you do my homework?

Despite the diverse outcomes there is a common pattern to these IoT devices or "things." They have sensors to "observe" the environment and collect data. This data may be simple sensor readings like temperature measurements, to complex unstructured datatypes like sound and video. Some processing is done on the device itself, which is called *edge processing*. IoT devices usually have a very limited processing and storage capability due to their low cost. For larger processing and comparing to historical data, these devices upload data to a remote server or the Cloud. Newer advanced IoT devices have built-in connectivity to the Cloud with options like Wi-Fi, Bluetooth, or cellular. Low-power (and low-cost) devices usually use a gateway to connect and upload data to the Cloud. At the Cloud, the data can be processed on bigger, faster computers often arranged into large clusters in data centers. Also, we can combine the device data with historical data from the same device and from many other devices. This can generate new and more complex outcomes not possible at the edge alone. The results generated are then downloaded back to the device using the same connectivity options. These IoT devices may also need to be managed remotely with timely software updates and configuration—that is also done through the Cloud. Figure 1.2 shows a very high-level overview with the scale of data handled at each level.

We are putting billions of smart connected devices on the Internet. We have smartphones capturing, storing, and transferring terabytes of photos and videos. Security cameras collect video feeds 24×7. GPS devices, RFID tags, and fitness trackers continuously monitor, track, and report motion. We have moved our library off the shelves and into hundreds of eBooks on our Kindles. We moved from tapes and CDs to MP3s to downloaded music libraries on apps. Netflix consumes 15% of the world's Internet bandwidth. And all this is only the consumer Internet.

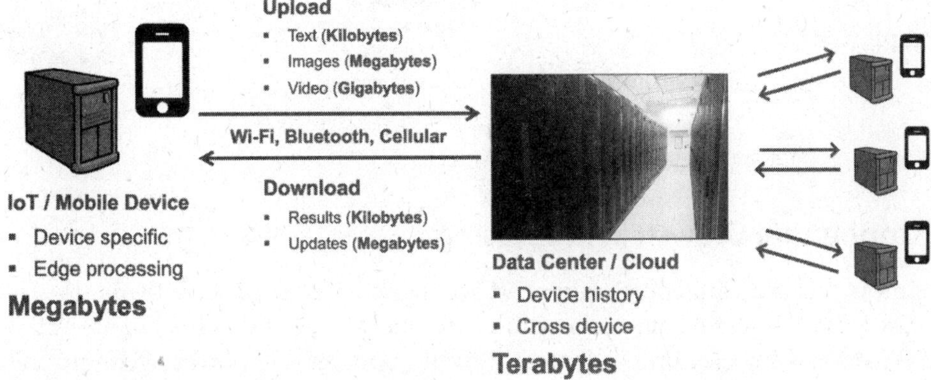

Figure 1.2: Data volumes on the consumer Internet

Rise of the Machines

There is a parallel data revolution happening in the industrial world with even bigger outcomes. This is a whole new Internet being championed by companies like General Electric, Siemens, Bosch, etc., especially for industrial applications. It's known as the Industrial Internet or Industry 4.0 in Europe. Instead of smaller consumer devices, heavy machinery like gas turbines, locomotives, and MRI machines are transformed into smart devices and connected to the Internet. These machines are upgraded with advanced sensors, connectivity, and processing power to enable edge analytics and connectivity to the industrial Cloud. Industrial machines generate terabytes and petabytes of data every day, probably much more than consumer devices. This needs to be processed in real-time to understand what the machine is telling us and how we can improve its performance. We need to be able to, by observing sensor data, determine that an aircraft is due for service and should not be sent on a flight. Our MRI scanners should have extremely high accuracy to be able to capture images that can provide enough evidence for a doctor to diagnose a condition.

You can clearly see from Figure 1.3 that the scales of data increase in the industrial world along with the criticality of processing the data and generating outcomes in time. We can wait a couple of seconds for our favorite *Black Mirror* episode to buffer up. But a few seconds' delay in getting MRI results to a doctor may be fatal for the patient!

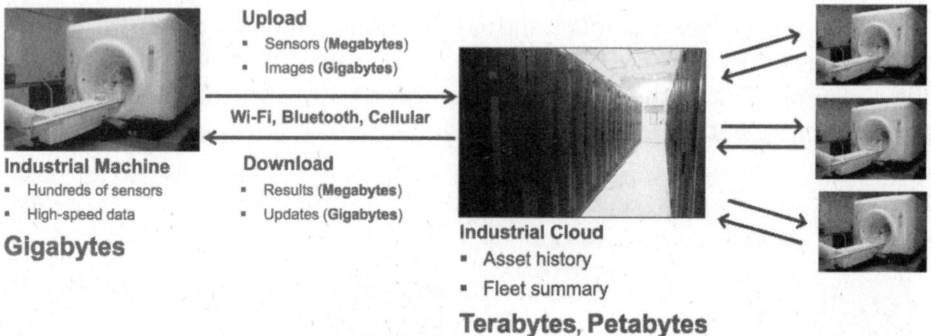

Figure 1.3: Data volumes on the industrial Internet

Exponential Growth in Processing

This is the Big Data revolution and we are all a part of it. All this data is of little use, unless we have a way to process it in time and extract value out of it. We are seeing an unprecedented growth in processing power of computing devices and a similar rise in storage capacity. Moore's Law of electronics states that the processing power of a computing device doubles every two years due to improvements in electronics. Basically, we can pack twice the number of transistors in the same form factor and double the processing power. Modern computing technology is making this law pretty much obsolete. We are seeing a growth of 10–100 times each year in processing power using advanced processors like NVIDIA GPU, Google TPU, and specialized FPGAs integrated using the System-on-Chip (SoC) technology. When we think of a computer, it is no longer a bulky screen with a keyboard and a CPU tower sitting on a table. We have microprocessors installed in televisions, air conditioners, washing machines, trains, airplanes, and more. Data storage volumes are rising from terabytes to petabytes and exabytes and now we have a new term introduced to describe Big Data, the *zettabyte*. We are getting good at improving processing on the device (edge) and moving the more intensive storage and processing to the Cloud.

This growth in data and processing power is driving improvements in the type of analysis we do on the data. Traditionally, we would program the computing devices with specific instructions to follow and they would diligently run these algorithms without question. Now we expect these devices to be smarter and use this large data to get better outcomes. We don't just want predefined rules to run all the time—but we want to achieve outcomes we talked of earlier. These devices need to think like a human. We are expecting computers to develop a visual and audio perception of the world through voice and optical sensors. We expect computers to plan our schedules like a human assistant would—to tell us in advance if our car will have issues based on the engine overheating and respond to us like a human with answers to questions we ask.

A New Breed of Analytics

All this needs a whole new paradigm shift in the way we conceptualize and build analytics. We are moving from predefined rule-based methods to building Artificial Intelligence (AI) in our processing systems. Our traditional algorithmic methods for building analytics cannot keep up with the tremendous increase in the volume, velocity, and variety of data these systems handle. We now need specialized applications that were so far thought only possible by the human brain and not programmed in computers. Today, we have computers learning to do intelligent tasks and even out-performing humans at them. Dr. Andrew Ng, Stanford Professor and the founder of Coursera, famously said, "AI is the new electricity." During the Industrial Revolution, just as electricity touched every industry and every aspect of human life and totally transformed it—we are seeing AI doing the exact same thing. AI is touching so many areas of our lives and enabling outcomes that were considered impossible for computers. Big Data and AI are transforming all aspects of our lives and changing the world!

Examples of AI performing smart tasks are recognizing people in photos (Google Photos), responding to voice commands (Alexa), playing video games, looking at MRI scans to diagnose patients, replying to chat messages, self-driving cars, detecting fraudulent transactions on credit cards, and many more. These were all considered specialized tasks that only humans could do. But we now have computer systems starting to do this even better than humans. We have examples like IBM's Watson, an AI computer beating the chess grandmaster. Self-driving trucks can take cross-country trips in the United States. Amazon Alexa can listen to your command, interpret it, and respond with an answer—all in a matter of seconds. The same holds for the industrial Internet. With many recent examples—like autonomous trucks and trains, and power plants moving to predictive maintenance and airlines able to anticipate delays before takeoff—we see AI driving major outcomes in the industrial world. See Figure 1.4.

Figure 1.4: AI for computer vision at a railway crossing

AI is starting to play a role in areas that no one would have thought of just 2 or 3 years ago. Recently there was news about a painting purely generated by AI that sold for a whopping $432,500. The painting sold by Christie's NY was titled "Edmond de Belamy, from La Famille de Belamy." This painting was generated by an AI algorithm called *Generative Adversarial Networks* (GAN). You will see examples and code to generate images with AI in Chapter 6. Maybe you can plan your next painting with AI and try to fetch a good price!

Another interesting AI project was done by the NVIDIA researchers to take celebrity face images and generate new ones. The result was some amazing new images that looked absolutely real, but did not belong to any celebrity. They were fakes! Using random numbers and patterns learned by "watching" real celebrity photos, the super-smart AI was able to create indistinguishable fakes. We will see cool AI examples like these in Chapter 6.

What Makes AI So Special

Imagine a security camera system at a railway crossing. It captures terabytes of video feeds from multiple cameras 24×7. It synchronizes feeds from several cameras and shows them on a screen along with timing information from each video. Now a human can look at this feed live or play back a specific time to understand what happens. In this case, the computer system handles the capturing and storing of data in the right format, synchronizing several feeds and displaying them on a common dashboard. It performs these tasks extremely efficiently without getting tired or complaining.

A human does the actual interpretation of the videos. If we want to check if there are people crossing the track as a train is about to approach, we rely on a human to check this in the feed and report back. Similar surveillance systems are used to detect suspicious behavior in public spaces or fire hazards on a ship or unattended luggage at an airport. The final analysis needs to be done by the human brain to pick up the patterns of interest and act on them. The human brain has amazing processing power and built-in intelligence. It has the intelligence to process hundreds of images per second and interpret them to look for items of interest (people, fires, etc.). The drawback is that humans are prone to fatigue over time and tend to make errors. Over time, if a security guard continuously watches live feeds, he or she is bound to get tired and may miss important events.

Artificial Intelligence is all about building human-like intelligence into computing systems. With the security feed example, along with displaying the synchronized video feeds, the system can also recognize significant activities, which builds an AI system. To do this, the system needs more than just large data and processing power. It needs some smart algorithms that understand and extract patterns in data and use these to make predictions on new data. These smart algorithms constitute the "brain" of our AI system and help it perform human-like activities.

Normal computer systems are very good at performing repetitive tasks. They need to be explicitly programmed with the exact instructions to perform actions on data and they will continuously run these actions on any new data that comes in the system. We program these instructions in code and the computer has no problem executing this code over and over millions of times. Modern computing systems can also handle parallel processing by running multiple jobs simultaneously on multi-core processors. However, each job is still a predetermined sequence programmed in it. This is where the earlier activity of processing video feeds and showing on a display fit perfectly. You can feed the system with footage from hundreds of cameras simultaneously and it will keep formatting the video, store it, and display it on-screen without any loss—as long as the computing resources (CPU, memory, and storage) are adequate. We can have hundreds of video feeds coming into the system and it will do an excellent job storing them, synchronizing them, and displaying them on-screen for us.

However, in order to understand these videos and extract valuable knowledge from them, it needs a totally different capability. This capability that we as humans have taken for granted is known as intelligence...and is a pretty big deal for computers. Intelligence helps us look at videos and understand what is happening inside them. Intelligence helps us read hundreds of pages of a book and summarize the story to a friend in a few words. Intelligence helps us learn to play a game of chess and over time get good at it. If we can somehow push this intelligence into computers then we have a lethal combination of speed and intelligence, which can help us do some amazing things. This is what Artificial Intelligence is all about!

Applications of Artificial Intelligence

AI has found many applications in our lives. As we speak, more AI applications are being developed by smart engineers to improve different aspects of our lives.

A very popular application of AI is in *knowledge representation*. This involves trying to replicate the human brain's super-ability to store large volumes of information in a manner that's easy to retrieve and correlate with so as to answer a question. If I ask you about your first day at your first ever job you probably remember it pretty well and hopefully have fond memories. You may not do so well remembering, say, the 15th day, unless something major happened then. Our brain is very good at storing large volumes of information that is relevant along with a context for it. So, when needed it can quickly look up the right information based on the context and retrieve it. Similarly, an AI system needs to convert volumes of raw data into knowledge that can be stored with context and easily retrieved to find answers. A good example of this is IBM's Watson, which is a supercomputer that is able to learn by reading millions of documents over the Internet and storing this knowledge internally. Watson was able to use this knowledge to answer questions and beat human experts at the game of *Jeopardy!*. IBM is also teaching Watson medical diagnosis knowledge so that Watson can help develop medical prescriptions like a doctor. See Figure 1.5.

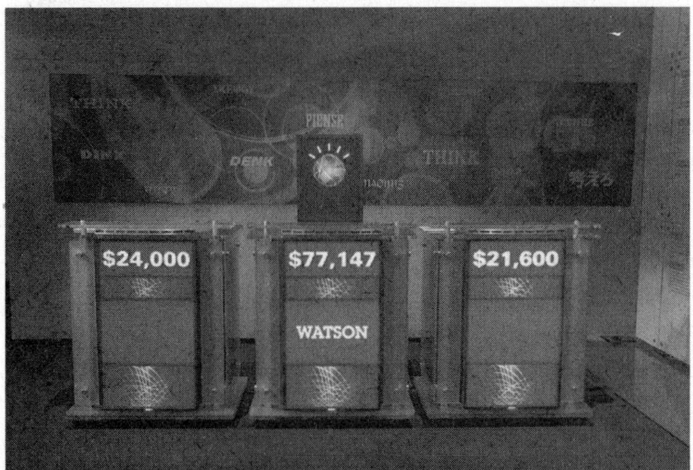

Figure 1.5: IBM Watson beating *Jeopardy!* champions
(*Source*: Wikimedia)

Another popular and even cooler application of AI is in building a sense of perception in machines. Here the computer inside of a machine collects and interprets data from advanced sensors to help the machine understand its environment. Think of a self-driving car that uses cameras, LiDAR, RADAR, and ultrasound sensors to locate objects on the road. Self-driving cars have AI computers that help them look for pedestrians, cars, signs, and signals on the road and make sure they avoid obstacles and follow traffic rules. Figure 1.6 shows Google's self-driving car, Waymo.

Figure 1.6: Google's self-driving autonomous car
(*Source*: Wikimedia)

AI can also be used for strategy and planning, where we have smart agents that know how to interact with real-world objects and achieve given objectives. This could be an AI beating the Grandmaster at a game of chess or an industrial agent or robot picking up your online orders from an Amazon warehouse and preparing your shipment in the fastest manner.

More applications of AI include recommendation engines like Amazon uses, which propose the next items you may be interested in based on your purchase history. Or Netflix recommending a movie you will like based on past movies you have seen. Online advertisement is a huge area where AI is used to understand patterns in human activity and improve visibility to products for sale. Google and Facebook automatically tagging photos of your friends is also done using AI.

Video surveillance is another area that is being revolutionized by AI. Recently many police teams have started using AI to identify persons of interest from video footage from security cameras and then track these people. AI can do much more than just find people in security footage. We are seeing AI understand human expressions and body posture to detect people with signs of fatigue, anger, acts of violence, etc. Hospitals use camera feeds with AI to see if patients are expressing high levels of stress and inform the doctor. Modern cars, trucks, and trains use driver cameras to detect if a driver is under stress or getting drowsy and then try to avoid accidents.

Last but not least, the industry that was one of the foremost to start adopting it and is making the most of the latest advances in AI is video gaming. Almost all modern games have an AI engine that can build a strategy for gameplay and play against the user. Some of the modern games have such an amazing engine that it captures the flawless rendition of the real world. For example, in my favorite game, *Grand Theft Auto V*, the railway crossing interactions are extremely realistic. The AI inside the game captures all aspects of stopping the traffic, flashing crossing lights, passing the train, and then opening the gates to allow traffic to pass, absolutely perfectly. Using methods like Reinforcement Learning, games can learn different strategies to take actions and build agents that can compete with humans and keep us entertained.

The field of AI that has really jumped in prominence and attention over the past years is Machine Learning (ML). This will be our area of focus for this book. ML is all about learning from data, extracting patterns, and using these patterns to make predictions. While most people put ML as a category under AI, you will find that modern ML is pretty much a major influencer in different areas of AI applications. In fact, you may struggle to find AI without some learning element of ML. If you think back to the different AI applications we discussed, ML touches all of them in some way or another.

IBM Watson builds a knowledge base and learns from this using Natural Language Processing (an area of ML) to be good at prescribing solutions.

Self-driving cars use ML models—more specifically Deep Learning (DL) models—to process huge volumes of unstructured data to extract valuable knowledge like location of pedestrians, other cars, and traffic signals. An agent playing chess uses Reinforcement Learning, which is again an area of ML. The agent tries to learn different policies by observing games of chess over and over again and finally gets good enough to beat a human. This can be compared to how a child learns to play the game too, but in a highly accelerated fashion. Finally, the robot finding your items and preparing your order is mimicking what 10 or more warehouse workers would be doing—of course, without the lunch break!

One topic gaining a lot of attention in the world of AI is *Artificial General Intelligence* (AGI). This is an advanced AI that is almost indistinguishable from humans. It can do almost all the intellectual tasks that a human can. Basically, it can fool humans into thinking that it's human. This is the kind of the stuff you will see on TV shows like *Black Mirror* or *Person of Interest*. I remember during a 2018 Google event that CEO Sundar Pichai demonstrated how their virtual assistant could make an appointment calling a restaurant (see Figure 1.7). The reservations attendant could not tell that a computer was on the other end of the line. This demo spun off many AI ethics debates and lots of criticism of Google for misleading people. Sure enough, Google issued an apology and released an AI ethics policy basically saying they won't use AI for harm. However, the fact remains that AI capability is maturing by the day and will greatly influence our lives more and more.

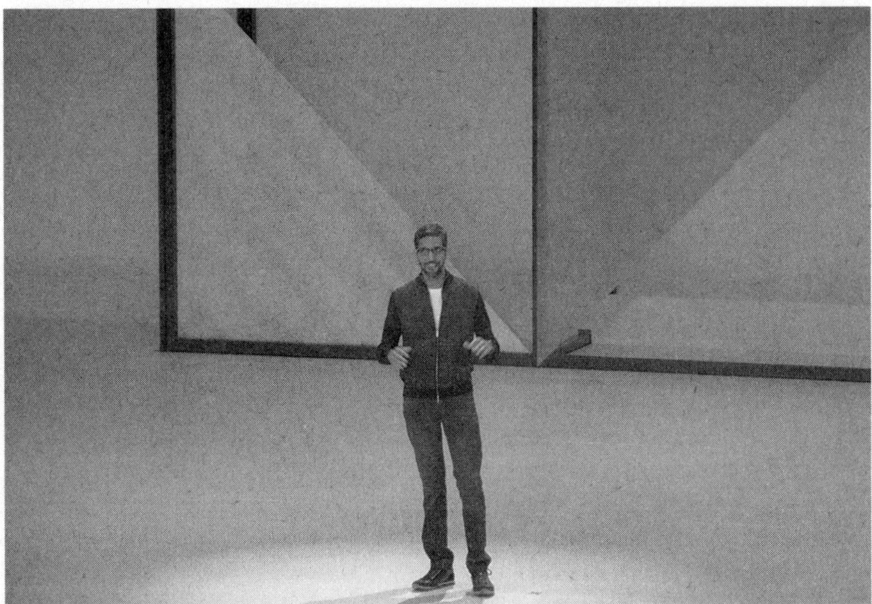

Figure 1.7: Google CEO demonstrating Duplex virtual assistant fooling the reservations attendant
(*Source*: Wikimedia)

Building Analytics on Data

Development of analytics depends on the problem you are trying to solve. Based on the intended outcome you are chasing, you first need to understand what data is available, what can be made available, and what techniques you can use to process it. Data collected from the system under investigation may be human inputs, sensor readings, existing sources like databases, images and videos from cameras, audio signals, etc. If you are building a system from scratch, you may have the freedom to decide which parameters you want to measure and what sensors to install. However, in most cases you will be dealing with digitizing an existing system with limited scope to measure new parameters. You may have to use whatever existing sensors and data sources are available.

Sensors measure particular physical characteristics and convert them into electrical signals and then into a series of numbers to analyze. Sensors measure characteristics of a system under study like motion, temperature, pressure, images, audio, video, etc. These are usually located at strategic positions so as to give you maximum details about the system. For example, a security camera should be placed so that it covers the maximum area you want to watch over. Some cars have ultrasound sensors attached at the back that measure distance from objects to help you when you're reversing. These physical characteristics are measures and converted into electrical signals by sensors. These electrical signals then flow through a signal processing circuit and get converted into numbers that you can analyze using a computer.

If our system already has sensors collecting data or existing databases with system data, then we can use this historical data to understand our system. Otherwise, we may have to install sensors and run the system for some time to collect data. Engineering systems also use simulators to generate data very similar to how a real system would. We can then use this data to build our processing logic—that is our analytic. For example, if we want to build temperature control logic to simulate thermostat data, we can simulate different temperature variations in a room. Then we pass this data through our thermostat analytic—which is designed to increase or decrease heat flow in the room based on a set temperature. Another example of simulation may be generating data on different stock market conditions and using that to build an analytic that decided on buying and selling stock. This data collected either from a real system or simulator can also be used to train an AI system to learn patterns and make decisions on different states of the system.

Whether you are building an AI- or non-AI–based analytic—the general pattern for building is the same—you read inputs from data sources, build the processing logic, test this logic on real or simulated data, and deploy it to the system to generate desired outputs. Mathematically speaking, all these inputs and outputs whose values can keep varying over time are called variables. The inputs are usually called *independent variables* (or Xs) and the outputs are called *dependent variables* (or Ys). Our analytic tries to build a relationship between our dependent and independent variables. We will use this terminology in the rest of the book as we describe the different AI algorithms.

Our analytic tries to express or map our Ys as a function of our Xs (see Figure 1.8). This could be a simple math formula or a complex neural network that maps independent variables to dependent ones. We could know the details of the formula—meaning that we know the intrinsic details about how our system behaves. Or the relationship may be a black box where we don't know any details and only use the black box to predict outputs based on inputs. There may be an internal relationship between our dependent variables or Xs. However, typically we choose to ignore that and focus on the X-Y relationships.

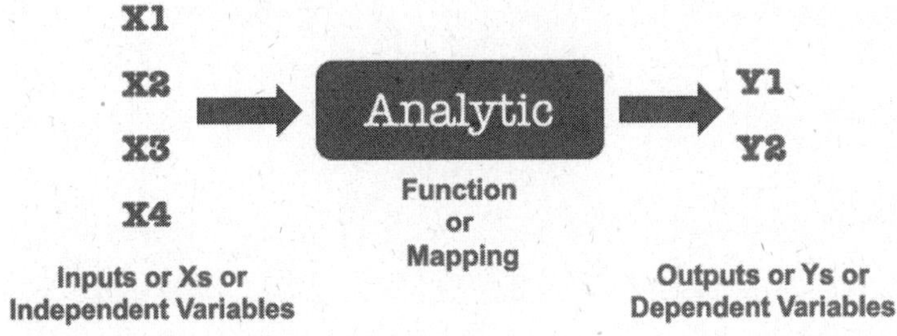

Figure 1.8: Expressing Ys as a function of Xs

Types of Analytics: Based on the Application

The job of the analytic is to produce outputs by processing input data from the system so humans can make decisions based on the system. It is extremely important to first understand the question we want to ask the system, before jumping into building the analytic. Based on the question we are asking, there may be four categories of analytics. The following sections explain some examples with the questions they try to answer.

Descriptive Analytics: What Happened?

These are the simplest kind but are also very important because they try to clearly describe the data. The outputs here may be statistical summaries like mean, mode, and median. We could have visual aids like charts and histograms that help humans understand patterns in the data. Many business intelligence and reporting tools like Tableau, Sisense, QlikView, Crystal Reports, etc., are based on this concept. The idea is to provide users with a consolidated view of their data to help them make decisions. The example in Figure 1.9 shows which months we had a higher than usual monthly spending.

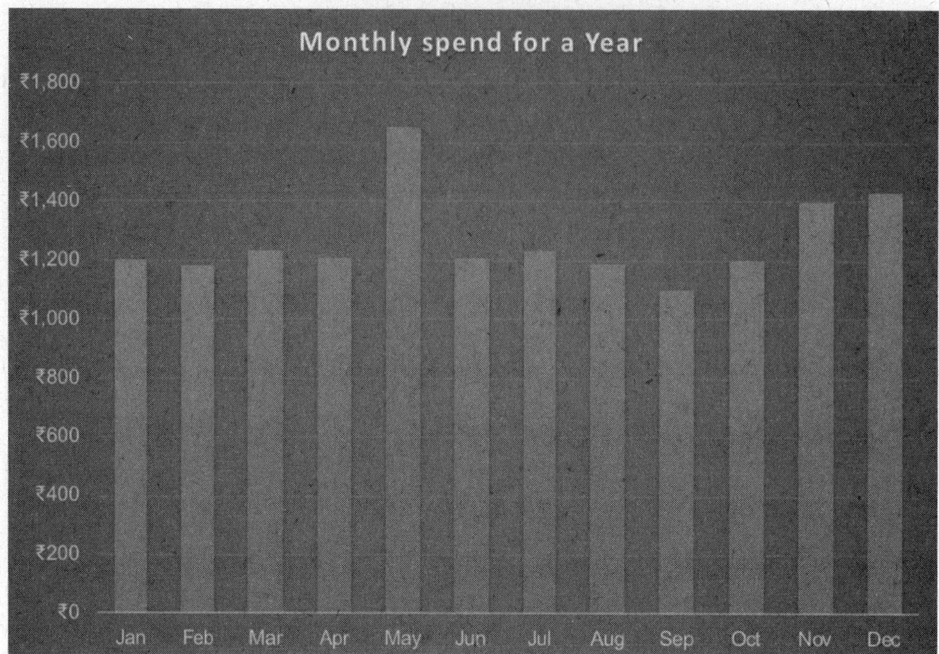

Figure 1.9: Describe the data to humans

Diagnostic Analytics: Why Did It Happen?

Here we try to diagnose something that happened and try to understand why it happened. The obvious example is when a doctor looks at your symptoms and diagnoses the presence of a disease. We have systems like WebMD that try to capture this amazing human intelligence that doctors possess and give us a quick initial diagnosis. Similarly, healthcare machines like MRI scanners use diagnostic analytics to try to isolate patterns of disease. This type of analytic is also very popular in industrial applications for diagnosing machines. Using sensor data, industrial control and safety systems use diagnostic rules to detect the presence of a failure occurring and try to stop the machine before major damage occurs.

We may use the same tools used in descriptive analytics like charts and summaries to diagnose issues. We may also use techniques like inferential statistics to identify root causes of certain events. In inferential statistics, we establish a hypothesis or assumption saying that our event is dependent on certain Xs in our problem. Then we collect data to see if we have enough data evidence to prove this assumption.

The analytic here will normally provide us with evidence regarding a particular event. The human still has to use her intuition to decide why the event occurred and what needs to be done. The example in Figure 1.10 shows how the engine oil temperature kept increasing, which might have caused the engine failure.

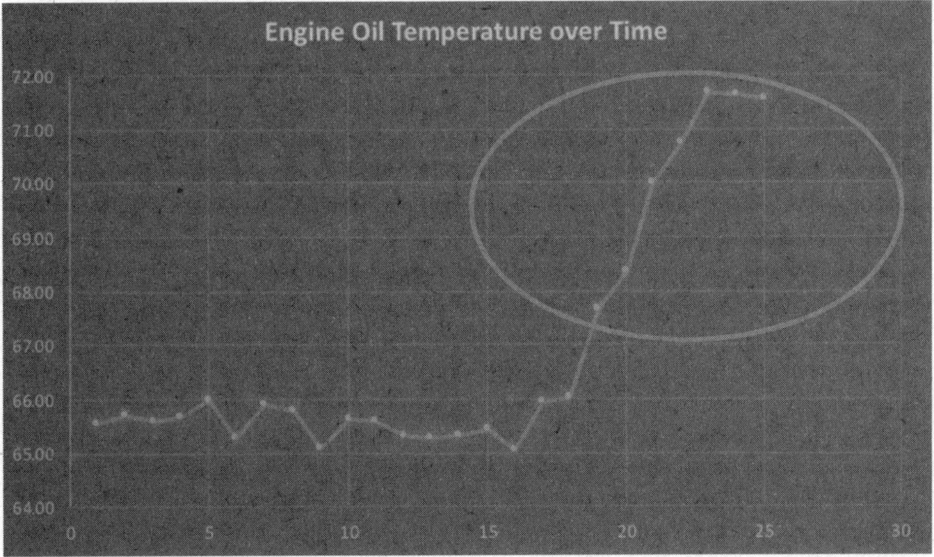

Figure 1.10: Diagnose an issue using data

Predictive Analytics: What Will Happen?

The previous two AI applications dealt with what happened in the past or in hindsight. Predictive analytics focus on the future or foresight. Here we use techniques like Machine Learning to learn from historical data and build models that predict the future. This is where we will primarily use AI to develop analytics that make predictions. Since we are making predictions here, these analytics extensively use probability to give us a confidence factor. We will cover this type of analytic case in the rest of the book.

The example in Figure 1.11 shows weather websites analyzing history data patterns to predict the weather.

Figure 1.11: Weather forecasting
(*Source*: weather.com)

Prescriptive Analytics: What to Do?

Now we take prediction one step further and prescribe an action. This is the most complex type of analytic and is still an active area of research and also some debate. Prescriptive can be looked as a type of predictive analytic; however, for an analytic to be prescriptive, it also clearly states an action the human must take. In some cases, if the confidence on the prediction is high enough, we may allow the analytic to take action on its own. This analytic depends heavily on the domain for which you are trying to make the prediction. To build impactful prescriptive analytics, we need to explore many advanced AI methods.

The example in Figure 1.12 shows how Google Maps prescribes the fastest route by considering traffic conditions.

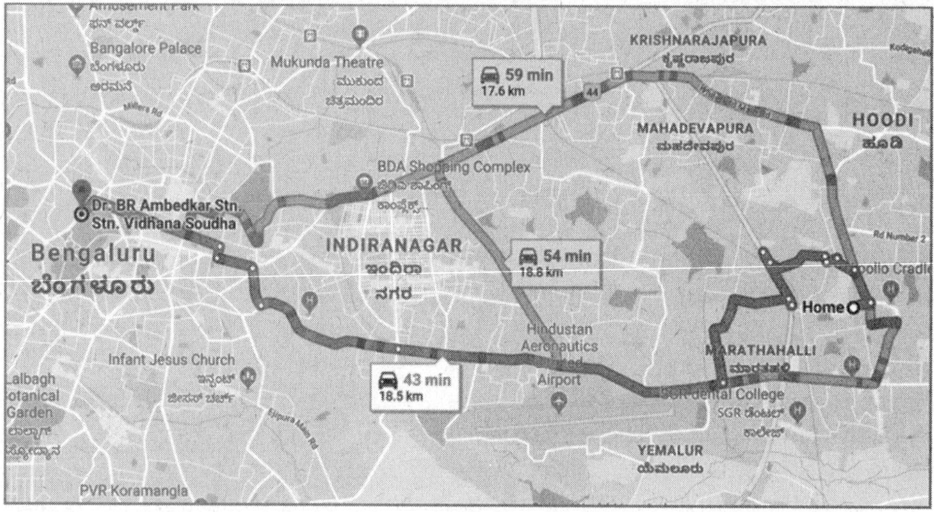

Figure 1.12: Route to work
(*Source*: Google Maps)

Figure 1.13 shows the types of analytics at a high level. We see that the complexity rises from descriptive to prescriptive and the assistance to human decision-making also increases—with prescriptive having potential to drive complete automation. I used examples from different domains to stress that analytics is a general discipline applicable in multiple domains—Healthcare, Engineering, Finance, Weather, etc. If you rethink each example, we tend to ask ourselves these questions and calculate the answers in our brain.

We look at our bank statements for different months and use descriptive analytics to deduce that we spent more money in a certain month compared to others. Then we dig deeper and try to diagnose why that was—maybe there was a family vacation that led to increased expenses. We use mental models to correlate our daily events such as consumption of certain cuisines like Thai food (rich in fish oil) to allergy symptoms we may have encountered. We all become weather experts by making inferences like, "It usually rains in Bangalore during the evenings in August." And we often get these predictions right. Finally, we know of our expert mechanics who can sense overheating or certain noises in the car's engine and prescribe actions like oil changes or that the water level is low.

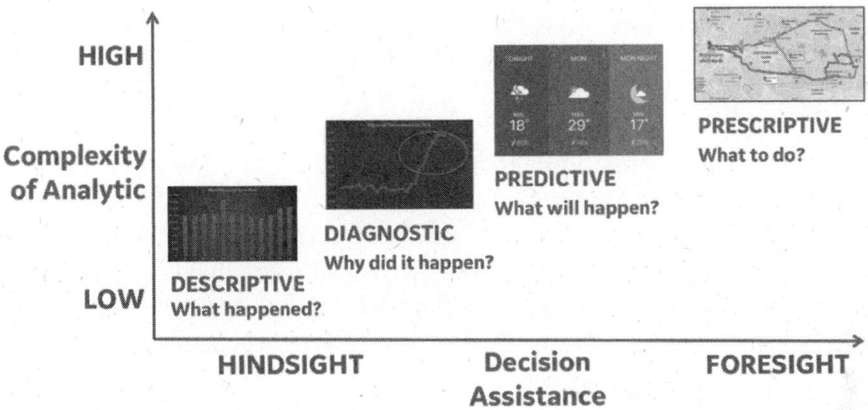

Figure 1.13: Types of analytics

Each analytic has a case for AI. We are making these smart decisions in our brain and we can build AI systems that can do the same. We can build an AI system that tries to delegate these thought processes to the computer and help us get the insights as fast as possible with maximum accuracy. This is what we will do with AI-based analytics. AI can be applied to any of the analytics applications to improve upon the results.

Types of Analytics: Based on Decision Logic

A different way to classify analytics that is more common in the industry is based on the way the decision logic is encoded in the analytic. Based on how we write the logic, we may have the following two types of analytics.

Rules-Based or Physics-Based Analytics

Rules-based (also referred to as Physics-based) is the more traditional approach to building analytics. Here you need to know how the different independent variables are related to form your dependent variables (see Figure 1.14). This approach is common when you have a good understanding of the system internals and understand how the variables relate. You use this knowledge and program explicit equations that the computer then calculates.

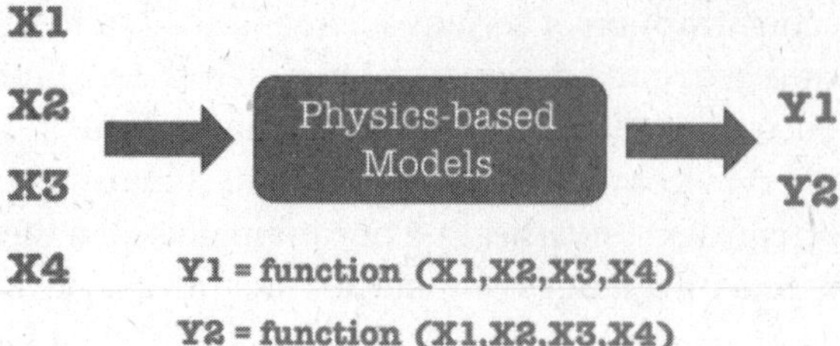

Figure 1.14: Rules-based analytics models

Data-Driven Models

Here we don't fully understand the system under study. We use historical data to derive patterns and encode these patterns into artifacts called *models*. With more and more data, the models get good at making predictions and form the internals of our analytic (see Figure 1.15). As you may have guessed, this approach is gaining huge popularity with growth in data being collected from real-world systems. This is also going to be the focus of this book.

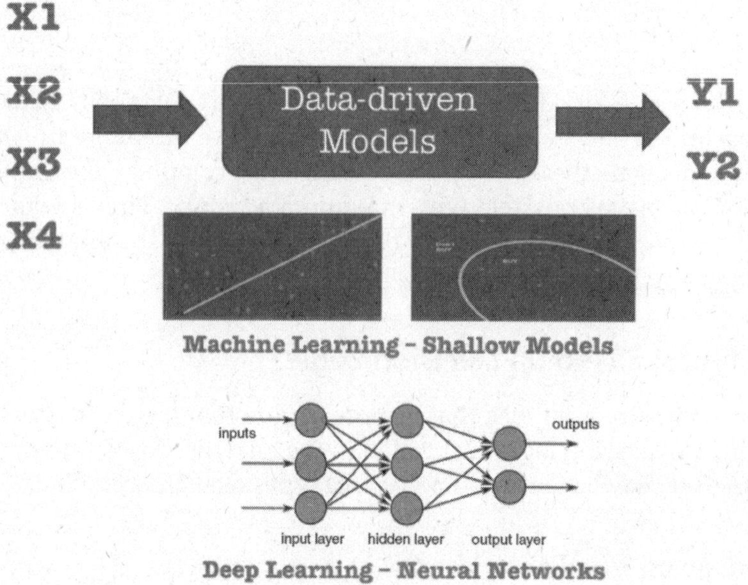

Figure 1.15: Data-driven analytics models

Building an Analytics-Driven System

Finally, let's look at a simple example of analytic development. This is by no means a full system with all details. We will just talk about it at a high level to whet your thinking on how the core analytic forms part of a bigger system and what the system considerations are. Keeping these in mind is very important when you are developing any type of analytic. Also, we will talk about three concepts that will help us decide the type of analytic to be developed.

Let's take an example of a system to measure the calories burned by a person while exercising. The outcome we are interested in is the number of calories burned—this is our dependent variable, our Y. To measure this, we want to consider the independent variables we can measure—our Xs. If we can establish our dependent variable as a function of the independent variables, we have an analytic.

To measure the exercise, we need to measure the motion that happens during the exercise. The motion is directly proportional to the outcome, which is the number of calories burned. The more you move, the more calories you burn. We could measure motion in several ways, discussed next.

Subject Walking on a Treadmill

We make the subject—our person of interest—run on a treadmill (see Figure 1.16). We find the distance run and try to use this to calculate the amount of exercise. Based on the distance, time, and weight of the individual, we can develop an equation that measures the calories burned in that period. This is a rules-based analytic since you know exactly how the Xs relate to the Ys. This is a case of "known knowns"—we know all the variables and their relationships.

Figure 1.16: Person on treadmill
(*Source*: Wikipedia)

Fitbit Motion Tracking

We can use a Fitbit to measure the motion of the hand and correlate that to calories. Fitbit measures acceleration in three directions (see Figure 1.17). It is very difficult to relate this acceleration directly to steps walked or run and then to calories. For this problem, a data-driven approach like Machine Learning is usually taken. We take samples from many people walking and measure the acceleration values corresponding to actions like walking and running. We use this data to train an ML model. After learning from a large volume of data, the ML model becomes good enough to start predicting the number of steps taken from raw acceleration data. This data of steps taken can then be mapped to calories burned. ML gets us into the area of "known unknowns." We know the Xs that affect our outcome but don't know the relationship to our Y. We use data to determine that relation.

Figure 1.17: Fitbit wrist device
(*Source*: Wikipedia)

Using External Cameras

Now what if we decide to use a camera to monitor a person while he is walking or running (see Figure 1.18)? No sensors are attached to the person and there is no special equipment like a treadmill. The sensor data we have here is video footage of the person walking. The video is basically a sequence of images and each image is digitized as an array of pixel intensity values. This is unstructured data because we only have a big blob of data without formal columns. From this big blob of data, how do we identify where the person is and measure his motion? This is where Deep Learning (DL) comes into play. DL builds large models with many layers of learning that helps decode this large unstructured data and extract knowledge. This is an area where we deal with "unknown unknowns." There are too many Xs and we don't know how they relate to Ys. We will cover Deep Learning in detail in Chapter 4 and also show examples of building, training, and using a model developed in Keras.

Figure 1.18: Cameras tracking motion
(*Source*: Wikipedia)

Summary

This concludes Chapter 1. We talked about how our world is being transformed by digitization, both in the consumer and industrial spaces. We see exponential growth in volumes of data generated by devices, more than a hundred times growth in processing power and rise of Artificial Intelligence (AI) to give us a new breed of applications that "learn" from experience. The next chapter explores AI further and talks about the most popular AI application—something that is transforming all other applications of AI—Machine Learning.

CHAPTER

2

Machine Learning

Chapter 1 provided an overview of some of the emerging trends in the industry around Big Data and Artificial Intelligence. We talked about software getting smarter with the application of Artificial Intelligence. In this chapter, we specifically focus on the most popular AI technique for infusing smarts into software—Machine Learning (ML). We see examples of using ML to capture patterns in data and capture these patterns in artifacts called *models*. We see the three types of ML techniques and discuss applications of each. Finally, in this chapter we review some code examples of building ML models from simple datasets. The code is highly commented, so you can start your own Colaboratory or Jupyter Notebook environment and run the code.

Finding Patterns in Data

As you saw in Chapter 1, AI is all about making computers develop human-like intelligence. This intelligence can help computers do knowledge representation, learning, planning, perception, language understanding, and more. One of the key areas of AI is Machine Learning, which is all about finding patterns in the data. The human brain is excellent at finding patterns. However, it is not very good at handling lots and lots of data.

Let's look at an example in Listing 2.1. Can you correctly guess the next number in the series?

Listing 2.1: A Sequence of Integers

```
2     4     6     8     10    12    14    16    18    20
22    24    28    30    32    34    36    38    40    ?
```

You should have no trouble looking at this data and finding the pattern. This is the powerful natural intelligence your brain has. You see that they are all even numbers in increments of 2. To capture this pattern in data, all the machine needs to do is build a rule that says add 2 to the previous number and that's the next number. Pretty simple, huh?

Wait a minute. Some of you may have noticed that the number 26 is missing in this sequence. Our brain is great at finding patterns but as we process more data we tend to miss things. If there is too much data, we usually get things wrong over time due to human error and fatigue. In this simple example, some of you may have actually noticed the missing 26 and probably attributed it to a printing mistake—but its omission was intentional!

Now look at the set of numbers in Listing 2.2. We are no longer dealing with integers but with real numbers with decimal points. This makes it more difficult.

Listing 2.2: A Sequence of Real Numbers

```
2.84   2.91   2.14   1.24   1.04   1.72
2.66   2.99   2.41   1.46   1.00   1.46   2.42   2.99   2.65   1.71
1.04   1.25   2.15   2.91
```

Just by looking at this sequence, it's pretty difficult for our brains to find patterns. We can make some sense of the data increasing and decreasing but cannot do much with it. Now for a computer, this new data is almost the same as the previous list of integers. With a minimal increase in processing power, a computer can analyze this new data. However, it still needs a human-like capability to find the pattern. In other words, it needs some level of Artificial Intelligence to find a pattern. This is where Machine Learning (ML) comes in the picture. So why is ML a big deal? If we train computers to find patterns in huge volumes of Big Data without getting tired and making human-like mistakes, we can get lots of intelligent work done quickly and highly accurately.

Now let's plot the data from the previous example and see what we find. No coding or any fancy tools. We will only use Excel. We take these numbers and plot the points on a chart in Excel. Immediately we see a pattern emerging. The values increase and decrease periodically and form a wave. So, there is a prominent pattern in the data and we only see this with help of a visual aid—a chart (see Figure 2.1).

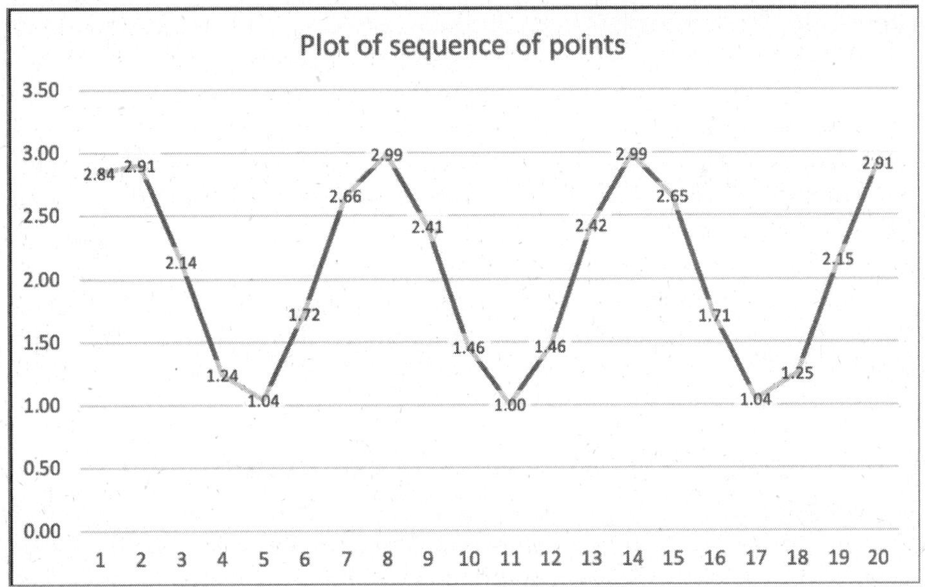

Figure 2.1: Charting these real numbers shows a pattern

Many business intelligence and reporting tools work on this basic principle—they process data, calculate important statistical summaries, and show results on intuitive visual aids (mostly charts) that help us understand the data and look for patterns. However, they still rely on humans to make the final decision by processing all this information. This approach is usually referred to as *descriptive analytics.*

Machine Learning goes beyond descriptive analytics, into the realm of *predictive analytics.* We find patterns in data and store these patterns in an artifact called a *model.* The model can now be used for making predictions on new data. The process of building a model is called *training.* Even before we start actually training, we need to collect data and identify the algorithm we will use for training.

In order to make accurate predictions on the new data, our model needs to learn all the patterns in the data. It needs to understand all the variations that the real data will encounter. Otherwise, it will have limited capability and will be less accurate. Also, the quality of data used to build the model is very important. Here ML follows the GIGO—Garbage In Garbage Out—rule. You need to feed the model with good data, or it will learn incorrect patterns.

Take the earlier example of integers. If we had fed the ML model with a sequence with the missing 26, it would think that it is a true pattern and start learning that. That would affect the accuracy of the model. There are more steps in the ML model lifecycle. We usually focus on the algorithm, but equally important (and sometimes more important) are the data collection, preparation, and model deployment and monitoring steps. The real world keeps changing, so a model deployed in production may not be relevant over time due to changes to the environment. A solid monitoring strategy and feedback cycle is very important when you deploy ML models in production. We will talk about this issue in the next chapter.

Let's focus on some of the popular algorithms and techniques in ML. Here I describe some common techniques in simple terms with examples and sample code. I also provide links for websites that provide these techniques in details.

The Awesome Machine Learning Community

Before we start—a word on the Machine Learning community. The ML community is truly amazing and provides a huge amount of data and information for free. They publish an amazing amount of content regarding algorithms and techniques and most of it is available for free. Many times it includes sample code. It's a really fun discipline to learn with lots of involvement across the globe. You can find many magazines, articles, and communities open to listening to your problem and helping with solutions.

Moreover, websites like Kaggle.com host ML competitions where they provide real-world problems with sample datasets (see Figure 2.2). Anyone in the world can register and join these competitions and be in line to win thousands of dollars. They don't care which country you are from or what your academic background is—the only thing that matters is how well you can solve the data science problem. Truly making the world a much smaller place!

For explaining the different algorithms, I use some publicly available datasets.

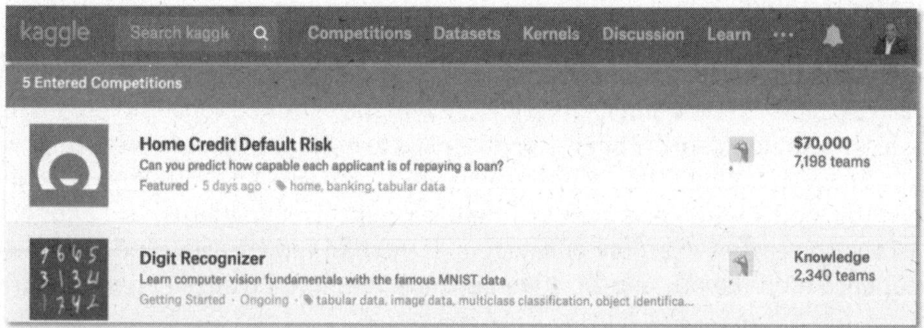

Figure 2.2: Kaggle hosts data science competitions and gives free datasets (*Source*: kaggle.com)

Again, thanks to the amazing ML community, we have many good datasets that can be used for learning ML methods. We will use datasets provided by the University of California, Irvine's Center for Machine Learning and Intelligent Systems (see Figure 2.3).

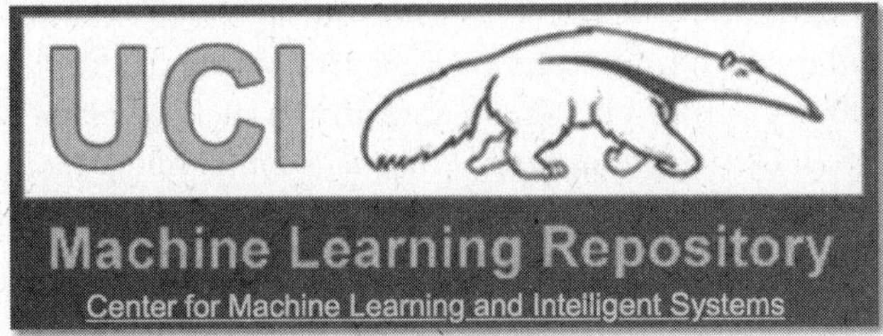

Figure 2.3: UCI Machine Learning repository
(*Source*: uci.edu)

Types of Machine Learning Techniques

Machine Learning is that one field of AI that touches and influences almost every other discipline. In fact, in the last five years there is hardly any area of the consumer and industrial Internet that has not been transformed by ML. All the AI examples we saw earlier—like tagging photos, recommender systems, playing games like chess, and self-driving cars—use some form of learning methods. ML can be classified into three areas, discussed in the following sections.

Unsupervised Machine Learning

In this case, we do not have any data on the results that are expected from our analysis. This is a more classical approach to finding patterns and trying to determine what the data is "telling" us. We focus on finding generic patterns in the dataset and using these to gain insights. Unsupervised learning algorithms can be divided into three categories.

Clustering

Clustering is all about dividing the dataset into clusters or groups with similar characteristics. Based on the variation in data in different features/columns, we try to determine what data points are similar and put them in a cluster. For example, if we have a class of students with different heights, we could divide them into tall, medium, and short categories. Clustering techniques analyze the data statistically to find groups of similar points. Let's discuss some common clustering methods.

K-Means is a popular method where you specify K number of clusters and the algorithm finds optimal clusters by assigning points to each cluster by distance from the centroid of each cluster. We will see a code example of clustering later in this chapter, when we analyze a dataset of houses using the K-Means algorithm.

Another popular algorithm is called *DBSCAN (Density-Based Spatial Clustering of Applications with Noise).* With it, we don't need to specify the number of clusters as in K-Means. The algorithm finds regions in feature space where the density of points is high. Other popular clustering algorithms include *Hierarchical Clustering* and *t-SNE* (*t—Distributed Stochastic Neighbor Embedding*). Each has a different way of finding clusters, but the basic idea is the same—they find data points that are statistically similar and group them as a cluster.

Dimensionality Reduction

Another popular unsupervised learning method is called *dimensionality reduction.* The idea here is to reduce the number of features/columns in your dataset. Too many features are difficult to handle and visualize. Also, you may end up focusing on features that are not of interest. For example, if we have 10 features describing a medical dataset—maybe 10 measurements of a sample of patients like blood pressure, cholesterol, sugár, etc.—it would probably be easier if we had just two or three features. We could plot these and look at the variation in data. That is what is done by dimensionality reduction. It reduces the size of the dataset while trying to capture and maintain the variation between these features in records. So, if one patient had significantly different readings from the others, after dimensionality reduction, the record for that patient will also be equivalently different from the others. The end results obtained by analyzing our dataset with hundreds of features and a fewer number of features after dimensionality reduction should be the same.

One of the most popular techniques for reducing the number of dimensions in a dataset is *principal component analysis* (PCA). The idea of PCA is to capture the variation between the features of the dataset. It transforms the dataset into a new dataset of principal components. The first principal component tries to capture the maximum variation between the features, followed by the next. The principal components themselves are independent of each other. Hence, we could take a large dataset with hundreds of features and select the top two or three principal components to see most of the major variation in the data. Now these two or three features are easy to deal with—we could plot them or process them more easily than with hundreds of features. Another use of PCA I have seen is to hide data. Since the data is fully converted from its original form, we could use it to hide the original set of features while providing this data to third parties. This is particularly handy when we have sensitive data like financial or medical records.

Anomaly Detection

One unsupervised learning technique that is often used by data scientists is *anomaly detection*. This technique uses simple statistical calculations like mean and standard deviation to find outliers in the data. For example, say you are tracking money spent on monthly groceries and, on average, you spend $200 with a deviation of plus or minus $50, so the values are between $150 and $250. Then, all of a sudden, you spend $300 in one month. That could be flagged as an anomaly. More complex anomaly detection involves considering contextual relationships. A monthly expense of $250 is not considered an anomaly, unless it happens at a time when the expenses have been below $200 for several years. In this context, $250 might be treated as an anomaly.

More complex anomaly detection involves using techniques like clustering, which we learned about earlier in this chapter. We could group our good (non-anomalous) data into a single cluster with each point represented by a distance from the cluster centroid. The distance is calculated considering all the features in the dataset, which can get pretty complex. If new data is far away from the centroid, we could label it an anomaly.

Supervised Machine Learning

Here we supervise how the model learns by giving it labeled data. The labeled data contains the expected values of outputs of (Ys) for each data point of features (Xs). For example, from the medical records dataset, we may have data showing which patients have a condition like hypertension. Now we can establish a relationship among the Xs—blood pressure, sugar, cholesterol, etc.—to the presence or absence of hypertension (the Y). This is supervised learning. Usually the thing that we are looking for is considered a *positive*. So, if we are looking for patients with hypertension, those patient data points are positives (absolutely nothing to do with the sentiment of the word—data scientists are weird that way!). Here the output labels are very important. If we incorrectly label a patient with healthy metrics as positive, our model will learn the wrong patterns and make false predictions. It's like teaching a child bad stuff like stealing is good!

The ML model generated by supervised learning is basically a relationship between the Xs and the Ys. It's a function or an analytic that we saw in Figure 1.9 from Chapter 1. In other words, we are mapping the Xs to the Ys and the function or relation that gives us this mapping is called the *model*. Once you have the model, you can give it the Xs and it will predict the Ys for those specific inputs. The way this internal relationship is stored in the model uses special parameters called *weights*. Whether you have a simple linear regression model or a complex *neural network*, it is essentially a way of representing inputs as a function of outputs using weights.

When we first define a model and initialize these weights, the model will not be able to predict the Ys correctly. We need to conduct a process of training the model so that it can learn patterns from training data. This learning process basically involves optimizing these internal weights so that the model can make predictions close to expected results. So ultimately the ML problem boils down to an optimization problem where you are adjusting weight parameters of the model to make it fit the training data.

For optimization, we need an objective function that we must minimize or maximize. Here our objective function is called a *Cost* or *Error* function that measures the difference in predicted and expected outputs. Our model training process tries to minimize this cost function iteratively. We use a popular optimization technique called *gradient descent* to optimize the weights. In this method, we use the partial derivative or gradient of the cost function with respect to each weight to calculate a correction to be applied to that weight. This correction is expected to improve the weight so that the model makes better predictions. In optimization terms, this correction will take us closer to the objective or minima.

We iterate through our training data and keep correcting the model weights. This is also called the *model training* process. The amount by which the weight improves is controlled by a parameter called the *learning rate*. Parameters that are not learned during training are called *hyper-parameters* and we need to define them at the beginning of the training process. We look at all these concepts in detail in the next section with an example on linear regression.

Supervised ML is normally divided into two areas, discussed next.

Regression

Regression aims at predicting values. The labeled data is made up of the values of the expected outputs or Ys. For example, say we are predicting the stock price of a company over the next week or the currency exchange rate for the U.S. dollar versus the Indian Rupee—these Ys are the actual values that we will predict. Our model will give us the result in numbers like $9.58—the prediction for the stock price of General Electric. These are our labels. The units for these values depend on the units we use for inputs. So as our training data, we use the stock values (in dollars) from last the six months. The prediction will also be in the same unit. The Ys we provide are real numbers and our model tries to map Xs to predict the actual values of Ys.

Classification

Here the goal is to predict a *class* as an output. There are two or more classes that can be the outcome and the algorithm maps input Xs to predict a class. The earlier example of predicting patients with hypertension from their medical records is an example of classification. The output here is usually expressed as a *probability* of membership in a particular class.

For our earlier example of predicting hypertension, there are two possible outcomes—hypertension or no hypertension. This is a case of binary classification and our output Y will be 1 for a case with hypertension (positive) and 0 for a healthy patient (negative). Our predictor model will usually give us a number between 0 and 1, such as 0.95. We then map that to the right class by determining if it's close to 0 or 1. So 0.95 is rounded to 1 and 0.05 to 0.

If we deal with multiple class predictions then we may have multiple Ys. For example, say we are looking for hypertension and diabetes. In that case, we have two Ys—Y1 for the probability of hypertension and Y2 for the probability of diabetes. We need to feed data in this format and a good trained model will output results by predicting the values of Y1 and Y2 between 0 and 1. We will see examples of this later in this chapter.

Reinforcement Learning

This is very different from the earlier two areas. In RL, we try to build agents that learn patterns and can take actions. These agents "observe" the real world as a person makes decisions and tries to learn the policies used for making these decisions. For example, you may have read about AI beating humans at chess and Go—that's using RL. Also, all your favorite video games like *Call of Duty* and *GTA* have an AI engine that's using RL.

It's best to understand the ML methods using real examples. I start with a very simple example to explain the concept. Each method has several algorithms to build a model. In this book, we will not go into the details of every algorithm. My focus is to show how you apply the algorithm and get results and then evaluate your results. I have many references that explain each algorithm in detail.

We will first start with a very basic dataset. Then we will get into some more detailed datasets from UCI. I share the Python code for each algorithm using the popular Scikit-Learn library. The code will be heavily commented so you can easily re-create it in a different language.

All right, let's get started.

Solving a Simple Problem

We will start by analyzing a housing prices dataset. The data shows houses sold in Bangalore with size and locality as features (Xs). The price is what we will predict (Y). The size is in square meters (referred to as the *area* in the dataset) and the locality rating is a subjective value provided based on different factors, like closeness to amenities, schools, crime rate, etc. In the real world, many times you will not have the complete data you need. In that case, you may need to create features that represent the concepts you want to measure and find ways of measuring them. That's what we have done with the locality feature. This is called *feature engineering* and is a separate area of study in ML. Feature engineering is a major activity in the overall ML development lifecycle. We cover it in detail in Chapter 9. For now, we will use the clean and prepared data shown in Figure 2.4, available as a comma-separated value (CSV) file, for our analysis.

Area in sq meters	Locality rating (1-10) 10=best	Price in Lakh Rupees (INR)
100	4	30
250	5	80
105	6	40
260	6	60
150	8	100
180	9	120
225	4	60
95	5	40
220	5	80
160	9	110

Figure 2.4: Sample dataset we will analyze

This is a very tiny dataset meant for us to understand the concepts. In reality you will need hundreds and thousands of points to build effective models. The more data the better, usually. Also, here all the data is complete—there is no missing data. Real life is always noisy and you will have data points missing, duplicate data, etc. You will have to work on data cleansing to get rid of bad data or replace it with a good representation, like mean or median or interpolation of values around a point. Again, this is a dedicated field of study called *data cleansing*—we will not go into depth about it here.

Here we have labeled the data with the price of house as the Y and the size/area and locality as the Xs. By looking at the data, we can draw some inferences. For example, as area/size increases so does price, and a better locality demands a better price. However, it is not easy to understand the effect of both the Xs together on our Y. That's what we will try do with ML. First let's plot the area and locality and see if we notice any patterns (see Figure 2.5). The plot shows us some distinct grouping of data. We see three sets of clusters developing in the data. We will explore if we can use ML techniques to extract this pattern without needing human intelligence. In other words, let's start building our first Artificial Intelligence model.

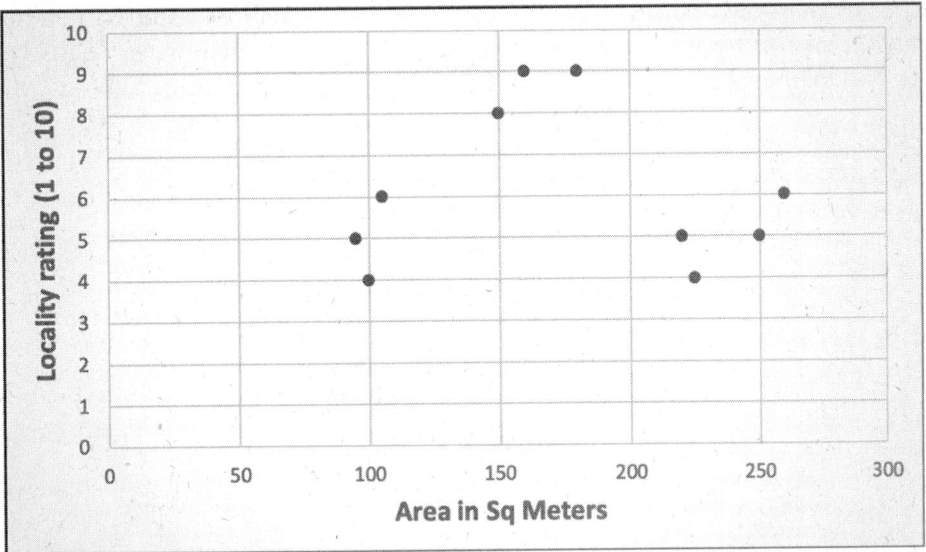

Figure 2.5: Chart of the sample dataset

Unsupervised Learning

Let's just look at two features—size (or area) and locality—and see if we find any patterns. We will intentionally not include price because we want to see if size and locality influence the price. We will start with unsupervised learning, in particular the clustering method. Say we want to divide these houses into three groups—high-priced, medium, and low-priced. We know the number of clusters we want, so we can use the K-Means algorithm. The principle behind K-Means is to find K number of clusters in the dataset and separate the data into these clusters. The clusters are organized so that relative to all features, the data is grouped such that similar data points are together in a cluster. For each cluster, the centroid mean is used as the representation. For any point in the dataset, the shortest distance to the cluster centroid determines to which cluster it is assigned.

We will use this same concept and find clusters in our data. First let's use the Pandas library to load our dataset. The dataset is loaded from a CSV file that is stored on disk or Cloud storage like S3 or Google. Pandas loads the data and creates an in-memory object called a *data frame*.

A data frame is a common way of representing structured data in data science tools like Pandas and R. A data frame stores the data like a table with features as columns with distinct headings and rows with data. They are optimized so that we could easily search for data by querying a feature/column and getting the matching data points or records. Also, since they are stored as binary objects they can be used to run statistical calculations like mean, median, etc., quickly. We will load data from the CSV file into a Pandas data frame. See Listing 2.3.

Listing 2.3: Code to Read a CSV File Using Python and the Pandas Library

```
# Pandas - my favorite tool for Data loading & manipulating
import pandas as pd
# Read a csv file and show the records
features = pd.read_csv('data/house.price.csv')
features.head(10)
```

Area	Locality	Price
100	4	30
250	5	80
105	6	40
260	6	60
150	8	100
180	9	120
225	4	60
95	5	40
220	5	80
160	9	110

Now we will apply the K-Means algorithm to divide the dataset into clusters and assign each record to a particular cluster. We will apply this to our independent variables or Xs—which are area/size and locality. The intent is to see if the clustering can find patterns and then we will relate these patterns to pricing. We do not use the Ys to supervise our algorithm. This is a case of unsupervised learning. See Listing 2.4.

Listing 2.4: Apply K-Means Algorithm and Divide Data into Three Clusters

```
# We will use the K-Means algorithm
from sklearn.cluster import KMeans
# We will only consider 2 features and see if we get a pattern
cluster_Xs = features[['Area', 'Locality']]
# How many clusters we want to find
NUM_CLUSTERS = 3
# Build the K Means Clusters model
model = KMeans(n_clusters=NUM_CLUSTERS)
```

```
model.fit(cluster_Xs)
# Predict and get cluster labels - 0, 1, 2 ... NUM_CLUSTERS
predictions = model.predict(cluster_Xs)
# Add predictions to the features data frame
features['cluster'] = predictions
features.head(10)
```

Area	Locality	Price	cluster
100	4	30	1
250	5	80	2
220	5	80	2
105	6	40	1
260	6	60	2
150	8	100	0
180	9	120	0
225	4	60	2
95	5	40	1
160	9	110	0

The result is interesting. We see a grouping of points for the three clusters corresponding to the three groups we saw in the chart earlier. We see houses with specific combinations of area/size and locality as clusters 0, 1, and 2. The logic that our brain can see by looking at the visual aid (the chart) was determined by the clustering algorithm on its own (see Figure 2.6). This was a very simple and limited dataset. By just observing the data in Figure 2.6, you can see that the houses with a similar size/area and locality rating are grouped together. However, in the real world, when you have thousands of data points and hundreds of features, you cannot easily find these patterns through observation. This is where a clustering algorithm can quickly find patterns in complex data.

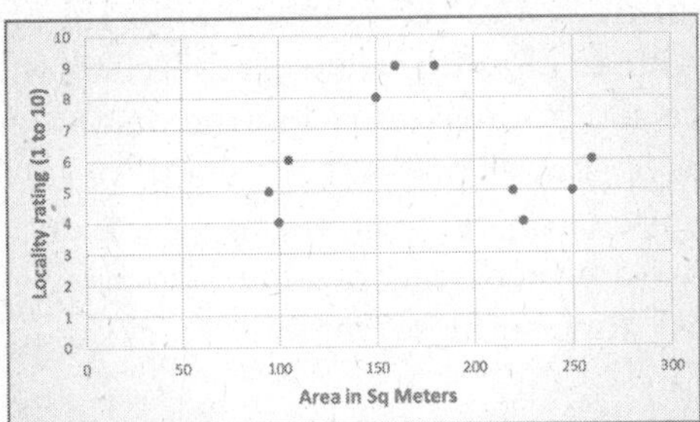

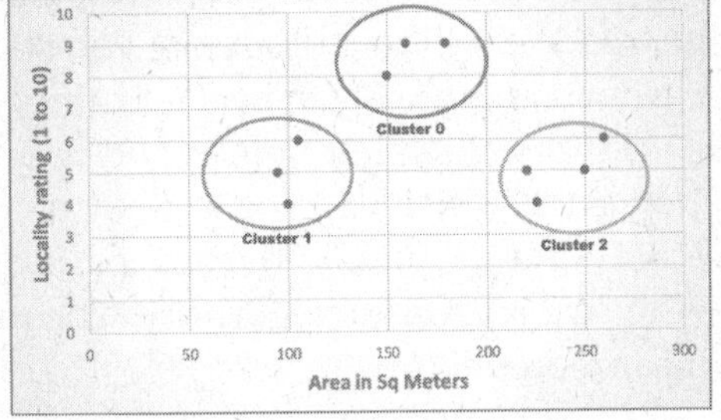

Figure 2.6: Clusters shown on the initial data chart

Now let's sort our results on the cluster value and see if we find any relationship to the price (see Listing 2.5).

Listing 2.5: Separate the Data into Clusters and See Relations

```
features_sorted = features.sort_values('cluster')
print(features_sorted)
```

Area	Locality	Price	cluster
150	8	100	0
180	9	120	0
160	9	110	0
100	4	30	1
105	6	40	1
95	5	40	1
250	5	80	2
220	5	80	2
260	6	60	2
225	4	60	2

We see the houses in a cluster following a similar pricing structure. Our algorithm captured the variation in the data using area/size and locality and organized the data into groups. These groups show the same variation with respect to a third value of price. In the real world, you will not have clean separation like this. You will need to experiment with different parameters like number of clusters to look for and see what combination gives you the best results.

The number of clusters in this case is a fixed value we provide to the algorithm and is not something that the algorithm learns. These parameters are called *hyper-parameters* in ML. Hyper-parameters normally depend on the algorithm we use. In K-Means, our hyper-parameter is the number of clusters. If we use Random Forests, it will be the number of trees and the maximum height of the tree. We will cover Random Forests with an algorithm later in this chapter.

Now using unsupervised learning, we saw some patterns in the data. We see clusters of similar houses and they have similar prices. Let's see if we can apply supervised learning to find the relationship between the area/size and locality and the price of the house. Since we are predicting a value—Price—we will use a regression algorithm. The most popular and simplest algorithm is linear regression.

Supervised Learning: Linear Regression

Linear regression tries to extract a linear relationship from the Xs by fitting a line through the data. Let's take an even simpler example with just one X and one Y and plot the data. See Figure 2.7.

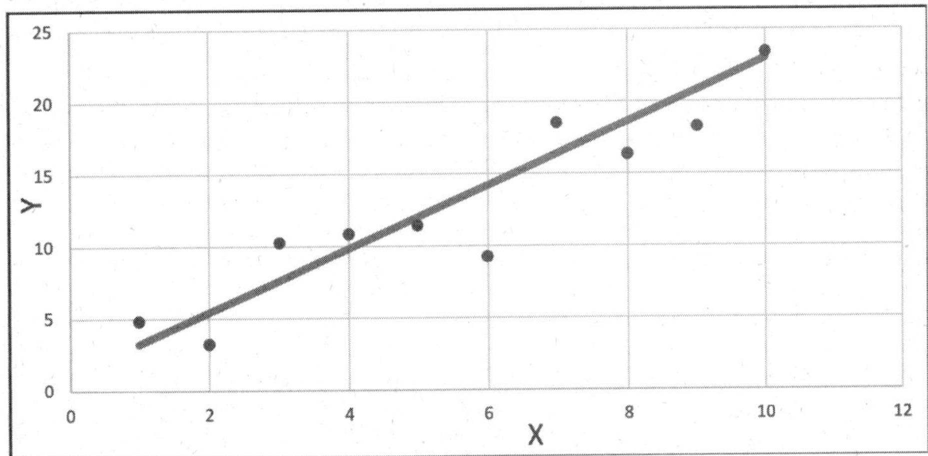

Figure 2.7: Linear regression tries to map X and Y values to a straight line

For a simple case with just one X variable, the linear regression equation can be written as shown in Listing 2.6.

Listing 2.6: The Most Basic Linear Regression Equation

$$Y = \mathbf{w} * X + \mathbf{b}$$

where **w**s the weight and b is the bias term.

What this means is that Y is expressed as a linear function of X. So as X increases, Y will increase and vice versa. This is the simplest of relationships between variables. In the real world, very few cases will show a clean linear relationship that can be expressed as a simple equation. However, data scientists sometimes make an assumption of linearity and try to fit a linear equation to get results quickly. Linear regression usually takes less processing power since there are many statistical shortcuts to solving these problems. These are built into an ML library like Scikit-Learn to make life easy for us.

w and **b** are the weights that we want to learn. **w** is a regular weight associated with a variable (X), while **b** is known as the bias. Even if the variable becomes zero, the bias term will still give us some value of Y. The bias is equivalent to some assumptions made by the model on predicted outcome even in absence of the influence of inputs.

We collect many samples of X and Y values and use these to calculate **w** and **b**. Using basic statistics, we use the X and Y samples collected to find these weight or parameter values. **w** is the slope of the line and **b** is the intercept point.

In the simple dataset with just one X and one Y, we will keep changing the weights **w** and **b** to see if the line fits the data well. Let's see some examples. We start with zero values and then slowly change values to see how the line starts fitting our data. In the final figure shown in Figure 2.8, the values of **w** and **b** seem to be a good assumption for a linear model.

You can see that we will never get a straight line that passes through every data point. The fourth line is our best model. This is the model that gives us minimum error—that is, the minimum distance between the model line and every point in our dataset.

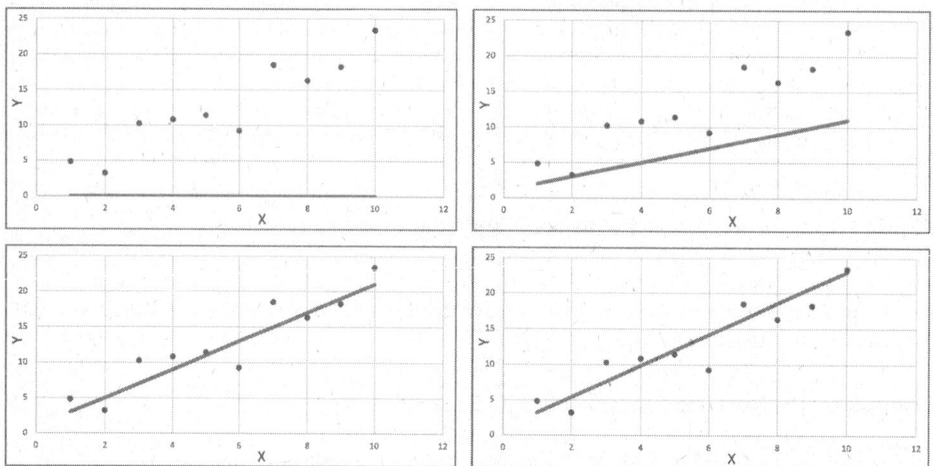

Figure 2.8: Varying slope (w) and intercept (b) values gives us different lines that try to fit our data

This is how we fit a model on our dataset. However, we normally don't use a manual approach like this because it would take forever. We have clever optimization techniques that help us fit and get the best model. We will see this through an example. Let's look back at our area/size and locality dataset from Listing 2.3.

If we want to fit a linear regression model on this information, we will want to express a relation like the one shown in Listing 2.7.

Listing 2.7: Expressing Area, Locality, and Price Data in Linear Form

Price = Linear function of (Area, Locality)
OR
Price = **w1** (Area) + **w2** (Locality) + **b**

We see that this is very similar to the single X problem we saw earlier. Now we have two X values. Our job as part of the training process is to find the optimal values for weights **w1**, **w2** and bias **b**. Again, since we are assuming a linear relation this is a pretty straightforward problem. As we get into more complex ML and DL problems, we will start looking at non-linear relationships and use very complex equations with many variables. However, the ML training technique you learn here is applicable to those problems as well.

We have a very small dataset with 10 points. Before starting any ML analysis, it is recommended to divide the data into training and validation datasets. The training set contains most of the records, which we will use to build our model. After building the model, we want to see how effective it is with data it has never seen before. That will be done by running the model against the validation set. The code in Listing 2.8 takes the top eight points for training and the remaining two for validation. In practice, we will use functions in the Scikit-Learn library to do this separation at random. We will cover that in the next example.

Listing 2.8: Divide the Data into X,Y Training and Test Sets

```
# Separate first 8 points as Validation set (0-7)
X_train = features[["Area","Locality"]].values[:7]
Y_train = features[["Price"]].values[:7]
# Separate last 2 points as Validation set
X_test = features[["Area","Locality"]].values[7:]
Y_test = features[["Price"]].values[7:]
```

We will use the training dataset to learn the weights of the model and the validation dataset to check that the model predicts unseen data properly. Let's understand the model training process. Model training basically involves adjusting weight values (w, b) such that they best fit our training dataset.

How do we decide what best fit is? For that we need a Cost function. The Cost function is basically a way to measure how much our prediction is off from the expected value.

Let's say we choose some random weights initially, just as we did with the single X problem. Based on these values we can pass each of the eight data points from our training set through the model (our equation) and get the corresponding predicted Y values. These predicted Y values will most likely be different from the expected Y values in our training set. Our Cost function needs to quantify the difference between predicted and actual values in the training set. If we are predicting numerical outputs (Regression), we can find a difference of the expected and actual for each training point and combine the difference. If we are predicting a Class membership (Classification), we could use a function that quantifies our error in classification. The Cost function is also known as the Error function—simple because it helps us quantify the error in our predictions.

Now that we passed all our training data through the initial model, our task is to adjust the weights so that we get better at predicting. In other words, we need to adjust weights so that our Cost or Error function reduces. We can now use the Cost function as our objective function for optimization. We optimize the weight values so as to minimize the Cost function. This now becomes a classical optimization problem. We can use popular optimization methods like gradient descent to get the optimal weights—ones that "fit our training data to minimize cost."

Gradient Descent Optimization

Gradient descent is a popular optimization technique used for training ML algorithms. This is a general-purpose optimization technique where you try to modify the weights and bias terms so as to build a relationship between your independent variables (Xs) and dependent variables (Ys). We start with an initial approximation of weights and bias terms and build an initial model. We run all the Xs through this model and predict the Ys. We compare predictions to actual and find the errors. Next, we find the *gradient* of the Cost function we found earlier with respect to each weight and bias term. The gradient is basically the partial derivative of the Cost function with respect to each weight/bias term. Now this gradient will give you the direction and magnitude of how much that particular weight or bias influences your Cost. Using this value, you adjust the weight and bias terms in a direction that reduces Cost. We also account for a *learning rate*, which is a factor that controls the size of step we take to modify the weight or bias. If we take too big steps we may overshoot our minimum value, but if we take too small steps our convergence to the minimum value may take a long time. Let's apply this to our linear regression example.

For the simple linear regression example earlier, we want to optimize the values of **w0**, **w1**, and **b** in order to minimize the Cost function. When the Cost is the minimum our model gives us the best predictions. Our Cost function has to capture the difference between the predicted and actual values in the training dataset. We don't really care about the sign of the difference—but the actual value of distance. Hence, for linear regression the Cost function we use is either Mean Absolute Error or Mean Squared Error. Let's see the steps in gradient descent, shown in Figure 2.9.

At a high-level, this is how the gradient descent algorithm works:

- Initiate the weight values to zero or random values. Make a prediction on each X value and get the predicted outcome—let's call it Y'.
- Compare Y' with the actual Y value from training data and find the error, which is equal to Y-Y'.

- Positive and negative errors may cancel each other—so either take absolute error or squared error so that the sign of error doesn't affect the calculation.
- Find the mean of the total error term using one of the following terms:

```
Mean Absolute Error (MAE)
= Sum of |Y - Y'| / # training samples

Mean Square Error (MSE)
= Sum of (Y - Y')2 / # training samples
This is our Cost function!
```

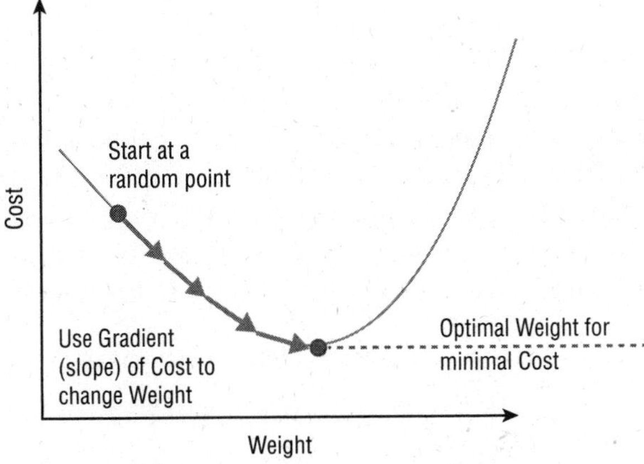

Figure 2.9: Gradient descent to find the optimal weight and bias terms

Use any one of these Cost functions and try to minimize this Cost (objective) by adjusting the weights—**w0** and **w1**. Now this becomes an optimization problem with **w0** and **w1** as terms you modify.

Calculate the partial derivative (the gradient) of the Cost function with respect to the weight we want to modify. As shown in the chart in Figure 2.9, the gradient is a Calculus term that gives us the slope of the curve. Gradient tells us in which direction we should modify the weight value (shown with the arrow).

The amount by which we should modify the gradient is controlled by a constant parameter known as the *learning rate*. If we choose a high learning rate then we may miss the minimum value and overshoot to the other side of curve. A small learning rate will make the learning process very slow since weights don't get changed much. In general, 0.05 is a good learning rate to start with.

Now use the gradient to adjust the weights **w0** and **w1**. Use the learning rate to control how much the weights change at each iteration. Keep optimizing until the Cost is minimum:

```
w0 = w0 - lambda * d(Cost)/dw0
w1 = w1 - lambda * d(Cost)/dw1
```

Here lambda is the learning rate. **d** is the notation for derivative.

We adjust weights after all the training points have been evaluated for specific weight values. Then we repeat this for new weights and again adjust the weights. This iterative process keeps getting us close to minimum values of the Cost function. We may end our training after so many iterations or once our error is below a particular value.

Applying Gradient Descent to Linear Regression

Let's apply linear regression to our data and find the model weights. Now you see the code in Listing 2.9 is pretty simple and all the complex details of gradient descent are hidden from you—you don't even specify a learning rate. Also, Scikit-Learn uses some statistical shortcuts to quickly calculate the optimum **w0** and **w1** values based on training data. However, as we progress to complex models—especially models that combine many learning units together into a network—we will have to carefully configure optimization parameters. These networks of learning units—also referred to as *neural networks* in ML—are excellent at learning complex non-obvious patterns in data, but need lots of manual tuning. We discuss tuning these factors (called *hyper-parameters*) in Chapter 4.

Listing 2.9: Fit Linear Regression Model on Data Using Scikit-Learn Internal Functions

```
# Use Scikit-Learn's built-in function to fit Linear Regression Model
sklearn.linear_model import LinearRegression
model = LinearRegression()
model.fit(X_train, Y_train)
print("Model weights are: ", model.coef_)
print("Model intercept is: ", model.intercept_)

# Predict for one point from Test set
print('Predicting for ', X_test[0])
print('Expected value ', Y_test[0])
print('Predicted value ', model.predict([[95,5]]))

Model weights are:  [[ 0.20370091 13.56708023]]
Model intercept is:  [-46.39589056]
Predicting for  [95  5]
Expected value  [40]
Predicted value  [[40.79109689]]
```

We fit a linear regression model to our training data and it predicts the equation that relates house price to the area/size and locality. The equation is:

```
Price = 0.2037 (Area) + 13.5670 (Locality) - 46.3958
```

We can also manually solve this using the preceding equation for Area = 95 and Locality = 5:

```
Price = 0.2037 (95) + 13.5670 (5) - 46.3958 = 40.7910
```

This is how linear regression works. Of course, this was an extremely simple dataset. We see that for a complex dataset we may not be able to fit data accurately with a linear model. The metric of MSE or MAE is used to evaluate regression models and when we are left with high values then possibly we have to look at other models. We could look at other regression models like Support Vector Regression, which uses different way to form a model and check for MSE or MAE.

If we keep getting high error values with linear models, then usually we need to start looking at more complex non-linear models. Most popular in the non-linear regression methods are *neural networks*. Using neural networks, you can capture the non-linearity in the data and try to find models that give you a low error value. Also, for complex models like neural networks we will see a very clever algorithm called *back-propagation* that helps us propagate the error between actual and predicted values through the network and quickly calculate gradient values for the Cost function with respect to each weight and bias term. This algorithm developed by Geoffrey Hinton totally revolutionized the field of AI and brought neural networks into prominence. So much so that today they are considered the de facto standard for solving complex problems like computer vision and text and speech recognition.

We talk more about neural networks and back-propagation later in this chapter.

Supervised Learning: Classification

Now let's talk about the other form of supervised ML—a more popular and common one in real-world ML—which is *classification*. In classification, your outcome or dependent variable is not a value but a membership in a class. The outcome can take an integer value from 0 to the number of classes. Extending the earlier example, let's say you have data for location and price of houses and you want to predict if you will buy this or not. This is a common decision we encounter. Our brain makes a mental model of this decision and as we see new data of houses, we decide to buy or not. Now using Machine Learning, we will try to build a model of this decision. This is the most common form of ML problems in the real world. You will have to understand the various features and decide what class each belongs to. We will show a few examples with code to solve this.

This particular problem is a binary classification problem and the output variable can have one of two values—Buy or Don't Buy. We represent this as 0 (Don't Buy) and 1 (Buy). Let's say the data we collected looks like Figure 2.10 when plotted. We have the Price on the y-axis and the location rating (1–10) on the x-axis.

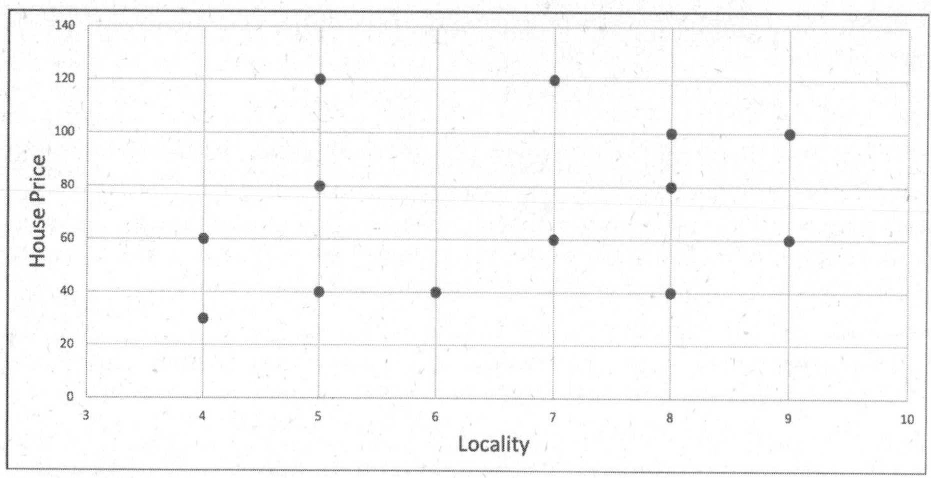

Figure 2.10: Plot of house price versus location

A couple of very basic decisions would be to consider only one feature or independent variable. Let's only consider location or price and make a decision. We will define a decision boundary that will help us decide. Figures 2.11 and 2.12 show two such decisions.

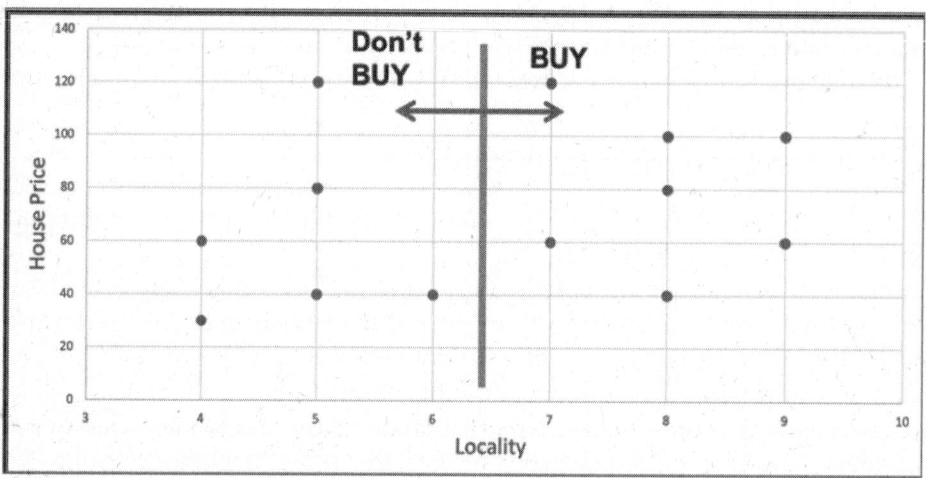

Figure 2.11: Decision based only on location

Figure 2.11 shows a decision that anything above a particular locality rating we will buy, while Figure 2.12 says that if the house has a price below a particular value, we will buy it.

But, in reality we have to consider both factors together. We can try to fit a linear relation between the variables. So just like the earlier linear regression, we fit a line between the points, but instead of predicting a value, our line tries to separate the data into two classes, as shown in Figure 2.13.

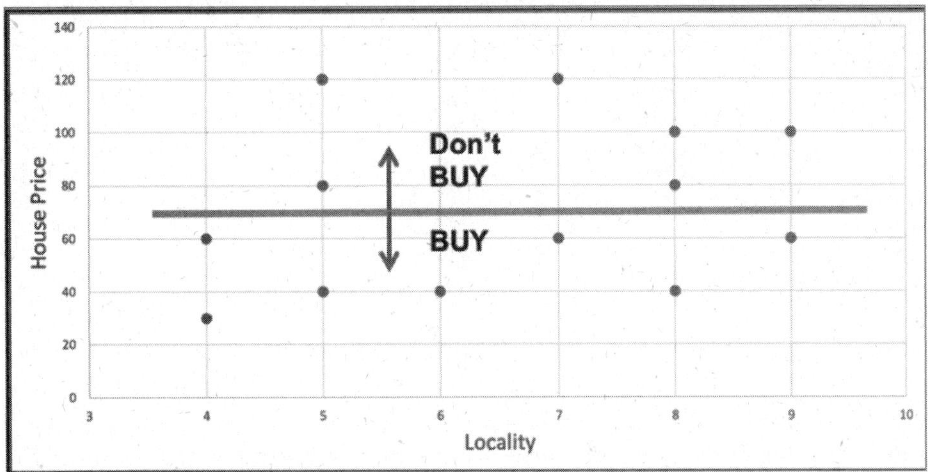

Figure 2.12: Decision based only on price

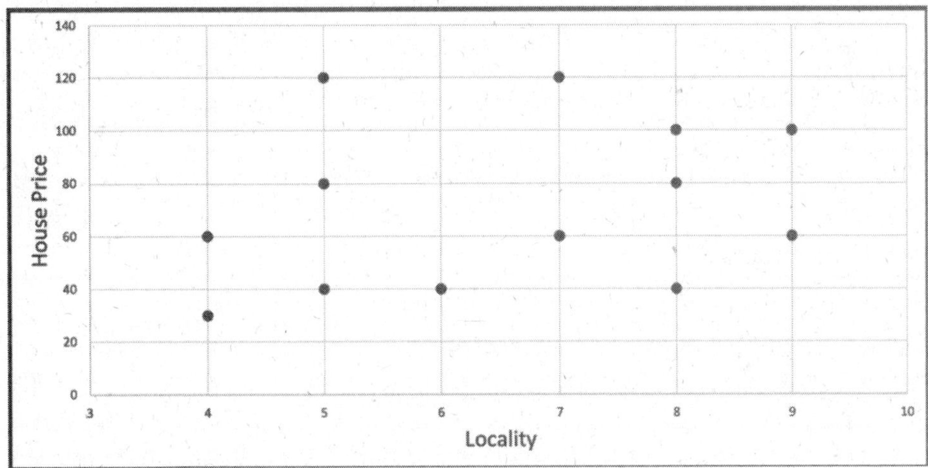

Figure 2.13: Linear decision boundary for buy vs. no-buy decisions

The line is our decision boundary and it separates the points into two classes—buy and don't buy. This approach is known as a logistic regression. For any new point, we can predict a buy or not decision based on where it lies with respect to the model line. Though we use the term "regression," this technique is a classification technique.

Mathematically, logistic regression does the following:

```
Buy/NotBuy = LogisticFunction(function(Price, Locality))
```

An alternative way of looking at this is visually as a network, as shown in Figure 2.14.

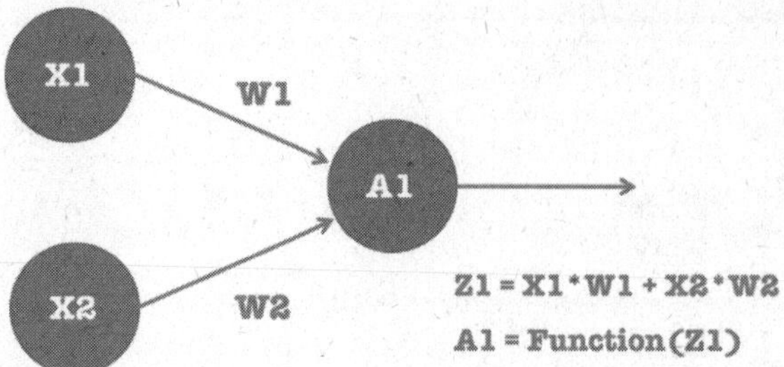

Figure 2.14: Simple network representation of the logistic regression equation

First, we learn a linear relationship between the variables (new variable Z1)—just like in linear regression. Then we convert that linear term into a number between 0 and 1 using a function. Here we use a function known as a logistic function or Sigmoid function. I will not go into the formula but essentially it produces a result (variable A1) between 0 and 1. This is analogous to a threshold. Of the Z1 value, which is the linear weighted sum if above a certain threshold—the value gets close to 1; otherwise, it is close to 0. This threshold is what the ML algorithm learns. It uses the results produced—A1—to classify data points into one of two classes. This is a binary classification since we have two classes represented by 0 and 1. We can extend this to multi-class problems using neural networks. We will see this with examples in Chapter 4.

We use this activation value A1 to classify our data point. If this number is close to 1, then result is one class and if it's close to 0, it's the other class. Depending on the training data, the class membership is decided between 0 and 1. Let's look at a real example and some code.

Let's collect the house area/size, location, and price data and add one more column for Buy or Not. This column will have 0 if you will not buy and 1 if you will buy. Now we want the computer to predict your mental model of why you will predict buy or not. There could be several criteria for buy and don't buy. Based on the data given to us, let's try to build a model that predicts if we will buy a house; see Figure 2.15.

As with the earlier example, let's separate the data into training and validation sets. We take the last two points as test data points, as shown in Listing 2.10.

Listing 2.10: Simple Separation of Training and Validation Sets

```
# Separate first 8 points as Validation set (0-7)
X_train = features[["Area","Locality","Price"]].values[:8]
Y_train = features["Buy"].values[:8]

# Separate last 2 points as Validation set (0-7)
X_test = features[["Area","Locality","Price"]].values[8:]
Y_test = features["Buy"].values[8:]
```

Area	Locality	Price	Buy
100	4	30	0
250	5	80	1
220	5	80	1
105	6	40	1
150	8	100	0
180	9	120	0
225	4	60	0
95	5	40	1
260	6	60	1
160	9	110	0

Figure 2.15: Our new dataset with expectation of buy and don't buy

Now we will fit a logistic regression model on this training data. Then we use the trained model to make a prediction on the two testing data points. See Listing 2.11.

Listing 2.11: Fit a Logistic Regression Model on the Data

```
from sklearn.linear_model import LogisticRegression

model = LogisticRegression()
model.fit(X_train, Y_train)

# make a prediction on test data
Y_pred = model.predict(X_test)

# print expected results
print(Y_test)
# print the predictions
print(Y_pred)

# Separate last 2 points as Validation set (0-7)
X_test = features[["Area","Locality","Price"]].values[8:]
print(Y_test)
```

Here are the results:

```
[1 0]
[1 0]
```

From the very limited data, we get pretty good results. However, logistic regression has the limitation that it cannot capture the non-linear relationship in the data. For example, if we wanted to get a decision boundary like the one shown in Figure 2.16, logistic regression will not help.

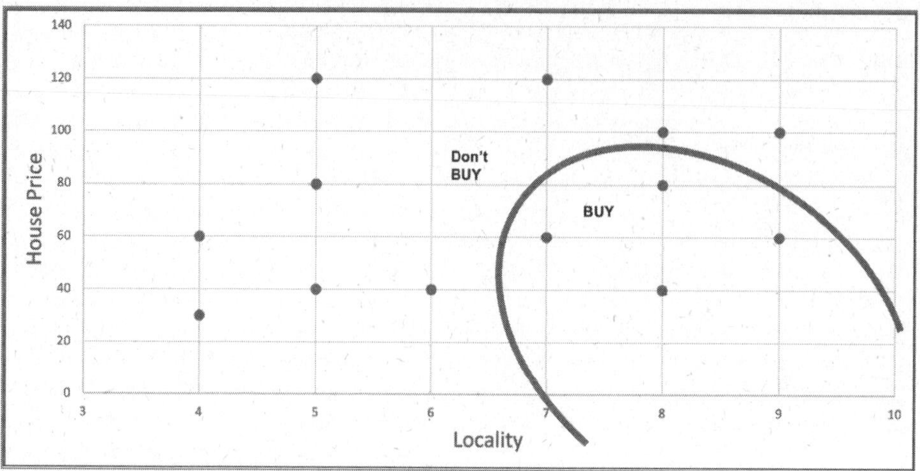

Figure 2.16: Non-linear decision boundary

This decision boundary has a non-linear relationship between the variables, so advanced classification methods need to be employed. Some of these are K-means, decision trees, random forests, and the more complex *neural networks*.

Analyzing a Bigger Dataset

Let's now look at a more complicated example with a bigger dataset to understand other classification methods.

The dataset we will use is a publicly available one from UCI—the Wine Quality dataset. The feature columns in the dataset are different chemical attributes of different wines like Ash, Alcohol, etc. The outcome or dependent variable is a class of wine that has been decided by human experts by sampling the wines. Each row is a new wine type and the class is allocated by expert opinion among three classes. We want to build a model that can map the expertise of the human wine expert and express class as a function of features. Figure 2.17 shows a sample of the dataset.

The complete dataset has 11 column features and one outcome column, which is the quality of wine. The total records in the dataset are 1599. Let's use different classification methods to try to build the wine class prediction model. See Listing 2.12.

fixed acidity	volatile acidity	citric acid	residual sugar	chlorides	free sulfur dioxide	total sulfur dioxide	density	pH	sulphates	alcohol	QUALITY
7.4	0.7	0	1.9	0.076	11	34	0.9978	3.51	0.56	9.4	5
7.8	0.88	0	2.6	0.098	25	67	0.9968	3.2	0.68	9.8	5
7.8	0.76	0.04	2.3	0.092	15	54	0.997	3.26	0.65	9.8	5
11.2	0.28	0.56	1.9	0.075	17	60	0.998	3.16	0.58	9.8	6
7.4	0.7	0	1.9	0.076	11	34	0.9978	3.51	0.56	9.4	5
7.4	0.66	0	1.8	0.075	13	40	0.9978	3.51	0.56	9.4	5
7.9	0.6	0.06	1.6	0.069	15	59	0.9964	3.3	0.46	9.4	5
7.3	0.65	0	1.2	0.065	15	21	0.9946	3.39	0.47	10	7
7.8	0.58	0.02	2	0.073	9	18	0.9968	3.36	0.57	9.5	7
7.5	0.5	0.36	6.1	0.071	17	102	0.9978	3.35	0.8	10.5	5
6.7	0.58	0.08	1.8	0.097	15	65	0.9959	3.28	0.54	9.2	5
7.5	0.5	0.36	6.1	0.071	17	102	0.9978	3.35	0.8	10.5	5
5.6	0.615	0	1.6	0.089	16	59	0.9943	3.58	0.52	9.9	5
7.8	0.61	0.29	1.6	0.114	9	29	0.9974	3.26	1.56	9.1	5
8.9	0.62	0.18	3.8	0.176	52	145	0.9986	3.16	0.88	9.2	5
8.9	0.62	0.19	3.9	0.17	51	148	0.9986	3.17	0.93	9.2	5
8.5	0.28	0.56	1.8	0.092	35	103	0.9969	3.3	0.75	10.5	7
8.1	0.56	0.28	1.7	0.368	16	56	0.9968	3.11	1.28	9.3	5
7.4	0.59	0.08	4.4	0.086	6	29	0.9974	3.38	0.5	9	4
7.9	0.32	0.51	1.8	0.341	17	56	0.9969	3.04	1.08	9.2	6
8.9	0.22	0.48	1.8	0.077	29	60	0.9968	3.39	0.53	9.4	6
7.6	0.39	0.31	2.3	0.082	23	71	0.9982	3.52	0.65	9.7	5
7.9	0.43	0.21	1.6	0.106	10	37	0.9966	3.17	0.91	9.5	5
8.5	0.49	0.11	2.3	0.084	9	67	0.9968	3.17	0.53	9.4	5

Figure 2.17: Sample of the Wine Quality dataset

Listing 2.12: Load the Wine Quality Dataset into a Pandas Data Frame

```
# Pandas is my favorite tool for Data loading and munging
import pandas as pd
# Read a csv file and show the records
features = pd.read_csv('data/winequality-red.csv')
features.describe()
```

	fixed acidity	volatile acidity	citric acid	residual sugar	chlorides	free sulfur dioxide	total sulfur dioxide	density	pH	sulphates	alcohol	quality
count	1599.000000	1599.000000	1599.000000	1599.000000	1599.000000	1599.000000	1599.000000	1599.000000	1599.000000	1599.000000	1599.000000	1599.000000
mean	8.319637	0.527821	0.270976	2.538806	0.087467	15.874922	46.467792	0.996747	3.311113	0.658149	10.422983	5.636023
std	1.741096	0.179060	0.194801	1.409928	0.047065	10.460157	32.895324	0.001887	0.154386	0.169507	1.065668	0.807569
min	4.600000	0.120000	0.000000	0.900000	0.012000	1.000000	6.000000	0.990070	2.740000	0.330000	8.400000	3.000000
max	15.900000	1.580000	1.000000	15.500000	0.611000	72.000000	289.000000	1.003690	4.010000	2.000000	14.900000	8.000000

Figure 2.18: Summary of the wine data frame

First we will separate our "features" data frame into X and Y frames. Then we will separate these further into training and testing frames. Unlike earlier, now we will use a built-in function to randomly split data into 80-20 for training and testing. See Listing 2.13.

Listing 2.13: Code to Separate the Data and Build Training and Validation Datasets

```
# separate the Xs and Ys
X = features # all features
X = X.drop(['quality'],axis=1) # remove the quality which is a Y
Y = features[['quality']]
print("X features (Inputs): ", X.columns)
print("Y features (Outputs): ", Y.columns)

X features (Inputs):
['fixed acidity', 'volatile acidity', 'citric acid', 'residual sugar',
'chlorides', 'free sulfur dioxide', 'total sulfur dioxide', 'density',
'pH', 'sulphates', 'alcohol']

Y features (Outputs):   ['quality']

from sklearn.model_selection import train_test_split
# split the data into training and test datasets -> 80-20 split
X_train, X_test, Y_train, Y_test = train_test_split(X, Y,test_size=0.2)
print("Training features: X", X_train.shape, " Y", Y_train.shape)
print("Test features: X", X_test.shape, " Y", Y_test.shape)
```

Here are the results:

```
Training features: X (1279, 11)  Y (1279, 1)
Test features: X (320, 11)  Y (320, 1)
```

We divided the data first into X and Y data frames. X has our 11 input features and Y is a single output for the prediction we want to make—the quality of the wine. Then we split them each into 1279 training points and 320 testing points. We will use the training data frames to build our classification models and test to compare its performance.

Metrics for Accuracy: Precision and Recall

Before we get started with training, let's discuss the metrics we will use. Metrics are very important to compare different algorithms and models and see which is accurate. Also, by adjusting the hyper-parameters, we can achieve significant improvement in prediction, which again needs to be measured and benchmarked.

The accuracy of Machine Learning models is measured using two popular metrics—precision and recall. Figures 2.19 and 2.20 explain the two.

Precision is what we usually attribute to accuracy. If we are playing a game of darts and hit three bull's-eye targets out of four attempts, our precision is 3/4 or 0.75 or 75%. It's what we use in our everyday lives as a metric of accuracy.

Recall is more complex. It is concerned with the overall outcome we wish to achieve and how our model performs against this. Many times, precision and recall are conflicting metrics—you may have to lower your precision to improve recall.

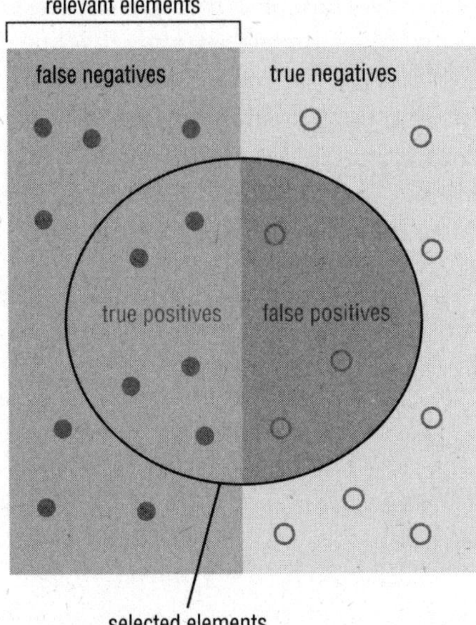

Figure 2.19: Precision and recall concepts
(*Source*: Walber – Wikipedia)

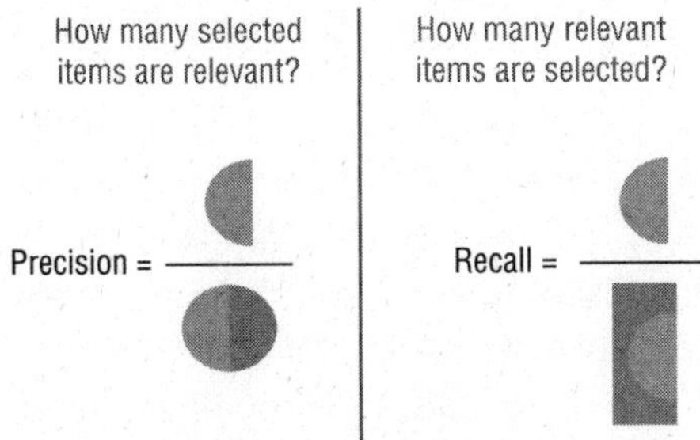

Figure 2.20: Precision and recall formula
(*Source*: Walber – Wikipedia)

Let's take an example. Say you are playing a shooting game like *Call of Duty*. You are in a combat zone facing five enemy shooters. You fire three bullets and take down three of the enemy shooters. Your accuracy is three out of three, which is 100%. However, you have not eliminated the problem. There are still two shooters who can get you. So the high accuracy doesn't really help unless you solve the problem. That is why accuracy alone is not enough and you need a different metric—*recall*.

In this scenario, your recall is 3/5 which is 60%. Precision focuses on how good you are, while recall tells you if the problem is actually solved. Now say you fire three more shots. You miss one and hit the two remaining targets with the next two shots. Precision tells you how many selected items are relevant. Out of six total shots, five are relevant. Your precision is five out of six, which is

83%. Recall tells us how many relevant items are selected. So out of five shooters, all are shot. Recall is five out of five, or 100%. In this example, we sacrificed our precision to improve the recall.

Let's consider these metrics in terms of true and false positives and negatives.

For the first case with three shots fired, your true positives (shots hitting targets) was three, and your false positives (misses) were zero, which makes the precision 100%. The formula for precision is as follows:

```
Precision = True Positives / (True Positives + False Positives)
```

And the formula for recall is:

```
Recall = True Positives / (True Positives + False Negatives)
```

In our example of the *Call of Duty* game:

```
True Positives = Shots fired that got Enemies
False Positives = Shots fired but missed
False Negatives = Enemies that did not get hit
```

If you notice, the false negatives are more the property of the environment—while true and false positives measure your skill. If you want to get all the enemies, you need to take more shots and thus risk lowering your precision.

When you took three more shots and got the two enemies, but missed one shot, your new metrics are:

```
Precision = 5/(5+1) = 83.3%

Recall = 5/(5+0) = 100%
```

You sacrificed your precision to go after more enemies and achieve 100% recall. As a data scientist, you will often face this scenario. It's not enough to achieve a high precision. You also need to focus on solving the problem at hand.

Now let's get back to building our classification ML model. This is the more popular application of ML, where you predict the outcome as a particular class. Most Deep Learning techniques you will see later are also classification models, but are more complex.

Comparison of Classification Methods

First, we will apply logistic regression to classify our Wine Quality data from earlier. Since we have a good division of wine types, we will use precision as our main metric for evaluating the model. We will do training on (`X_train,Y_train`) and will use (`X_test,Y_test`) to evaluate the model generated. We will build the model and predict for `X_test` and compare predictions to the ground truth. *Ground truth* is the expected value that we want our model to start predicting—in this case Y _ test.

In more complex techniques like Deep Learning, when we deal with unstructured data like images, our ground truth is usually what a human can decipher from this data. For example, say we want to separate images containing Pepsi and Coca-Cola logos. We need a human to look at these images and mark which ones contain which logo. We will discuss this exact example in Chapter 5. For this example, we have a clear ground truth value defined by the Y _ test array. See Listing 2.14.

Listing 2.14: Logistic Regression Classifier on Wine Quality Dataset

```
from sklearn.linear_model import LogisticRegression
# build the Model
model = LogisticRegression()
# fit our Training data
model.fit(X_train, Y_train)
# predict Y values for X_testy
Y_pred = model.predict(X_test)
# compare with Y_test and record the Precision
print("Precision for Logistic Regression: ", precision_score(Y_test, Y_
pred, average='micro'))
```

Here are the results:

```
Precision for Logistic Regression:  0.590625
```

We get a 60% precise classifier using logistic regression. Now let's apply a few more algorithms to build models.

First, we will use a K-Nearest Neighbors (KNN) classifier. This is a very simple classifier. It simply learns to predict the class using the K nearest neighbors. For any new point—based on K points that are nearest to it—it will try to predict the class. See Listing 2-15.

Listing 2.15: K-Nearest Neighbors Classifier on Wine Quality Dataset

```
from sklearn.neighbors import KNeighborsClassifier
# Train the KNN Model
model = KNeighborsClassifier(n_neighbors=20)
model.fit(X_train, Y_train)
# predict for X_test
Y_pred = model.predict(X_test)
# compare with Y_test
print("Precision for KNN: ", precision_score(Y_test, Y_pred,
average='micro'))
```

Here are the results:

```
Precision for Logistic Regression:  0.496875
```

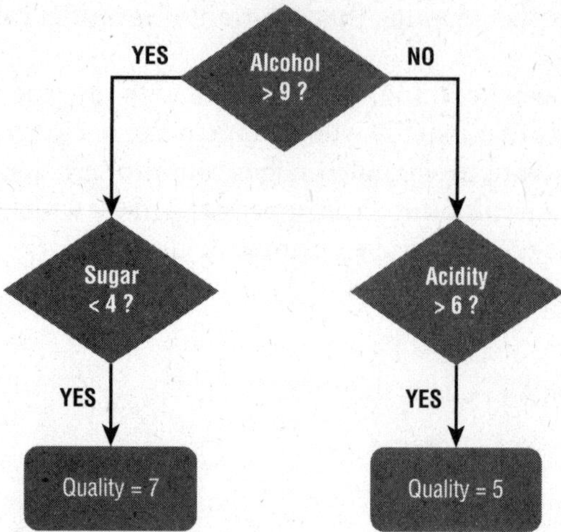

Figure 2.21: Sample example of a decision tree

KNN looks at your whole training set and, for each new point, gives a score based on the nearest neighbors. It is usually pretty time-consuming and may not give you the best accuracy. Let's look for a different algorithm.

Now let's look at a popular algorithm called the *decision tree*. As the name suggests, this method builds a tree of decisions that help divide the data into classes. At each branch we make a decision pertaining to one particular feature. For example, we may have a simple tree like the one in Figure 2.21 to decide on basic prediction. This is a very simple example—in reality, a decision tree algorithm like CART tries different possible combinations of features to get good separation of your training data.

Luckily, most ML libraries have pretty good implementation of decision tree algorithms and we can use them without going into details. Listing 2.16 shows how we call one in Python.

Listing 2.16: Decision Tree Classifier on Wine Quality Dataset

```
from sklearn import tree
from sklearn.metrics import precision_score
# build the Decision Tree Model
model = tree.DecisionTreeClassifier()
# fit your training data to the Model
model.fit(X_train, Y_train)
# predict for the test dataset
Y_pred = model.predict(X_test)
# find the precision of the prediction
print("Precision for Decision Tree: ", precision_score(Y_test, Y_pred,
average='micro'))
```

Here are the results:

```
Precision for Decision Tree:  0.59375
```

We can build and visualize the whole decision tree using the code in Listing 2.17. This can get pretty complicated. But if you want to visualize the decision tree, it is done as shown here.

Listing 2.17: Plotting the Decision Tree Classifier on Wine Quality Dataset

```
from sklearn.tree import export_graphviz
# Export as dot file
export_graphviz(model,
                out_file='tree.dot',
                feature_names = X_train.columns,
                class_names = str(range(6)),
                rounded = True, proportion = False,
                precision = 1, filled = True)
```

This will generate a `tree.do` file that you will need to convert to PNG using the following command:

```
>> dot -Tpng tree.dot -o tree.png
```

Now you have `tree.png`, which looks like Figure 2.22. This is about 20% of the whole diagram. You can try the diagram and see how it divides your data.

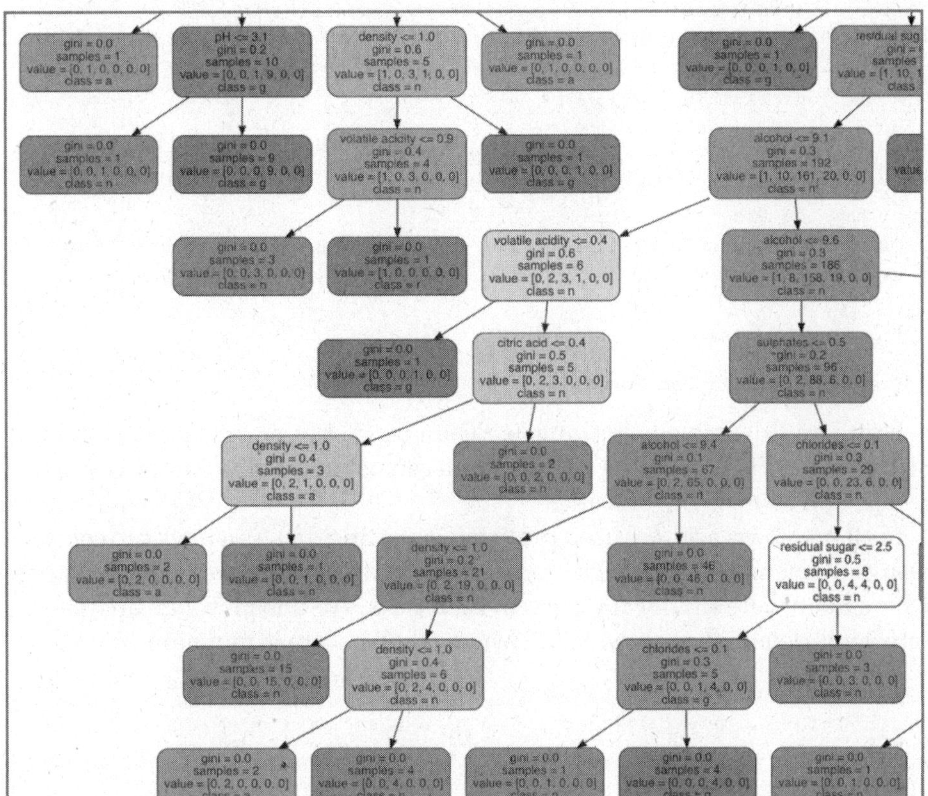

Figure 2.22: Sample decision tree

Coming back to the ML model metrics, our precision is better than KNN but still not very high. Usually these direct ML methods like logistic regression, KNN, and decision trees give you weak classification, unless your data is very simple, like in our house price example. You have to try some other methods to improve accuracy.

One technique often used is called the *Ensemble* method. In this technique we combine predictions from many weak classifiers and try to build a strong classifier. The Ensemble technique applied to the Decision Tree algorithm gives us a new algorithm—called *Random Forest*. The idea of the Random Forest is to take a subset of features at random and a subset of data points, again at random. Use this reduced data to build a decision tree. Construct multiple decision trees with subsets of features and rows, and at the end combine the outputs to make a prediction. This combination may be a mode (most common prediction class) in case of a classifier. We can also use a Random Forest to build a regression model—here we get the mean of the individual tree outputs.

Let's apply Random Forest to our data. Again, an excellent library like Scikit-Learn makes it absolutely simple to apply Random Forest (see Listing 2.18).

Listing 2.18: Random Forest Classifier on Wine Quality Dataset

```
from sklearn.ensemble import RandomForestClassifier
# build the Model with 100 random Trees
model = RandomForestClassifier(n_estimators=100)
# fit your training data
model.fit(X_train, Y_train)
# make prediction for testing data
Y_pred = model.predict(X_test)
# show the Precision value
print("Precision for Random Forest: ", precision_score(Y_test, Y_pred,
average='micro'))
```

Here are the results:

```
Precision for Random Forest:  0.740625
```

Using an Ensemble technique, we get a much better precision. Ensemble techniques are not restricted to trees—you can use other algorithms to combine results and form string classifiers.

In all previous cases, we used precision on testing data as a metric to compare results. Remember we did not worry about recall because we had an example where there were significant items in each class. We don't have an anomaly or rare items detection case, which is where recall becomes more important.

Bias vs. Variance: Underfitting vs. Overfitting

Now we discuss the cause for error in ML models. Error can happen due to bias or variance. Let's understand bias and variance using a basic example.

Let's say you have to throw five darts at a dartboard. Figure 2.23 shows the results that you get on the first attempt.

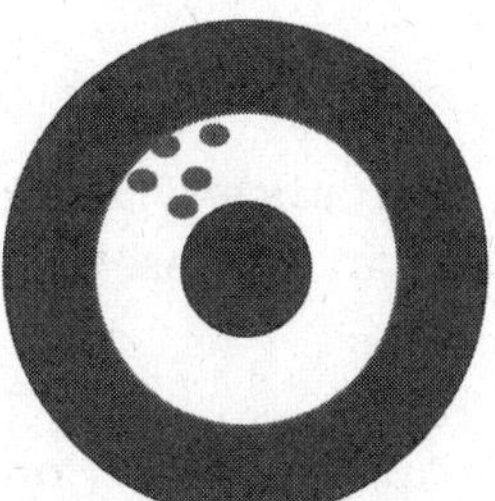

Figure 2.23: Shooting darts with high bias to the top left

You are very good at hitting the top-left side of the board. But you are still far away from your target—the center of the board. This is the case of high bias. You are biased toward a particular location and need to work on reducing this bias to get close to the target. Irrespective of the number of attempts (Xs) you will keep getting a similar Y.

Now you adjust your stance and practice a few more shots. Then you try the five darts again. Say you get result shown in Figure 2.24.

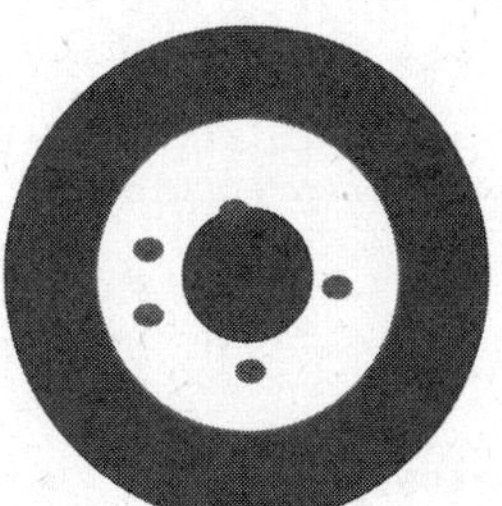

Figure 2.24: Shooting darts with high variance across the board

You are no longer biased toward hitting the top left, but your darts are distributed all over the board. So, there is a lot of variation in the results you get—this is a case of high variance.

Now you work on your aim for some more hours and finally start hitting the target. What you have done is controlled your bias and variance so that you

Figure 2.25: Adjusting bias and variance to get your bull's-eye!

start hitting the target. Although variance and bias seem contradictory, there are ways to control both so you get an optimal solution, which in this case is to hit the bull's-eye! (See Figure 2.25.)

Let's see an example with real data.

We will take the case of logistic regression. Now instead of precision only on the testing data we will find it for the training and testing data. See Listing 2.19.

Listing 2.19: Logistic Regression Classifier on Wine Quality Dataset

```
from sklearn.linear_model import LogisticRegression
# build the Logistic Regression Model
model = LogisticRegression()
# fit Model on your data
model.fit(X_train, Y_train)
# make prediction on training data and get precision
Y_pred = model.predict(X_train)
print("Precision for LogisticRegression on Training data: ", precision_
score(Y_train, Y_pred, average='micro'))
# make prediction on testing data and get precision
Y_pred = model.predict(X_test)
print("Precision for LogisticRegression on Testing data: ", precision_
score(Y_test, Y_pred, average='micro'))
```

Here are the results:

```
Precision for LogisticRegression on Training data:  0.58561364

Precision for LogisticRegression on Testing data:  0.590625
```

We see that for both training and testing data our precision is pretty much the same. Why is this? We trained the model on training data, so it should have fit better on training, right? Well this is a case of underfitting.

Underfitting means the model does not fit well on both training and test data. This happens because of a property of the ML model known as *bias*. Bias refers to the assumptions the model makes and if it has high bias, the model does not learn very well from the data. Some amount of bias is necessary for the model, or the model will be highly susceptible to input data variations and any bad data points will cause the model to make mistakes. Figure 2.26 shows an example of a model with high bias, which underfits. This is usually the problem with linear regressors and classifiers.

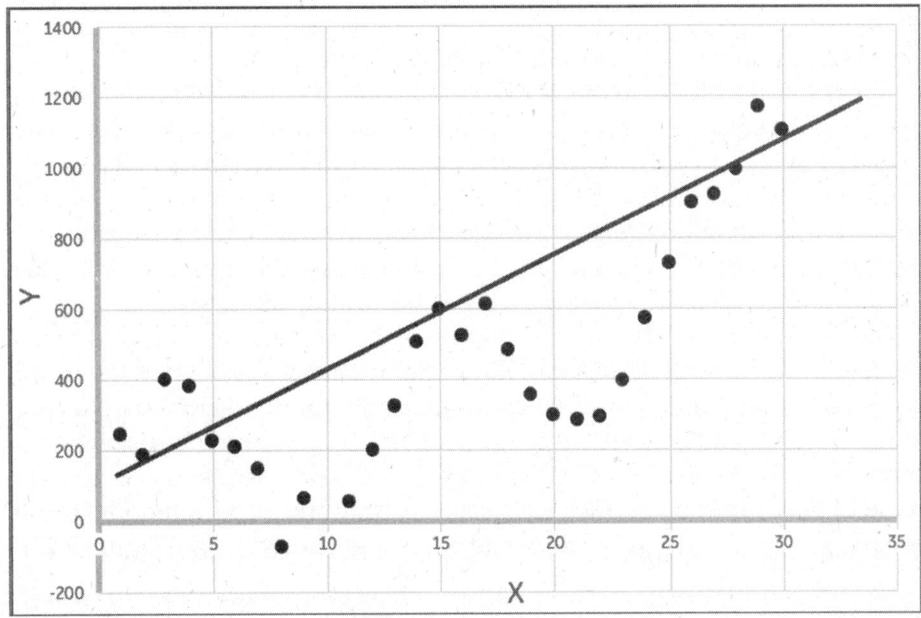

Figure 2.26: Linear regressor underfitting our data

Now let's take the case of a Random Forest (see Listing 2.20). Now instead of precision only on the testing data, we will find it for both the training and testing data.

Listing 2.20: Decision Tree Classifier on Wine Quality Dataset

```
from sklearn import tree
from sklearn.metrics import precision_score
# build the Decision Tree Classifier Model
model = tree.DecisionTreeClassifier()
# fit Model on your data
model.fit(X_train, Y_train)
# make prediction on training data and get precision
Y_pred = model.predict(X_train)
print("Precision for Decision Tree on Training data: ", precision_
score(Y_train, Y_pred, average='micro'))
# make prediction on testing data and get precision
Y_pred = model.predict(X_test)
print("Precision for Decision Tree on Testing data: ", precision_
score(Y_test, Y_pred, average='micro'))
```

Here are the results:

```
Precision for Decision Tree on Training data:  1.0

Precision for Decision Tree on Testing data:  0.634375
```

Now you notice a very interesting thing. The model gives you 100% precision on training data but for testing data the precision drops. This model has learned all the training patterns extremely well. But when it sees new data (which it has not seen before), it cannot generalize on the test dataset. Such a model is said to have high variance and is overfitting on the training data.

A real-world analogy to this is like studying for an exam and only learning the textbook questions by heart. Then, if a question comes from somewhere other than the textbook, you cannot answer it. Rather, if you learn the actual concepts in the textbook, you will know how to solve any problem in that domain. Now you can easily generalize this knowledge and answer questions not directly from the textbook. That's kind of how the ML model learns. We want it to generalize well on unseen data, which we provide as the testing dataset.

The variance of an ML model determines the model's capability to change prediction with variation in input data. High variance means that the model keeps adjusting outputs to fit the input data and doesn't really learn the patterns. Variance and bias are inversely proportional. As you increase bias, the variance will decrease and vice versa. Usually a data scientist has to accept a tradeoff between the variance and bias. Decision trees and Random Forests usually show a very high variance and a tendency to overfit (see Figure 2.27).

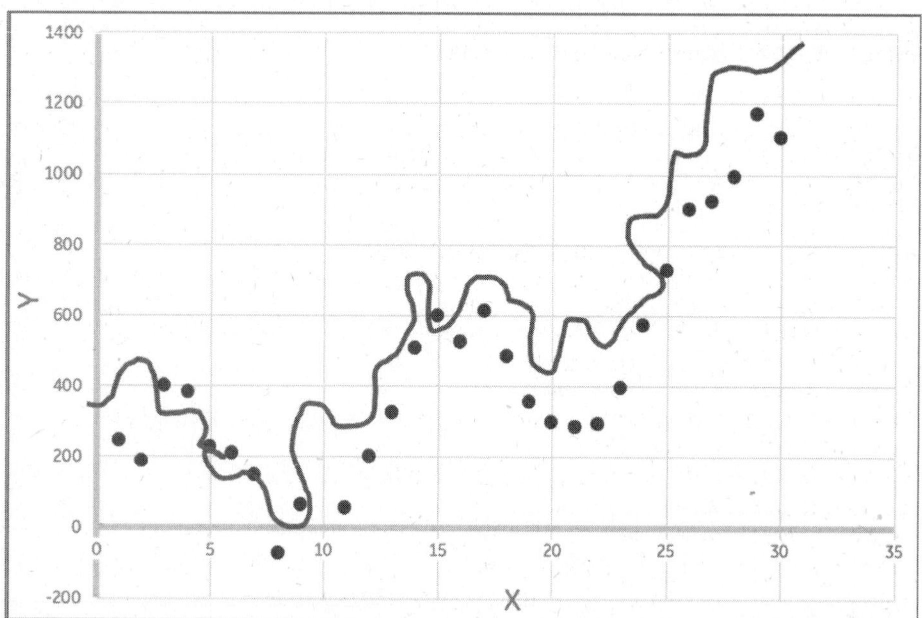

Figure 2.27: Overfitting on the training data

A data scientist usually looks at different models that fit the data and evaluates the bias and variance to establish a good tradeoff. We see that linear models tend to underfit and show high bias. Models like decision trees tend to overfit and show higher variance. You have to try several models on your dataset and see the metrics on training and testing data to evaluate the model performance. The idea is to build an optimal model that can fit your data well, as shown in Figure 2.28. Usually, based on the nature of real-world data, you will most likely need a non-linear model to capture all the variations in data without getting too biased.

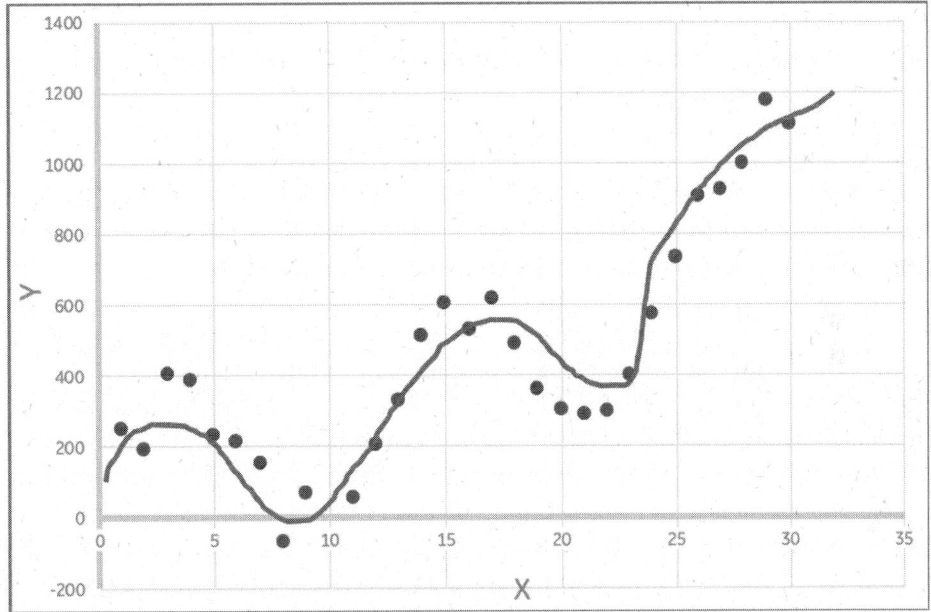

Figure 2.28: A good fit and well-trained model!

The other option sometimes used by data scientists is to use a linear model but be aware of the bias errors and try to compensate for them using some domain knowledge of the problem. For example, in Figure 2.26, if we know that for lower values of X (say X < 25), the predicted Y values are higher than the actual values on average by 10%. And for higher values of X (say X > 25) the predicted values tend to be 10% lower than the ones expected. This is a non-linear relationship our linear model cannot be expected to learn. However, we could put a rule of thumb or empirical factor in our calculation to add 10% of Y for predictions where X < 25 and subtract 10% of Y where X > 25. This adjustment will get us closer to the actual prediction, but involves some domain knowledge.

However, as your features increase and dataset gets more complex—particularly unstructured data like images, text, and audio—you will need to start evaluating more complex models that fit the data better and capture all the non-linearities. This is the beginning of a huge field inside Machine Learning called Deep Learning (DL). We cover DL in detail in Chapters 4 and 5.

Reinforcement Learning

And finally, a few words about *Reinforcement Learning (RL)*. Before that let's talk about *Avengers: Infinity War*. As of writing this book, it's 2018 and we are still figuring how our mighty heroes will return from the infamous snap of finger by Thanos. However, let's talk about my favorite Avenger—Dr. Strange.

In the movie, just before the final battle, Dr. Strange runs in his mind 14,000,605 scenarios of how the battle will play out. He finds that out of all those scenarios there is exactly one in which the Avengers end up defeating Thanos. Now this is kind of what Reinforcement Learning does. It builds agents that work against an environment, which can simulate actions and give you results. So over time an agent takes many actions and compares results, and it finds out which actions give favorable results and which don't. It learns a policy on how to take actions that will give maximum rewards in the long term. In Dr. Strange's case, he just had a single policy that would give him the desired end goal. But when we play game of chess, there are many ways by which we can win the game.

Now you can compare this to supervised learning. There is some supervision; however, the agent learns by taking different actions through trial and error. There is no finite training set that is prepared beforehand, as is the case with Supervised Learning. Different RL algorithms use different techniques to train and learn an optimal policy that guides them to take actions against a given environment. The key to RL is that there is no fixed dataset that the algorithm learns from. Instead, RL tries to build an agent that interacts with an environment and, based on the feedback, it learns which actions to take. See Figure 2.29.

Reinforcement Learning is a special branch of ML that's probably the closest to Artificial Intelligence in its true or traditional sense. It's the process of building a system that can observe and start making decisions like humans.

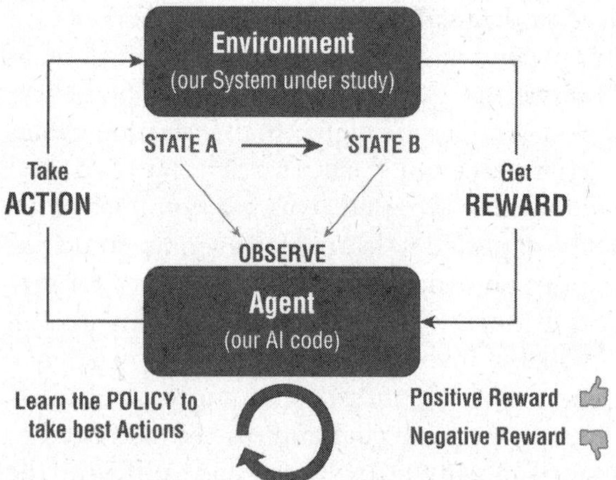

Figure 2.29: How Reinforcement Learning works

RL is often considered one of the core Artificial Intelligence techniques because it is analogous to the way the human brain learns. Imagine a child learning to walk. The child keeps trying different ways to get up, establish balance, and walk. If the method is wrong, the child falls down, which is basically a negative reward or negative reinforcement. If the child is successful and takes a few steps, that's a positive reinforcement and the child's brain learns how to reproduce those exact actions. Every time the child falls, it's a negative reinforcement that tells him not to use that method. If you think closely, the child's brain does not take random movements while walking. It trains from "experience" and builds a "policy" of how to move while walking—a policy that the brain remembers for the rest of one's life.

In a similar manner, the agent in RL is given an environment to train against. It takes actions on the environment that change the state of the environment and produce a positive or negative reinforcement. These actions taken during the learning process may be taken at random but the learning process is much more effective if we consider the long-term reward for the actions.

There are two types of RL algorithms: model-based and model-free. Let's look at these next.

Model-Based RL

With this approach, we build or have a model of the environment we are building our agent to control. This model can help us answer questions like what result (new state) we will get when taking an action A on the environment in state S to get a reward R. The term *model* here is used for the environment rather than an ML model of the agent itself—one which we are trying to build. This is a mathematical model that captures the dynamics of the environment. Now we can use a planning algorithm to find the optimal action at any state to get the maximum reward. Basically, we can try several combinations of actions for each state and use the model to get the next state and reward and find the optimal rewarding policy. It comes down to a pure optimization problem.

In the real world, however, it's very difficult to get a true model of your environment. You have to consider the internal physics of the system you are dealing with. Then there are so many noise factors to consider. It becomes highly impractical to build a model of a system that can capture all the states, as well as their transitions and the rewards for different actions. Hence, these techniques are useful for limited and highly simplistic systems.

Let's consider a simple analogy to understand this a little better. Say that Fred is borrowing money from his friend, Anna. Anna has $200 and Fred can ask for any amount. Anna will accept or reject his ask based on some internal rule she has in her mind. Fred doesn't know what is going on inside of Anna's mind, so he doesn't know how much money to ask for.

Here we can think of Anna as our environment E. The state S of environment E is defined by a single variable—the amount of money Anna has. The initial state is that Anna has $200 with her, that is s0 = 200. Fred is our RL agent who takes an action A on the environment E. The action in this case is asking for a certain amount of money. Based on the amount of money he asks for, Anna will provide a reward R, which may be positive (accepts the ask) or negative (rejects the ask). So, our job is to figure out how much money Fred can ask Anna for, without her saying no. Figure 2.30 shows this concept.

Figure 2.30: A simple analogy for Reinforcement Learning

Model-based RL is where we know the internal dynamics of our environment. In this example, if we know what Anna is thinking and how much money she is willing to part with, we have a simple solution to how much we should ask her for. Say Anna feels that as long as she has at least $100, then she is good. Fred can ask for up to $100 and she will most likely say yes. Here we have the environment E modeled and we know its internal workings. It's a highly simplified example, but the bottom line is that we know enough about the environment E to influence our action A and find a simple solution.

However, the real world is not so simple. There are many variables and constraints to consider as well as factors affecting how the environment behaves. It is very difficult to find the right model of the environment.

Consider a real-world example of driving a car. We want an agent that controls the throttle position and braking so that we can drive from point A to point B. There are too many variables involved. We have to consider the dynamics of the actual car and its components like engine, brakes, throttle, etc. We have to consider wind resistance and ground friction. We have to consider safety features like spotting pedestrians and other vehicles and avoiding them. You can see how quickly this problem becomes big and it's almost impossible to accurately model such a complex environment. Hence, we need an alternate means of building our agents other than using deterministic models. That is where model-free RL agents come into play. In fact, model-free agents are the most popular RL methods for practical applications.

Model-Free RL

In this case, we don't have a model of the environment. Rather we take a trial-and-error approach to determine the patterns for how the environment behaves. We run trials on the real system or a simulator and observe the results and learn from these observations. Through trial and error, our agent learns the patterns of actions that maximize rewards for particular states.

Let's consider an example of this approach with our friends Fred and Anna. Without any knowledge of how Anna decides on giving money out, Fred is left with no option but to try out a few requests, as shown in Figure 2.31.

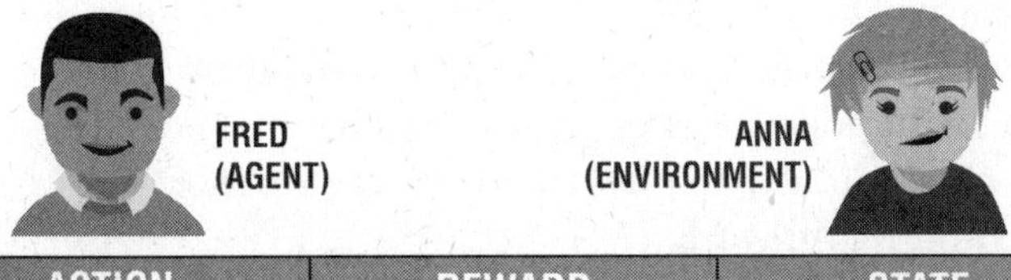

ACTION	REWARD	STATE
		$200 (Initial state)
Ask for $20	Accept +	$180
Ask for $40	Accept +	$140
Ask for $50	Reject –	$140
Ask for $30	Accept +	$110
Ask for $20	Reject –	$110
Return $20	Accept +	$130
Ask for $20	Accept +	$110

Figure 2.31: Learning from reinforcements received from the environment

You can see that since Fred does not know what Anna is thinking—or the agent does not know the model of the environment—he keeps taking actions and tries to understand how Anna will react. He initially starts asking for small amounts, such as $20 and $40, and increases his ask until he gets rejected. After a rejection, he makes his ask smaller until he gets acceptance again. He also tries a new approach where he returns $20 and asks for it so that he knows how much Anna will give away.

This is the process of learning a policy that Fred is going through. The policy is what will drive his actions and, through this trial-and-error approach, Fred or our agent learns a good action-making policy. The different RL algorithms like SARSA, Q-Learning, and Deep Q Networks (DQN) take different approaches to analyzing the data and learning a good policy. The key thing that affects how an algorithm learns is how it strikes a balance between exploitation and exploration. Let's look at this in some detail:

- *Exploitation* means focusing on the current positive reinforcement and continuing actions along the same policy. So, if Fred got a positive reinforcement when he asked for $40 and then a negative response when he asked for $50, he can learn that as a policy and stop right there. From here, he can assume that Anna will not part with anything more than $140. Now he can keep exploiting this further by returning and borrowing the same amounts by following a strict policy that Anna's net has to be above $140. In some problems, exploitation may serve as a good strategy, especially when you arrive at a good solution immediately. However, in this case you can see that it is not.

- *Exploration* is when you deviate from the current policy and try something new. After being rejected for $50, Fred explores the environment further and asks for a lower amount, $30. This time he gets acceptance so the exploration approach worked. Now he can keep exploring further and try to arrive at a better policy. Again, we see that the final policy he learns in Figure 2.31 is not optimal. He could try to borrow $10 more after Anna's net reaches $110 and it will work.

RL algorithms may use different types of policies to determine the right action for the agent based on the state. For example, a *random policy* will have the agent take random actions. In this case, Fred will keep borrowing and returning random amounts of money until he learns the threshold amount beyond which Anna won't lend. Another policy may be a *greedy policy*, where Fred keeps asking for more money and chooses actions that get him the most immediate rewards.

This is how model-free RL works. The agent tries several exploration and exploitation strategies to find an optimal policy, which can be used to take further actions. Let's next discuss a couple of the most popular RL model-free algorithms used in practice—*Q-Learning* and *DQN*.

Q-Learning

The idea of Q-Learning is to choose a policy that maximizes long-term rewards. The concept here is to use a calculation, called the *Q-Value*, that measures the long-term reward achieved by taking a particular action when the environment is at a particular state. Hence, the Q-Learning table, or *Q-Table*, has a number of rows equal to the number of possible states and a number of columns for all the possible actions. It is usually initialized with all zero values. The cells with unrelated states and actions remain at zero.

Now we run the training or learning process, where we run each trial from start to end and find the rewards collected. For each trial, we calculate the Q-Value for each state-action combination using an equation called the *Bellman equation*. Figure 2.32 shows this Bellman equation. We will not go into details on the equation here, but I do provide references at end of the book for it. The idea is that the Bellman equation helps calculate a long-term reward for that state-action combination based on the results of that trial. Since this is an *iterative* learning process, after each trial, the appropriate Q-Value for that state-action cell is updated.

Let's consider a simple example to understand this better and more practically. Say you have a problem of traveling from point S (for start) to point E (end). You

$$Q^{new}(s_t, a_t) \leftarrow (1-\alpha)\cdot \underbrace{Q(s_t, a_t)}_{\text{old value}} + \underbrace{\alpha}_{\text{learning rate}} \cdot \overbrace{\left(\underbrace{r_t}_{\text{reward}} + \underbrace{\gamma}_{\text{discount factor}} \cdot \underbrace{\max_a Q(s_{t+1}, a)}_{\text{estimate of optimal future value}} \right)}^{\text{learned value}}$$

Figure 2.32: Bellman equation for calculating long-term rewards

can travel different paths with middle points represented by M1, M2, etc. By traveling each path, you get a reward represented by a number. Now you have to find an optimal path to travel to maximize your rewards. This problem is represented as a Markov Decision Process (MDP) in Figure 2.33. MDP shows different states and the connections representing state transitions. It also captures the rewards for each state transition.

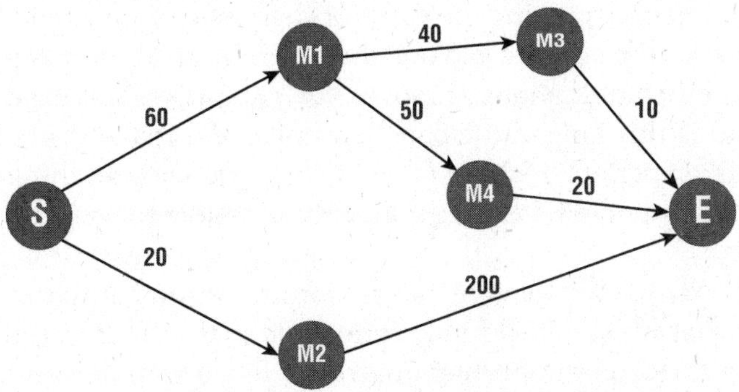

STATES		ACTIONS						
		S to M1	S to M2	M1 to M3	M1 to M4	M2 to E	M3 to E	M4 to E
	S	0.85	1.2	0	0	0	0	0
	M1	0	0	0.45	0.6	0	0	0
	M2	0	0	0	0	2	0	0
	M3	0	0	0	0	0	0.1	0
	M4	0	0	0	0	0	0	0.2

Figure 2.33: Example showing a Markov Decision Process (MDP) and a sample Q-Learning table

The MDP shows us two possible paths from state S to E. Keep in mind that if we know this MDP beforehand, this becomes a model-based RL problem and we can easily find the optimal path with maximum reward. We see that path S-M2-E is the most rewarding one. However, let's assume we don't know the MDP and through trial and error we have to find the best path. We will apply Q-Learning. We will take each path run and calculate the Q-Value for each state-action pair using the Bellman equation. Over the iterations, this Q-Value is updated in the table and you get a table like one in Figure 2.33.

NOTE **A word on the hyper-parameters we used in this example. Here we used a learning rate of 0.01 and a discount factor of 0.5. The discount factor tells us how important future rewards are compared to current rewards. As you know, money in the hand is worth more than what's been promised in the future. Applying the same logic, we apply a discount factor to future rewards.**

Since this is a very simple problem, we only have three trials to run and calculate Q-Values for updating the table. From the Q-Table, we see that for each state we can choose the best action based on a maximum Q-Value. So, we take the start state S and find the action that gives us the maximum Q-Value. That turns out to be S-M2 and then M2-E gives us the best path. There we have it—S-M2-E is our most rewarding path, and we found this in a model-free way.

In a real-world problem, you'll have too many variables and state-action combinations to consider. Imagine playing the game of chess with your friend. From the starting state where all pieces are laid out, there are almost an unimaginable number of moves and combinations of moves you can make. You need to know what your friend is thinking, anticipate her move, and make yours. Unless you are a genius like Sherlock Holmes (albeit fictitious), who can think 10–15 moves ahead of your opponent, it's pretty much impossible to consider all possible combinations.

Q-Learning, although extremely effective, has major limitations. It works well for a finite state set that we can build in a finite table that will fit in the computer's memory. However, as the problem becomes more complex and the number of states goes from a few hundred to millions, it becomes ineffective. You can easily see that if we don't have a value in the Q-Table for a particular state, the agent will not know what action to take.

To solve this problem, a new technique has gained popularity. It's called Deep Q Networks (DQN). Let's look at it now.

Deep Q Networks (DQN)

As we saw in the last section, Q-Learning can handle a finite set of states. For any *unseen* states, it cannot predict actions to take. With real-world systems, it is very difficult to plan for the entire state space and feed it to a Q-Learning algorithm. Hence, we need a way to predict the Q-Value given the state and action combination. This is done using a neural network called the *Deep Q Network*.

DQN trains a neural network for different combinations of state and action pairs and tries to build the Q-Value as a dependent variable of these. DQN can now predict a Q-Value for states that are not known to it and select the best action.

Another problem is that building a state space is often difficult. Say for a game of chess, modeling the different positions of chess pieces on the 8×8 board can be pretty challenging. A technique that is gaining popularity is feeding the images of the input medium like a chessboard and using this to decode the state. A neural network first decodes the state from an image, which is an array of pixel values. Then this decoded state is used to learn how to predict the Q-Value.

Figure 2.34 shows how the images are fed to the network and a Q-Value estimator is developed. The network uses *convolution* layers to extract features from images. These tell us where the pieces are located on the board. Then, using Supervised Learning, the prediction patterns are learned. The network starts to predict Q-Values for different state-action combinations. Based on highest Q-Value, we can select that action and plan our moves.

This is an active area of research. Companies like Google's DeepMind are actively investigating new techniques for building DQNs that can solve complex problems. One of the most significant achievements of DQN has been the AlphaGo program that defeated the champion of the game Go. Go is supposed to be more complex than chess, with many more combinations, and AlphaGo was able to predict the best action for all of these.

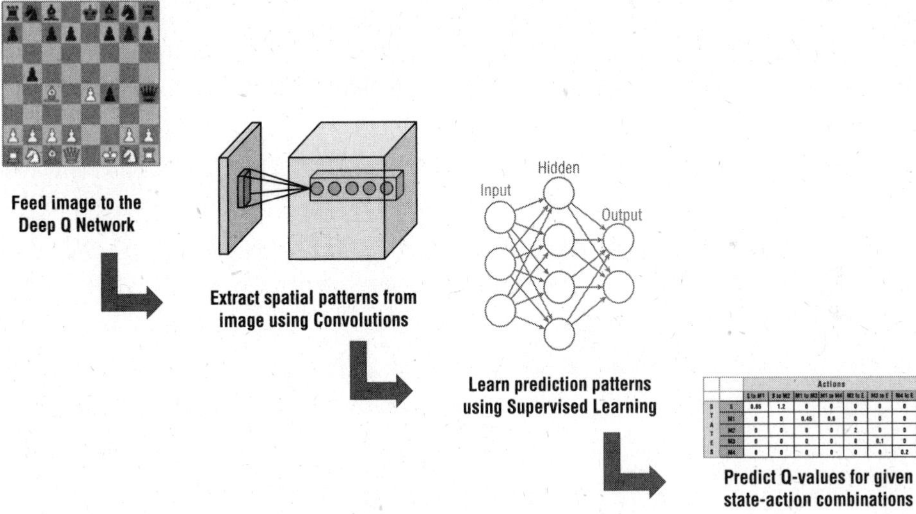

Figure 2.34: Deep Q Network to predict Q-Values

Deep RL is a highly active and growing area. We should expect many more innovations in this space helping us reach significant milestones in fields like medical treatment, robotics, and transportation. Of course, the video game industry has been one of the front runners of using these algorithms inside games.

That's all about Reinforcement Learning for now. We will now return to general ML techniques and specifically focus on Deep Learning.

Summary

All right, that's it on Machine Learning. I hope I was able to provide you with an overview of the methods and algorithms. The code examples showed how you can apply these techniques to your datasets. I hope you can use these methods on your data and find interesting patterns.

We discussed how ML is divided into unsupervised, supervised, and Reinforcement Learning. Unsupervised ML is about finding patterns in data without knowing the results or outcomes beforehand. This includes algorithms for clustering the data, reducing the dimensions (number of features), and detecting anomalies. Supervised ML uses labeled data to build a model that can make predictions on new data. This includes classification algorithms where we predict the membership of each data point to a particular class. The other method is regression, where we predict a numerical value based on input features. We saw examples of popular algorithms in each category. Finally, we talked about Reinforcement Learning, which uses an agent that learns patterns by interacting with an environment and receiving reinforcement (rewards) for taking actions.

In the next chapter, we explore the differences between structured and unstructured data, because this difference often determines which kinds of ML algorithms we use. Then, in Chapter 4, we start looking at neural networks, which use bigger and more complex models, but will be much more effective in capturing all sorts of non-linear patterns in your data.

CHAPTER

3

Handling Unstructured Data

In this chapter, we look in more detail at the differences between structured and unstructured data. This difference in type of data often drives the selection of certain classes of algorithms for ML. We see what makes unstructured data different and why it needs particular attention to handle it properly. We explore common types of unstructured data like images, videos, and text. We see which techniques and tools are available to analyze this data and extract knowledge from it. We see examples of converting structured data into features that can be used for training Machine Learning models.

Structured vs. Unstructured Data

As we saw in the previous chapter, the key to ML is providing good data that the model can learn patterns from and then make its own predictions on unseen data. We need to provide good clean data to the model in a way that it can learn from. *Structured data* is data in a state that can be easily consumed by a model. Here there is a fixed data structure to how you receive the data to feed to your model. Over time or over multiple data points, this structure does not change. Hence, you can map your features to this structure. Each data point can be thought of as a fixed size *vector*, with each dimension or row of the vector representing a feature.

Figure 3.1 shows two examples of structured data. The first is *timeseries* data obtained as sensor readings. Here you get the same vector data points over different intervals of time. The timestamp in this case is the key or index field (column) that is the unique identifier. We will not have two data points with the same exact timestamp (unless our data collection system has an error).

Structured Data Examples

Sensor readings: Timeseries

Timestamp	Value	Quality
21/01/18 0:20	22.4	1
21/01/18 0:30	22.5	1
21/01/18 0:40	22.3	1
21/01/18 0:50	22.3	1
21/01/18 1:00	22.25	1
21/01/18 1:10	22.2	1
21/01/18 1:20	22.15	1
21/01/18 1:30	22.1	1
21/01/18 1:40	22.05	1
21/01/18 1:50	22	1
21/01/18 2:00	21.95	1
21/01/18 2:10	21.9	1
21/01/18 2:20	21.85	1

Key or Index

Loan history: Tabular or Columnar data

Custimer ID	Loan Amout	Term	Interest	Income	Purpose
111123	5000	36 months	10.65	24000	credit_card
112333	2500	60 months	15.27	30000	car
111378	2400	36 months	15.96	12252	small_business
111866	10000	36 months	13.49	49200	other
111994	5000	36 months	7.9	36000	wedding
112121	3000	36 months	18.64	48000	car
112249	5600	60 months	21.28	40000	small_business
112376	5375	60 months	12.69	15000	other
112504	6500	60 months	14.65	72000	debt_consolidation
112631	12000	36 months	12.69	75000	debt_consolidation
112759	9000	36 months	13.49	30000	debt_consolidation
112886	3000	36 months	9.91	15000	credit_card
113014	10000	36 months	10.65	100000	other
113141	1000	36 months	16.29	28000	debt_consolidation
113269	10000	36 months	15.27	42000	home_improvement
113396	3600	36 months	6.03	110000	major_purchase
113524	6000	36 months	11.71	84000	medical
113651	9200	36 months	6.03	77385.19	debt_consolidation
113779	21000	36 months	12.42	105000	debt_consolidation
113906	10000	36 months	11.71	50000	credit_card

Key or Index

Figure 3.1: Structured data examples—timeseries and tabular data

The example in Figure 3.1 is *tabular* or *columnar* data that shows the history of loans given by a financial institution. It is usually recommended to have a unique key like a customer ID in this case, so we can have fast searches based on the key. However, for the same customer, you may have two loans and you'll end up with two entries for the same customer ID. In that case, it is recommended you have a unique key like a loan ID.

Now you can see that each of the data points is a finite length vector of numbers that can be fed into the ML model for training. Similarly, after the model is developed for prediction or inference, the data in the same formal structure can be fed to the model. The features that are used for training map directly to the columns in the structured data. Of course, you may still need to cleanse the data.

For example, the timeseries data always comes with a quality value set by the *data acquisition system (DAQ)*. If the data acquisition system gets the sensor data correctly, it will assign a quality flag of good—in this case 1. An example could be a DAQ with sensor wires connected at different input/output (I/O) points. If a wire is loose and the signal does not come from the sensor to the DAQ box, it will set the flag as bad. One data cleansing step will be to get rid of all the bad-quality data points.

Other examples of structured data include *clickstreams*, which are collected whenever users click website links; *weblogs*, which are logs of website statistics collected by web servers; and of course, *gaming data*, which captures every step you take and every bullet you fire in *Call of Duty*!

Now let's talk about *unstructured data*. This could be images or videos collected from cameras. A video stream may be obtained from cameras and stored into common video files like MP4s and AVIs. Text data may be collected from email messages, web searches, product reviews, *tweets*, social media postings, and more. Audio data may be collected just through sound recorders on cell phones or by placing acoustic sensors at strategic locations to get the maximum sound signal.

Unstructured data is called so because the data points do not follow a fixed structure. An image may come in as an array of pixel intensity values. Text may be encoded as a sequence of characters in special encodings like ASCII (American Standard Code for Information Interchange). Sound may come in as a set of pressure readings. There is no fixed structure to this data. You cannot read data from the pixel arrays and say that the image has a person in it, for example.

There are usually two popular ways to handle unstructured data, as shown in Figure 3.2.

- The first approach is to extract *features* from the unstructured data. This involves cleansing the data, removing noise, and finding the key features. In Figure 3.2, we see unstructured data as a big blob. After cleansing, you can extract structured features—analogous to LEGO blocks. These LEGO blocks can then be assembled to build the result, such as a house.
- The second approach is to use a method called *end-to-end* learning. This is analogous to a ready-made mold of a house in which you fit the unstructured data. You don't have to do any cleansing or preparation—you just get the right mold and fit the data into it to get your desired shape. Of course, you need the right mold for the particular result you are trying to get. End-to-end models are where Deep Learning really shines. Here the mold is analogous to the appropriate DL architecture that is used to build your model. This is getting standardized very fast. A DL architecture called *Convolutional Neural Networks (CNN)* has been universally accepted as a standard for all image and video tasks. Similarly, while handling text and speech data, since this data comes as a sequence of inputs, the universally accepted architecture here is *Recurrent Neural Networks (RNN)*. We will cover the DL techniques in detail in Chapters 4 and 5.

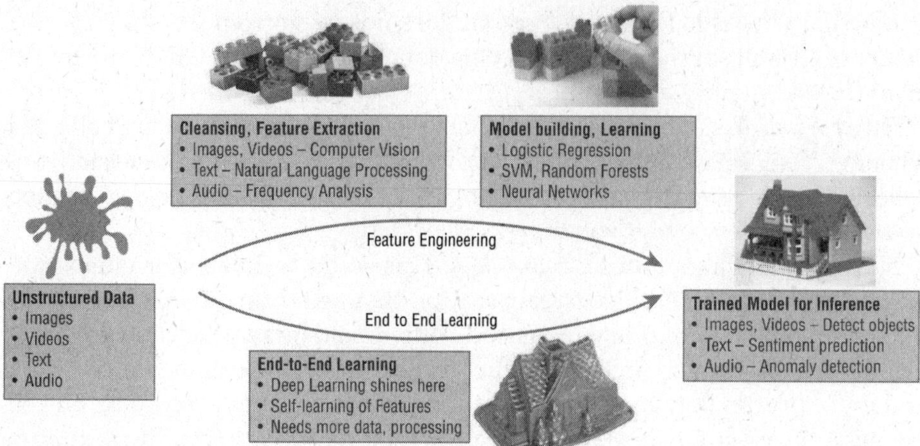

Figure 3.2: Two paths to handling unstructured data

In reality, you may not find a silver bullet using either approach. The end-to-end approach looks good but will not work in all cases. You will have to use trial and error to see what best fits your needs and datatypes. Sometimes you may have to use a hybrid approach. You may have to cleanse the data to some level and then feed it into a DL model. Although RNNs are best for sequence data, you may find CNN used for sequence data after some preprocessing. The method or combination of methods usually depends on the problem domain and this is where the experience of data scientists comes into play. For now, let's explore each type of unstructured data and the common methods of handling it.

Making Sense of Images

When a computer reads an image, it is usually captured from a *digital camera* or a *scanner* and stored in digital form in computer memory. When we take a photo with a digital camera, our camera has an optical sensor that captures light from a scene, renders this inside our camera, and saves the image as a series of numbers—basically a large sequence of 0s and 1s. In raw form, a two-dimensional image is basically a matrix or array of pixel values. Here each pixel value represents intensity of a particular color. However, it does not have a human-readable value like wine alcohol percentage or quality rating. This data is usually referred to as unstructured. The individual values have less significance but as a whole they complement each other and form the bigger domain object like an image.

First, let's look at an example of how a computer captures and stores unstructured data. Say we have an image of a handwritten digit, as shown in Figure 3.3. This is an image from the open handwriting image dataset—considered the "Hello World" for Deep Learning problems—known as MNIST. This has a training set of 60,000 examples and a test set of 10,000 examples. It is a subset of a larger set available from NIST. The digits have been size-normalized and centered in a fixed-size image. This dataset is made available by Yann Lecun at the website `http://yann.lecun.com/exdb/mnist`.

Figure 3.3: An image of a handwritten digit 5 in 28×28 resolution

The image we have in Figure 3.3 is a 28×28 pixel image. That means this image is represented in digital format—in the computer's memory—as a two-dimensional array of pixels with 28 rows and 28 columns. The value of each element of the array is a number from 0 to 255 representing the intensity of black or white color, with 255 being all white and 0 being black. 150 will be a gray cell. Figure 3.4 expands this image to show exactly how these pixel intensity values look.

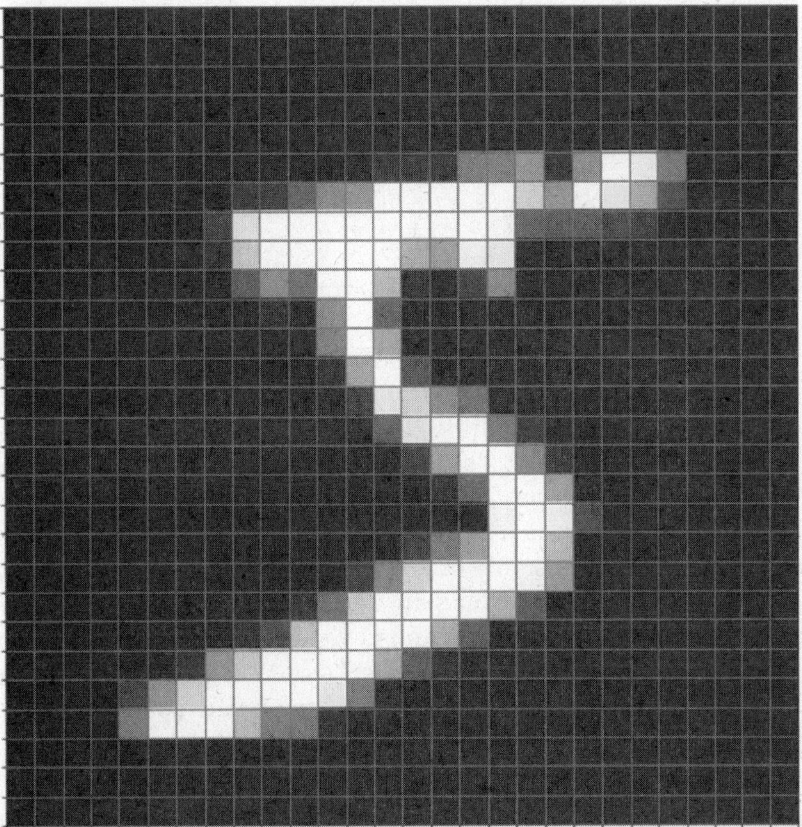

Figure 3.4: The image expanded to show the 28×28 pixel array in detail

We see in the expanded image in Figure 3.4 the details of the color values for each of the 28×28 pixels in the array. The border is shown to differentiate the pixels. The white, black, or shade of gray value for each pixel is represented by a number between 0 and 255. Figure 3.5 shows the raw data.

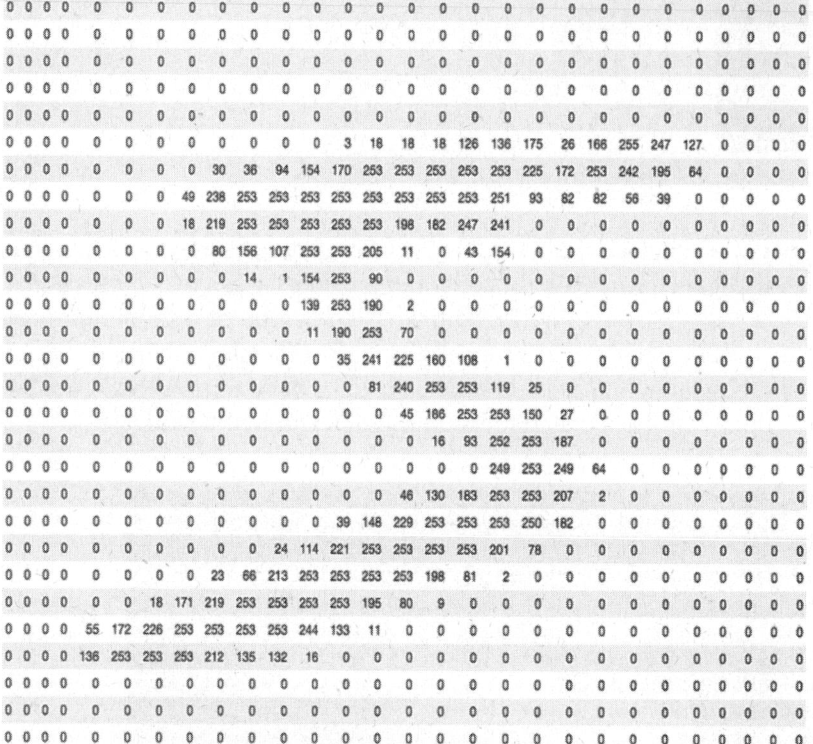

0	0	0	0	0	0	0	0	0	0	0	0	0	0	0	0	0	0	0	0	0	0	0	0	0	0	0	0
0	0	0	0	0	0	0	0	0	0	0	0	0	0	0	0	0	0	0	0	0	0	0	0	0	0	0	0
0	0	0	0	0	0	0	0	0	0	0	0	0	0	0	0	0	0	0	0	0	0	0	0	0	0	0	0
0	0	0	0	0	0	0	0	0	0	0	0	0	0	0	0	0	0	0	0	0	0	0	0	0	0	0	0
0	0	0	0	0	0	0	0	0	0	0	0	0	0	0	0	0	0	0	0	0	0	0	0	0	0	0	0
0	0	0	0	0	0	0	0	0	0	0	0	3	18	18	18	126	136	175	26	166	255	247	127	0	0	0	0
0	0	0	0	0	0	0	0	30	36	94	154	170	253	253	253	253	253	225	172	253	242	195	64	0	0	0	0
0	0	0	0	0	0	0	49	238	253	253	253	253	253	253	253	253	251	93	82	82	56	39	0	0	0	0	0
0	0	0	0	0	0	0	18	219	253	253	253	253	253	198	182	247	241	0	0	0	0	0	0	0	0	0	0
0	0	0	0	0	0	0	0	80	156	107	253	253	205	11	0	43	154	0	0	0	0	0	0	0	0	0	0
0	0	0	0	0	0	0	0	0	14	1	154	253	90	0	0	0	0	0	0	0	0	0	0	0	0	0	0
0	0	0	0	0	0	0	0	0	0	0	139	253	190	2	0	0	0	0	0	0	0	0	0	0	0	0	0
0	0	0	0	0	0	0	0	0	0	0	11	190	253	70	0	0	0	0	0	0	0	0	0	0	0	0	0
0	0	0	0	0	0	0	0	0	0	0	0	35	241	225	160	108	1	0	0	0	0	0	0	0	0	0	0
0	0	0	0	0	0	0	0	0	0	0	0	0	81	240	253	253	119	25	0	0	0	0	0	0	0	0	0
0	0	0	0	0	0	0	0	0	0	0	0	0	0	45	186	253	253	150	27	0	0	0	0	0	0	0	0
0	0	0	0	0	0	0	0	0	0	0	0	0	0	0	16	93	252	253	187	0	0	0	0	0	0	0	0
0	0	0	0	0	0	0	0	0	0	0	0	0	0	0	0	0	249	253	249	64	0	0	0	0	0	0	0
0	0	0	0	0	0	0	0	0	0	0	0	0	0	46	130	183	253	253	207	2	0	0	0	0	0	0	0
0	0	0	0	0	0	0	0	0	0	0	0	39	148	229	253	253	253	250	182	0	0	0	0	0	0	0	0
0	0	0	0	0	0	0	0	0	0	24	114	221	253	253	253	253	201	78	0	0	0	0	0	0	0	0	0
0	0	0	0	0	0	0	0	23	66	213	253	253	253	253	198	81	2	0	0	0	0	0	0	0	0	0	0
0	0	0	0	0	0	18	171	219	253	253	253	253	195	80	9	0	0	0	0	0	0	0	0	0	0	0	0
0	0	0	0	55	172	226	253	253	253	253	244	133	11	0	0	0	0	0	0	0	0	0	0	0	0	0	0
0	0	0	0	136	253	253	253	212	135	132	16	0	0	0	0	0	0	0	0	0	0	0	0	0	0	0	0
0	0	0	0	0	0	0	0	0	0	0	0	0	0	0	0	0	0	0	0	0	0	0	0	0	0	0	0
0	0	0	0	0	0	0	0	0	0	0	0	0	0	0	0	0	0	0	0	0	0	0	0	0	0	0	0
0	0	0	0	0	0	0	0	0	0	0	0	0	0	0	0	0	0	0	0	0	0	0	0	0	0	0	0

Figure 3.5: Image array as raw data with pixel intensity values

Figure 3.5 is how a computer sees this image. You can see most pixels have a 0 value, representing a black color. The values with white and gray form a pattern of the digit 5. Also keep in mind that since this is a grayscale image, the values of pixel arrays are just a single integer. If we had a color image then these pixel array values would be arrays with RGB values. That is, each cell would be an array with values for red, green, and blue color intensities.

Also, a computer understands only 0s and 1s. When this image is stored in computer memory, the pixel array values are not stored as numbers—139, 253, etc. They get converted to sequences of 0s and 1s. Using the appropriate number encoding used by the computer, each integer is stored as a sequence of bits (0 or 1)—usually as a sequence of eight bits—that can capture values from 0 to 255. Hence 255 is the highest value, which is assigned to the color white.

You can actually see this in the array in Figure 3.5. Our brain is so amazing that it finds the pattern even in this huge array of values. But how does the computer extract this knowledge from this pixel array? For that, it needs a human-like intelligence, which is delivered using Machine Learning algorithms.

The features for this dataset are the pixel array values, so a total of 28 × 28 = 784 pixels. It will be extremely difficult to get a regular Machine Learning correlation between values of the pixels and digits we want to predict.

This is how the image is processed by the computer; however, it does not make sense to store such a large array for each image. Practically, we compress the image from the large array into a compressed format that is optimized for storage. We know these compressed storage formats as file extensions—*GIF (Graphics Interchange Format)*, *JPG/JPEG (Joint Photography Experts Group)*, and *PNG (Portable Network Graphics)*. These file extensions have their own ways of compressing data and saving images. You can use a *computer vision* or *image processing* library like *OpenCV* or *PIL (Python Imaging Library)* to read files from these formats and convert them into arrays for processing. Let's look at some examples.

Computer Vision

Computer vision is all about *seeing* things in images. We process images and extract knowledge from them. We can do things like find geometrical objects such as lines, rectangles, circles, etc., in images. We can look at colors of different objects and try to separate them. The knowledge extracted, which may be geometry or colors, can be used to prepare features that will be used to train our ML model. Hence, computer vision helps us in feature engineering to extract important knowledge from the large image array. Let's look at this through some examples.

We will use one of the most popular image-processing libraries called *OpenCV*. This was developed at Intel and then open sourced. Currently this is maintained as an open source solution at `opencv.org`. OpenCV is written in C++, but has APIs available in other languages like Python and Java. We will of course use Python as before. You can install it from the website. Incidentally, OpenCV comes preinstalled when you start a Notebook at Google Colaboratory.

Here we will cover some of the basic CV steps that will help you do some preprocessing on images. You can find a whole lot more examples at the OpenCV website at `https://docs.opencv.org/4.0.0/d6/d00/tutorial_py_root.html`.

Now we will look at some key computer vision tasks that are done to load and process images. We will do these in OpenCV. We will first load an image from disk, display it, and manipulate the pixels to show how it changes (see Listing 3.1). We will use a free and openly available image from Wikipedia—the Mona Lisa. The Mona Lisa is a painting by the Italian Renaissance artist Leonardo da Vinci. It's been described as "the best known, the most visited, the most written about, the most sung about, the most parodied work of art in the world." It is worth almost $800 million today. The image of Mona Lisa we will use is available at `https://en.wikipedia.org/wiki/Mona_Lisa`. You can save this as `monalisa.jpg` on your local drive. See Figure 3.6.

Listing 3.1: Load an Image as an Array, then Resize and Display It

```
# import opencv library and print the version
# a version above 3.0 is recommended
import cv2
print("OpenCV Version: ", cv2.__version__)

# import numpy library
import numpy as np

# import matplotlib charting library
import matplotlib.pyplot as plt

# show charts inline in notebook
%matplotlib inline

# Load a JPG image as an array
my_image = cv2.imread('monalisa.jpg')
# convert the image from BGR to RGB color space
my_image = cv2.cvtColor(my_image, cv2.COLOR_BGR2RGB)

# Show size of the array
print("Original image array shape: ", my_image.shape)

# Show values for pixel (100,100)
print ("Pixel (100,100) values: ", my_image[100][100][:])

# Resize the image
my_image = cv2.resize(my_image, (400,600))
plt.imshow(my_image)
plt.show()

# Show size of the array
print("Resized image array shape: ", my_image.shape)

# convert the image from RGB to BGR color space
my_image = cv2.cvtColor(my_image, cv2.COLOR_RGB2BGR)
# Save the new image
cv2.imwrite('new_monalisa.jpg', my_image)

# convert the image to greyscale
my_grey = cv2.cvtColor(my_image, cv2.COLOR_RGB2GRAY)
print('Image converted to grayscale.')
plt.imshow(my_grey,cmap='gray')
plt.show()
```

Here are the results:

```
OpenCV Version:  3.4.2
Original image array shape:  (1024, 687, 3)
```

```
Pixel (100,100) values:  [145 152  95]

Resized image array shape:  (600, 400, 3)

Image converted to grayscale.
```

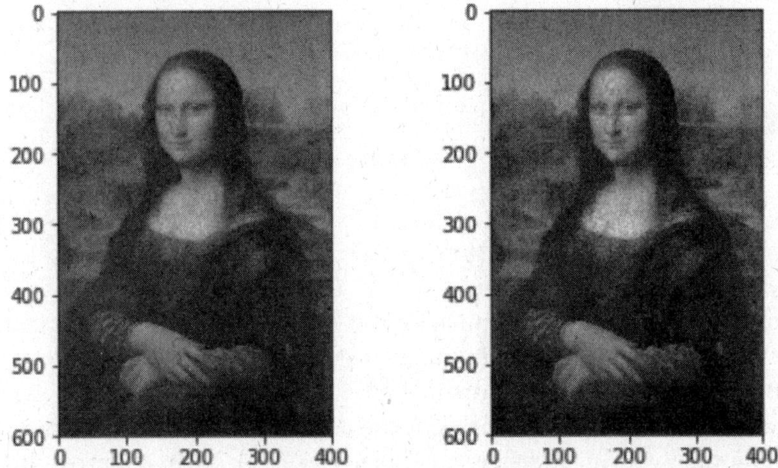

Figure 3.6: Load image using OpenCV and convert it to grayscale

We have loaded the image using the OpenCV library (CV2) and we have it as an array. We resized the image to a 400-pixel width and 600-pixel height image and displayed it using the Matplotlib charting library.

Finally, we save the modified image as a new JPG file called `new_monalisa.jpg`. This new image has 400×600 pixels—that is, 240,000 pixels. Each pixel has three values, indicating three color channels. Each color value representing red, blue, and green has an 8-bit integer value between 0 and 255. So the total size of the image should be 240,000 × 3 × 8 bits = 720,000 × 8 bits, which is 720,000 bytes or 720 *kilobytes* (kb). If you look at the new file generated (it's called `new_monalisa.jpg`), it's about 124KB. That's the level of compression JPG encoding provides us with.

One thing you will notice in this code is that we changed the color spaces back and forth. Color spaces determine how the information about colors is encoded in a digital image. The most popular way of representing color is using three values—one each for red, green, and blue (RGB) elements. Any color can be represented as a combination of these three colors. The RGB color model is an additive color model in which red, green, and blue values are added together in various ways to reproduce a broad array of colors. So red is represented as (255,0,0), green as (0,255,0), and blue as (0,0,255). As you see in Figure 3.7, a combination of red and green gives us yellow, green and blue gives cyan, and blue and red gives pink.

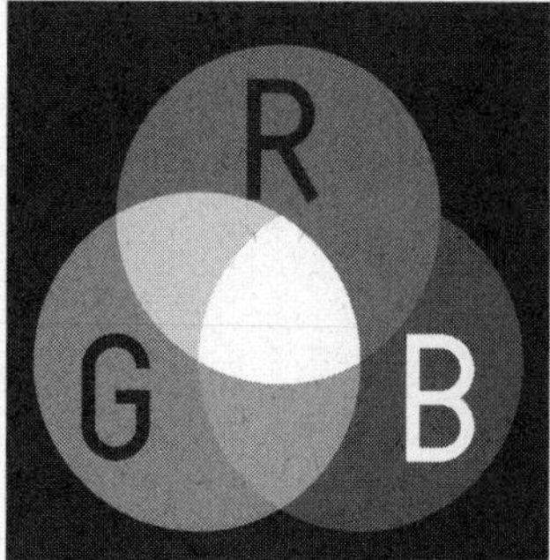

Figure 3.7: RGB color space source Wikipedia
(*Source*: SharkD)

Listing 3.2 shows some examples of how the additive nature of the RGB color space works. You see that you can mix colors and get new colors. Black and white are extremes with all 0 or 255 values for the RGB color channels. You can try several combinations and see what you get. Keep in mind that here the *resolution* or *granularity* of the digital colors is 8 bits. Hence, for any channel, the maximum number we can use to represent the color is 255. This is the most common resolution. However, sharper systems use a 16- or 24-bit color resolution and these can represent even more variation in colors.

Listing 3.2: Example of an RGB Additive Color Space

```
RED                 = (255,0,0)

GREEN               = (0,255,0)

BLUE                = (0,0,255)

RED (255,0,0)   + GREEN (0,255,0) = YELLOW (255,255,0)

BLUE (0,0,255) + GREEN (0,255,0) = CYAN (0,255,255)

RED (255,0,0)   + BLUE (0,0,255)  = YELLOW (255,0,255)

BLACK               = (0,0,0)

WHITE               = (255,255,255)
```

There are other color spaces used by different systems. For example, OpenCV loads and saves images in the BGR color space instead of RGB. Hence, we need to convert the color space after reading or before storing to save it in the correct format. Some of the other popular color spaces are YPbPr and HSV. YPbPr is a color space used in video electronics, particularly with component video cables. HSV (Hue, Saturation, Value) is also a popular color space usually representing colors in a true sense and not additive like RGB.

Now, let's do some processing on this image, as shown in Listing 3.3. We first convert the image into grayscale or black-and-white. Then we fill a portion of the image as a black rectangle. Then we crop a portion of the image and fill it elsewhere. We do these as array operations. Figure 3.8 shows the results.

Listing 3.3: Perform Array Operations on the Image

```
# import opencv library and print the version
import cv2
print("OpenCV Version: ", cv2.__version__)

# import numpy library
import numpy as np

# import matplotlib charting library
import matplotlib.pyplot as plt
# show charts inline in notebook
%matplotlib inline

# Load a JPG image as an array
my_image = cv2.imread('new_monalisa.jpg')
# convert the image from BGR to RGB color space
my_image = cv2.cvtColor(my_image, cv2.COLOR_BGR2RGB)

# draw a black filled rectangle at top left
my_image[10:100,10:100,:] = 0
plt.imshow(my_image)

# draw a red filled rectangle at top right
my_image[10:100,300:390,:] = 0
# fill in the red channel with maximum value (255)
my_image[10:100,300:390,0] = 255
plt.imshow(my_image)

# get the face as region of interest - roi
roi = my_image[50:250,125:250,:]
# resize the roi
roi = cv2.resize(roi,(300,300))
# draw the roi pixels elsewhere in image
my_image[300:600,50:350,:] = roi
plt.imshow(my_image)
```

Now we will use OpenCV's built-in functions for drawing some geometries and text on the image. We will first make a copy of the original image in memory, which we call `temp_image`, and then we process this to show the results. For showing the results, we define a dedicated function. This will get rid of the axes when the image is shown and set the image size. Let's see this action in Listing 3.4. Figure 3.9 shows the results.

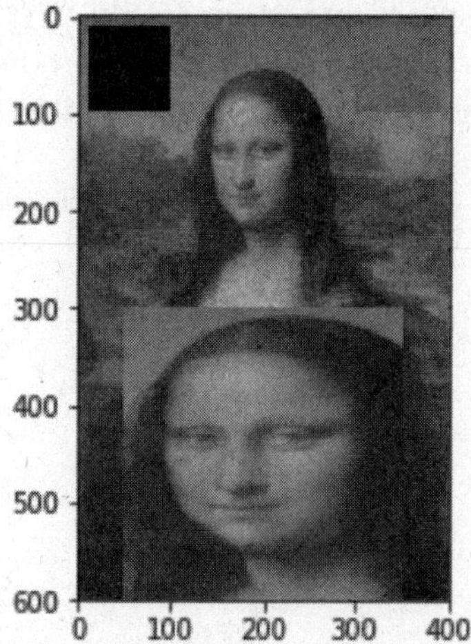

Figure 3.8: Results of array operations on the image

Listing 3.4 Perform Computer Vision Operations on the Image

```
# Load a JPG image as an array
my_image = cv2.imread('new_monalisa.jpg')
# convert the image from BGR to RGB color space
my_image = cv2.cvtColor(my_image, cv2.COLOR_BGR2RGB)

# define a function to show image
# takes parameters p_image and p_title
def show_image(p_image, p_title):
    plt.figure(figsize=(5,10))
    plt.axis('off')
    plt.title(p_title)
    plt.imshow(p_image)

# make a copy of the image
temp_image = my_image.copy()

# draw a line of blue color = (0,0,255) in RGB colorspace - line width
is 5px
cv2.line(temp_image, (10,100), (390,100), (0,0,255), 5)

# draw a rectangle at coordinates of line 5px
cv2.rectangle(temp_image, (200,200), (300,400), (0,255,255), 5)

# draw a circle - for filled option set linewidth -1
cv2.circle(temp_image,(100,200), 50, (255,0,0), -1)

# draw some text on the image
font = cv2.FONT_HERSHEY_SIMPLEX
cv2.putText(temp_image,'Mona Lisa',(10,500), font, 1.5, (255,255,255),
2, cv2.LINE_AA)
```

```
# call our function to display image
show_image(temp_image,'Result 1: Draw geometry and text')
```

Figure 3.9: Results of the OpenCV operations on the image

Now we will use OpenCV's functions for doing some image-cleansing operations. These can be pretty handy when you're dealing with noisy images, which is often the case when you get field images. Many times, the color may not store important information about the image. You may be interested in understanding the geometry, and in that case, a grayscale image is fine. So first we convert our image to grayscale and then perform a thresholding operation on it.

Thresholding is a very important operation in computer vision. It is basically a filtering operation that checks for pixel intensity up to a particular value. Anything below that value is removed. This way, we only get specific details like bright areas of the image.

Let's see this action in Listing 3.5. Figure 3.10 shows the result.

Listing 3.5: Perform Computer Vision Thresholding Operation on the Image

```
# make a copy of the original image
temp_image = my_image.copy()

# convert to grayscale
gray = cv2.cvtColor(temp_image, cv2.COLOR_RGB2GRAY)

# create threshold for the image using different algorithms
# last parameter here is the algorithm - we will check for pixel
intensity > 100
ret,thresh1 = cv2.threshold(gray,100,255,cv2.THRESH_BINARY)
```

```
ret,thresh2 = cv2.threshold(gray,100,255,cv2.THRESH_BINARY_INV)
ret,thresh3 = cv2.threshold(gray,100,255,cv2.THRESH_TRUNC)
ret,thresh4 = cv2.threshold(gray,100,255,cv2.THRESH_TOZERO)
ret,thresh5 = cv2.threshold(gray,100,255,cv2.THRESH_TOZERO_INV)

# set an array of titles for above algorithm results
titles = ['Original Image','BINARY Threshold','BINARY_INV
Threshold','TRUNC Threshold','TOZERO Threshold','TOZERO_INV Threshold']
# create an array of results images
images = [gray, thresh1, thresh2, thresh3, thresh4, thresh5]

# now we will plot these images as an array
plt.figure(figsize=(15,15))
for i in np.arange(6):
    plt.subplot(2,3,i+1),plt.imshow(images[i],'gray')
    plt.title(titles[i])
    plt.axis('off')
plt.show()
```

Figure 3.10: Results of thresholding operations on the image

Now we will perform two operations that can greatly help you make images smooth and remove noise. We will use a process called *convolution* to run a filter or kernel over the image. The filter will have a particular structure that will help process the image and transform it. Using special kinds of filters, we can do operations like smooth or blur the image or sharpen it. These are the operations often done by image processing software like Photoshop and mobile photo editors.

We will use two filters/kernels of the following type. These will be uniformly applied over the entire image array and we will see how the results transform the image:

```
Kernel_1 = 1/9 * [  [1,1,1],
[1,1,1],
[1,1,1]]

Kernel_2 =        [   [-1,-1,-1],
[-1,+9,-1],
[-1,-1,-1]]
```

Let's see this action in Listing 3.6. Figure 3.11 shows the results.

Listing 3.6: Run Kernel/Filters on the Image to Blur and Sharpen

```
# make a copy of the original image
temp_image = my_image.copy()
show_image(temp_image,'Original image')

# first apply the kernel for smoothing or blurring
kernel = np.ones((3,3),np.float32)/9
result = cv2.filter2D(temp_image,-1,kernel)

# apply burring twice to see better effect
result = cv2.filter2D(result,-1,kernel)
result = cv2.filter2D(result,-1,kernel)
show_image(result,'Result: Blurring filter')

# apply sharpening filter
kernel_sharpening = np.array([[-1,-1,-1],
                              [-1, 9,-1],
                              [-1,-1,-1]])
result = cv2.filter2D(temp_image,-1,kernel_sharpening)
show_image(result,'Result: Sharpening filter')
```

You can use these techniques to cleanse the images you collect of noise. Smoothing helps get rid of unwanted noise in images. In some cases, if the images are too blurry, you can use a sharpening filter to make the features look more prominent.

Figure 3.11: Results of applying 2D filters to the image

Another very useful technique that is often used is to extract geometry information from images. You can take a grayscale image and extract the edges from it. This helps remove unwanted details like colors, shading, etc., and focuses only on the prominent edges. Listing 3.7 shows the code and Figure 3.12 shows the result.

Listing 3.7: Run a Canny Edge Detector Algorithm to Detect Edges

```
# make a copy of the original image
temp_image = my_image.copy()

# convert to grayscale
gray = cv2.cvtColor(temp_image,cv2.COLOR_RGB2GRAY)

# run the Canny algorithm to detect edges
edges = cv2.Canny(gray,100,255)

plt.figure(figsize=(5,10))
plt.axis('off')
plt.title('Result: Canny Edge detection')
plt.imshow(edges, cmap='gray')
```

We will see one last example that may be helpful when you handle image data. We earlier saw an example where we took a small region of interest (ROI) from a bigger image. However, in that case, we knew the exact coordinates that corresponded to the face of Mona Lisa. Now we will see a technique to detect faces directly. This is an ML technique that is included with the OpenCV library. We will cover details of the ML methods in the next chapter; however, let's talk a little about this method.

Figure 3.12: Results of applying Canny edge detection

OpenCV comes with an algorithm that can look at images and automatically detect faces in them. This algorithm is called *Haar Cascades*. The idea here is that it tries to use some knowledge of how a face looks in a big array of pixels. It tries to capture knowledge like the fact that our eyes are usually darker than the rest of our face, the region between the eyes is bright, etc. Then, using a cascade of learning units or classifiers, it identifies the coordinates of a face in an image. These classifiers for detecting faces, eyes, ears, etc. are already trained for you and made available on the OpenCV GitHub at `https://github.com/opencv/opencv/tree/master/data/haarcascades`.

Take a look at the face detection in action in Listing 3.8. Figure 3.13 shows the result.

Listing 3.8: Use Haar Cascades to Detect a Face in an Image

```
# make a copy of the original image
temp_image = my_image.copy()

# convert to grayscale
gray = cv2.cvtColor(temp_image,cv2.COLOR_RGB2GRAY)

# load the face cascade model from xml file
face_cascade = cv2.CascadeClassifier('haarcascade_profileface.xml')
```

```
# find faces and draw green rectangle for each face found
faces = face_cascade.detectMultiScale(gray,1.3,5)
for (x,y,w,h) in faces:
    roi_color = temp_image[y:y+h, x:x+w]
    # show the roi detected
    show_image(roi_color, 'Result: ROI of face detected by Haar Cascade
Classifier')
    cv2.rectangle(temp_image,(x,y),(x+w,y+h),(0,255,0),2)

# show the image with face detected
show_image(temp_image, 'Result: Face detection using Haar Cascade
Classifier')
```

Figure 3.13: Results of detecting a face using the Haar Cascade Classifier

These preprocessing steps can greatly cleanse your noisy images and help you extract valuable information, which can then be used to train the ML model. Using smoothing and edge detection, you can get rid of the background and only give the model relevant information to work with. Similarly, say you are building a face detection analytic—like the one that iPhone uses to unlock with face identification. The first step would be to reduce the large image into a much smaller and more manageable region of interest, which can be processed much faster by your face recognition model.

There are lots more algorithms and methods that computer vision libraries like OpenCV provide. If your data involves images, then you can look at details of some of the other methods like extracting Hough lines, circles, matching image templates, etc. They are available at `https://docs.opencv.org/4.0.0/d6/d00/tutorial _ py _ root.html`.

Next, we'll look at how we can handle video data. Again, we will use computer vision methods to do so.

Dealing with Videos

Videos are basically sequences of images over time. They can be like a timeseries of image data. Typically, you extract the frames at specific times from a video and process them using regular computer vision or ML algorithms. Now you may feel that storing all these images in sequence may make the video files extremely huge. A typical video will have around 24 or 30 frames per second (fps), which indicates that every second there will be 30 images. You can see how the file sizes would typically grow enormous. That's where the video formats come into play.

Just like image storage formats like JPG, GIF, and PNG compress the pixel arrays into binary formats, video compression and decompression (*codec*) will compress the sequence of images that create a video. Common video codecs used are XVid, DivX, and the current most popular, H.264. These codecs define how the frames are encoded to maximize storage and minimize loss.

Along with a codec, another specification the video has is the type of *container* used. This is also known as the *format*. The container stores the contents of the video file encoded by the respective codec. Popular container formats are AVI, MOV, and MP4. Not all MP4 files are encoded by the same codec. Some may need a special codec and hence your video player may need to download a special codec—although the extension is the same—.MP4. Sometimes the video content may be available as a stream rather than as a container. Here also a similar codec is used, only the content is streaming. That's how you get content delivered over YouTube and Netflix.

Computer vision libraries like OpenCV provide codec support to decode these video files and extract frames. OpenCV can also connect to a live stream from a source like a camera and extract video. Check out the example code in Listing 3.9. It is difficult to show the actual results in a book, but you can run the example on your machine.

Listing 3.9: Extract Frames from Video for Processing

```
import cv2 as cv

# open video capture
cap = cv2.VideoCapture('sample_video.mp4')

# frame counter
counter = 0
```

```
# while the video file is open
while(cap.isOpened()):
    # read a frame
    ret, frame = cap.read()

    # write frame number
    counter += 1
    print(counter)

    # convert the frame to grayscale
    new_frame = cv2.cvtColor(frame, cv2.COLOR_RGB2GRAY)

    # show every 30th frame
    if counter%30 == 0:
        plt.imshow(new_frame)
        plt.show()

# release the video file
cap.release()
```

This code will read a video file, extract the frames (images), convert the frames to grayscale, and write every 30th frame out. Assuming 30 frames per second, you should get a frame per second. After you have the images or frames, you can run the same computer vision algorithms to extract valuable information.

Next, we cover handling another interesting datatype—text.

Handling Textual Data

Data in text format is one of the most common forms of unstructured data around us. We don't often consider text as a data source; however, analyzing text can give us rich insights into several aspects, particularly human behavior.

You have probably had this experience yourself. The other day, I searched for reviews of a new PlayStation game on Google. The next thing I knew, I started getting bombarded with advertisements of games in the same genre. I also got an email from Amazon recommending more games. When I entered my search query, Google had an algorithm that extracted the meaning of my search query and *learned* that I am interested in that product. Then it passed that information to other algorithms that found similar products and provided me with recommendations. That is the magic of modern advertising. Companies like Google, Facebook, and Twitter have advertisements as one of their major revenue sources. They continuously analyze volumes of text content generated from product reviews, social media postings, and tweets to extract valuable information about the lifestyles of their customers. Many times, this information is sold to third parties, who can mine this data and extract valuable insights. Text mining is a major activity where companies try to extract value from text content using advanced *Natural Language Processing (NLP)* algorithms.

Another example of analyzing text data is the *chatbot*, which understands text messages sent by customers and responds appropriately by searching through huge databases of text. Here the chatbot needs to be smart enough to understand what the customer asked for and respond correctly. Many online support services employ chatbots and you may not even know that you are not talking to a human on the other end. Text analysis is also extensively used for filtering emails and identifying *spam* content. This is a classification problem where, based on the content of the message, we give it a label of spam or not.

What makes text data unique is that it comes in as a sequence of characters, unlike an image, which is one big blob or array of data. Text content comes in as a sequence and has to be processed so that the meaning or context can be derived. In the computer memory, text data is encoded using several types of encoding. It could be a proprietary encoding like a Microsoft Word file or an open encoding specified by American Standard Code for Information Interchange (ASCII). Now this sequence of text data has to be analyzed for meaning.

As we saw in Figure 3.2 for text data, you can follow one of the same two approaches. You can denoise the data and extract features using specialized text processing techniques like NLP. Or you can feed the text as a vector to Deep Learning models that learn to extract this information.

For NLP, one of the most popular libraries is NLTK (Natural Language Tool Kit). NLTK is written in the Python programming language. It was developed by Steven Bird and Edward Loper from the Department of Computer and Information Science at the University of Pennsylvania. Details about this library are available at `https://www.nltk.org`.

Let's look at some examples of processing text data to cleanse it and extract features from it. We will look at an example of using an end-to-end DL approach in the next chapter. Here we will also see an example of a *Recurrent Neural Network (RNN)*.

Natural Language Processing (NLP)

NLP is about processing text data to cleanse and extract valuable information from it. If we can understand the meaning of the text and do some action, then it is termed as a different activity called *Natural Language Understanding (NLU)*. NLP usually deals with low-level actions and NLU deals with higher level ones. The chatbot case we discussed earlier is an example of NLU. However, many times we generalize and for all text analysis, use the term NLP.

Let's look at some basic concepts about NLP. Text is stored in groups called *documents*. Documents contain words, which are called *tokens*. We could group tokens from a document together into smaller groups separated by a full-stop called *sentences*. A sentence is usually a sequence of tokens that carries some meaning and should be processed together and in order. A group of similar documents is called a *corpus*. Many corpora are available online for free to test our NLP skills. NLTK itself comes with corpora like *Reuters* (news), *Gutenberg* (books), and *WordNet* (word meanings) that have specific content.

Let's look at some quick and simple examples with sample NLTK code, which you can easily apply to your data to analyze text.

First, we will work on cleansing the data. We will convert the text to lowercase and then *tokenize* the text to extract words and sentences. Then we will remove some commonly occurring stop words. Stop words like *the*, *a*, and *and* usually don't add value to overall the context or meaning of a sentence. Finally, we will create a frequency plot to identify the most common words. This can easily give us the gist of words of importance and help in summarizing the content. You can look at this effort in Listing 3.10.

Listing 3.10: NLP Methods to Cleanse Text Data and Extract Basic Information

```
import nltk

# this will be the text document we will analyze
mytext = "We are studying Machine Learning. Our Model learns patterns
in data. This learning helps it to predict on new data."
print("ORIGINAL TEXT = ", mytext)
print('----------------------')

# convert text to lowercase
mytext = mytext.lower()

# first we will tokenize the text into word tokens
word_tokens = nltk.word_tokenize(mytext)
print("WORD TOKENS = ", word_tokens)
print('----------------------')

# we can also extract sentences if needed
sentence_tokens = nltk.sent_tokenize(mytext)
print("SENTENCE TOKENS = ", sentence_tokens)
print('----------------------')

# lets remove some common stop words
stp_words = ["is","a","our","on",".","!","we","are","this","of","and",
"from","to","it","in"]
print("STOP WORDS = ", stp_words)
print('----------------------')

# define cleaned up tokens array
clean_tokens = []

# remove stop words from our word_tokens
for token in word_tokens:
    if token not in stp_words:
        clean_tokens.append(token)
```

```
print("CLEANED WORD TOKENS = ", clean_tokens)
print('----------------------')

from nltk.stem import WordNetLemmatizer
lemmatizer = WordNetLemmatizer()
from nltk.stem import PorterStemmer
stemmer = PorterStemmer()

# define cleaned up and lemmatized tokens array
clean_lemma_tokens = []
clean_stem_tokens = []

# remove stop words from our word_tokens
for token in clean_tokens:
    clean_stem_tokens.append(stemmer.stem(token))
    clean_lemma_tokens.append(lemmatizer.lemmatize(token))

print("CLEANED STEMMED TOKENS = ", clean_stem_tokens)
print('----------------------')

print("CLEANED LEMMATIZED TOKENS = ", clean_lemma_tokens)
print('----------------------')

# get frequency distribution of words
freq_lemma = nltk.FreqDist(clean_lemma_tokens)
freq_stem = nltk.FreqDist(clean_stem_tokens)

# import plotting library
import matplotlib.pyplot as plt
%matplotlib inline

# set a font size
chart_fontsize = 30

# plot the frequency chart
plt.figure(figsize=(20,10))
plt.tick_params(labelsize=chart_fontsize)
plt.title('Cleaned and Stemmed Words', fontsize=chart_fontsize)
plt.xlabel('Word Tokens', fontsize=chart_fontsize)
plt.ylabel('Frequency (Counts)', fontsize=chart_fontsize)
freq_stem.plot(20, cumulative=False)
plt.show()

# plot the frequency chart
plt.figure(figsize=(20,10))
plt.tick_params(labelsize=chart_fontsize)
plt.title('Cleaned and Lemmatized Words', fontsize=chart_fontsize)
plt.xlabel('Word Tokens', fontsize=chart_fontsize)
plt.ylabel('Frequency (Counts)', fontsize=chart_fontsize)
freq_lemma.plot(20, cumulative=False)
plt.show()
```

Here are the results:

```
ORIGINAL TEXT =  We are studying Machine Learning. Our Model learns
patterns in data. This learning helps it to predict on new data.
----------------------

WORD TOKENS =  ['we', 'are', 'studying', 'machine', 'learning', '.',
'our', 'model', 'learns', 'patterns', 'in', 'data', '.', 'this',
'learning', 'helps', 'it', 'to', 'predict', 'on', 'new', 'data', '.']
----------------------

SENTENCE TOKENS =  ['we are studying machine learning.', 'our model
learns patterns in data.', 'this learning helps it to predict on new
data.']
----------------------

STOP WORDS =  ['is', 'a', 'our', 'on', '.', '!', 'we', 'are', 'this',
'of', 'and', 'from', 'to', 'it', 'in']
----------------------

CLEANED WORD TOKENS =  ['studying', 'machine', 'learning', 'model',
'learns', 'patterns', 'data', 'learning', 'helps', 'predict', 'new',
'data']
----------------------

CLEANED STEMMED TOKENS =  ['studi', 'machin', 'learn', 'model', 'learn',
'pattern', 'data', 'learn', 'help', 'predict', 'new', 'data']
----------------------

CLEANED LEMMATIZED TOKENS =  ['studying', 'machine', 'learning',
'model', 'learns', 'pattern', 'data', 'learning', 'help', 'predict',
'new', 'data']
----------------------
```

If you follow the code and results in Listing 3.10, we take a set of sentences through a series of cleansing steps. We make the text lowercase, tokenize the text into words, and remove any stop words. Then for each token we apply two normalization techniques in parallel—*stemming* (see Figure 3.14) and *lemmatization* (see Figure 3.15). Both these techniques try to remove different versions of the same word and try to make the text simple. They try to remove multiple versions of the same base word such as *learns, learning,* and *learned* for the base word *learn.*

Stemming is a more heuristic technique, where common suffixes are chopped off, like *s, es,* and *ing*. However, in doing so, sometimes the true meaning of the word is lost. In the results for stemming, you see some non-words like *machin* and *studi.* Lemmatization, on the other hand, tries to derive the actual root word and keeps the results as valid words. Hence, we see valid words as a result of lemmatization. This is usually preferred when you process text.

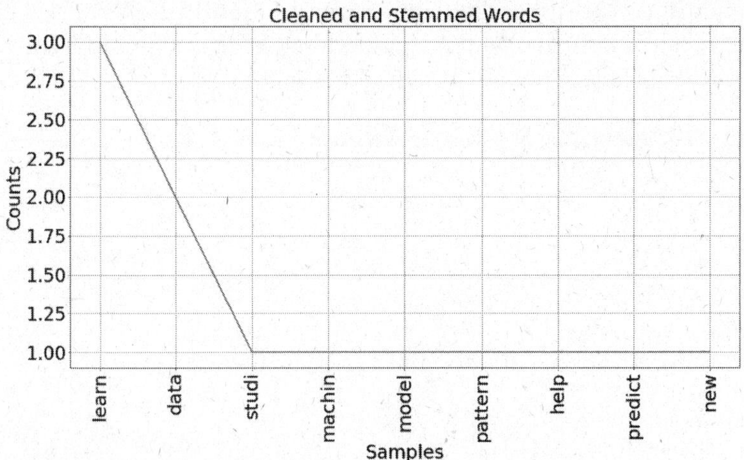

Figure 3.14: Frequency chart of common words—stemmed

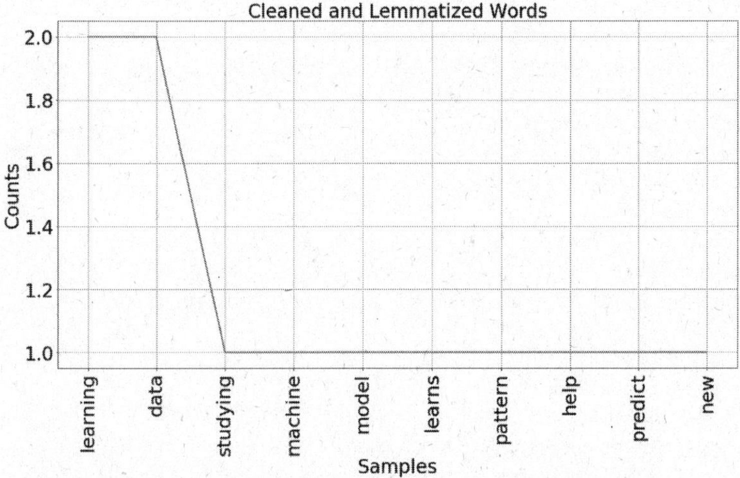

Figure 3.15: Frequency chart of common words—lemmatized

Finally, we get a frequency of most common words and plot it—both stemmed and lemmatized. This gives us a high-level summary of the most frequently occurring words and helps us get a gist of the text. We have a very small amount of text here, but when you apply this approach to a large document or corpus, you can clearly see the key terms popping up with high frequency.

After cleansing the text data, we will explore how to extract some useful information. We will look at two very useful text processing concepts called *parts of speech (POS) tagging* and *Named Entity Recognition (NER)*. Here, we are extracting contextual information about the text, so the sequence of words is very important. The sequence in which words are arranged helps the algorithm understand what part of speech each word represents.

POS tagging takes a word-tokenized sentence and identifies the parts of speech, like nouns, verbs, adverbs, etc. A detailed list of tag names added by NLTK to words and their meanings is shown in Listing 3.11.

Listing 3.11: List of Parts of Speech Tags and Their Abbreviations, as per NLTK

```
CC coordinating conjunction
CD cardinal digit
DT determiner
EX existential there (like: "there is" ... think of it like "there
exists")
FW foreign word
IN preposition/subordinating conjunction
JJ adjective 'big'
JJR adjective, comparative 'bigger'
JJS adjective, superlative 'biggest'
LS list marker 1)
MD modal could, will
NN noun, singular 'desk'
NNS noun plural 'desks'
NNP proper noun, singular 'Harrison'
NNPS proper noun, plural 'Americans'
PDT predeterminer 'all the kids'
POS possessive ending parent's
PRP personal pronoun I, he, she
PRP$ possessive pronoun my, his, hers
RB adverb very, silently,
RBR adverb, comparative better
RBS adverb, superlative best
RP particle give up
TO, to go 'to' the store.
UH interjection, errrrrrrrm
VB verb, base form take
VBD verb, past tense took
VBG verb, gerund/present participle taking
VBN verb, past participle taken
VBP verb, sing. present, non-3d take
VBZ verb, 3rd person sing. present takes
WDT wh-determiner which
WP wh-pronoun who, what
WP$ possessive wh-pronoun whose
WRB wh-adverb where, when
```

Named Entity Recognition takes POS one step further by identifying real-world entities like *person, organization, event,* etc., from words. Take a look at the quick example in Listing 3.12.

Listing 3.12: Parts of Speech Tagging and Named Entity Recognition on Text

```
# define the sentence that will be analyzed
mysentence = "Mark is working at GE"
```

```
print("SENTENCE TO ANALYZE = ", mysentence)
print('----------------------')

# now we will map parts of speech (pos) for the sentence
word_tk = nltk.word_tokenize(mysentence)
pos_tags = nltk.pos_tag(word_tk)
print("PARTS OF SPEECH FOR SENTENCE = ", pos_tags)
print('----------------------')

entities = nltk.chunk.ne_chunk(pos_tags)
print("NAMED ENTITIES FOR SENTENCE = ", entities)
print('----------------------')
```

Here are the results:

```
SENTENCE TO ANALYZE =  Mark is working at GE
----------------------

PARTS OF SPEECH FOR SENTENCE =  [('Mark', 'NNP'), ('is', 'VBZ'),
('working', 'VBG'), ('at', 'IN'), ('GE', 'NNP')]
----------------------

NAMED ENTITIES FOR SENTENCE =  (S (PERSON Mark/NNP) is/VBZ working/VBG
at/IN (ORGANIZATION GE/NNP))
----------------------
```

Here you can see that *Mark* and *GE* were tagged as proper nouns and *is* and *working* were tagged as verbs. When we do NER, it identifies Mark as a *person* and GE as an *organization*. As you analyze bigger volumes of text, this technique can be invaluable to extracting key named entities.

Word Embeddings

So far, we have kept the text as is and applied some NLP techniques to cleanse the data, find word frequencies, and extract information like parts of speech and named entities. However, for more complex processing, we will need to convert the text into *vectors* or *arrays* that can help us extract more value. This is just like the case of images we convert into an array of pixel intensity values for better processing. Now we will see how we can convert text into arrays. The key thing with text data is that for extracting a value, we need to treat it like a sequence. We need to process the words in order so that the contextual information is captured correctly.

One of the most basic ways to create a word vector is using *one-hot encoding*. One-hot encoding is used often to represent categorical data, where each data point belongs to a particular category. So, here we have a large binary array with elements equal to all possible categories. For any data point, all the elements are zero values except for the one that represents the category of that data point—which has a value of 1. Listing 3.13 shows an example. We will first create a vocabulary of all the words that are relevant. This is obtained by analyzing all the words in our corpus. Here, that's just a small amount of text. Then, using this vocabulary, we can build one-hot encoded vectors.

Listing 3.13: Simple Example of One-Hot Encoded Words

```
# define the sentence that will be analyzed
mytext = "AI is the new electricity. AI is poised to start a large
transformation on many industries."

# we will first tokenize the text
word_tk = nltk.word_tokenize(mytext)
words = [w.lower() for w in word_tk]

# create a vocabulary of all relevant words
vocab = sorted(set(words))

print("VOCABULARY = ", vocab)
print('----------------------')

# create one hot encoded vectors for each word
for myword in vocab:
    test_1hot = [0]*len(vocab)
    test_1hot[vocab.index(myword)] = 1
    print("ONE HOT VECTOR FOR '%s' = "%myword, test_1hot)
```

Here are the results:

```
VOCABULARY =  ['.', 'a', 'ai', 'electricity', 'industries', 'is',
'large', 'many', 'new', 'on', 'poised', 'start', 'the', 'to',
'transformation']
----------------------

ONE HOT VECTOR FOR '.' =  [1, 0, 0, 0, 0, 0, 0, 0, 0, 0, 0, 0, 0, 0, 0]
ONE HOT VECTOR FOR 'a' =  [0, 1, 0, 0, 0, 0, 0, 0, 0, 0, 0, 0, 0, 0, 0]
ONE HOT VECTOR FOR 'ai' =  [0, 0, 1, 0, 0, 0, 0, 0, 0, 0, 0, 0, 0, 0, 0]
ONE HOT VECTOR FOR 'electricity' =  [0, 0, 0, 1, 0, 0, 0, 0, 0, 0, 0, 0,
0, 0, 0]
ONE HOT VECTOR FOR 'industries' =  [0, 0, 0, 0, 1, 0, 0, 0, 0, 0, 0, 0,
0, 0, 0]
ONE HOT VECTOR FOR 'is' =  [0, 0, 0, 0, 0, 1, 0, 0, 0, 0, 0, 0, 0, 0, 0]
ONE HOT VECTOR FOR 'large' =  [0, 0, 0, 0, 0, 0, 1, 0, 0, 0, 0, 0, 0, 0,
0]
ONE HOT VECTOR FOR 'many' =  [0, 0, 0, 0, 0, 0, 0, 1, 0, 0, 0, 0, 0, 0,
0]
ONE HOT VECTOR FOR 'new' =  [0, 0, 0, 0, 0, 0, 0, 0, 1, 0, 0, 0, 0, 0,
0]
ONE HOT VECTOR FOR 'on' =  [0, 0, 0, 0, 0, 0, 0, 0, 0, 1, 0, 0, 0, 0, 0]
```

```
ONE HOT VECTOR FOR 'poised' =  [0, 0, 0, 0, 0, 0, 0, 0, 0, 0, 1, 0, 0,
0, 0]
ONE HOT VECTOR FOR 'start' =  [0, 0, 0, 0, 0, 0, 0, 0, 0, 0, 0, 1, 0, 0,
0]
ONE HOT VECTOR FOR 'the' =  [0, 0, 0, 0, 0, 0, 0, 0, 0, 0, 0, 0, 1, 0,
0]
ONE HOT VECTOR FOR 'to' =  [0, 0, 0, 0, 0, 0, 0, 0, 0, 0, 0, 0, 0, 1, 0]
ONE HOT VECTOR FOR 'transformation' =  [0, 0, 0, 0, 0, 0, 0, 0, 0, 0, 0,
0, 0, 0, 1]
```

As you can see, for a very small text set like this with a couple sentences, we get pretty big vectors. As we look at corpora with vocabularies of thousands or millions of words, these vectors can get extremely large. Hence this method is not recommended.

Another way of representing text is using *word frequencies* for full sentences or documents. We first define a vocabulary for the corpus, and then for each sentence or document we count the frequency of each word. Now we can represent each sentence or document as an array with the count of each word occurring. We could convert the count into percentages to show the relative importance of words. The problem with this approach will be that many stop words like *and*, *the*, *to*, etc. will have very high frequencies.

An alternative approach that is popular is called *term frequency–inverse document frequency* (TF-IDF). This is a numerical statistic that is intended to reflect how important a word is to a document in a collection or corpus. This method assigns frequency terms for words but also compares with words occurring in different documents in the corpus. So, if more documents in the corpus contain the word then it's more likely to be a stop word and is given smaller value. On the other hand, if we have a term that is frequent in a particular document but not in other documents, then most likely that's a subject area for that document. That's the concept of TF-IDF. The problem with TF-IDF is that again the vector can get pretty big due to high vocabulary size. Also, it does not capture the context of the word. It does not consider the sequence of words to try to capture the context.

Modern systems use a method called *word embeddings* to convert words into vectors. Here the embedding values are so assigned that similar words tend to appear together. This concept is known as *topic modeling*. We will use a popular open source library that focuses on topic modeling called *Gensim*. Gensim was developed and is maintained by the Czech natural language processing researcher Radim Řehůřek and his company RaRe Technologies. Details are available at `https://radimrehurek.com/gensim/index.html`.

Gensim can be installed using the Python pip installer, as follows:

```
pip install --upgrade gensim
```

We will now look at a very popular algorithm for learning word embeddings, called *Word2Vec*. Word2Vec is a *neural network* model that learns the context of words and builds dense vectors that represent each word with its context. First you will need to train this model on your data and then start using it to get word embeddings. You can download and use pretrained word embedding models on general corpora and use them. We will see an example of building an embedding on our dataset. Unlike the one-hot encoded vectors, which were sparse, here the vectors we get are dense with fixed lengths. Hence, they can easily represent words with limited storage and can be processed very fast. Internally, Word2Vec uses a combination of two learning models—continuous bag of words (CBOW) and skip-grams. The details of how these algorithms work can be found in this wonderful research paper: `https://arxiv.org/pdf/1301.3781.pdf`.

For now, we will look at the implementation of creating word embeddings from our text. Take a look at the example in Listing 3.14.

Listing 3.14: Learn Word Embeddings from Text—word2vec

```
# import the word2vec model
from gensim.models import Word2Vec

# this will be the text document we will analyze
mytext = "AI is the new electricity. AI is poised to start a large
transformation on many industries."
print("ORIGINAL TEXT = ", mytext)
print('----------------------')

# convert text to lowercase
mytext = mytext.lower()

# we can also extract sentences if needed
sentence_tokens = nltk.sent_tokenize(mytext)
print("SENTENCE TOKENS = ", sentence_tokens)
print('----------------------')

# lets remove some common stop words
stp_words = ["is","a","our","on",".","!","we","are","this","of","and",
"from","to","it","in"]

# define training data
sentences = []
for sentence in sentence_tokens:
    word_tokens = nltk.word_tokenize(sentence)

    # define cleaned up tokens array
    clean_tokens = []

    # remove stop words from our word_tokens
    for token in word_tokens:
        if token not in stp_words:
            clean_tokens.append(token)
```

```
sentences.append(clean_tokens)

print ("TRAINING DATA = ", sentences)
print('----------------------')

# train a new word2vec model on our data - we will use embedding size 20
word2vec_model = Word2Vec(sentences, size=20, min_count=1)

# list the vocabulary learned from our corpus
words = list(word2vec_model.wv.vocab)
print("VOCABULARY OF MODEL = ", words)
print('----------------------')

# show the embeddings vector for some words
print("EMBEDDINGS VECTOR FOR THE WORD 'ai' = ", word2vec_model["ai"])
print("EMBEDDINGS VECTOR FOR THE WORD 'electricity' = ", word2vec_
model["electricity"])
```

Here are the results:

```
ORIGINAL TEXT =  AI is the new electricity. AI is poised to start a
large transformation on many industries.
----------------------

SENTENCE TOKENS =  ['ai is the new electricity.', 'ai is poised to start
a large transformation on many industries.']
----------------------

TRAINING DATA =  [['ai', 'the', 'new', 'electricity'], ['ai', 'poised',
'start', 'large', 'transformation', 'many', 'industries']]
----------------------

VOCABULARY OF MODEL =  ['ai', 'the', 'new', 'electricity', 'poised',
'start', 'large', 'transformation', 'many', 'industries']
----------------------

EMBEDDINGS VECTOR FOR THE WORD 'ai' =  [ 2.3302788e-02  9.8732607e-03
4.6109618e-03  5.3516342e-03
 -2.4620935e-02 -5.2335849e-03 -8.8206278e-03  1.3721633e-02
 -1.8686499e-04 -2.2845879e-02  3.5632821e-03 -6.0331034e-03
 -2.2344168e-03 -2.3627717e-02 -2.3793013e-05 -1.3868282e-02
 -3.0636601e-03  1.0795521e-02  1.2196368e-02 -1.4501591e-02]

EMBEDDINGS VECTOR FOR THE WORD 'electricity' =  [-0.00058223 -0.00180565
-0.01293694  0.00430049 -0.01047355 -0.00786022
 -0.02434015  0.00157354  0.01820784 -0.00192494  0.02023665  0.01888743
 -0.02475209  0.01260937  0.00428402  0.01423089 -0.02299204 -0.02264629
  0.02108614  0.01222904]
```

The Word2Vec model has learned some vocabulary from the current small amount of text we provided. It trained itself on this data and now can provide us with embeddings for specific words. The embeddings vector does not mean anything to us. However, it has been built by observing patterns among the words and the order or sequence in which they appear. These embeddings can be used to analyze words mathematically, show similarities, and apply Deep Learning analysis.

The embeddings vector here has 20 dimensions, so when we display the vector, it has 20 rows. Word embedding in 20 dimensions is difficult for us to visualize. We can make sense of vectors in two dimensions and plot them on a chart. Let's try to do this.

We will use an unsupervised learning technique called *Principal Component Analysis (PCA)* to reduce the 20-dimensional vector into two-dimensional vectors. Although there is loss of information when we do this, the two-dimensional vector tries to capture the maximum variations in data points as displayed in 20 dimensions. PCA is an unsupervised ML technique for dimensionality reduction, as we discussed in Chapter 2. Let's look at an example of applying PCA to word embeddings to plot the words on a chart, as shown in Listing 3.15. The actual plot of words is shown in figure 3.16.

Listing 3.15: Reduce Dimension of Word Embeddings and Plotting the Words

```
# import the PCA library from scikit-learn
from sklearn.decomposition import PCA

# build training data using word2vec model
training_data = word2vec_model[word2vec_model.wv.vocab]
# use PCA to convert word vectors to 2 dimensional vectors
pca = decomposition.PCA(n_components=2)
result = pca.fit_transform(training_data)

# create a scatter plot of the 2 dimensional vectors
plt.figure(figsize=(20,15))
plt.rcParams.update({'font.size': 25})
plt.title('Plot of Word embeddings from Text')
plt.scatter(result[:, 0], result[:, 1], marker="X")

# mark the words on the plot
words = list(word2vec_model.wv.vocab)
for i, word in enumerate(words):
    plt.annotate(word, xy=(result[i, 0], result[i, 1]))

plt.show()
```

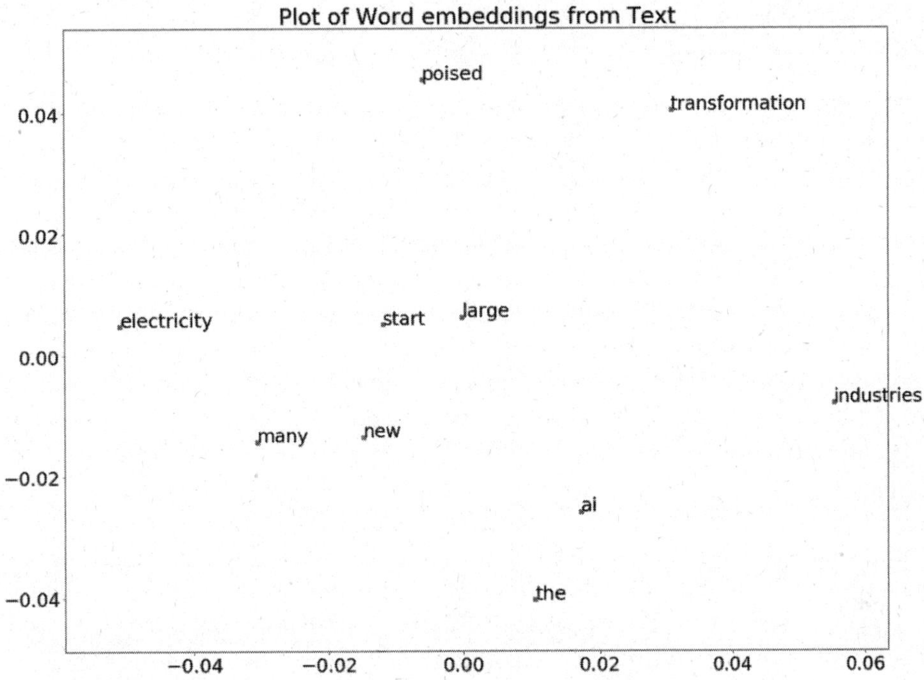

Figure 3.16: PCA to reduce dimensions and plot word embeddings

We don't get much insight from these word embeddings because we have a very small amount of text. However, if you have large text corpus on which you train the Word2Vec model, you will start seeing relationships between similar words. A pretrained model with around 3 million words from the Google news dataset is available from Google for free. You can download this model and use the embeddings to establish relationships between words. Also, you can perform word math using these words converted to vectors of 300 dimensions.

For example, a very popular example cited in many books on word embeddings is getting embeddings for the words *king*, *man*, and *woman*. You can then use vector math to solve this equation:

```
(king - man) + woman
```

The answer to this math equation is the vector embedding for the word *queen*. So, you are able to extract meaning or context from these words and use it to show relationships.

We will see an example of using a word embedding to get vectors and feed it to a sentiment analysis Deep Learning model in the next chapter. For now, let's get back to the last unstructured datatype we will look at—audio.

Listening to Sound

Audio data is all around us and it can provide valuable insights. We have the obvious audio data in the form of speech that humans use to communicate. If we can process sound and extract knowledge stored in it, that can drive some amazing outcomes. Our ears are pretty good at analyzing sound waves, recognizing different tones, and extracting information. Modern AI systems try to replicate this power of humans to process and understand sound. *Amazon Alexa* and *Google Home* are prime examples of systems that process sound waves and decode the information present in them. So, if we ask Alexa, "What's the capital of India?," it will process this audio signal received using its built-in microphone, extract information from this signal to understand the question as text, then send this question as text to a remote Cloud service hosted on Amazon Web Services.

This service does the NLP processing we saw in the previous section to understand what the user has asked. It searches its rich knowledgebase that has structured data that can be easily queried. Once an answer is found, it's coded as text and sent to your Alexa device. This text is then encoded into sound and Alexa responds to you in a few seconds. This flow is shown at a high level in Figure 3.17.

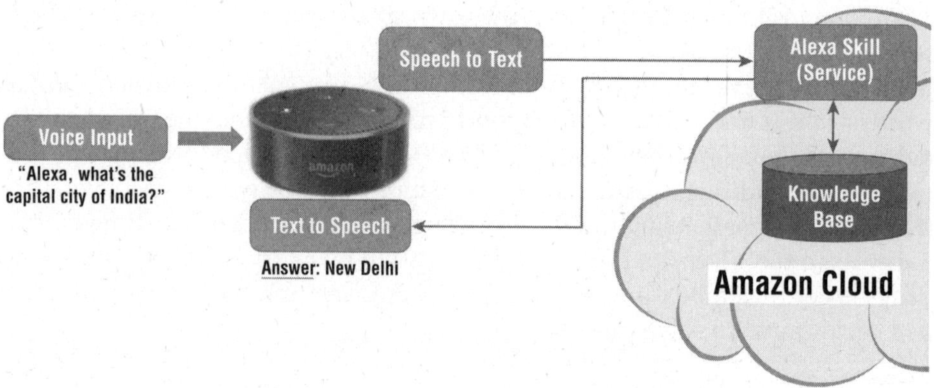

Figure 3.17: High-level flow of Alexa answering a question

Systems that process sound or audio data need to extract information from this data—particularly for outcomes like speech to text and text to speech. These are usually special types of models called *sequence-to-sequence* models that convert a sequence of data (speech or text) into another sequence. These models are also used in translation from one language to another. This is an active area of research and many companies and startups have invested top dollars in solving this problem. However, to start building models, the sound signal first needs to be converted into a vector that can be analyzed by the computer—just like we did with the text data. Let's see how to do that.

Sound waves are basically *pressure waves* that are generated by vibration and these pressure waves travel through a medium, which could be solid, liquid, or gas. As shown in Figure 3.18, a wave in a time domain will have different pressure values over time. However, this complex signal is composed of many smaller constituent signals of constant frequency—basically sine waves. If we analyze these pressure waves in a frequency domain, we can find the frequency constituents in the signal and these components carry information in the wave.

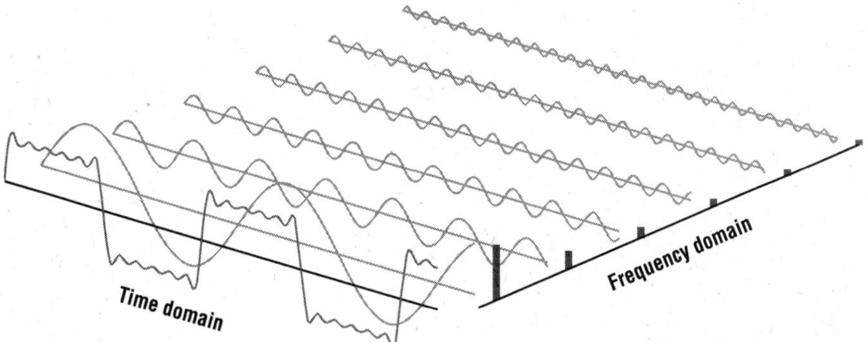

Figure 3.18: Frequency domain reveals the hidden information inside waves

To extract information from a sound wave, we use microphones or acoustic sensors that sample these pressure waves. These waves are sampled at very high frequencies, like 44.1 Kilohertz (KHz) to get all the frequency components from the wave. You probably have seen this sampling frequency mentioned in streaming applications like online radio stations. Converting sound waves into a frequency domain also helps us vectorize the sound sequences and use them for further analysis in ML and DL models. Let's see an example of converting sound into a vector of numbers.

We will take a sound sample from a car engine and analyze it. This sample was taken using a simple microphone on a cell phone—no complex acoustic sensor. We will first read the signal from the sound file and see how the time domain signal is noisy and does not provide any insights (see Figure 3.19). Then we will convert it to a frequency domain using an algorithm called *Fast Fourier Transform (FFT)*—see Figure 3.20. We won't cover details about the FFT algorithm, but the underlying concept is that it converts signals from time to frequency domains. You can see the example code in Listing 3.16.

Listing 3.16: Analyze a Sound Sample from a Car Using FFT

```
# import the libraries for reading sound files
from scipy.io import wavfile
# import numpy to do the fft
import numpy as np
# import plotting libraries
```

```
import matplotlib.pyplot as plt
%matplotlib inline

# We will take sample wav file with car engine sound
# this is about 15 second clip recorded from engine running at around
2000 RPM
AUDIO_FILE = "sound_sample_car_engine.wav"

# load the file - get frequency and the data array
sampling_freq, sound_data = wavfile.read(AUDIO_FILE)

# show the shape of data read
print ("Sampling frequency = ", sampling_freq, "\nShape of data array
= ", sound_data.shape)

# normalize sound values between -1 to +1
sound_data = sound_data / (2.**15)

# lets just take a single audio channel
if len(sound_data.shape) == 1:
    s1 = sound_data
else:
    s1 = sound_data[:,0]

# get time domain representation of the sound pressure waves
timeArray = np.arange(0, s1.shape[0], 1.0)
timeArray = timeArray / sampling_freq
timeArray = timeArray * 1000  #scale to milliseconds

# show the plot of sound signal in time domain
plt.figure(figsize=(20,10))
plt.rcParams.update({'font.size': 25})
plt.title('Plot of sound pressure values over time')
plt.xlabel('Time in milliseconds')
plt.ylabel('Amplitude')
plt.plot(timeArray, sound_data, color='b')
plt.show()

# number of points for fft
n = len(s1)
p = np.fft.fft(s1) # take the Fourier transform

# only half the points will give us the frequency bins
nUniquePts = int(np.ceil((n+1)/2.0))
p = p[0:nUniquePts]
p = abs(p)

# create the array of frequency points
freqArray = np.arange(0, float(nUniquePts), 1.0) * float(sampling_freq)
/ n;
```

```
# convert the frequency from hertz to engine RPM
MAX_RPM = 20000
NUM_POINTS = 20

# remove points above max RPM
maxhz = MAX_RPM/60
p[freqArray > maxhz] = 0

# plot the frequency domain plot
plt.figure(figsize=(20,10))
plt.rcParams.update({'font.size': 25})
plt.title('Plot of sound waves in frequency domain')
plt.plot(freqArray*60, p, color='r')
plt.xlabel('Engine RPM')
plt.ylabel('Signal Power (dB)')
plt.xlim([0,MAX_RPM])
plt.xticks(np.arange(0, MAX_RPM, MAX_RPM/NUM_POINTS),
size='small',rotation=40)
plt.grid()
plt.show()
```

Here are the results:

```
Sampling frequency =  44100

Shape of data array =  (672768, 2)
```

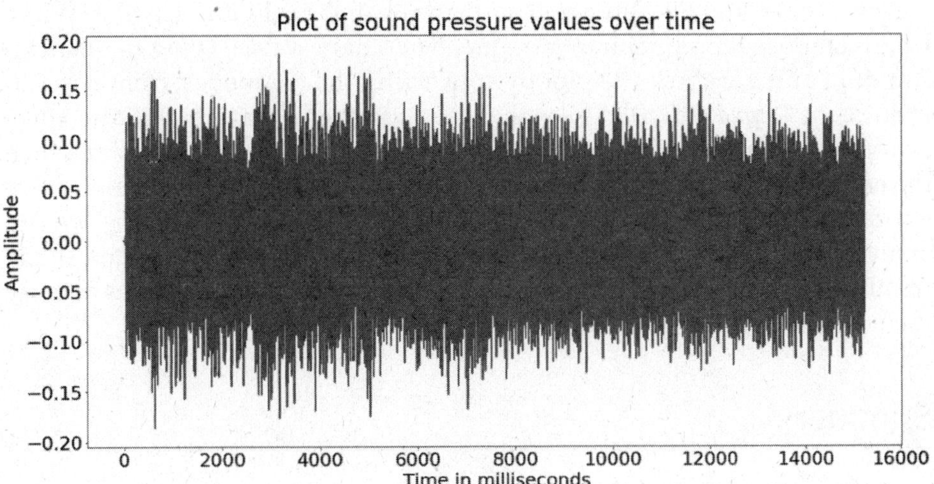

Figure 3.19: Time domain plot of sound from car engine

We read the sound sample (around 15 seconds) from a WAV file. WAV is a common and simple extension for audio data. Modern files are compressed into MP3 extensions, but that needs additional drivers to be read. WAV can be easily read by our sound analysis library, Scipy. We see that the sampling rate for audio is 44100 Hertz or 44.1KHz, which is pretty common. We first create a plot of the time domain signal—that is, the pressure amplitude variation over time. We see that the blue plot is pretty noisy and we don't really get much from it.

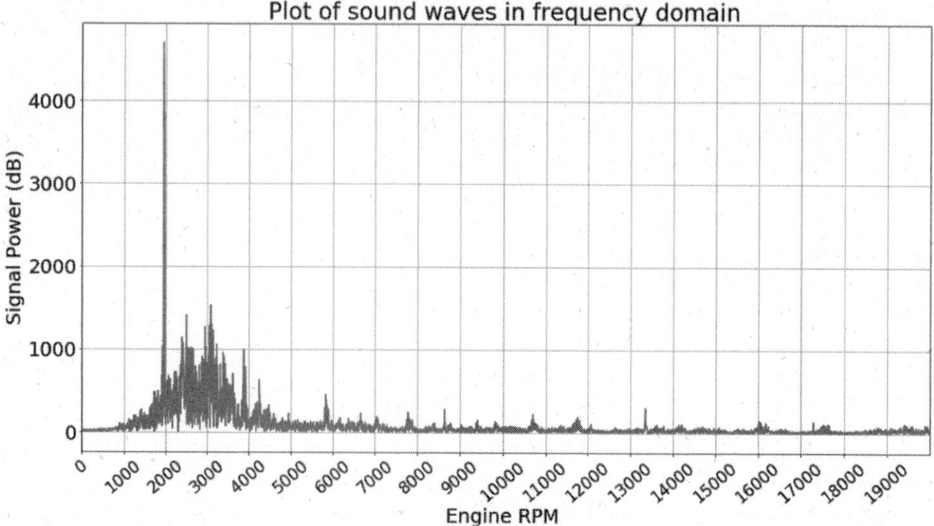

Figure 3.20: Frequency domain plot for car engine sound signal

Now we use the FFT library from NumPy and build an FFT plot. When we decompose the signal into a frequency domain we see some frequencies standing out. We show the plot by converting the frequency from hertz to *rotations per second (RPM).* We see that the audio signal has a significant spike at a frequency around 2000 RPM. This corresponds to the frequency at which the engine was rotating when the signal was collected. This is just one value we decode from the audio signal. Without knowing about the engine, we can analyze the sound and find the rotating frequency. Similarly, we can use the frequency data encoded in the sound signal to vectorize sound values and use them for training our ML and DL models.

Summary

In this chapter, we looked at the differences between structured and unstructured data. We went into details of specific types of unstructured data and how to convert this data into vectors and arrays for processing. We saw how images are represented as pixel intensity arrays and how, using computer vision techniques, we can cleanse the data and extract information. We saw how the same methods can be extended to video, which is a timeseries of images. We saw how to handle text data using natural language processing (NLP) and extract information. Finally, we saw an example of analyzing audio data using frequency analysis. These methods can be used on their own to extract valuable information from unstructured data. They also serve as good preprocessing techniques to make data ready for processing by advanced ML and DL algorithms.

CHAPTER

4

Deep Learning Using Keras

In Chapter 2, you learned about Machine Learning algorithms and techniques. You saw code samples of how to build ML models and evaluate your models using metrics of precision and recall. These models were pretty straightforward to understand with some clever ways of capturing patterns in the data. This chapter gets to the much more complex types of learning models. These models have many learning units organized in layers and many such layers—making the architecture "deep." Though they are complex to build and train, you will see how effective they are at handling big and complex unstructured data like images. Finally, you will use one of the most popular Deep Learning libraries today—called *Keras*—to build models that can classify images of handwritten digits and learn to label these digits. I am hoping that these simple examples trigger some big ideas in your mind. You can reuse this code to apply learning to your images to build deep models in your domain area.

Handling Unstructured Data

We saw data used in earlier problems like wine quality analysis. Here each column had a particular significance and meaning. We used the term *feature* to describe each column and this was an important part of our learning method to understand how these features are correlated. We used techniques like normalization to scale the features so they were on the same value scale. Also, we saw that we could use fewer features to make our models learn faster. In short, we needed to know what our features were and our model captured a pattern between them. This was all *structured data*.

Now let's imagine an image. When a computer reads an image, it is normally captured by a digital camera or a scanner and stored in digital form in computer memory. When we take a photo with a digital camera, our camera has an optical sensor that captures light from a scene, renders this inside our camera, and saves the image as a series of numbers—basically a large sequence of 0s and 1s. In raw form a two-dimensional image is basically a matrix or array of pixel values. Here each pixel value represents intensity of a particular color. However, it does not have a human-readable value like wine alcohol percentage or quality rating. This data is usually referred to as unstructured. The individual values have less significance but as a whole they complement each other and form a bigger domain object like an image. The same goes for audio, video, and text data. You can see more examples of unstructured data and some basic steps to cleanse and extract information from them in Chapter 3. To analyze unstructured data like this, we need much more complex ML models with many learning units, known as neural networks.

Neural Networks

For complex and unstructured data, we build deeper models that use a combination of smaller individual learning units to form a bigger network. This network of learning units can learn complex patterns from a large number of features. This is called a *neural network*.

A common analogy that is used to represent this is the human brain, which contains a network of biological cells called *neurons* that are connected via *axons* and *dendrites*. If you recall from your biology textbooks, we have signals flowing into neurons through dendrites and processed outputs flowing to other neurons or muscles through axons. In fact, neural networks are heavily inspired by the structure of the human brain. Figure 4.1 shows a simple representation.

Similar to the human brain, these *artificial neural networks* contain processing units called *neurons* and connections between them. These networks are structured into layers, with each layer extracting valuable information from the data that is fed to it. These are Deep Learning networks and they have many layers of learning. They try to map the input space to a set of possible outcomes or classes. Let's look at a very simple neural network, shown in Figure 4.2. Let's understand some basics and then we will get into building more complex networks.

This neural network has three inputs in the first input layer. The second layer of neurons is the hidden layer, with three neurons again. The final layer is the output layer, with one neuron.

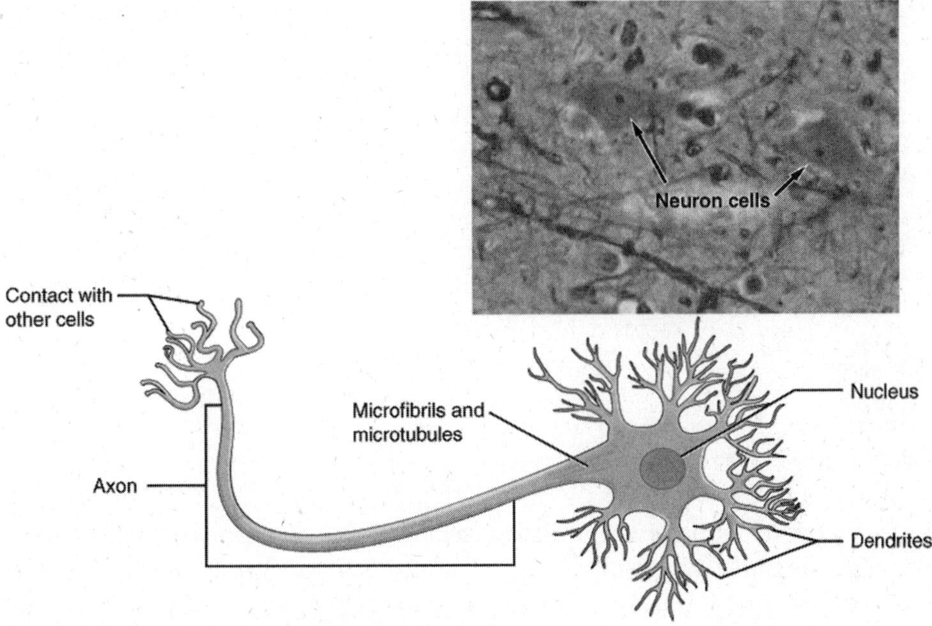

Figure 4.1: Biological neurons in the human brain
(*Source*: OpenStax college - Wikipedia)

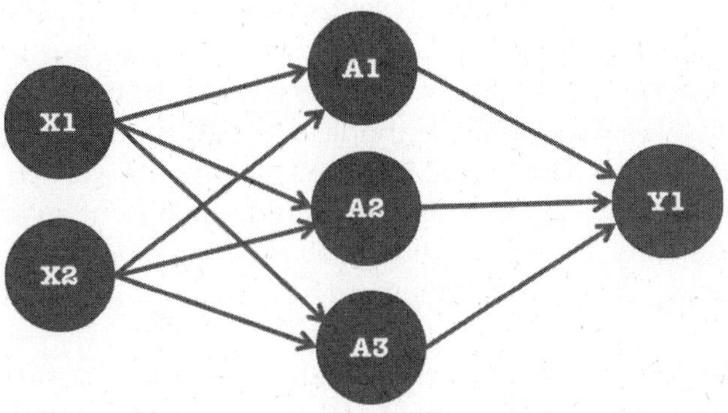

Figure 4.2: Simple neural network where learning units are connected as a network

Each neuron is a learning unit that may receive inputs from other neurons, perform some calculations, and send output to other neurons. The flow of information is shown by the arrows in Figure 4.2. Now let's look closer at what happens at the neuron stage.

Let's revisit our diagram from the logistic regression function in Chapter 2. We first calculated a weighted sum of inputs (Z1) and then applied a function to return a value A1 between 0 and 1. This result can also be called an *activation*.

This is exactly what is happening at each neuron in the neural network. You have inputs coming into each neuron, activations being calculated using weights, and an activation function—and these activations feed into the next neuron in the network. This is how neural networks work. See Figure 4.3.

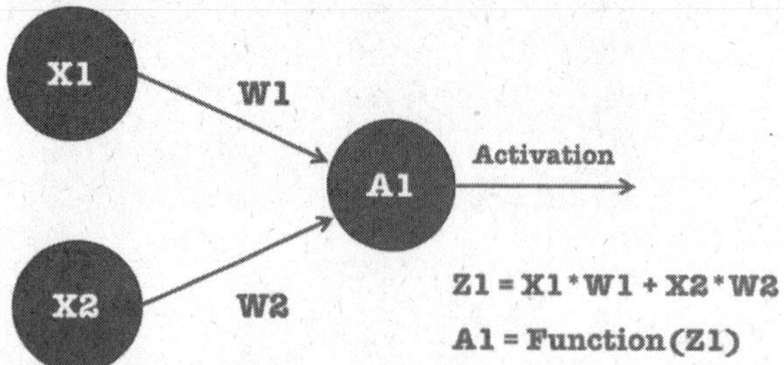

Figure 4.3: Processing at an individual neuron

This representation is often called a *computational graph* or *dataflow*. You have the nodes as circles where inputs are entered or some computation is done. The edges of this graph represent weights. You can look at this as a flow of data through the edges between nodes, with each node adding some processing to the data. Let's get back to our simple neural network in Figure 4.2.

A neural network has many neurons or learning units organized into layers. Inputs flow into each network layer and calculated outputs or *activations* move to the next layer. If we have a small number of layers, typically two or three in a network, we call them *shallow* networks. These take less processing time and can quickly calculate results. However, they cannot learn complex patterns, especially with unstructured data. The basic Machine Learning models we saw in Chapter 2 typically have two layers—one input and one output layer like linear and logistic regressions. These are the shallow learning models. We can find out what's going on inside them and they can be quickly trained—in a few milliseconds.

When we have to capture complex and non-linear patterns in the data that would not be possible by simpler shallow learning models, we need models with many layers called *Deep Learning models*. Deep Learning models learn in stages, or layers, with each layer extracting some pattern that is fed into the next layer.

For example, if you are learning to detect faces in an image, your deep network will take as input the pixel array of the image. Then, during the first stage, it may learn to detect lines and curves. Next, it will combine these to form figures like rectangles and circles. Finally, it will combine these to recognize any pattern of faces. This is the power that deep neural networks give us. They learn complex patterns in the data and capture non-linear relations extremely well.

The last layer of the neural network is the output layer, and the number of neurons there correspond to the number of outputs we want to learn. If we just want to make a prediction as to buy/don't buy based on housing variables, then our network will have a single neuron in the output layer with its value determining the buy decision. Now if we want to also predict another variable, we can add that as a neuron to the output layer. This new output should be considered in the training data we provide to the network while training. That's it—there is no special consideration needed and we can use the same network to predict two outputs instead of one.

The key difference between deep neural networks and the other ML algorithms we saw in Chapter 2 is that deep networks learn important features of the data on their own. We configure the inputs and outputs we seek, decide on the numbers of layers and neurons in each, and build a good training dataset. The network learns all the complex patterns in the data and establishes correlations between inputs and outputs. Basically, it maps the input space (Xs) to the output space (Ys). Hence, neural networks are often referred to as *blackboxes*, because they don't really tell us how they find these relations; they only predict outputs by internally capturing these relationships.

Because these networks are complex, we often analyze them by considering individual layers. Let's look at the neural network shown in Figure 4.2 again. We have an input layer with three neurons representing input Xs. There is one hidden layer with three neurons and an output layer with one neuron—the Ys.

Now this was just one example of a neural network and a pretty simple one at that. We only have layers where every neuron in the layer is connected to every other neuron in the subsequent layer. Such a layer of neurons is called a *fully-connected* or *dense* layer. In a dense layer, every neuron learns features by considering the output generated from every neuron from the previous layer. Hence, these layers tend to be memory consuming. In practice you will find these layers at the end of a deep network to learn from features extracted in earlier layers and make predictions. The earlier layers in a network may have more local connections to extract features. We look at some of these feature-extracting layers in Chapter 5, which discusses advanced Deep Learning.

The hidden and output layer neurons do exactly what we discussed earlier for a logistic regression unit. They get a weighted sum of inputs and apply an activation function. At each neuron these calculations are done and the results are fed forward to the next layer of neurons. This architecture, with all neurons feeding their output forward, is called a *feed-forward architecture*. At each layer, many calculations occur that are handled in parallel using multi-dimensional arrays. We will not go into detail about the equations, but it will help to get an understanding of weights in layers. Let's populate a few weights into our diagram, as shown in Figure 4.4.

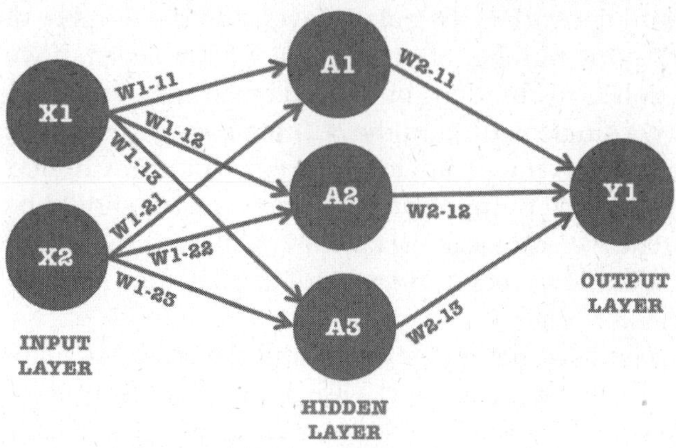

Figure 4.4: Neural network with weight values

You will see different conventions used in books and articles. Let's say we have the weight W1-32 for layer 1 and it connects neuron 3 from one layer to neuron 2 to the next layer. We can see that between the first hidden layer and input layer, we have (2 × 3), which is six weights. Then, between the output and hidden layers, we have (3 × 1), which is three weights. For this simple network, we have 6 + 3, which is nine weights. These are the weights that need to be "learned" during the training process.

Now let's add a special type of neuron to this network called a *bias neuron*. We saw the importance of bias in Chapter 2 in the linear regression equation. Bias helps the network learn certain assumptions about the data so that it does not depend only on the variables for generating results. All the inputs (X1, X2, X3) in our network are zero, which means both outputs (Y1, Y2) will always be zero, regardless of the weights. The network has no bias that influences its values in the absence of inputs.

All right, so let's add bias neurons to this network. Bias neurons don't do any calculations. We can just add a constant value of +1 and, just like other neurons, they have weights associated with them. See Figure 4.5. We will use the letter B to associate these weights.

The convention used here is B2-1, which is the weight associated with a bias neuron from the first layer to neuron 1 from the next layer. We have added bias neurons to the input and hidden layers. Adding to the output does not make sense since we don't calculate anything from this layer.

So, the total number of bias weights will be 3 + 1, which is four. Adding this to the previous nine weights, we have a total of 13 weights that this network has to learn. Now let's talk about the Activation functions.

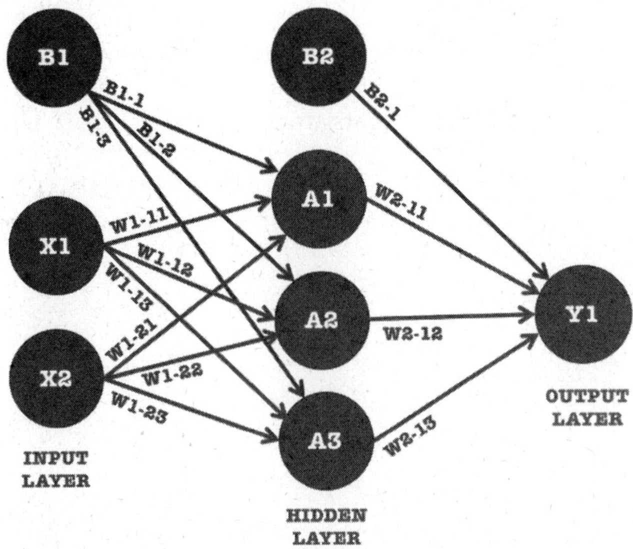

Figure 4.5: Neural network with weight and bias values

Activation functions take the weighted sum of inputs at each neuron and apply some non-linear function to them. Popular functions used are Tanh, Sigmoid, and ReLU (Rectified Linear Units). Each function helps in thresholding the output value based on the weighted sum of inputs. Usually you apply the same Activation function to a particular layer. So, every neuron in that layer uses the same Activation function. The "References" section at the end of the book includes a reference to material, with details on each Activation function. But as a rule of thumb, Tanh and ReLU are used for hidden layers and ReLU is more common. Sigmoid is mainly used for output layer neurons. Sigmoid produces a value between 0 and 1 so it can be used for classification problems.

Back-Propagation and Gradient Descent

Let see how neural networks are trained. I will avoid fancy formulas so you can understand the concepts clearly and then we will see a code example.

In Chapter 2 , we saw an overview of the gradient descent method to calculate gradients and optimize weights as part of the learning process. We follow the same process for training a neural network, but at a network level. The most popular algorithm used for training neural networks is called *back-propagation*. Back-propagation is essentially a smart way for calculating the partial derivatives (gradients) of the Cost function with respective to different weights.

The idea is to have a Cost function similar to mean squared error (MSE) that we saw during regression model training. Then we adjust the weights using Gradient Descent so as to minimize this Cost function. To do this, we calculate the partial derivative of the Cost function with respect to each weight value. Then, based on the error term, we use this partial derivative to find the magnitude and direction of the change in weight and apply the change. After every iteration, the Cost function is calculated and the weights are updated. See Figure 4.6.

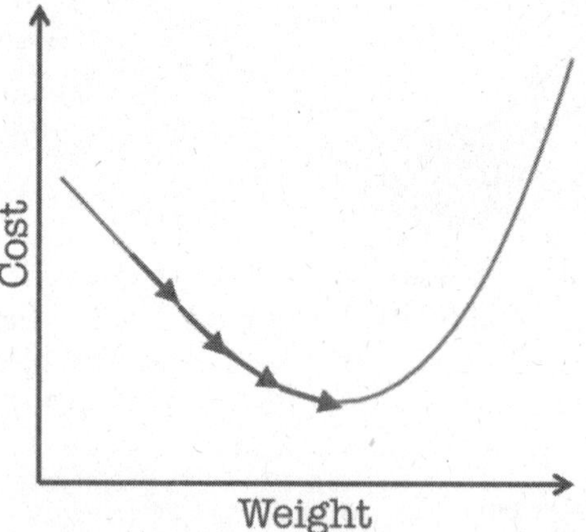

Figure 4.6: How Gradient Descent moves toward the minima

Before starting the training, we must establish a *cleansed* and *normalized* training dataset. This should contain data points with all our input features (Xs) and corresponding expected outputs (Ys). This will be treated as something referred to in the ML community as the *ground truth*. The model we train will try to learn patterns so it can be good enough to generate results as good as the ground truth. In other words, the ground truth is the standard that our ML model will aim to achieve.

Establishing the ground truth and defining a good training and testing set is a general starting point in the Machine Learning project lifecycle. We cover the ML lifecycle in detail in Chapter 9. For now, you can assume that we have the data for the Xs and Ys properly cleansed and available and we can use it as-is for training.

Here are the general steps involved in back-propagation training of neural networks:

1. Initialize the weight values to zero or random numbers. Run all the data points in consideration through the network and predict Ys of each X in the dataset.
2. Compare each Y value with the expected outcomes or the ground truth. Find the difference in the values. Based on the difference in values, calculate the error for each output term.
3. Establish a *Cost function*, which is basically a function of all the weights in the network—include weights at every layer of the network including

bias weights. The Cost function helps us define a metric to how far our model predictions are from the ground truth. The choice of Cost function is very important in training a good ML model.

4. The *Cost function* may be the same as the *mean absolute error (MAE)* or *mean square error* (MSE) that we used earlier. This Cost function is ideal when we are predicting a value and we can directly see how far away our predictions are from real values using the MAE or MSE. If we are predicting a class then the preferred Cost function is cross-entropy. Cross-entropy tries to minimize the information loss by doing a wrong classification and hence it helps capture the classification loss better.

   The objective of having a Cost function is to establish a relationship between the weights and the error in the prediction. So, as we tune the weights, the error reduces and we get an accurate model. (I provide a link to an article explaining different cost functions in detail in the "References" section at end of the book.)

5. As the name suggests, we back-propagate the error calculated through the network. As we go back from the outputs to the inputs, we update the weights using gradients of the Cost function with respect to the corresponding weight. This is the same gradient descent algorithm we saw in Figure 4.5, but we are now applying it to the whole network.

   We establish an overall Cost function of the network and, using partial derivatives, we calculate the gradient of this Cost function with respect to each weight. Now we start from the last layer and calculate the gradients from the errors between predicted values and ground truth. We *back-propagate* this error from last to first layer and thus calculate gradients for each neuron in every layer. The gradients are then used to adjust the weight values at each neuron connection in a layer. The details of this algorithm are excellently explained by Andrew Ng in his video from the ML class. I include a link to it in the "References" section at end of the book.

6. With all the weights adjusted, we run all the data points again and find the Error term. We iterate through this process until so many iterations are completed or until we achieve an acceptable Error value.

We will see this process in action with an example in Keras shortly.

Batch vs. Stochastic Gradient Descent

Gradient Descent applied to neural networks may be of the batch or stochastic type. We run back-propagation using training data points and adjust the weights. When all the training data points have passed through the entire network it is known as an *epoch*. In Batch Gradient Descent, we wait for a whole epoch to pass so our network has seen all the training data and then adjust weights. This usually takes a long time and needs to store variables in memory. This approach takes a long time, but it helps us find the optimum value for weights in one go. Usually, if we have a limited training dataset and lots of memory, we follow this approach.

The other type of gradient descent is *stochastic gradient descent (SGD)*, where we adjust weights after the pass of every data point through the network. Here, we don't store much data in memory and rapidly update weights. This is a very fast method, but we see fluctuations in the training because we tend to overshoot the local minima. This approach works when we have limited memory and a large training dataset to work with. We learn at every data point and update our model. The problem with this approach is that it's possible to get "lost" and move away from the minima, especially when we have some bad data points, which may cause major errors. Hence, in practice, we use a compromise of these two approaches.

That compromise is called *mini-batch gradient descent*. Here, we divide our data into smaller batches and update weights after each pass of each batch through the network. This is found to be a better approach to training neural networks. At each iteration of training, a smaller subset of the training data is loaded in memory to calculate errors and back-propagate that error to get gradients. Hence, the memory (RAM) used by the algorithm is less, as compared to loading the whole training dataset in memory. Also, we don't need to wait until all the training data is processed to see results. We usually see a faster convergence to the minima using this approach and reduce training time by a few magnitudes.

Neural Network Architectures

This particular neural network in Figure 4.4, where we have all layers as dense or fully-connected, is known as a *multi-layered perceptron (MLP)*. It is very good at learning patterns and has several applications especially around finding non-linear patterns in structured data. If you can have your data as a single-dimensional vector, then the MLP can quickly learn patterns due to its fully connected nature and make predictions. It works really well for structured data. We can apply MLP to unstructured data like images, but with some modification. Since the MLP handles data in single-dimensional layers, we have to convert the three-dimensional image data into a large flattened vector and feed it to the MLP. Hence, all the valuable spatial information that is stored in the three dimensions is lost and we have one large vector. There are some other deep architectures that extend the idea of MLP and are more suitable for specific types of unstructured data, which we discuss in Chapter 5. Before getting into their details, let's first build an example of an MLP neural network.

Welcome to TensorFlow and Keras

We can use libraries like Scikit-Learn to build a neural network, but for complex networks you will find many limitations especially around performance. Especially when you have to do massive parallel processing for a network, it makes sense to look at a Deep Learning framework like TensorFlow and PyTorch. These frameworks let us build computational or dataflow graphs by capturing the architecture in our neural network. These graphs can then be scheduled to run in parallel and on specialized hardware like CPU clusters or GPUs to train much faster than they would on a normal CPU machine. The frameworks have their own dedicated runtime, which could be a CPU or GPU cluster. They expose APIs in common languages like Java, Python, and C++, through which software applications can build, train, and run DL models.

TensorFlow is a framework developed by Google and is available as open source. Google has an active and agile team developing and maintaining TensorFlow and they release new versions every three to four months. Google internally also heavily uses TensorFlow for all sorts of image, video, text, and audio Deep Learning use cases.

Keras is a high-level API layer in Python written on the TensorFlow framework. It was developed by François Chollet, who now works at Google. With Keras you don't have to get into the nitty-gritties of defining the computational graphs. You focus on building the layers and defining configuration parameters like the type of layers, number of neurons, connections, etc. Keras internally handles building the computational graph for you.

NOTE **We use Keras with TensorFlow for all the DL examples in this book, mainly because it's very easy (and free) to spin up a Jupyter Notebook on Google Colaboratory with Keras and TensorFlow preinstalled and start coding. Thank you Google!**

PyTorch is a similar framework developed and maintained by Facebook. It heavily uses NumPy (Numerical Python), which is a powerful library for math processing in Python. PyTorch also defines computational graphs and has some of the simplicity of Keras built-in. It's more a matter of personal preference and time spent to decide which framework you choose. Your deep architectures should be able to be built and run on either TensorFlow or PyTorch.

Let's use Keras to build the MLP neural network. First, we will load a sample dataset that is provided with Keras called MNIST. This is a standard dataset for studying Machine Learning algorithms. It comes with defined training and test datasets. Let's load the data and show it as a plot using the Matplotlib library (see Figure 4.7). This code is pretty standard, as shown in Listing 4.1.

Listing 4.1: Load Handwritten Digits Dataset in TensorFlow and Keras

```
# import tensorflow, keras libraries
import tensorflow as tf
from tensorflow import keras

# Helper libraries
import numpy as np
import matplotlib.pyplot as plt

# load the mnist dataset provided by Keras
mnist = keras.datasets.mnist

# load the training and test data
(img_rows, img_cols) = (28,28)
(x_train, y_train),(x_test, y_test) = mnist.load_data()

# lets plot some data samples
plt.figure(figsize=(10,10))
for i in range(25):
    plt.subplot(5,5,i+1)
    plt.imshow(x_train[i], cmap=plt.cm.gray)
    plt.xlabel(y_test[i])
plt.show()
```

Figure 4.7: Sample from the MNIST training dataset

We see an example of the training dataset. Each of these has Xs, which are features, and Ys, which are the output. The Xs are 784 in number which correspond to 28×28 pixels of the images. The output Y is a number between 0 and 9, representing the digit that the image represents.

Let's use Python to understand the size of the X and Y features. This code is very important to clearly understand the features. It is recommended that the features have similar values. Hence, we normalize the pixel values, which can be between 0 and 255 to a number between 0 and 1. Similarly, the output Y is changed from an integer from 0–9 to a one-hot encoded vector. Basically, each Y is converted to a vector of size 10 with only the relevant element as 1 and all others as 0.

For example: `Y = 3` is converted to:

```
Y = [ 0,  0,  0,  1,  0,  0,  0,  0,  0,  0,  0 ]
```

Listing 4.2 shows standard code that does this.

Listing 4.2: Normalization of Training and Test Data to Learn Faster

```
from keras.utils import to_categorical

# one hot encode the results
y_train = to_categorical(y_train)
y_test = to_categorical(y_test)

# see the dimensions of the data
print('Training X dimensions: ', x_train.shape)
print('Training Y dimensions: ', y_train.shape)
print('Testing X dimensions: ', x_test.shape)
print('Testing Y dimensions: ', y_test.shape)

# normalize the data to values between 0 and 1
x_train, x_test = x_train / 255.0, x_test / 255.0
```

Here are the results:

```
Training X dimensions:  (60000, 28, 28)
Training Y dimensions:  (60000, 10, 2)
Testing X dimensions:  (10000, 28, 28)
Testing Y dimensions:  (10000, 10, 2)
```

Now that we have our dataset defined, let's look at the code that actually builds the neural network. We will first create the simple MLP we saw earlier. The input layer will have 784 inputs. This is created by taking the 28×28 image array and making it a single-dimension vector of size 784. This is done using the Flatten layer in Keras. You don't need to specify dimensions for the Flatten layer because it automatically calculates them using the input layer dimensions.

Next, we will use a hidden layer with 512 neurons. This layer is a dense layer signifying that every neuron from a previous layer is connected to every neuron from the next layer. We will use an ReLU activation function for this layer. As we discussed earlier, ReLU activation for hidden layers helps the network learn much faster.

Finally, we have the output layer, which is again a dense layer with 10 neurons. These 10 neurons signify the prediction of handwritten digits represented by the image—between 0 and 9. Here we use a Softmax Activation function so that we can get outputs between 0 and 1 in each of the 10 neurons. Also, Softmax applied to the whole layer gives us a total probability value for all neurons as 1. So, if the digit indicated in the image is a 5, the training set results will show a value of `Y_Train` as:

```
Y = [ 0,  0,  0,  1,  0,  0,  0,  0,  0,  0,  0 ]
```

After training, we expect our model to make a prediction such that the sum of all predictions is 1 (indicating 100% probability) and for digit 5, maximum probability has been allocated. After we build the model, we will show a summary of the model, as shown in Listing 4.3.

Listing 4.3: Our First Neural Network Code!

```
from keras.models import Sequential
from keras.layers import Dense, Flatten

# build a simple Neural Network
model = Sequential()
model.add(Flatten(input_shape=(28, 28)))
model.add(Dense(512, activation='relu'))
model.add(Dense(10, activation='softmax'))

# show summary
model.summary()

# assign the optimizer for the model and define loss function
model.compile(optimizer='adam',
              loss='categorical_crossentropy',
              metrics=['accuracy'])

# run the actual training
history = model.fit(x_train, y_train, epochs=1, validation_split=0.33)

# evaluate on test data
model.evaluate(x_test, y_test)
```

Here are the results:

```
_________________________________________________________________
Layer (type)                 Output Shape              Param #
=================================================================
flatten_6 (Flatten)          (None, 784)               0
_________________________________________________________________
dense_11 (Dense)             (None, 512)               401920
_________________________________________________________________
dense_12 (Dense)             (None, 10)                5130
```

```
Total params: 407,050
Trainable params: 407,050
Non-trainable params: 0
________________________________________________________________
Train on 40199 samples, validate on 19801 samples

Epoch 1/1
40199/40199 [==============================] - 7s 178us/step -
loss: 0.2389 - acc: 0.9298 - val_loss: 0.1346 - val_acc: 0.9606

10000/10000 [==============================] - 0s 44us/step

Evaluation on Test Dataset: [0.11573542263880372, 0.9653]
```

The number of hidden layers and neurons in a hidden layer are our hyperparameters. We will not learn these but modify them and see if they make our predictions better. What we will learn is the total number of weights to learn—also called trainable parameters. The model summary will show the number of trainable parameters. In the previous example, we see the total weights or trainable parameters set to 407,050. This calculation is pretty simple and can be used with any network:

```
First weight Layer size      = (Layer1 Neurons + 1) * Layer2 Neurons
                             = (784+1) * 512 = 401920

Second weights Layer size    = (Layer2 Neurons + 1) * Layer3 Neurons
                             = (512+1)*10 = 5130

Total weights of the Model   = 401920 + 5130 = 407050
```

As we did earlier, we will use training X and Y values to build the model and tune the weights. The testing values will be exclusively used for validation.

There you go. You have collected image data, normalized it, and trained your first neural network with 92% accuracy. Our MLP neural network structure is shown in Figure 4.8. We have 407,050 weights in this model to train. We have all dense layers, which we will indicate in blue. In the next chapter, as we deal with more types of layers, we will use different notations.

Some observations about the code and the results:

- We used the Adam optimizer. This is very common. Some other types are RMSProp, Adagrad, and SGD (Stochastic Gradient Descent). These are all variations of the traditional Gradient Descent optimization technique so that the model converges faster and our training process is faster. Adam is usually very popular, but you can try others and see if the results get better and faster.

- Since this was a multi-class classification problem, we used a categorical Cross-Entropy Loss function. We ran the training only for one epoch and got pretty good results. This was because the data was clean and of good quality. In reality, you will likely have bad data that will need cleansing and other processing.
- Another thing to notice is that MNIST was nice enough to give us training and testing data. However, when we trained the model, we also included a validation split of 0.33, which is 33%. So, we only used 67% of training data for training and got the model validated using 33% of data. Our results show us the training accuracy, loss and validation accuracy, and loss. Typically, we will tune hyper-parameters like number of layers and neurons in each and see if our validation accuracy increases.
- The testing dataset is used for evaluating our model and establishing benchmarks. The last line of code evaluates our model on test data and says it's 96.53% accurate. Now if we choose a new architecture or a new algorithm, this will be our benchmark to beat!

Now let's talk a little about the training, validation, and testing sets and about overfitting and underfitting.

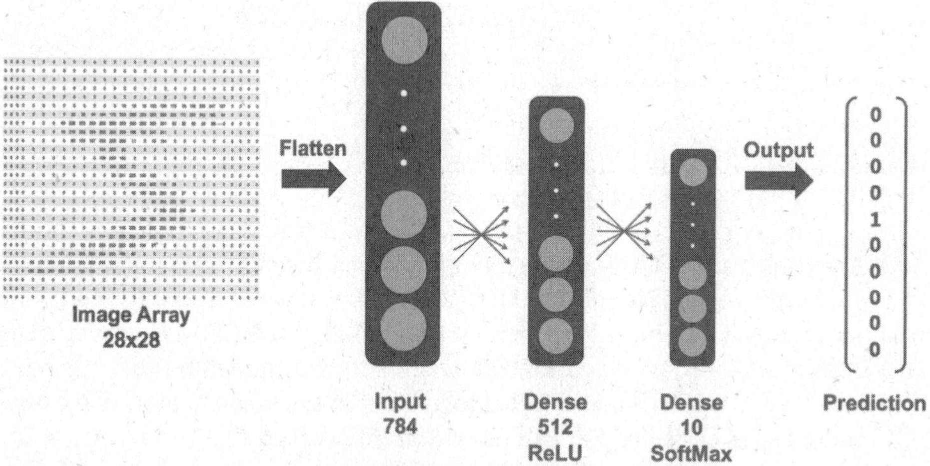

Figure 4.8: Summary of our neural network, multi-layered perceptron

Bias vs. Variance: Underfitting vs. Overfitting

You have seen the concepts of overfitting and underfitting in Chapter 2. Remember the darts example, shown again in Figure 4.9?

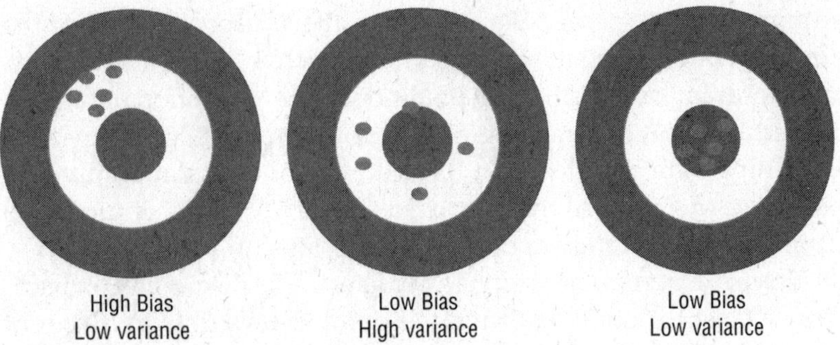

Figure 4.9: Darts example to explain bias and variance

Let's discuss how training and validation results give us an idea of underfitting and overfitting. Figure 4.10 shows an informal chart that can help us make some decisions while building neural networks.

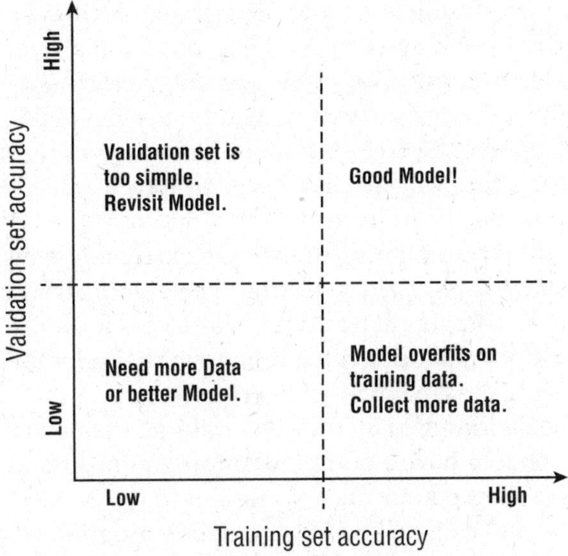

Figure 4.10: Training vs. validation set accuracy

As you build a new model, always use a separate training and validation dataset and find the accuracy of your model on each dataset. This concept is known as *cross-validation*. The idea is to give your model a set of data to train upon. Then you evaluate its metrics on a new dataset that it has never seen before, in order to see how effective it is.

There is a type of cross-validation that is popular in industry known as *K-fold cross-validation*. Here the idea is to divide your complete dataset into K groups and at each iteration use one of the K groups as a validation set and the rest of the data for training. This way, you keep changing the "unseen" data that the model learns from and over time it becomes more effective.

If you get high accuracy on training data but not on the validation data, then your model is overfitting on the training data. It is learning a bigger variance specific to the training data and does not translate to your validation dataset. In this case, you need to get more training data. There are also techniques to avoid overfitting, like *regularization* and *dropout*, that you can use.

Let's quickly look at what regularization is. We saw in the discussion on backpropagation how a Cost function is a function of all the weights in different layers of the network and helps us find optimum values for the network weights. If your model is overfitting on the training data, that means your weights are being too specific to your training data. The idea with regularization is to add some special terms with network weights to the Cost function, so the network doesn't converge very quickly. In other words, we are penalizing the weights so that they don't overfit to the training dataset and are more generic.

The second method to prevent overfitting is *dropout*. In dropout, during the training process, we randomly drop out a percentage of neurons from a layer and use the rest of the network for training. This helps prevent overfitting of the network by preventing certain neurons from getting tied to specific inputs. Since at any training iteration or epoch, there is a random number of neurons that will be dropped out (outputting zero values), the network is forced to learn patterns that are not dependent on specific training data or neurons.

Again, these concepts of regularization and dropout are extremely well explained with equations in Andrew Ng's video lecture. For practical ML, what I covered is good enough. You can now start using these layers in Keras. However, if you are interested in understanding what is happening under the hood, I highly recommend watching Andrew Ng's video classes.

If you get high accuracy on the validation data but your training data gives fewer promising results, you probably have a complex training dataset and a pretty simple validation set. We divided our data at random in our MNIST example. However, in real problems, you will need to build a validation set that has a good representation of your expected outputs. It is recommended to have all the variations you see in the validation set. This way, once you get good accuracy in validation you can be pretty confident that the model performs well on unseen data.

Finally, if you get poor accuracy on both the training and validation sets, that means you need more data or a better model, or sometimes both. By the same token, if you get good accuracy with both, you have a good model that has learned the patterns and works well on unseen data. That's what you should aim for!

For the MNIST example, an accuracy of above 90% is pretty good. We got that with all three datasets—training, validation, and testing. In the next chapter, we will see other model architectures like Convolutional Neural Networks (CNNs) and compare them to our MNIST model.

Summary

This chapter started building deep neural network models for analyzing image data. We used the Keras library on a TensorFlow framework to build our model. We saw cross-validation, where we separate training and testing data. We ran models that trained and we evaluated the accuracy metrics for our models. In the next chapter, we will start building more complex models. We will go beyond the MLP into Convolutional Neural Networks (CNNs) and show how they are much more effective in building deep models specifically for image analysis. In that chapter, we use different data—a fashion items images dataset. Hopefully, it will be interesting and you can try on some of your own image data.

CHAPTER 5

Advanced Deep Learning

In the previous chapter, we started building deep neural network models for analyzing images using Keras and TensorFlow. Now in this chapter we will start building models that extract complex visual *patterns.* We will go beyond the MLP into *Convolutional Neural Networks* (CNN) and show how they are much more effective in building deep models specifically for image analysis. We will use different data in this chapter—a fashion items images dataset. Hopefully it will be interesting and you can try on some of your own image data.

The Rise of Deep Learning Models

In the previous chapter, we saw one type of neural network called the *multi-layered perceptron* (MLP). These were the most common types of neural network used in the 1990s. However, these networks have many limitations.

MLP is good for a limited set of features, such as the less than one thousand in our example. As the number of features increases, since all neurons in dense layers are connected to all neurons in the next layer, the weights become very large. This makes the model difficult to train and requires a lot of processing power. As we add more layers with neurons in MLP, we don't see the effect of these layers much in the accuracy. So, adding more dense layers adds to complexity and training time, but doesn't really provide much benefit.

Also, we saw in our example that a 28×28 image was changed into a one-dimensional 784-element vector. This became the input layer for our network. However, when we flatten the two-dimensional layer, we lose many spatial relationships that the image carries. The two-dimensional structure carries relationships between pixels that help us understand the pattern the image contains. These are lost when we just flatten and give the inputs to an MLP.

We saw that in order to send unstructured data like images through an MLP, a large amount of feature extraction was needed to get meaningful results. This may be in the form of resizing large images to a smaller size, making images grayscale to reduce dimension, thresholding images to remove noise, etc. Many of these techniques fall in the domain of computer vision, which is basically a method to extract knowledge from images stored digitally as pixel arrays. Similar approaches were needed while handling other types of data like audio or text. In short, to get effective results from MLPs, a lot of feature extraction was needed. This process is known as *feature engineering*.

For a while in the 1990s, neural networks started going out of favor due to these limitations. However, in the early 2010s new discoveries in the types of network layers and architectures of neural networks started overcoming these limitations. Around the same time, there were tremendous improvements in processing power with advanced hardware like GPUs that could do thousands of linear Algebra calculations in parallel. This caused the advent of a new discipline under the Machine Learning umbrella known as *Deep Learning (DL)*. DL is technically a sub-branch of ML and more specifically a type of supervised learning. However, DL has been able show some amazing results in many challenging problems like image classification, natural language processing, speech recognition, voice synthesis, and many more. This makes DL a discipline of great importance and it is fast becoming the face of Artificial Intelligence. Again, since at its heart, DL is still a supervised learning method, all the concepts we learned about earlier, such as bias, variance, underfitting, and overfitting, are still valid for DL models.

New Kinds of Network Layers

One of the major improvements that DL introduces is new types of layers that help to build special types of models. These models work well on specific types of unstructured data like images or text. As we saw earlier, dense layers greatly increase the number of weights that need to be stored in the model. Also, they don't capture spatial relationships of the data, which are prominent in images. Let's look at how DL provides specialized layers and network architectures to help in image analysis. These types of networks are specialized neural networks known as Convolutional Neural Networks (CNNs). CNNs have been universally accepted as the best models available today for analyzing images and extracting knowledge from them. Let's look at these in detail.

Convolution Layer

As the name suggests, the major improvement in CNNs over regular MLP networks is the introduction of a new layer of neurons called a *convolution layer.* This layer specializes in extracting spatial patterns in pixel arrays. Let's look at this layer in detail.

Convolution is the operation of running a smaller matrix (known as a filter) over a larger data or signal matrix. At each run we do an element-wise multiplication of the two matrix elements and then add them. Consider convolution with the visual example shown in Figure 5.1.

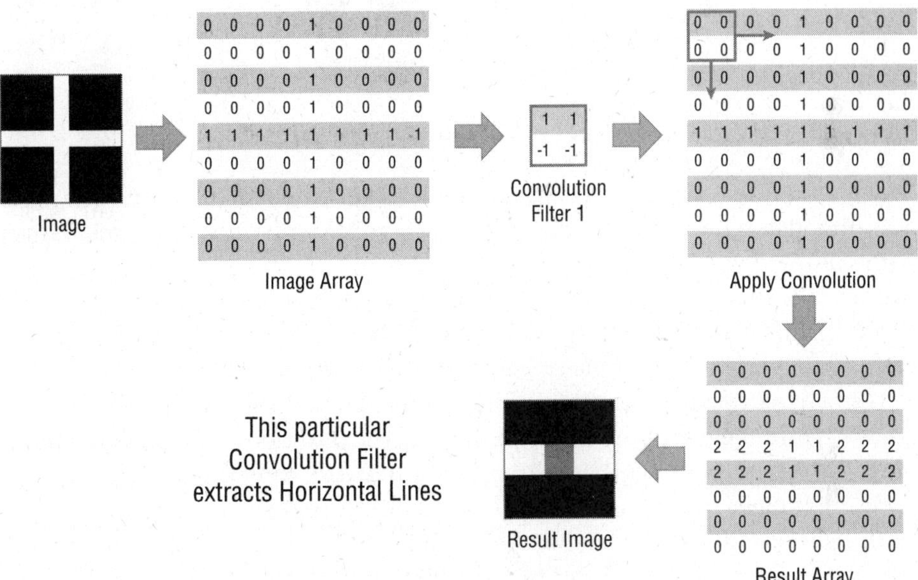

Figure 5.1: Simple convolution filter to extract horizontal lines

Our test image is a binary image with one horizontal and one vertical line, making a cross. This image is made up of 1s and 0s, indicating white and black pixels, respectively. We see the array representation of this image—with nine rows and nine columns. We choose a particular convolution filter (also called a *kernel*) of shape 2×2 and move it across the image. At each move we do element-wise multiplication and add the results. We get a new array that is of size 8×8. We see something interesting when we represent this new array as an image. We see the new convolved image only has the horizontal line highlighted. We were able to extract the pattern of horizontal lines from this image.

Now let's use a different filter and see what we can get. See Figure 5.2.

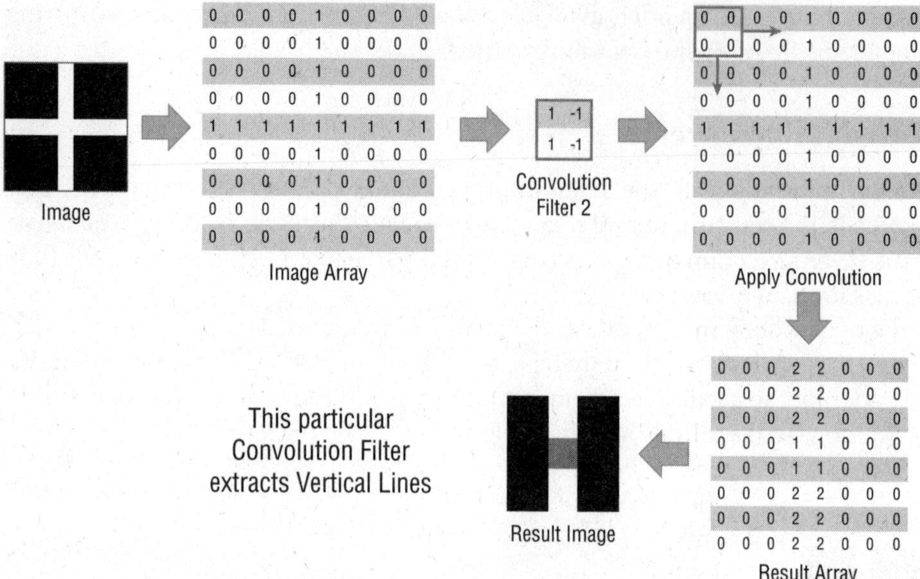

Figure 5.2: Simple convolution filter to extract vertical lines

Our next filter can detect vertical lines. It looks for particular patterns in the two-dimensional image and the result is an array with only the vertical lines with non-zero values.

If we take the two-dimensional image array as a layer in our neural network, applying this convolution filter will give us a new layer with only the vertical neurons activated. This is the concept of the convolution layer in CNNs.

The convolution layer is a three-dimensional layer. Two of its dimensions are the width and height of the input image. The third dimension is the number of filters we want our network to learn. As our network consumes the data points (training images in this case), it learns which features are of interest and starts learning those filters. Maybe the images you feed have many horizontal lines—then it will start learning the horizontal line filter we saw earlier. Typically, we use higher-order filters like 3×3, 5×5, or 7×7. The 2×2 filter was just an example to show how convolution works.

We saw in the previous examples that after applying a filter, the size of the image reduced a little bit. We went from a 9×9 image to an 8×8 one. This is a straightforward calculation. Basically:

```
New Image Dimension = Image Dimension - (filter size - 1)
```

This applies both to the width and height of the image. We normally use square filters—so the filter size is the same for both—three in 3×3 and five in 5×5. Many times, you don't want the convolution layer to change dimensions of your image. In that case, you add *padding*. With padding, the convolution operation basically returns an image of the same size as the input image, but with the patterns extracted by the convolution layer.

There are a few other layers of interest in CNNs and deep networks in general. We will go through a brief description and then explore them better with an example.

Pooling Layer

The key difference between MLP and CNN is that CNN works with two-dimensional image arrays and tries to extract spatial patterns using convolution layers. However, we need layers that can also reduce the dimension of images so we can improve upon the processing time. This is done using the *pooling layer.* All it does is down-sample the image based on a summary statistic like average or maximum. MaxPooling2D is a popular pooling layer that uses a pooling window like 2×2 or 4×4. It takes the maximum of the values in the window and assigns that to new image. It reduces the size of the image array by the amount of the window selected. For example, a 2×2 window will downsample a 100×100 image to 50×50.

We have already seen a flatten layer earlier that converts the two-dimensional array into a single-dimensional vector. The major difference in a CNN is that we use the flatten layer at the end of network after the convolution layers have extracted relevant patterns.

Now before we code an example, let's look at two special types of layers.

Dropout Layer

Many times, CNNs tend to overfit on the training data, with certain neurons always looking for fixed patterns in training data. One way to prevent this overfitting and increase the bias of the network is to use a special type of layer known as a dropout. A *dropout layer* basically drops a fixed percentage of neurons from our network at random during each training iteration or batch. So, a dropout of 0.3 means we randomly take 30% of neurons entering this layer and make their value zero. Now these neurons no longer play a role in learning. This way the network does not get a chance to overfit on training data because at any batch iteration any random neurons may be zero.

Batch Normalization Layer

We saw in the MLP example on the MNIST data earlier that we got training and test datasets with pixel intensity values between 0 and 255. We normalized these data points by dividing by 255, thus making the values between 0 and 1. This helps speed up the training process and our network converges faster. Another very popular way of speeding up training is to use a special layer known as a *batch normalization* layer. This layer basically does the normalization of data flowing through the network but at any layer. So instead of only normalizing input data, we also normalize data between layers so the network learns faster and we get good results.

Building a Deep Network for Classifying Fashion Images

All right, now let's see all this in action. We will take the earlier MNIST example and modify it to use CNN instead of MLP.

First, just as we saw earlier, let's load the data and look at the dataset. For this example, we will use a new dataset also provided by Keras—the fashion items dataset (see Figure 5.3). This dataset also has 28×28 grayscale training and test images like MNIST. These images are of fashion items rather than digits. Also, we will use a labels array to define labels for each item. See Listing 5.1.

Listing 5.1: Load a Different Dataset, One with Fashion Items

```
# import keras library
from tensorflow import keras

# Helper libraries
import numpy as np
import matplotlib.pyplot as plt
%matplotlib inline

# load the mnist dataset provided by Keras
dataset = keras.datasets.fashion_mnist

# labels for the images
class_names = ['T-shirt/top', 'Trouser', 'Pullover', 'Dress', 'Coat',
               'Sandal', 'Shirt', 'Sneaker', 'Bag', 'Ankle boot']

# load the training and test data
(img_rows, img_cols) = (28,28)
(x_train, y_train),(x_test, y_test) = dataset.load_data()

# lets plot some data samples
plt.figure(figsize=(10,10))
for i in range(25):
    plt.subplot(5,5,i+1)
    plt.xticks([])
    plt.yticks([])
    plt.grid(False)
    plt.imshow(x_test[i], cmap=plt.cm.gray)
    plt.xlabel(class_names[y_test[i]])

plt.show()
```

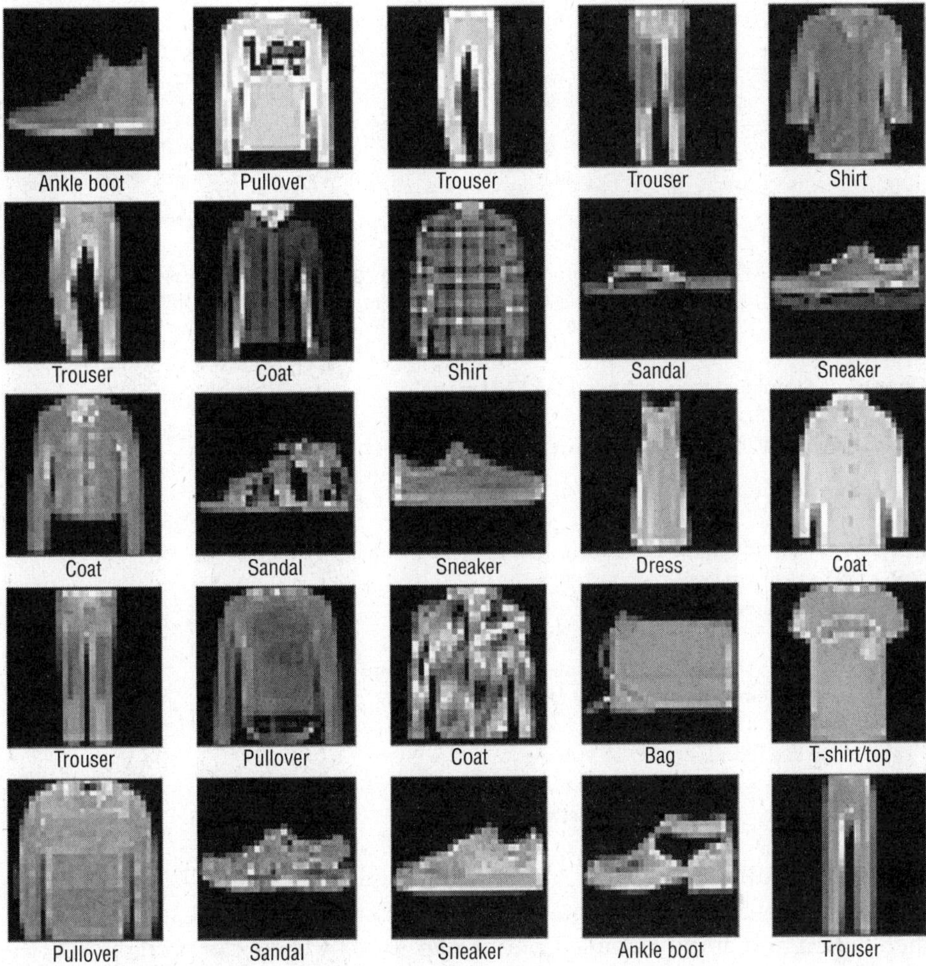

Figure 5.3: Samples from fashion images dataset

Now we will build a CNN using some of the layers we saw earlier. The concept of CNN is first to keep the image input in two dimensions and apply convolution and pooling. Then we flatten the data and build a dense layer to map to 10 outputs with a Softmax layer. The network's structure is shown in Figure 5.4.

Let's code this network. First, we do some preprocessing on the data. We convert the integer Y values to one-hot encoded array of 0s with only the prediction column with value 1. Next, we divide the values by 255 to normalize the data between 0 and 1. Finally, we use the numpy `expand_dims` function to change the array (or Tensor) from `(num_samples, 28, 28)` to `(num_samples, 28, 28, 1)`—one dimension. This does not change the data but reshapes the matrix to make it easier to feed the CNN. See Listing 5.2.

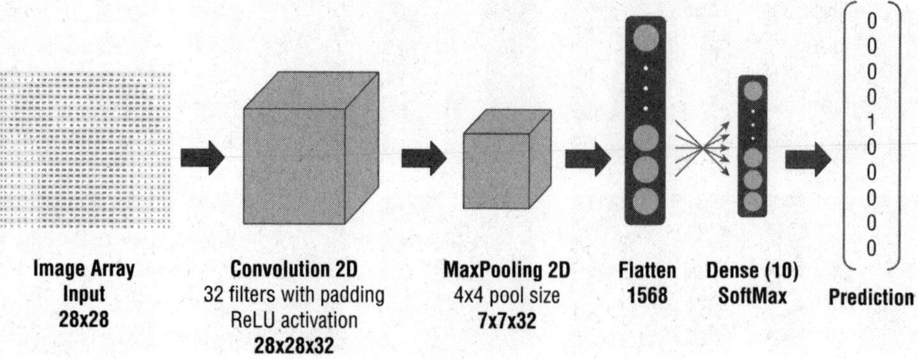

Figure 5.4: Simplified architecture of our CNN model

Listing 5.2: Load Dataset, Preprocess, and Split into Training and Testing

```
from keras.utils import to_categorical

# one hot encode the results
y_train = to_categorical(y_train)
y_test = to_categorical(y_test)

# normalize the data to values between 0 and 1
x_train, x_test = x_train / 255.0, x_test / 255.0

# customize data for CNN - make a 3D array
x_train_cnn = np.expand_dims(x_train, -1)
x_test_cnn = np.expand_dims(x_test, -1)
```

Now let's build the network. As shown in Figure 5.4, we will use a convolution layer with 32 filters and max pooling with a 4×4 pool size in 2D. We will then flatten and apply a dense layer of size 10 to indicate the predictions. See Listing 5.3.

Listing 5.3: Build a Convolutional Neural Network Model in Keras

```
from keras.models import Sequential
from keras.layers import Dense, Dropout, Flatten, Input
from keras.layers import Conv2D, MaxPooling2D


model = Sequential()
model.add(Conv2D(32, (3, 3), activation='relu',
                 input_shape=(28, 28, 1), padding='same'))
model.add(MaxPooling2D(pool_size=(4, 4)))
model.add(Flatten())
model.add(Dense(10, activation='softmax'))

# assign the optimizer for the model and define loss function
model.compile(optimizer='adam',
```

```
              loss='categorical_crossentropy',
              metrics=['accuracy'])

model.summary()
```

Here are the results:

```
_________________________________________________________________
Layer (type)                 Output Shape              Param #
=================================================================
conv2d_18 (Conv2D)           (None, 28, 28, 32)        320
_________________________________________________________________
max_pooling2d_17 (MaxPooling (None, 7, 7, 32)          0
_________________________________________________________________
flatten_11 (Flatten)         (None, 1568)              0
_________________________________________________________________
dense_12 (Dense)             (None, 10)                15690
=================================================================
Total params: 16,010
Trainable params: 16,010
Non-trainable params: 0
_________________________________________________________________
```

Let's compare the CNN model to the MLP we built earlier. One thing you notice immediately is that the total trainable parameters or weights in the CNN is 16,010, while the ones in the MLP were 407,050. That is the advantage of using convolution and pooling layers. They capture patterns but use way fewer weights. This is because the convolution layer reuses weights by having the same filter convolve over the previous layer again and again.

This makes the CNN model much lighter to load and faster to train and predict. Now let's train our model; see Listing 5.4.

Listing 5.4: Train the Model and Observe Accuracy and Loss

```
# run the actual training
history = model.fit(x_train_cnn, y_train, epochs=1)

# evaluate on test data
model.evaluate(x_test_cnn, y_test)

Epoch 1/1
60000/60000 [==============================] - 20s 338us/step - loss:
0.5202 - acc: 0.8176
10000/10000 [==============================] - 2s 211us/step

[0.4220195102214813, 0.847]
```

Since this is a more complex dataset than MNIST, we get a lower accuracy in the first epoch. You will get similar accuracy values using an MLP, but with a huge model size. As you increase the epochs, you will get more improvements in accuracy. We will plot the accuracy and loss over time with epochs. Let's run for 20 epochs and see how the loss and accuracy vary. See Listing 5.5.

Listing 5.5: Train the Model for 20 Epochs

```
# run the actual training
history = model.fit(x_train_cnn, y_train, epochs=20)
```

Here are the results:

```
Epoch 1/20
60000/60000 [==============================] - 19s 314us/step - loss:
0.3605 - acc: 0.8722
Epoch 2/20
60000/60000 [==============================] - 17s 278us/step - loss:
0.3234 - acc: 0.8851
Epoch 3/20
60000/60000 [==============================] - 15s 248us/step - loss:
0.3031 - acc: 0.8933
Epoch 4/20
60000/60000 [==============================] - 15s 250us/step - loss:
0.2893 - acc: 0.8971
Epoch 5/20
60000/60000 [==============================] - 15s 251us/step - loss:
0.2785 - acc: 0.9007
Epoch 6/20
60000/60000 [==============================] - 15s 256us/step - loss:
0.2679 - acc: 0.9052
Epoch 7/20
60000/60000 [==============================] - 16s 260us/step - loss:
0.2608 - acc: 0.9077
Epoch 8/20
60000/60000 [==============================] - 15s 247us/step - loss:
0.2536 - acc: 0.9095
Epoch 9/20
60000/60000 [==============================] - 15s 257us/step - loss:
0.2468 - acc: 0.9123
Epoch 10/20
60000/60000 [==============================] - 15s 247us/step - loss:
0.2420 - acc: 0.9133
Epoch 11/20
60000/60000 [==============================] - 15s 248us/step - loss:
0.2354 - acc: 0.9159
Epoch 12/20
60000/60000 [==============================] - 15s 246us/step - loss:
0.2320 - acc: 0.9165
Epoch 13/20
60000/60000 [==============================] - 15s 248us/step - loss:
0.2274 - acc: 0.9181
```

```
Epoch 14/20
60000/60000 [==============================] - 15s 248us/step - loss:
0.2227 - acc: 0.9200
Epoch 15/20
60000/60000 [==============================] - 15s 250us/step - loss:
0.2197 - acc: 0.9213
Epoch 16/20
60000/60000 [==============================] - 15s 247us/step - loss:
0.2158 - acc: 0.9236
Epoch 17/20
60000/60000 [==============================] - 15s 251us/step - loss:
0.2125 - acc: 0.9222
Epoch 18/20
60000/60000 [==============================] - 15s 247us/step - loss:
0.2099 - acc: 0.9254
Epoch 19/20
60000/60000 [==============================] - 15s 244us/step - loss:
0.2071 - acc: 0.9252
Epoch 20/20
60000/60000 [==============================] - 15s 244us/step - loss:
0.2038 - acc: 0.9267
10000/10000 [==============================] - 1s 115us/step
```

Now we will take the learning history data stored in the history variable and plot it. See Listing 5.6.

Listing 5.6: Plotting the Learning History to See How the Model Has Learned

```
import matplotlib.pyplot as plt
%matplotlib inline

# summarize history for accuracy
plt.plot(history.history['acc'])
#plt.plot(history.history['val_acc'])
plt.title('model accuracy')
plt.ylabel('accuracy')
plt.xlabel('epoch')
plt.legend(['train', 'test'], loc='upper left')
plt.show()

# summarize history for loss
plt.plot(history.history['loss'])
#plt.plot(history.history['val_loss'])
plt.title('model loss')
plt.ylabel('loss')
plt.xlabel('epoch')
plt.legend(['train', 'test'], loc='upper left')
plt.show()
```

Let's look at the plot of accuracy and loss over the epochs in Figure 5.5 below.

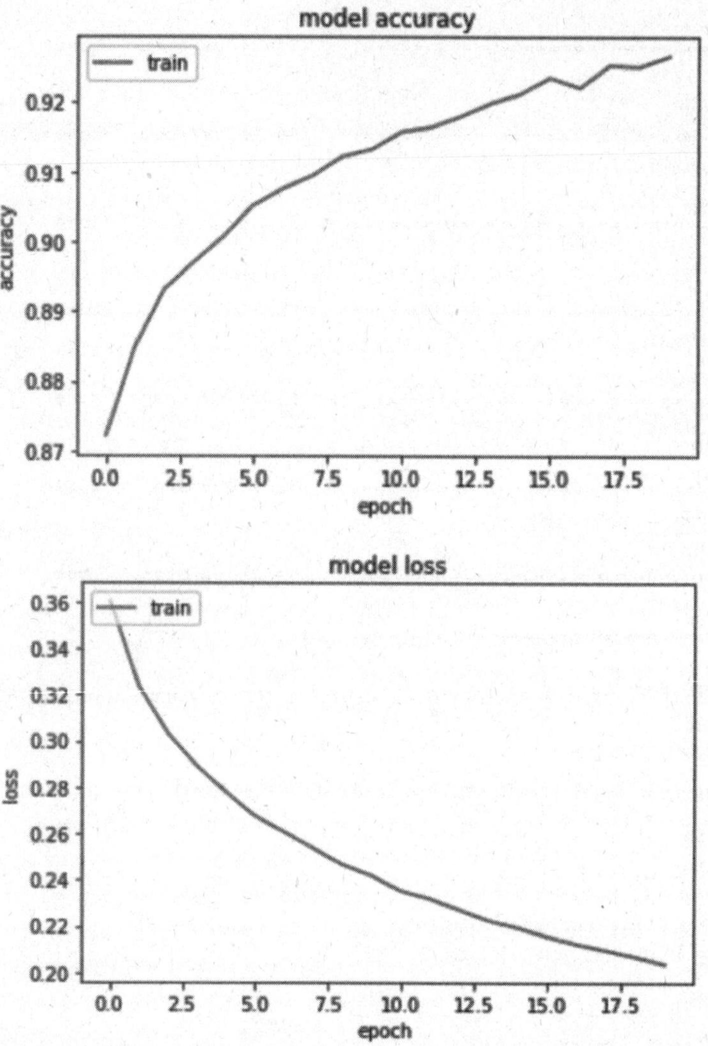

Figure 5.5: Model accuracy increases and loss decreases over the epochs

We see the model accuracy increase gradually over epochs and loss reduces. We can try different model architectures and hyper-parameters to see what gives us the best results on our dataset. This is mostly done by trial and error, but many veteran data scientists have their favorite methods of tuning hyper-parameters to get the best results. These hyper-parameters may be number of layers, type of layers, number of neurons in each layer, loss function, optimizer used, etc. Let's look at some common ways data scientists tune their models by adjusting architectures and hyper-parameters.

CNN Architectures and Hyper-Parameters

CNNs can easily get very complex with many layers of neurons and different parameters. There are a few common practices data scientists use that can help better tune hyper-parameters and save a lot of time. Because the models are complex and need large volumes of data to train, usually these take a lot of time and need specialized expensive hardware like GPUs to train.

First, we have to decide on the architecture of the neural network. This includes how many layers, what type of layers, and how many neurons in each layer. Earlier we saw a very simple network with one convolutional, one pooling, and one dense layer. However, that won't work when we have millions of images to classify into thousands of categories (yes people have tried that!). There are a few popular deep network architectures for CNN that have shown very good results on image classification problems. But how do we compare these? We need a standard image dataset to do so.

That's where ImageNet comes into the picture. This is a standardized image dataset with 14 million training images that are hand-annotated into about 20 thousand categories. There are also a few thousand separate validation and testing datasets for evaluating your image classification models. Interestingly, ImageNet was a community effort lead by Fei Fei Li who is (as of 2018) the Chief Scientist working at Google.

Now with ImageNet, data scientists across the world can come up with innovative deep network architectures and evaluate on a common and standard dataset. When you present your next Deep Learning model architecture, you confidently say you tested it on ImageNet with 70% accuracy and everyone will know what that is. There is also an annual ImageNet Large Scale Visual Recognition Challenge (ILSVRC) organized every year where computer vision and AI scientists from universities and companies across the world compete on ImageNet. Pretty awesome stuff!

Figure 5.6 shows the common standard image dataset. Extremely smart data scientists around the world have been developing innovative deep network architectures to solve the image recognition problem. All these architectures have been published in the public domain—especially those that have participated in and won the ILSVRC competition over the years.

Some of these popular architectures are AlexNet, VGG, ResNet, Inception, and more. I will provide some papers in the "References" section at the end of the book describing each of these in detail for those interested. Also, keep in mind that this is an area of active and ongoing research. So, as you are reading this book there may be a super-smart data scientist somewhere in the world coming up with the next great architecture that will out-perform all others.

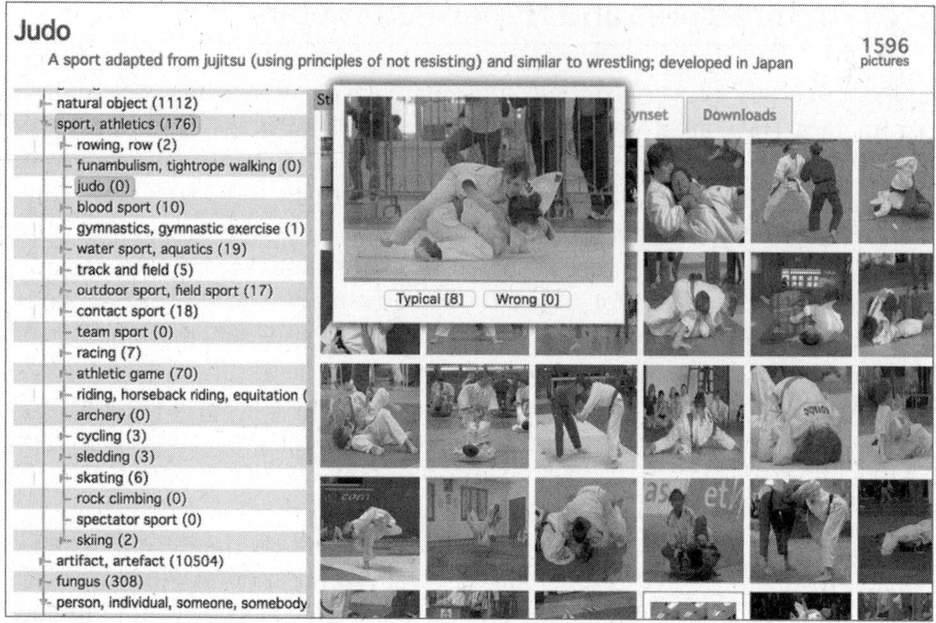

Figure 5.6: ImageNet categorized images (*Source*: Image-Net.org)

Typically, it is recommended to start with one of the proven architectures and fine-tune it for your requirements. The good news is that Keras comes packaged with most of these popular architectures. You can start with one of these and use it to train on your dataset. Moreover, Keras also gives you these models pre-trained on the most popular open data source for image classification—ImageNet!

You will typically start with a good, proven model architecture like VGG or ResNet or Inception, then tune the hyper-parameters to solve the particular problem you are dealing with. A couple other hyper-parameters we may think of tuning are the loss function and the type of optimizer to be used. Typically, cross-entropy or log loss is a popular loss function for classification problems. Cross-entropy loss could be binary or categorical depending on if the problem is to classify between two classes (binary) or multiple classes (categorical). We have seen the standard batch, stochastic, and mini-batch gradient descent optimizers. We may want to make the learning process faster by using different learning rates that work with these optimizers. Also, specialized optimizers like stochastic gradient descent (SGD) with Momentum, RMSProp, and Adam (which we used in the last example) may show better results. SGD with momentum tries to push the weight values (applies momentum) in the direction of the minima (optimal weights with minimum loss value). RMSProp tends to remove oscillations around certain weights while approaching the minima. Typically, Adam is more popular since it captures the effects of both Momentum and RMSProp. You may have to do lot of trial and error to arrive at the best optimizer for your problem.

The learning rate decides how big a step you take while modifying weights to approach the minima. A bigger learning rate may have you oscillating around the minima while a smaller rate may have you take a long time to reach it. Again, a lot of trial and error involved.

Making Predictions Using a Pretrained VGG Model

We will talk about a relatively simpler Deep Model—VGGNet by VGG (Visual Geometry Group) from the University of Oxford. The VGG network architecture was introduced by Simonyan and Zisserman in their 2014 paper "Very Deep Convolutional Networks for Large Scale Image Recognition" (you will find a link in the "References" section). The key features are that it only contains 3×3 convolution layers stacked on each other with 2×2 MaxPooling2D layers. This is a 2D convolution layer because we keep the layer width the same and convolve in 2 dimensions. There are two fully connected dense layers at the end that map to a thousand image categories.

We will now see some code examples. First, we will load a pretrained VGG-16 model in Keras and use it to make predictions on an image. Then we will look at data augmentation to generate lots of data from a few samples to help us train models better. Finally, we will use transfer learning to tune the last few layers of a pretrained VGG-16 model to adapt it to learn specific categories in our domain of data. This is something you may see a lot in the real world. We will actually take an example of a real-world logo detector that can read images and tell us which brand the logo belongs to. You will find that these general methods (and the code provided) can be directly applied to many common business problems. Do let me know if you find some cool use cases for these methods! Listing 5.7 shows the code.

Listing 5.7: Import a Popular VGG16 Model with Pretrained Weights

```
# import keras libraries
from tensorflow import keras

# import the pretrained VGG16 Model
from keras.applications.vgg16 import VGG16

# create the Model instance
model = VGG16()

# show summary
print(model.summary())
```

Here are the results:

```
Layer (type)                 Output Shape              Param #
=================================================================
input_1 (InputLayer)         (None, 224, 224, 3)       0
_________________________________________________________________
block1_conv1 (Conv2D)        (None, 224, 224, 64)      1792
_________________________________________________________________
block1_conv2 (Conv2D)        (None, 224, 224, 64)      36928
_________________________________________________________________
block1_pool (MaxPooling2D)   (None, 112, 112, 64)      0
_________________________________________________________________
block2_conv1 (Conv2D)        (None, 112, 112, 128)     73856
_________________________________________________________________
block2_conv2 (Conv2D)        (None, 112, 112, 128)     147584
_________________________________________________________________
block2_pool (MaxPooling2D)   (None, 56, 56, 128)       0
_________________________________________________________________
block3_conv1 (Conv2D)        (None, 56, 56, 256)       295168
_________________________________________________________________
block3_conv2 (Conv2D)        (None, 56, 56, 256)       590080
_________________________________________________________________
block3_conv3 (Conv2D)        (None, 56, 56, 256)       590080
_________________________________________________________________
block3_pool (MaxPooling2D)   (None, 28, 28, 256)       0
_________________________________________________________________
block4_conv1 (Conv2D)        (None, 28, 28, 512)       1180160
_________________________________________________________________
block4_conv2 (Conv2D)        (None, 28, 28, 512)       2359808
_________________________________________________________________
block4_conv3 (Conv2D)        (None, 28, 28, 512)       2359808
_________________________________________________________________
block4_pool (MaxPooling2D)   (None, 14, 14, 512)       0
_________________________________________________________________
block5_conv1 (Conv2D)        (None, 14, 14, 512)       2359808
_________________________________________________________________
block5_conv2 (Conv2D)        (None, 14, 14, 512)       2359808
_________________________________________________________________
block5_conv3 (Conv2D)        (None, 14, 14, 512)       2359808
_________________________________________________________________
block5_pool (MaxPooling2D)   (None, 7, 7, 512)         0
_________________________________________________________________
flatten (Flatten)            (None, 25088)             0
_________________________________________________________________
fc1 (Dense)                  (None, 4096)              102764544
_________________________________________________________________
fc2 (Dense)                  (None, 4096)              16781312
_________________________________________________________________
predictions (Dense)          (None, 1000)              4097000
=================================================================
```

```
Total params: 138,357,544
Trainable params: 138,357,544
Non-trainable params: 0
```

This is how the VGG-16 model looks. It has 16 layers. The initial layers are Conv2D and MaxPooling2D type. The last three layers are dense with two of them having 4096 neurons. The final layer has a thousand neurons for a thousand categories.

Now let's use this network to make a prediction. First, we will download a sample image from the Internet. I use an image of an electric train, shown in Figure 5.7. Download it using the exclamation mark (`!`) followed by the shell command `wget`. The `-O` option specifies the name of the file to be downloaded. See Listing 5.8.

Listing 5.8: Download a File Using a Shell Command Inside Notebook

```
# download a sample image from the Internet - use any URL you want
!wget -O mytest.jpg https://upload.wikimedia.org/wikipedia/commons/f/fe/
Amtrak_Train_161.jpg
```

This command will download the image from the URL and store it as a file called `mytest.jpg`.

Figure 5.7: Electric Locomotive image from Wikipedia
(*Source*: Lexcie Wikimedia)

Now we will use the pretrained model loaded to classify this image. We will use some prebuilt functions in Keras like `preprocess_input` to normalize the image so that it is provided in the form with which the VGG network can make the best predictions. We will also use the `decode _ predictions` function to make sense of what the model predicted. It will predict a class number between 0 and 999. This method will get us the right label, such as cat, dog, plane, train, etc. See Listing 5.9.

Listing 5.9: Make a Prediction Using the Neural Network on Your Downloaded Image

```
from keras.preprocessing.image import load_img
from keras.preprocessing.image import img_to_array
from keras.applications.vgg16 import preprocess_input
from keras.applications.vgg16 import decode_predictions
import numpy as np

# load image from file - VGG16 takes (244,244) input
myimg = load_img('mytest.jpg', target_size=(224, 224))

# convert image pixels to array
myimg = img_to_array(myimg)
myimg = np.expand_dims(myimg, axis=0)
print('Image shape to feed to VGG Net: ', myimg.shape)

# prepare image for the VGG model
myimg = preprocess_input(myimg)

# predict probability for all 1000 classes
pred = model.predict(myimg)
print('Predictions array shape: ', pred.shape)

# convert the probabilities to class labels
label = decode_predictions(pred)

# retrieve the most likely result, e.g. highest probability
label = label[0][0]

# print the classification
print('Predicted class: %s (%.2f%%)' % (label[1], label[2]*100))
```

Here are the results:

```
Image shape to feed to VGG Net:  (1, 224, 224, 3)

Predictions array shape:  (1, 1000)

Predicted class: electric_locomotive (86.93%)
```

Our pretrained network looked at a new image and predicted with 86.93% confidence that it was an electric locomotive. Pretty awesome!

In just about 15 lines of code, we can use any of these best-in-class Deep Learning models trained by top data scientists in the world for free in Keras to predict our images. That's why I think the Deep Learning community is truly awesome!

Data Augmentation and Transfer Learning

Now we will see two extremely useful techniques that data scientists use regularly to solve problems. I have met many data scientists who swear by these two methods—*data augmentation* and *transfer learning*. These will greatly help you save on the amount of data and processing time needed to build your models.

Data augmentation is a way to create more data from a limited set of data. Most often when we deal with a new problem domain, we have limited data. Using augmentation techniques, we can create more data that can be used to train our models. Some of these techniques include flipping the image, shearing, scaling in certain directions, zooming in, etc. For image analysis problems, you will normally need some sort of computer vision techniques to augment images and increase the size of your training set. Luckily our favorite Deep Learning framework—Keras—comes with built-in tools that can handle this augmentation. We will see those tools in an example shortly.

A second very popular method is called *transfer learning*. Here we take a pretrained model that has been trained to good accuracy on images from similar domains as the problem we are solving. As we discussed already, the model training process is basically finding optimal weights for our model so that it fits our training data the best. We may have a model that has been trained on a large standard dataset like ImageNet. Now instead of retraining the model on our dataset, we leverage existing knowledge that the model has learned from the previous training. So, in a way, we transfer learning from one problem domain to another. Basically, you are transferring the knowledge obtained from training a model on a large dataset to teach a new model with similar architecture on your specific smaller dataset. This saves you a lot of time compared to starting from scratch and building models.

Take the example of a typical CNN, as shown in Figure 5.8. We see that the early layers act as feature-extractors. In the case of images, these look for two-dimensional spatial patterns. For example, if we are exploring a dataset of images of human faces, these early layer neurons may be looking for edges or curves. Further down they may look for more fully formed features like contours. Even further, the layers will look for things like eyes, lips, etc. Finally, the dense or fully-connected layers will "learn" patterns by looking at these features and the expected outputs. This is how an array of pixels gets mapped to an array of predictions for what the image contains. That's Deep Learning for you!

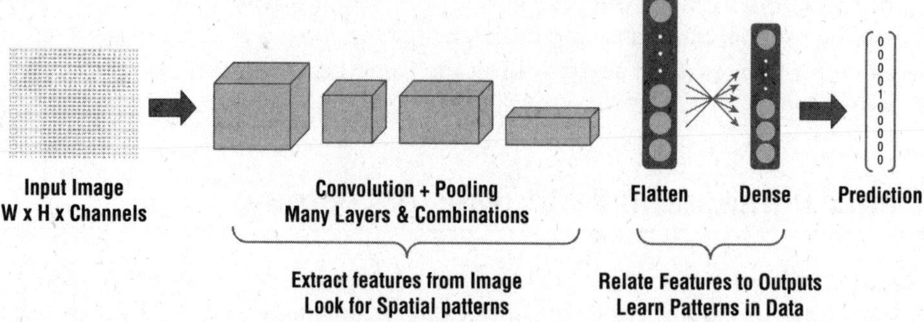

Figure 5.8: Typical CNN architecture where early layers extract spatial patterns and final dense layers learn from them

If we have a popular and proven architecture that's trained on a good diverse dataset like ImageNet, we know that this is very good at extracting features from image data—basically three-dimensional pixel value arrays. Now if we can use this feature-extractor and apply to our dataset, we can focus mainly on training the model to learn patterns in extracted features and relating them to desired outcomes. This greatly cuts down on our model development and training time. This is accomplished through transfer learning.

Let's dive into an example using data augmentation and transfer learning.

A Real Classification Problem: Pepsi vs. Coke

Let's take a real example to show the value of data augmentation and transfer learning during the Deep Learning model development process. Say we have a few images of the product logos of Pepsi and Coca-Cola (Coke). We want to build a basic Deep Learning classifier that can read an image and tell us if it is a logo of Pepsi or Coke.

You see that this is a classification problem on image data. A typical first step in such a problem is to collect thousands of images of the intended classes—Coke and Pepsi logos. These should cover all the variations in size, color, shapes, viewing angle, rotation, etc. Ultimately, we should train a classifier that can take any image containing a prominent logo of Pepsi or Coke and tell us which logo it is. It is a simple binary classification problem.

As we discussed in Chapter 1, we need to always consider an analytic in the context of the system it will be used in. Here, assume that the system is a mobile app where we will use a smartphone to take a photo and somehow call our trained model to get a classification on what the image contains—Pepsi or Coke. Since it's binary classification, our output will be a single digit—0 or 1. We can say 0 will indicate Coke and 1 will indicate Pepsi. We can choose any way of naming it, as long as we use this way to feed training data to our model.

So, if we choose Coke = 0 and Pepsi = 1, then all our training images for Coke should be marked 0 and Pepsi should be 1.

Now from the problem context, we can see that we may be using the cell phone at any angle to take pictures. Thus, we need to take training images from several different angles. Collecting this data seems a lot of work even for just two classes of images. This where we will use *data augmentation* to save time. We will take a few images—five training and five validation images for each class. Then we will use these limited datasets to convert thousands of images for training. During augmentation, we will use the contextual knowledge of the application to set parameters for how the images should be augmented.

Luckily, Keras provides some very good tools for image data augmentation. Figure 5.9 shows the folder structure we have created along with couple sample images for the logos in two classes. This is what we will feed to our Keras image augmentation methods. You see that there are two main folders, one for *training* and one for *validation* datasets. Each has folders representing the two classes we want to train for—in this case Pepsi and Coca-Cola. Keras tools are smart enough to observe this folder structure and pick the two classes. For other problems, we can increase the number of folders inside the training and validation folders.

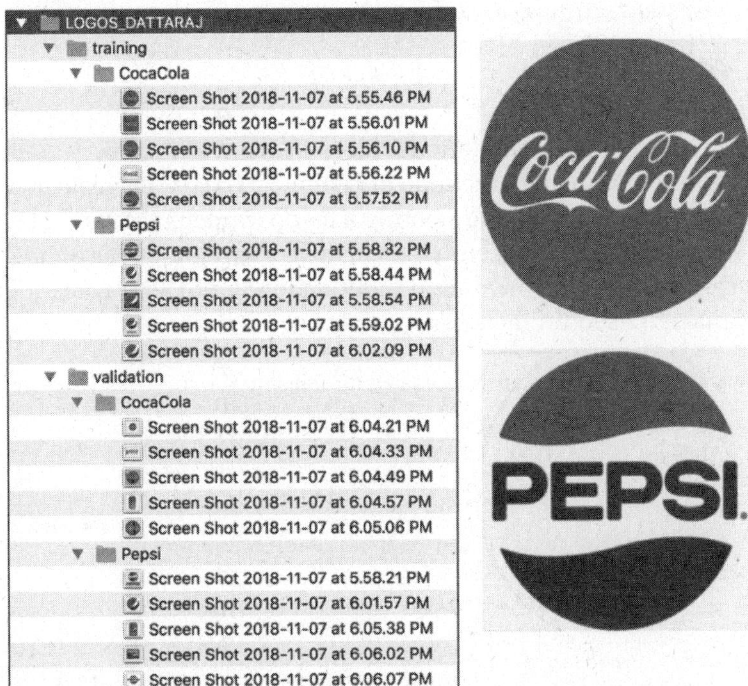

Figure 5.9: General folder structure for our problem of predicting two classes for images. Sample logo images from each class are shown.

I pretty much scraped these images from the web and put them in folders. They don't need to have the exact same width and height, but it's recommended that they be similar in ratio. Ultimately Keras data augmentation tools will convert these images to a standard width and height you specify. If the saved images are too different, they may look distorted.

You see that for training we just use five images of each class. We have similar images for validation also. It's highly recommended that for validation you use images that you will feed to your model in the actual application. If you are building a mobile app that will predict logos, it's better to use many mobile images from different orientations and zoom as validation images. It's usually recommended to apply data augmentation to training data and try to keep the validation data fixed. You may apply a very basic filter like scaling for this data, as we will do in the following example. I have made this small dataset with the folder structure available as a downloadable ZIP file in my S3 bucket. If you are using Google Colaboratory to run code, you can download and extract it using the commands shown in Listing 5.10.

Listing 5.10: Download Sample Images for This Example

```
# Download sample images in folder structure for Data Augmentation

!wget -O LOGOS_DATTARAJ.zip https://s3.ap-south-1.amazonaws.com/
dattaraj-public/LOGOS_DATTARAJ.zip

!unzip LOGOS_DATTARAJ.zip
```

Now we have the training and validation folders with a few images in each class. We will see how to use them in the code in Listing 5.11. We will create new images from our sample images by augmenting a few parameters and display these new augmented images on-screen. This will give you a good idea of how this works. You can use data augmentation independently of Deep Learning to generate new images based on the existing ones.

Listing 5.11: Data Augmentation to Generate New Images for Training

```
from keras.preprocessing.image import ImageDataGenerator
import matplotlib.pyplot as plt
%matplotlib inline

# specify the directories for training and validation images
training_dir = './LOGOS_DATTARAJ/training'
validation_dir = './LOGOS_DATTARAJ/validation'

# we will generate 1 image at a time - we could do so in batches
gen_batch_size = 1

# we will create a generator of generating training data
# we will apply transformations and rotations to new images
```

```
# idea is to capture different variations we see in real world
train_datagen = ImageDataGenerator(
                     rescale=1./255,
                     shear_range=0.2,
                     zoom_range=0.2,
                     fill_mode = "nearest",
                     width_shift_range = 0.3,
                     height_shift_range=0.3,
                     rotation_range=20,
                     horizontal_flip=False)



# this is a generator that will read pictures found in
# subfolders and indefinitely generate
# batches of augmented image data
train_generator = train_datagen.flow_from_directory(
                         training_dir,  # this is the target directory
                                target_size=(150, 150),
                           batch_size=gen_batch_size,
                                                      class_mode='binary'
                                  )
# since we use binary_crossentropy loss, we need binary labels

# generator will specify classes by index 0, 1
class_names = ['Coca-Cola', 'Pepsi']

# lets generate some images and plot them
print('Generating images now...')
ROW = 10
plt.figure(figsize=(20,20))
for i in range(ROW*ROW):
    plt.subplot(ROW,ROW,i+1)
    plt.xticks([])
    # run the generator to get the next image - we can do this forever!
          next_set = train_generator.next()
    plt.imshow(next_set[0][0])
    plt.xticks([])
    plt.yticks([])
    plt.grid(False)
    plt.xlabel(class_names[int(next_set[1][0])])

plt.show()
```

Here are the results:

```
Found 10 images belonging to 2 classes.
```

It's generating images now, as shown in Figure 5.10.

Figure 5.10: Results of data augmentation on a few logos

This is how you can generate thousands of images from a few sample images using data augmentation. You can experiment with the different generator settings to change the amount of variation that will exist in generated images. Augmentation is a very powerful feature and many other tools are available that can augment images. You can evaluate them and see what unique features they offer.

Now let's build our classification model for predicting the two logo classes. We will start with the VGG16 pretrained model like the earlier example. Now we will use transfer learning to reuse this model for our specific classification example. We will load the model in what Keras calls "headless" mode, so it will only load the feature-extractor layers and not the fully-connected learning layers. We will build our own fully-connected layers to learn patterns on our data. Let's see how, in Listing 5.12.

Listing 5.12: Load VGG16 Model and Modify It for Our Specific Problem

```
from keras.layers import Flatten
from keras.layers import Dense
from keras.layers import Dropout
```

```
from keras import Model
from keras import optimizers

# set a size of image we will feed to our Model as input
# this is the same size we should have our generator build images
img_width, img_height = 150, 150

# load VGG16 model in headless mode - include_top = False
model = VGG16(weights = "imagenet", include_top=False, input_shape =
(img_width, img_height, 3))

# Freeze all the feature-extractor layers which you don't want to train.
for layer in model.layers:
    layer.trainable = False

# Add custom Layers for our Binary Classification problem
x = model.output
x = Flatten()(x)
x = Dense(512, activation="relu")(x)
x = Dropout(0.5)(x)
x = Dense(64, activation="relu")(x)
predictions = Dense(1, activation="sigmoid")(x)

# create final Model which we will use
model_final = Model(input = model.input, output = predictions)

# show summary of this new Model
model_final.summary()
```

Here are the results:

```
_________________________________________________________________
Layer (type)                 Output Shape              Param #
=================================================================
input_2 (InputLayer)         (None, 150, 150, 3)       0
_________________________________________________________________
block1_conv1 (Conv2D)        (None, 150, 150, 64)      1792
_________________________________________________________________
block1_conv2 (Conv2D)        (None, 150, 150, 64)      36928
_________________________________________________________________
block1_pool (MaxPooling2D)   (None, 75, 75, 64)        0
_________________________________________________________________
block2_conv1 (Conv2D)        (None, 75, 75, 128)       73856
_________________________________________________________________
block2_conv2 (Conv2D)        (None, 75, 75, 128)       147584
_________________________________________________________________
block2_pool (MaxPooling2D)   (None, 37, 37, 128)       0
_________________________________________________________________
block3_conv1 (Conv2D)        (None, 37, 37, 256)       295168
_________________________________________________________________
```

```
block3_conv2 (Conv2D)        (None, 37, 37, 256)      590080
_________________________________________________________________
block3_conv3 (Conv2D)        (None, 37, 37, 256)      590080
_________________________________________________________________
block3_pool (MaxPooling2D)   (None, 18, 18, 256)      0
_________________________________________________________________
block4_conv1 (Conv2D)        (None, 18, 18, 512)      1180160
_________________________________________________________________
block4_conv2 (Conv2D)        (None, 18, 18, 512)      2359808
_________________________________________________________________
block4_conv3 (Conv2D)        (None, 18, 18, 512)      2359808
_________________________________________________________________
block4_pool (MaxPooling2D)   (None, 9, 9, 512)        0
_________________________________________________________________
block5_conv1 (Conv2D)        (None, 9, 9, 512)        2359808
_________________________________________________________________
block5_conv2 (Conv2D)        (None, 9, 9, 512)        2359808
_________________________________________________________________
block5_conv3 (Conv2D)        (None, 9, 9, 512)        2359808
_________________________________________________________________
block5_pool (MaxPooling2D)   (None, 4, 4, 512)        0
_________________________________________________________________
flatten_1 (Flatten)          (None, 8192)             0
_________________________________________________________________
dense_1 (Dense)              (None, 512)              4194816
_________________________________________________________________
dropout_1 (Dropout)          (None, 512)              0
_________________________________________________________________
dense_2 (Dense)              (None, 64)               32832
_________________________________________________________________
dense_3 (Dense)              (None, 1)                65
=================================================================
Total params: 18,942,401
Trainable params: 4,227,713
Non-trainable params: 14,714,688
_________________________________________________________________
```

Notice the earlier layers in the model are the same as VGG16. We added the later layers `flatten_1`, `dense_1`, `dense_2`, and `dense_3`. `Dense_3` has just one output neuron signifying our output, which can be 0 or 1 based on the image being a Coca-Cola or Pepsi logo. Notice that we also include a dropout layer, where 50% of the neurons get dropped so that the model does not overfit on training data. This is very important since we have limited training data and are generating new images only through augmentation. Overfitting can be a problem here.

Now let's use these generators to directly feed data to the model and train it. We will also create a validation generator that will not use a whole lot of augmentation. We will only scale the image so that the pixel values are between 0 and 1 for ease of learning. See Listing 5.13.

Listing 5.13: Create Training and Validation Generators to Load and Normalize Images from Directory

```
# validation images here
validation_dir = './LOGOS_DATTARAJ/validation'

# we will generate 1 image at a time - we could do so in batches
gen_batch_size = 1

# we will create a generator of generating validation data
# we will apply only scaling to this generator nothing else
validation_datagen = ImageDataGenerator(rescale=1./255)

# this is a similar generator, for validation data
validation_generator = validation_datagen.flow_from_directory(
                validation_dir,
                target_size=(150, 150),
                batch_size=gen_batch_size,
                class_mode='binary')
```

Here are the results:

```
Found 10 images belonging to 2 classes.
```

Our validation folder also has five images of each class for validation. We don't use any augmentation and just use rescaling to load these images. That's a recommended practice.

Now we will use a single line of code to apply both our training and validation generators to our model and do the training. We will use one thousand steps per epoch for training, which means we will generate one thousand images and use them for training. For validation, we will generate one hundred images. We will run the training for two epochs only. Here we go, as shown in Listing 5.14.

Listing 5.14: Do the Model Training Using Generators

```
# Train the model
model_final.fit_generator(
          train_generator,
          steps_per_epoch = 1000,
          epochs = 2,
          validation_data = validation_generator,
          validation_steps = 100
          )
```

Here are the results:

```
Epoch 1/2
1000/1000 [==============================] - 32s 32ms/step - loss:
0.2738 - acc: 0.9490 - val_loss: 0.7044 - val_acc: 0.8000

Epoch 2/2
1000/1000 [==============================] - 28s 28ms/step - loss:
0.0156 - acc: 0.9970 - val_loss: 1.6118 - val_acc: 0.9000
```

You can see that our training data accuracy is pretty high. For validation data, the accuracy keeps improving over the epoch. We can get much better accuracy by getting more data and using a good representative set for training as compared to validation.

Now let's make a couple of predictions using our trained model, as shown in Listing 5.15.

Listing 5.15: Make Predictions with Our New Model

```
# Download 2 test images to validate our Model

!wget -O test1.jpg https://encrypted-
tbn0.gstatic.com/images?q=tbn:ANd9GcSgQDqAfUoTXRosjwPjUh0TCUfnNK2G2OMVh7
NEc1hdrz8-1dY3

!wget -O test2.jpg https://encrypted-
tbn0.gstatic.com/images?q=tbn:ANd9GcQAHyl61P__
bIru0lYLq0MjEcjP10i7hMRWB9JbQ71dLwOLPZg9

###### NOW MAKE THE PREDICTION ######

from keras.preprocessing.image import load_img
from keras.preprocessing.image import img_to_array
from keras.applications.vgg16 import preprocess_input
import numpy as np

# function that reads image, shows it on-screen and makes prediction
def predict_for(img_name):
    # load image from file - VGG16 takes (244,244) input
    myimg = load_img(img_name, target_size=(150, 150))
    plt.imshow(myimg)
    plt.show()

    # convert image pixels to array
    myimg = img_to_array(myimg)
    myimg = np.expand_dims(myimg, axis=0)

        # prepare image for the VGG model
        myimg = preprocess_input(myimg)

        # predict probability for all 1000 classes
        pred = int(model_final.predict(myimg)[0][0])
            print('Prediction for %s: %s'%(img_name, class_names[pred]))

predict_for('test1.jpg')
predict_for('test2.jpg')
```

Now we have a pretty good model that can tell two logos apart. Let's look at some testing done in Figure 5.11.

Prediction for test1.jpg: Coca-Cola

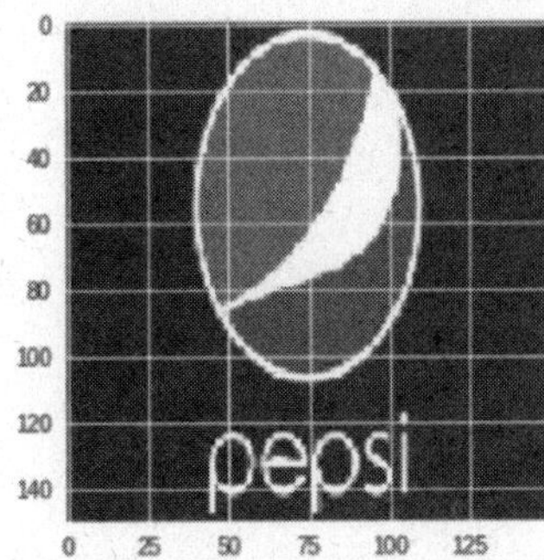

Prediction for test2.jpg: Pepsi

Figure 5.11: Predictions for test1.jpg: Coca-Cola and test2.jpg: Pepsi

We will save this as a model file. Keras uses the HDF5 or H5 format to store data. This is the Hierarchical Data Format (HDF), which is good at storing arrays. Some other engines may store models as JSON or YAML files. When we save models, we are saving two things—the architecture of the network and the weights associated with it. The one containing the weights is usually the bigger file. With H5 you can save both in a single file. See Listing 5.16.

Listing 5.16: Save the Trained Model to an H5 File

```
# save the trained Model to a H5 file
      model_final.save('my_logo_model.h5')
```

Now we load this saved model into a new variable and use this to make predictions about a new image, just as we did earlier. See Listing 5.17.

Listing 5.17: Load the Saved Model from an H5 file and Make Predictions

```
from keras.models import load_model

# load Model from saved H5 file
new_model = load_model('my_logo_model.h5')

# download an image to test our model on
image_url    = "http://yourblackworld.net/wp-content/uploads/2018/02/
pepsi-cans.jpg"

!wget -O test.jpg {image_url}

# Now let's do the prediction on this image with new model

# function that reads an image and makes prediction
def new_predict_for(img_name):
    # load image from file - VGG16 takes (244,244) input
    myimg = load_img(img_name, target_size=(150, 150))
    plt.imshow(myimg)
    plt.show()

    # convert image pixels to array
    myimg = img_to_array(myimg)
    myimg = np.expand_dims(myimg, axis=0)

    # prepare image for the VGG model
    myimg = preprocess_input(myimg)

    # predict probability for all 1000 classes
    pred = int(new_model.predict(myimg)[0][0])
    print('Prediction for %s: %s'%(img_name, class_names[pred]))

new_predict_for('test.jpg')
```

There you have it. We have a model that is trained to "see" images and tell us if the image contains a logo of Coca-Cola or of Pepsi. This can be used on new images to make predictions on what logo is present in them.

Recurrent Neural Networks

So far, we looked at image data and how to build neural networks for decoding patterns from images. Convolutional Neural Networks (CNN) is the proven architecture for extracting knowledge from image data. As we learned in Chapter 3, another common type of unstructured data is text data. Text data comes as a sequence of words and, to analyze this data, special kinds of networks are required. These are not the *feed-forward* kind, where each layer is connected only to the next network layer. The new architecture we look at is called a *recurrent neural network* (RNN). Figure 5.12 shows this architecture.

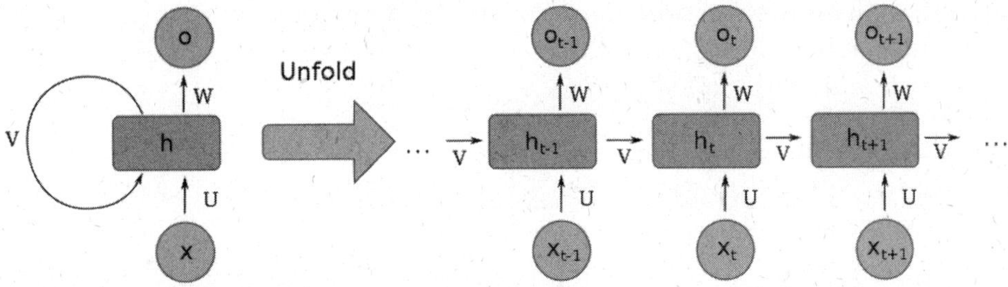

Figure 5.12: Architecture of a Recurrent Neural Network
(*Source*: François Deloche – Wikipedia)

Recurrent networks don't have all forward-feeding connections. At each layer, the output value is tapped and fed back to the next input in the sequence. Hence, the input for this network comes from the sequence and the value coming back from the previous layer. This is illustrated in Figure 5.12, by unfolding the network to show values over a sequence of time steps—X_{t-1}, X_t, X_{t+1}. Due to this characteristic of passing part of the value from the previous item in the sequence to the next, this network can *remember* key values while it's learning. This is very much like how our human brain processes sequences. When we interpret sequences like text or speech, we remember previous information and use it to make sense of future values. For example, I am sure you remember items like neural networks from previous chapters and hopefully that's helping you interpret this new knowledge.

One problem with RNN is that it cannot remember values for a long time. This is where a special type of RNN, called *Long Short-Term Memory* (LSTM), comes in handy. LSTM uses a gated architecture to remember key items over long sequences. We will not go into details of the gated architecture of LSTM but I do provide references at end of the book on this topic. We can use LSTM layers as a new type of layer in Keras that will work well with sequence data like text.

We talked in Chapter 3 about how text is represented. We saw that we could take a body of text like a sentence as an integer array based on the vocabulary of all words used. Then we can convert this array into dense word embeddings for each word in the sequence. We saw how these word embeddings capture the context of using these words and helps us do word math.

Now we will convert the words into embeddings and feed these as a sequence to our LSTM model to learn information. We will handle a particular case study to detect sentiments in sentences. Sentences can have a positive or negative sentiment, depending on the type and order of words used to form them.

We will first use a dataset available in Keras, called *IMDB*. This is a dataset of movie reviews that's been converted into integer arrays using a standard vocabulary. We will use a Keras embeddings layer to convert these integers into word embedding vectors and learn how to classify sentiments. Then we will run the same example on our own text and see if it predicts the sentiment correctly. Let's get started.

First, we load the dataset and explore it. As mentioned, the sentences come as an integer array along with a label of positive or negative for the sentiment. Let's explore the data in Listing 5.18.

Listing 5.18: Load the IMDB Dataset

```
# load keras libraries, layers and the imdb dataset
from keras.preprocessing import sequence
from keras.models import Sequential
from keras.layers import Dense, Embedding
from keras.layers import LSTM
from keras.datasets import imdb

# decide maximum number of words to load in dataset
max_features = 20000

# decide maximum words in a sentence and batch size
maxlen = 50
batch_size = 32

# load the data
print('Loading data...')
(x_train, y_train), (x_test, y_test) = imdb.load_data(num_words=max_features)

# pad the sequences
x_train = sequence.pad_sequences(x_train, maxlen=maxlen)
x_test = sequence.pad_sequences(x_test, maxlen=maxlen)

print('x_train shape:', x_train.shape)
print('x_test shape:', x_test.shape)
```

Here are the results:

```
Loading data...
Pad sequences (samples x time)
x_train shape: (25000, 50)
x_test shape: (25000, 50)
```

Now we will explore the data. We will see the integer array and use vocabulary to get the full sentences. Let's look at this in Listing 5.19.

Listing 5.19: Explore the Text Dataset

```
# show a data sample
print("Sample of x_train array = ", x_train[0])
print("Sample of y_train array = ", y_train[0])

# get the vocabulary used for converting words to numbers
imdb_vocab = imdb.get_word_index()
```

```
# create a small vocabulary with only top 20 items and print it
# this is just to understand how the vocabulary looks
small_vocab = { key:value for key, value in imdb_vocab.items() if value < 20 }
print("Vocabulary = ", small_vocab)

# function to get the sentence from integer array
# reverse look-up words in vocabulary
def get_original_text(int_arr):
    word_to_id = {k:(v+3) for k,v in imdb_vocab.items()}
    word_to_id["<PAD>"] = 0
    word_to_id["<START>"] = 1
    word_to_id["<UNK>"] = 2

    id_to_word = {value:key for key,value in word_to_id.items()}
    return ' '.join(id_to_word[id] for id in int_arr)

# define sentiments array
sentiment_labels = ['Negative', 'Positive']

print("-------------------------")
print("SOME SENTENCE AND SENTIMENT SAMPLES")
# print some of the training data
for i in range(5):
    print("Training Sentence = ", get_original_text(x_train[i]))
    print("Sentiment = ", sentiment_labels[y_train[i]])
    print("----------------------")
```

Here are the results:

```
Sample of x_train array =  [2071   56   26  141    6  194 7486   18    4
226   22   21  134  476   26  480    5  144   30 5535   18   51   36
28  224   92   25  104  4  226   65   16   38 1334   88   12   16  283
5   16 4472  113   103   32   15   16 5345   19  178   32]

Sample of y_train array =  1

Vocabulary =  {'with': 16, 'i': 10, 'as': 14, 'it': 9, 'is': 6, 'in': 8,
'but': 18, 'of': 4, 'this': 11, 'a': 3, 'for': 15, 'br': 7, 'the': 1,
'was': 13, 'and': 2, 'to': 5, 'film': 19, 'movie': 17, 'that': 12}

-------------------------
SOME SENTENCE AND SENTIMENT SAMPLES
-------------------------

Training Sentence =  grown up are such a big profile for the whole film
but these children are amazing and should be praised for what they have
done don't you think the whole story was so lovely because it was true
and was someone's life after all that was shared with us all
Sentiment =  Positive
----------------------
```

```
Training Sentence =  taking away bodies and the gym still doesn't close
for <UNK> all joking aside this is a truly bad film whose only charm is
to look back on the disaster that was the 80's and have a good old laugh
at how bad everything was back then
Sentiment =  Negative
-----------------------

Training Sentence =  must have looked like a great idea on paper but on
film it looks like no one in the film has a clue what is going on crap
acting crap costumes i can't get across how <UNK> this is to watch save
yourself an hour a bit of your life
Sentiment =  Negative
-----------------------

Training Sentence =  man to see a film that is true to Scotland this
one is probably unique if you maybe <UNK> on it deeply enough you might
even re evaluate the power of storytelling and the age old question of
whether there are some truths that cannot be told but only experienced
Sentiment =  Positive
-----------------------

Training Sentence =  the <UNK> and watched it burn and that felt better
than anything else i've ever done it took American psycho army of
darkness and kill bill just to get over that crap i hate you sandler for
actually going through with this and ruining a whole day of my life
Sentiment =  Negative
-----------------------
```

Now we will build the model and do the training. Notice the use of the embedding and LSTM layers instead of the previous Conv2D and Dense layers. See Listing 5.20.

Listing 5.20: Build and Train the LSTM Model

```
# build the model
model = Sequential()
model.add(Embedding(max_features, 128))
model.add(LSTM(128, dropout=0.2))
model.add(Dense(1, activation='sigmoid'))

# try using different optimizers and different optimizer configs
model.compile(loss='binary_crossentropy',
              optimizer='adam',
              metrics=['accuracy'])

# train the model
model.fit(x_train, y_train,
          batch_size=batch_size,
          epochs=2,
          validation_data=(x_test, y_test))
```

```
score, acc = model.evaluate(x_test, y_test,
                batch_size=batch_size)
print('Test score:', score)
print('Test accuracy:', acc)
```

Here are the results:

```
Train on 25000 samples, validate on 25000 samples

Epoch 1/2
25000/25000 [==============================] - 126s 5ms/step - loss:
0.4600 - acc: 0.7778 - val_loss: 0.3969 - val_acc: 0.8197

Epoch 2/2
25000/25000 [==============================] - 125s 5ms/step - loss:
0.2914 - acc: 0.8780 - val_loss: 0.4191 - val_acc: 0.8119
25000/25000 [==============================] - 26s 1ms/step

Test score: 0.41909076169013976
Test accuracy: 0.81188
```

We will save the model as an H5 file called `imdb _ nlp.h5`. We will not use the saved model file right away. We will use this file in Chapter 8 ("Deploying AI Models as Microservices"). For now, we will use the trained model in memory to predict new text. We see that prediction will be a value between 0 and 1. If the value is close to 0, the sentiment is positive. Otherwise, it's negative. See Listing 5.21.

Listing 5.21: Make Predictions on Our Sentences

```
from keras.preprocessing.text import text_to_word_sequence

# first we will save the model
model.save('imdb_nlp.h5')

# get the word index from imdb dataset
word_index = imdb.get_word_index()

# define the documents
my_sentence1 = 'really bad experience. amazingly bad.'
my_sentence2 = 'pretty awesome to see. very good work.'

# define function to predict sentiment using model
def predict_sentiment(my_test):
    # tokenize the sentence
    word_sequence = text_to_word_sequence(my_test)

    # create a blank sequence of integers
    int_sequence = []
```

```
    # for each word in the sentence
    for w in word_sequence:
    # get the integer from word_index (vocabulary) and add to list
        int_sequence.append(word_index[w])

    # pad the sequence of numbers to input size expected by model
    sent_test = sequence.pad_sequences([int_sequence], maxlen=maxlen)

    # make a prediction using our Model
    y_pred = model.predict(sent_test)
        return y_pred[0][0]

# show results for sentences
print ('SENTENCE : ', my_sentence1, ' : ', predict_sentiment(my_
sentence1), ' : SENTIMENT : ', sentiment_labels[int(round(predict_
sentiment(my_sentence1)))] )
print ('SENTENCE : ', my_sentence2, ' : ', predict_sentiment(my_
sentence2), ' : SENTIMENT : ', sentiment_labels[int(round(predict_
sentiment(my_sentence2)))] )
```

Here are the results:

```
SENTENCE :  really bad experience. amazingly bad.  :
0.8450574  : SENTIMENT :  Negative

SENTENCE :  pretty awesome to see. very good work.  :
0.21833718  : SENTIMENT :  Positive
```

There you have it. We classified images to detect logos and classified text to identify the sentiment of the sentences. There is a lot more to Deep Learning and Keras than what we covered in this chapter. We have just scraped the surface. Hopefully I have stirred your interest in this area and given you enough to start playing in this field with your own datasets. By using tools like Google Colaboratory, you can run your code on the best of hardware environments like GPU and TPU without any cost. All the best!

Summary

In this chapter, we moved from the basics into some advanced concepts in Deep Learning. We looked at concepts like data augmentation and transfer learning, which can help you work with limited data and reuse knowledge from existing proven model architectures. We also saw an example of building a model to learn about image data containing product logos and used it to make real-world predictions.

We will now take a break from Deep Learning. The next chapter starts looking at the history of software applications and how microservices and Cloud applications are developed using containers. We will explore Kubernetes, which is fast becoming the platform of choice for managing lifecycles of containers and providing a Container-as-a-Service paradigm. Modern applications—especially Cloud-native ones—get packaged as containers and can be scheduled by Kubernetes. We will see all this magic in the next chapter.

CHAPTER

6

Cutting-Edge Deep Learning Projects

Deep Learning is revolutionizing our world with some amazing results by processing images, text, speech, and video. It is extracting knowledge and insights from unstructured data. We saw examples of processing images and text data using Deep Learning in Chapter 5. In this chapter, we take that understanding to the next level and look at some interesting projects. These are innovative solutions folks have developed and shared with the community. These solutions have become very popular due to their unique nature, and you may have read a few news articles on these promoting AI. We will see cool projects like repainting photos in styles of famous painters and generating fake images that look indistinguishable from the real ones. We will see an example of detecting fraud in credit card transactions using unsupervised Deep Learning. Although the outcomes here are unique, the underlying Deep Learning techniques and concepts remain the same. As long as you have followed the concepts in the previous chapters, you should understand these well. Maybe reading about these projects will trigger an innovative spark in your mind and you will come up with the next big AI solution. Here's hoping for that!

Neural Style Transfer

One of the big AI headlines of 2018 was a painting that sold for about $400,000 that was painted entirely by Artificial Intelligence. Many researchers are actively evaluating algorithms that learn patterns for creating art and using them to build new paintings. It's fascinating and a lot of fun. Let me show you an example of doing this. This example learns patterns from famous paintings and applies it to the photo we supply. To be specific, we will copy the style of a famous painting and draw it with our content, a photo. This is called *neural style transfer.* This topic has been very popular among computer vision researchers and many methods have evolved to solve this problem. There are a few websites and also a mobile app called Prizma that does this in real time on your photos. Let's see how this works.

We know that Deep Learning involves building deep neural networks that extract high-level features from low-level ones—particularly low-level ones like pixel intensity arrays. As the model learns to identify patterns from image data, it learns many aspects of the picture, like the way pixels arrange themselves to form edges, curves, and surfaces. Now if we train the network on a digitized image of a painting, there is a good chance that the network will learn features like brushstrokes that the painter used to create the painting. This is the idea behind neural style transfer. In a nutshell, the process can be described as shown in Figure 6.1. This figure is from the wonderful paper describing this approach entitled "A Neural Algorithm of Artistic Style," by Leon A. Gatys, Alexander S. Ecker, and Matthias Bethge.

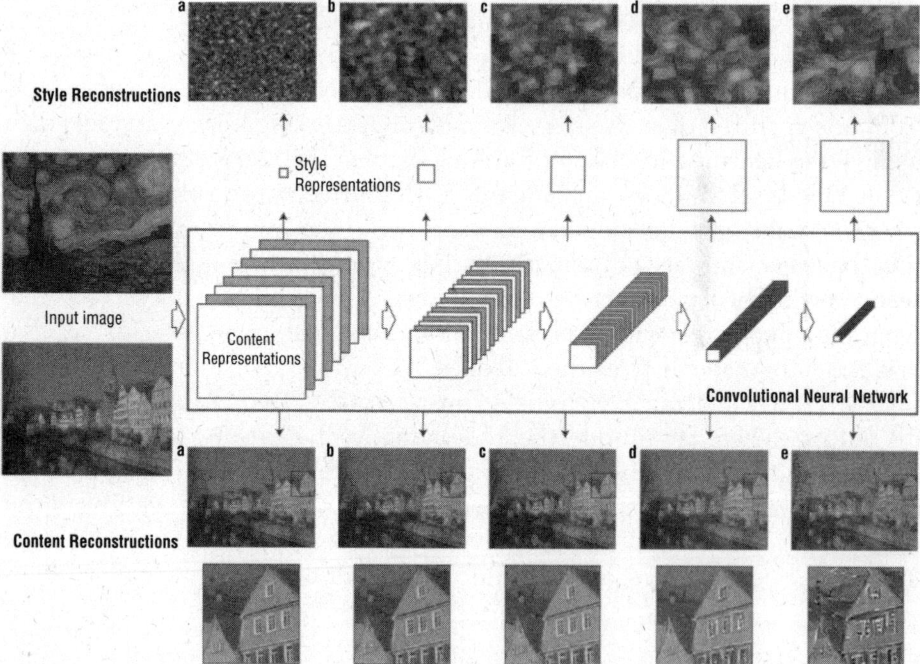

Figure 6.1: General idea of how neural style transfer works

Figure 6.1 is from the original paper published by Gatys, Ecker, and Bethge. Here we see that there are two images. One is the content image, which is the photo of buildings. The other is the style image, which is the famous painting by Vincent van Gogh called *The Starry Night*. We see that the initial layers of the Convolutional Neural Network (CNN) has fewer filters and bigger pixel arrays. As we move down the network and we reduce the size of elements using pooling layers, we see an increase in filters. Hence the depth of the layer's volume increases. The layers down the line learn higher-level feature-sets from the images. At the same time, within a layer of filters, if we analyze the variation and try to correlate the filters, we get the style information of the image. Hence, down the line of the network, the style information that's captured also increases.

The method we will use is a style image, which will be a famous painting. The content image will be our image to process. We will define a style distance and content distance. These are both loss functions that we will try to optimize. The overall concept with an example is shown in Figure 6.2.

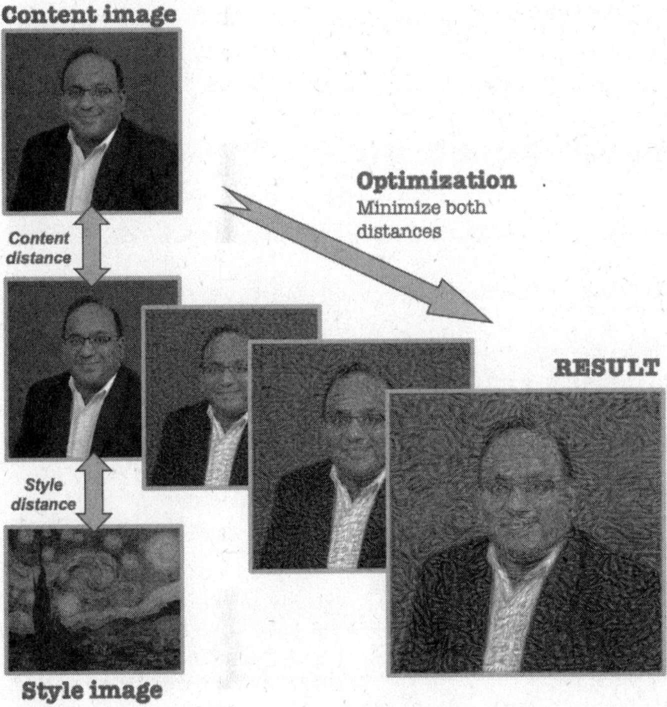

Figure 6.2: Example of neural style transfer

The general idea is to calculate the style distance and content distance between two images using certain feature layers of a deep network like CNN. We will use a popular VGG19 model trained on ImageNet data. VGG19 is a standard Deep Learning architecture that has 16 convolution layers and three fully connected layers. These are the weight layers and there are a few pooling layers in the middle. Let's look at the following code. I show and explain individual blocks of code and then put it all together to give you the full program.

The code in the following sections is highly inspired from Google's Keras/TensorFlow example for style transfer. You can look this code up in your TensorFlow installation or on GitHub at `https://github.com/keras-team/keras/blob/master/examples/neural_style_transfer.py`.

There is also an excellent Medium post that covers this in detail by Raymond Yuan at `https://medium.com/tensorflow/neural-style-transfer-creating-art-with-deep-learning-using-tf-keras-and-eager-execution-7d541ac31398`.

Let's start with Listing 6.1. We will import a pretrained VGG19 model on the ImageNet data. We will also set an *eager execution* to "on" for TensorFlow so it does not create computation graphs but directly executes the code to get fast results.

Listing 6.1: Load VGG19 Model and Describe It

```
# import tensorflow libraries
import tensorflow as tf
# load the easy execution library
import tensorflow.contrib.eager as tfe
import time

# enable eager execution - this should be done at start of program
tf.enable_eager_execution()
print("Eager execution: {}".format(tf.executing_eagerly()))

# load the model from keras with imagenet weights
vgg19 = tf.keras.applications.vgg19.VGG19(include_top=False,
weights='imagenet')
vgg19.trainable = False
vgg19.summary()
```

Here are the results:

```
Eager execution: True
_________________________________________________________________
Layer (type)                 Output Shape              Param #
=================================================================
input_3 (InputLayer)         (None, None, None, 3)     0
_________________________________________________________________
block1_conv1 (Conv2D)        (None, None, None, 64)    1792
_________________________________________________________________
block1_conv2 (Conv2D)        (None, None, None, 64)    36928
_________________________________________________________________
block1_pool (MaxPooling2D)   (None, None, None, 64)    0
_________________________________________________________________
```

```
block2_conv1 (Conv2D)        (None, None, None, 128)   73856
_________________________________________________________________
block2_conv2 (Conv2D)        (None, None, None, 128)   147584
_________________________________________________________________
block2_pool (MaxPooling2D)   (None, None, None, 128)   0
_________________________________________________________________
block3_conv1 (Conv2D)        (None, None, None, 256)   295168
_________________________________________________________________
block3_conv2 (Conv2D)        (None, None, None, 256)   590080
_________________________________________________________________
block3_conv3 (Conv2D)        (None, None, None, 256)   590080
_________________________________________________________________
block3_conv4 (Conv2D)        (None, None, None, 256)   590080
_________________________________________________________________
block3_pool (MaxPooling2D)   (None, None, None, 256)   0
_________________________________________________________________
block4_conv1 (Conv2D)        (None, None, None, 512)   1180160
_________________________________________________________________
block4_conv2 (Conv2D)        (None, None, None, 512)   2359808
_________________________________________________________________
block4_conv3 (Conv2D)        (None, None, None, 512)   2359808
_________________________________________________________________
block4_conv4 (Conv2D)        (None, None, None, 512)   2359808
_________________________________________________________________
block4_pool (MaxPooling2D)   (None, None, None, 512)   0
_________________________________________________________________
block5_conv1 (Conv2D)        (None, None, None, 512)   2359808
_________________________________________________________________
block5_conv2 (Conv2D)        (None, None, None, 512)   2359808
_________________________________________________________________
block5_conv3 (Conv2D)        (None, None, None, 512)   2359808
_________________________________________________________________
block5_conv4 (Conv2D)        (None, None, None, 512)   2359808
_________________________________________________________________
block5_pool (MaxPooling2D)   (None, None, None, 512)   0
=================================================================
Total params: 20,024,384
Trainable params: 0
Non-trainable params: 20,024,384
```

Next, we select certain layers of features as our style and content layers. These layers will be used to extract features learned by the VGG19 model on the images. These features will give us an idea of both the content and style of the respective images. As stated earlier, our objective is to minimize the style and content distances—also referred to as *costs*—since we will be doing optimization. Let's select some of these layers by their names in the description. You can experiment with different layers. We will use the convolution layer in block_5 to compare the content and use multiple convolution layers for style comparison, as shown in Listing 6.2. Using these feature layers, we will build a new model called `style_model` that only returns these layers. We are no longer interested in predictions made by the model.

Listing 6.2: Build a New Model Outputting Layers for Style and Content Comparison

```
# Content layer where we will pull our feature maps
content_layers = ['block5_conv2']

# Style layer we are interested in
style_layers = ['block1_conv1',\
                'block2_conv1',
                'block3_conv1',
                'block4_conv1',
                'block5_conv1'
                ]

# get counters for style and content layers
num_content_layers = len(content_layers)
num_style_layers = len(style_layers)

# Get output layers corresponding to style and content layers
style_outputs = [vgg19.get_layer(name).output for name in style_layers]
content_outputs = [vgg19.get_layer(name).output for name in content_
layers]
model_outputs = style_outputs + content_outputs

# Build model
style_model = tf.keras.models.Model(vgg19.input, model_outputs)
```

Next, we download two images—one for content and one for style (see Figure 6.3). We convert these into arrays and display them, as shown in Listing 6.3.

Listing 6.3: Load Images for Style and Content

```
# download style and content image files
!wget -O mycontent.jpg https://pbs.twimg.com/profile_
images/872804244910358528/w5H_uzUD_400x400.jpg

!wget -O mystyle.jpg https://upload.wikimedia.org/wikipedia/
commons/thumb/e/ea/Van_Gogh_-_Starry_Night_-_Google_Art_Project.
jpg/1920px-Van_Gogh_-_Starry_Night_-_Google_Art_Project.jpg

# import the plotting libraries
import matplotlib.pyplot as plt
%matplotlib inline

# import numpy
import numpy as np
# import preprocessing functions for preparing image
from keras.preprocessing import image
from keras.applications.vgg19 import preprocess_input
```

```
content_path = 'mycontent.jpg'
style_path = 'mystyle.jpg'

# load content and style images in memory
content = image.load_img(content_path, target_size=(224, 224))
style = image.load_img(style_path, target_size=(224, 224))

# convert style and content images as arrays
content_x = image.img_to_array(content)
content_x = np.expand_dims(content_x, axis=0)
content_x = preprocess_input(content_x)

style_x = image.img_to_array(style)
style_x = np.expand_dims(style_x, axis=0)
style_x = preprocess_input(style_x)

# show the images loaded
plt.subplot(1, 2, 1)
plt.axis('off')
plt.title('Content image')
plt.imshow(content)

plt.subplot(1, 2, 2)
plt.axis('off')
plt.title('Style image')
plt.imshow(style)
plt.show()
```

Figure 6.3: Style and content images we will use for this demo

Listing 6.4 shows some helper functions that will be used to calculate the loss for content and style and the gradients that we will use for optimization.

Listing 6.4: Helper Functions for Calculating Loss

```
# define a few helper functions

# get real pixel values from normalized result generated by model
def deprocess_img(processed_img):
```

```
    x = processed_img.copy()
    if len(x.shape) == 4:
        x = np.squeeze(x, 0)
    # perform the inverse of the preprocessing step
    x[:, :, 0] += 103.939
    x[:, :, 1] += 116.779
    x[:, :, 2] += 123.68
    x = x[:, :, ::-1]
    # remove any values below 0 and above 255
    x = np.clip(x, 0, 255).astype('uint8')
    return x

# define the content loss as distance between content and target
def get_content_loss(base_content, target):
    return tf.reduce_mean(tf.square(base_content - target))

# to get style loss first we should calculate gram matrix
def gram_matrix(input_tensor):
    # make the image channels first
    channels = int(input_tensor.shape[-1])
    a = tf.reshape(input_tensor, [-1, channels])
    n = tf.shape(a)[0]
    # gram matrix is obtained by multiplying matrix with transpose
    gram = tf.matmul(a, a, transpose_a=True)
    return gram / tf.cast(n, tf.float32)

# calculate the style loss
def get_style_loss(base_style, gram_target):
    # we scale the loss at a given layer by the size of the feature map
and the number of filters
    height, width, channels = base_style.get_shape().as_list()
    gram_style = gram_matrix(base_style)

    return tf.reduce_mean(tf.square(gram_style - gram_target))

# calculate total loss
def compute_loss(model, loss_weights, init_image, gram_style_features,
content_features):
    style_weight, content_weight = loss_weights

    # our model is callable just like any other function
    model_outputs = model(init_image)
    style_output_features = model_outputs[:num_style_layers]
    content_output_features = model_outputs[num_style_layers:]

    style_score = 0
    content_score = 0
```

```
    # accumulate style losses from all layers
    weight_per_style_layer = 1.0 / float(num_style_layers)
    for target_style, comb_style in zip(gram_style_features, style_
output_features):
        style_score += weight_per_style_layer * get_style_loss(comb_
style[0], target_style)

    # accumulate content losses from all layers
    weight_per_content_layer = 1.0 / float(num_content_layers)
    for target_content, comb_content in zip(content_features, content_
output_features):
        content_score += weight_per_content_layer* get_content_
loss(comb_content[0], target_content)

    style_score *= style_weight
    content_score *= content_weight
    # Get total loss
    loss = style_score + content_score
    return loss, style_score, content_score

# function to compute gradients
def compute_grads(cfg):
    with tf.GradientTape() as tape:
        all_loss = compute_loss(**cfg)
    # Compute gradients wrt input image
    total_loss = all_loss[0]
    return tape.gradient(total_loss, cfg['init_image']), all_loss

# compute our content and style feature representations
def get_feature_representations(model, content_path, style_path):
    # batch compute content and style features
    style_outputs = model(style_x)
    content_outputs = model(content_x)
    # get the style and content feature representations from our model
    style_features = [style_layer[0] for style_layer in style_
outputs[:num_style_layers]]
    content_features = [content_layer[0] for content_layer in content_
outputs[num_style_layers:]]
    return style_features, content_features

# display image function
def display_result(p_image):
    plt.figure(figsize=(8,8))
    plt.axis('off')
    plt.imshow(p_image)
    plt.show()
```

Next, we define the main function that we will call to do the style transfer optimization. We specify the number of iterations and provide weights for the content and style. See Listing 6.5.

Listing 6.5: Run the Main Style Transfer Function

```
# main function to actually run the style transfer
def run_style_transfer (num_iterations=1000, content_weight=1e3, style_
weight=1e-2):
    # we will set layers as not trainable since we are not learning
    model = style_model
    for layer in style_model.layers:
        layer.trainable = False

    # get the style and content feature representations (from our
specified intermediate layers)
    style_features, content_features = get_feature_representations
(style_model, content_path, style_path)
    gram_style_features = [gram_matrix(style_feature) for style_feature
in style_features]

    # set initial image as our content image
    init_image = content_x.copy()
    init_image = tfe.Variable(init_image, dtype=tf.float32)
    # lets build an Adam optimizer
    opt = tf.train.AdamOptimizer(learning_rate=2.0, beta1=0.99,
epsilon=1e-1)

    # for displaying intermediate images
    iter_count = 1

    # our best result
    best_loss, best_img = float('inf'), None

    # define loss terms and build a config object
    loss_weights = (style_weight, content_weight)
    cfg = {
            'model': style_model,
            'loss_weights': loss_weights,
            'init_image': init_image,
            'gram_style_features': gram_style_features,
            'content_features': content_features
        }

    # for displaying results
    num_rows = 2
    num_cols = 5
    display_interval = num_iterations/(num_rows*num_cols)
    start_time = time.time()
    global_start = time.time()

    # means of each channel for normalization
    norm_means = np.array([103.939, 116.779, 123.68])
```

```
    min_vals = -norm_means
    max_vals = 255 - norm_means

    # perform optimization and get the intermediate generated images
    # work with init_image and modify it through optimization
    imgs = []
    for i in range(num_iterations):
        grads, all_loss = compute_grads(cfg)
        loss, style_score, content_score = all_loss
        opt.apply_gradients([(grads, init_image)])
        clipped = tf.clip_by_value(init_image, min_vals, max_vals)
        init_image.assign(clipped)
        end_time = time.time()

        if loss < best_loss:
            # update best loss and best image from total loss.
            best_img = deprocess_img(init_image.numpy())

        if i % display_interval== 0:
            start_time = time.time()
            # define title for image
            print ('Iteration: {}'.format(i))
            print ('Total loss: {:.4e}, '
                   'style loss: {:.4e}, '
                   'content loss: {:.4e}, '
                   'time: {:.4f}s'.format(loss, style_score, content_
score, time.time() - start_time))

            # use the .numpy() method to get the concrete numpy array
            plot_img = init_image.numpy()
            plot_img = deprocess_img(plot_img)
            display_result(plot_img)

    print('Total time: {:.4f}s'.format(time.time() - global_start))
    return best_img, best_loss
```

Finally, we run the code to do the actual optimization and see how our original content photo gets transformed, as shown in Listing 6.6. We will pause every few iterations and see how the modified image looks. See Figure 6.4.

Listing 6.6: Do the Actual Optimization and Style Transfer

```
best, best_loss = run_style_transfer(num_iterations=50)
```

There you have it—we took an image and applied the style of a famous painting to it. You can modify your images with different paintings to get some cool effects. Or you could download apps like Prizma and see this effect in action. Or why don't you code up a Prizma-type app of your own?

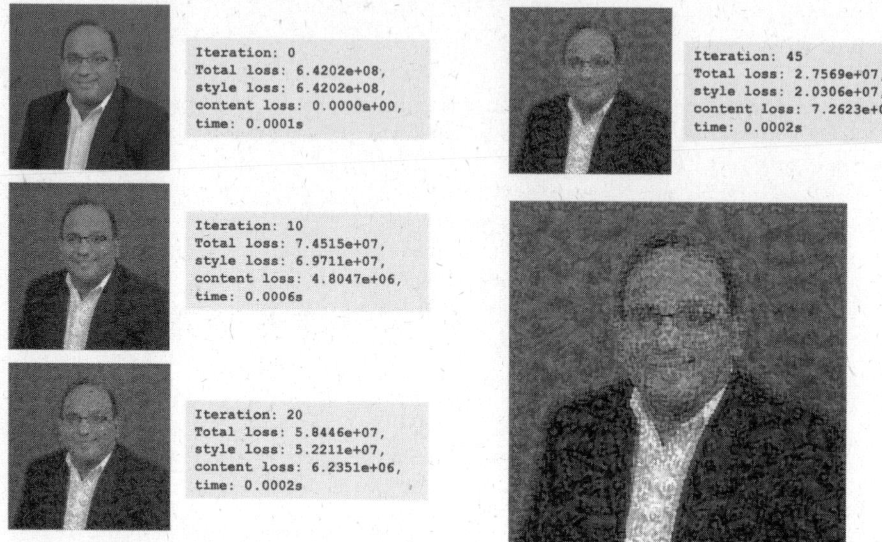

Figure 6.4: Results of neural style transfer

This particular example and its code are available as a Google Colab Notebook at this link:

`https://colab.research.google.com/drive/1_tHUYgO_fIBU1JXdn_mXWCDD6n-jLyNSu`

Next, let's look at another interesting application of Deep Learning. You probably have heard of this one a lot in the news recently—using neural networks to create photos.

Generating Images Using AI

One of the big news items in 2018 related to AI was a new algorithm developed by researchers from NVIDIA that could generate fake celebrity photos. These photos were so realistic that any human could be fooled into thinking they were real. However, these were all fake photos generated by a super-smart AI algorithm by identifying patterns in real photos. These are special types of algorithms called *generative models* that learn the *probability distribution* of input data and then generate new data.

We will use a popular generative model called *generative adversarial networks (GAN)* for generating new images. Before we talk about GAN, remember that a neural network—whether it is shallow or deep—learns to encode an image array into a limited dimensions vector. This vector can be seen as a compressed encoding of our original image. This is shown in Figure 6.5.

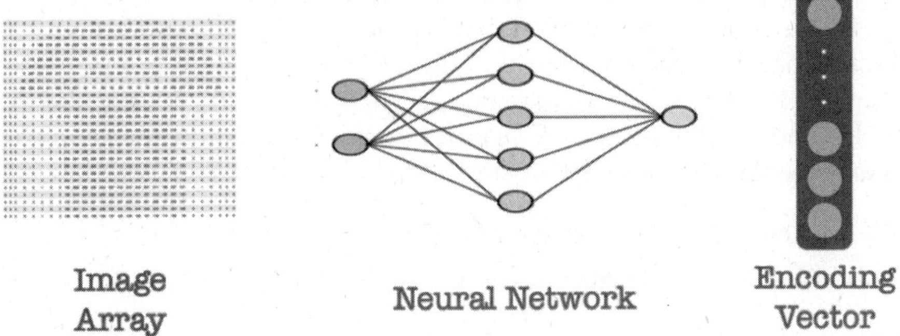

Figure 6.5: Neural network captures encoding of image

Now let's talk about GANs. The concept of how a GAN works is illustrated in Figure 6.6 with an art forger-inspector analogy. We have two neural networks—one *generator* (G) and one *discriminator* (D). The generator creates images, starting with a random encoding vector. It does the reverse process of encoding shown in Figure 6.5. From an encoding vector, it generates an image. This is analogous to an art forger, who generates forgeries of paintings.

Next, we have a discriminator network that is analogous to an art inspector, who checks if the image is genuine or fake. This network takes one image at a time from real and generated sections and learns to classify it as real or fake. If the image generated by G is accepted by D as real, then G gets rewarded. If D finds a fake, then it gets the reward. These two networks are now competing against each other. Hence, it's called adversarial. Over time, as both networks train, G gets good at generating fakes identical to the real images. That's what we are looking for. This concept is illustrated in Figure 6.6.

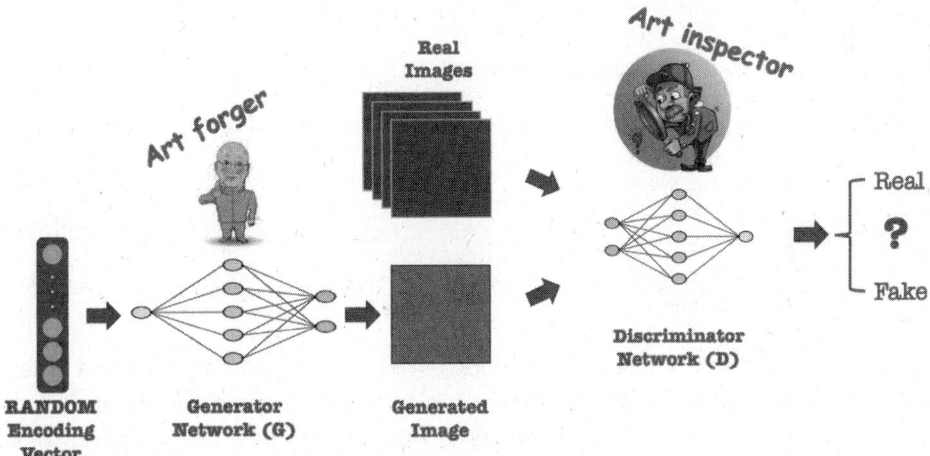

Figure 6.6: Art-forger analogy for generative adversarial networks

Let's see this in action with a simple example using a very simple dataset. We will use the fashion items dataset that is provided with Keras. This is a set of grayscale images of fashion elements with each image at 28×28 pixels. These are pictures of 10 fashion objects, like coats, T-shirts, shoes, etc. (see Figure 6.7). First, we load needed libraries, then we load the dataset and show some sample images to explore the dataset. See Listing 6.7.

Listing 6.7: Load the Images and Show Dataset Samples

```
# import tensorflow and math libraries
import tensorflow as tf
import numpy as np

# import plotting libraries
import matplotlib.pyplot as plt
%matplotlib inline

# print the version of tensorflow - higher than 1.0 preferred
print(tf.__version__)

# create a directory for our generated images
!mkdir images

# import the fashion dataset from keras
fashion_mnist = tf.keras.datasets.fashion_mnist

# extract the training and testing data
(X_train, Y_train), (X_test, Y_test) = fashion_mnist.load_data()

# set class names for images
class_names = ['T-shirt/top', 'Trouser', 'Pullover', 'Dress', 'Coat',
               'Sandal', 'Shirt', 'Sneaker', 'Bag', 'Ankle boot']

# plot first 25 images to see how they look
plt.figure(figsize=(20,20))
for i in range(25):
    plt.subplot(5,5,i+1)
    plt.xticks([])
    plt.yticks([])
    plt.grid(False)
    plt.imshow(X_train[i], cmap=plt.cm.binary)
    plt.xlabel(class_names[Y_train[i]], fontsize=25)
```

Next, we build the two neural networks—one for the generator (G) and other for the discriminator (D). G will take a random encoding vector as input and generate an image sized at 28×28 for us. D takes a 28×28 image and gives us a single result of true (for real image) or false (for generated image). You can see this in Listing 6.8.

Figure 6.7: Displaying the fashion items dataset

Listing 6.8: Build the Generator and Discriminator Networks

```
# import keras libraries to create neural networks
from keras.layers import Input, ReLU
from keras.models import Model, Sequential
from keras.layers.core import Dense
from keras.optimizers import Adam

# set the encoding dimension - we will convert our image array to 128
dimension vector
ENCODING_SIZE = 128

# normalize the training data
X_train = X_train.astype(np.float32)/255.

# define the optimizer
adam = Adam(lr=0.0002, beta_1=0.5)

# now build the Generator that creates images
generator = Sequential()
generator.add(Dense(256, input_dim=ENCODING_SIZE, kernel_
initializer='random_uniform'))
```

```
generator.add(ReLU())
generator.add(Dense(512))
generator.add(ReLU())
generator.add(Dense(1024))
generator.add(ReLU())
generator.add(Dense(784, activation='tanh'))
generator.compile(loss='binary_crossentropy', optimizer=adam)
print('------ GENERATOR ------')
generator.summary()

# now build the Discriminator that classifies an image
discriminator = Sequential()
discriminator.add(Dense(1024, input_dim=784, kernel_initializer='random_
uniform'))
discriminator.add(ReLU())
discriminator.add(Dense(512))
discriminator.add(ReLU())
discriminator.add(Dense(256))
discriminator.add(ReLU())
discriminator.add(Dense(1, activation='sigmoid'))
discriminator.compile(loss='binary_crossentropy', optimizer=adam)
print('------ DISCRIMINATOR ------')
discriminator.summary()

# combine both networks in a single model
discriminator.trainable = False
ganInput = Input(shape=(ENCODING_SIZE,))
x = generator(ganInput)
ganOutput = discriminator(x)
gan_model = Model(inputs=ganInput, outputs=ganOutput)
gan_model.compile(loss='binary_crossentropy', optimizer=adam)
```

Here are the results:

```
------ GENERATOR ------
_________________________________________________________________
Layer (type)                 Output Shape              Param #
=================================================================
dense_1 (Dense)              (None, 256)               33024
_________________________________________________________________
re_lu_1 (ReLU)               (None, 256)               0
_________________________________________________________________
dense_2 (Dense)              (None, 512)               131584
_________________________________________________________________
re_lu_2 (ReLU)               (None, 512)               0
_________________________________________________________________
dense_3 (Dense)              (None, 1024)              525312
_________________________________________________________________
re_lu_3 (ReLU)               (None, 1024)              0
```

```
_________________________________________________________________
dense_4 (Dense)              (None, 784)               803600
=================================================================
Total params: 1,493,520
Trainable params: 1,493,520
Non-trainable params: 0


------ DISCRIMINATOR ------
_________________________________________________________________
Layer (type)                 Output Shape              Param #
=================================================================
dense_5 (Dense)              (None, 1024)              803840
_________________________________________________________________
re_lu_4 (ReLU)               (None, 1024)              0
_________________________________________________________________
dense_6 (Dense)              (None, 512)               524800
_________________________________________________________________
re_lu_5 (ReLU)               (None, 512)               0
_________________________________________________________________
dense_7 (Dense)              (None, 256)               131328
_________________________________________________________________
re_lu_6 (ReLU)               (None, 256)               0
_________________________________________________________________
dense_8 (Dense)              (None, 1)                 257
=================================================================
Total params: 1,460,225
Trainable params: 1,460,225
Non-trainable params: 0
```

Now we will write two functions—one to plot the result images created by G during training and the other to perform the actual training by feeding real and fake images to the model. Then we run the training and, after every epoch, show a section of the images that were created. You can see this in Listing 6.9.

Listing 6.9: Do the Training of D and G on Images We Have

```
# plot the generated images on an array
def plotGeneratedImages(epoch, examples=100, dim=(10, 10), figsize=(10,
10)):
    # create random encoding vector to generate images
    noise = np.random.normal(0, 1, size=[examples, ENCODING_SIZE])
    generatedImages = generator.predict(noise)
    generatedImages = generatedImages.reshape(examples, 28, 28)

    # plot the array of images
    plt.figure(figsize=figsize)
    for i in range(generatedImages.shape[0]):
        plt.subplot(dim[0], dim[1], i+1)
```

```
        plt.imshow(generatedImages[i], cmap='gray_r')
        plt.axis('off')
    plt.tight_layout()
    plt.show()

# train the generative model
def train(epochs=1, batchSize=128):
    # get the number of samples in a batch
    batchCount = int(X_train.shape[0] / batchSize)
    print ('Epochs:', epochs)
    print ('Batch size:', batchSize)
    print ('Batches per epoch:', batchCount)

    # for each epoch
    for e in range(1, epochs+1):
        print ('-'*15, '\nEpoch %d' % e)
        # for each
        for idx in np.arange(0,batchCount):
            if idx%10 == 0:
                print('-', end='')

            # get a random set of input noise and images
            noise = np.random.normal(0, 1, size=[batchSize, ENCODING_SIZE])
            imageBatch = X_train[np.random.randint(0, X_train.shape[0],
                                        size=batchSize)]

            # generate fake fashion images
            generatedImages = generator.predict(noise)
            imageBatch = np.reshape(imageBatch,(batchSize, 784))
            X = np.concatenate([imageBatch, generatedImages])

            # labels for generated and real data
            yDis = np.zeros(2*batchSize)
            # one-sided label smoothing
            yDis[:batchSize] = 0.9

            # train the discriminator
            discriminator.trainable = True
            dloss = discriminator.train_on_batch(X, yDis)

            # train the generator
            noise = np.random.normal(0, 1, size=[batchSize, ENCODING_SIZE])
            yGen = np.ones(batchSize)
            discriminator.trainable = False
                gloss = gan_model.train_on_batch(noise, yGen)

          plotGeneratedImages(e, examples=25, dim=(5,5))
```

```
# train for 20 iterations or epochs
train(20)
```

Here are the results:

```
Epochs: 200
Batch size: 128
Batches per epoch: 468
```

The images generated by this training process are shown in Figure 6.8 below. As we train by increasing epochs, the generated images get closer to the intended target. We start seeing patterns of fashion objects. We can keep training to improve the images and make them sharper.

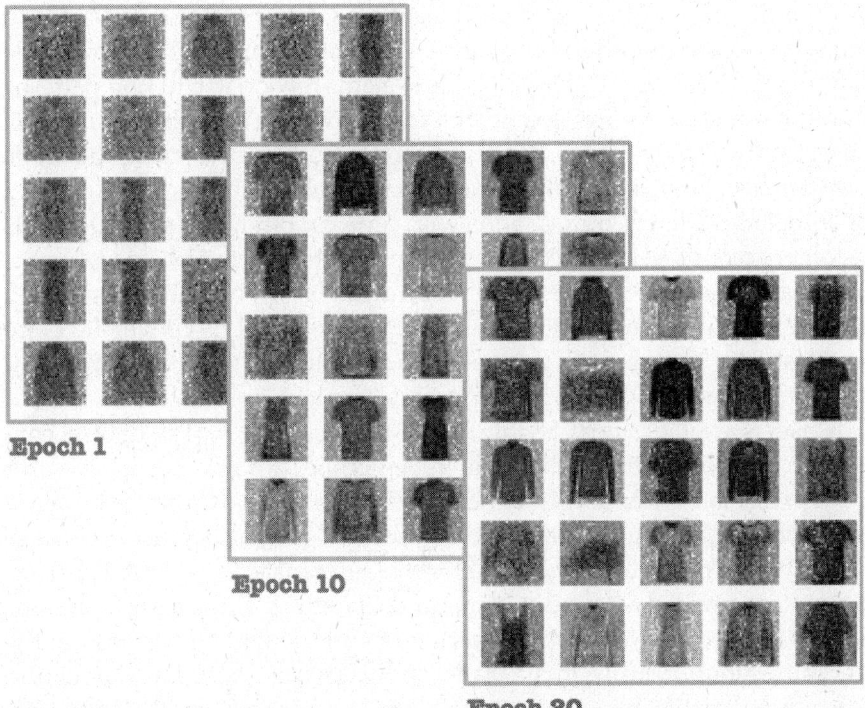

Figure 6.8: Results from GAN trained to generate fashion images

NVIDIA used celebrity photos to help the GAN model learn from known faces. After a few hours of training, the model was able to capture patterns that form faces. Then the model was able to output some generic faces that looked very much like known celebrities, but were *fake* people.

Credit Card Fraud Detection with Autoencoders

The previous two examples used unstructured data in the form of images. Now let's look at an example of structured tabular data. We will look at a dataset of financial transactions made using credit cards and try to identify patterns of fraudulent transactions. This particular use case is extremely common in the financial world. Perhaps you have received a call from your credit card bank stating that there was a suspicious transaction and they want to verify it was actually done by you. The transaction is usually flagged using some sort of ML model.

Traditionally, banks have used predefined rules for flagging suspicious transactions. For example, there could be a rule that if there is a sudden transaction from a different country, flag that for your approval. Or, if there is a purchase from a store that is not one you usually visit, flag that. Setting fixed rules to cover all sorts of cases for all individuals is extremely difficult and it's possible to get lots of false positives. Hence, modern systems rely on ML to find patterns of fraudulent transactions and predict if a transaction is fraudulent or normal.

We will explore an unsupervised learning method for analyzing this data, called *autoencoder*. First, let's look at the dataset. The dataset is structured and tabular. It includes a list of transactions with time, amount, and several details like customer account, vendor account, government taxes, etc. For this example, we will use a dataset that is generously made available in the public domain by the Machine Learning Group (`http://mlg.ulb.ac.be`) of ULB (Université Libre de Bruxelles). This dataset was generated as a research study by Andrea Dal Pozzolo, Olivier Caelen, Reid A. Johnson, and Gianluca Bontempi.

The dataset is available as a CSV file called `creditcard.csv`. The dataset contains transactions made by credit cards in September 2013 by European cardholders. It presents transactions that occurred in two days, where we have 492 frauds out of 284,807 transactions. The dataset is highly unbalanced, because the positive class (frauds) accounts for 0.172% of all transactions. Three features or columns are provided—Amount, Time, and Class. The Time feature contains the seconds elapsed between each transaction and the first transaction in the dataset. The Amount feature is the transaction amount and the Class feature is the response variable. It indicates 1 for fraud and 0 for a normal transaction.

The dataset has 28 columns named V1, V2, V3 . . . to V28. These represent the customer and vendor details for each transaction. However, using a dimensionality reduction technique called *Principal Component Analysis* (PCA), we have been given just these 28 V-features. This is also to hide the customer and vendor details in the interest of privacy. We can assume these 28 features are of importance and start analyzing the data. Figure 6.9 shows the data loaded in Excel.

We will use a special type of neural network to solve this problem, called an *autoencoder*. This is an unsupervised learning network that basically tries to reproduce the inputs given to it. The idea is to read the input vector and *encode* it using an encoder neural network into a smaller dimension vector called *encoding vector*. Then this smaller dimension encoding vector is *decoded* back into the input vector. The input is compressed and stored as a small encoding vector. This method has also been applied to data compression.

Time	V1	V2	V3	V4	V5	V6	V7	V8	V9	V10	V11	V27	V28	Amount	Class
0	-1.36	-0.073	2.5363	1.3782	-0.338	0.4624	0.2396	0.0987	0.3638	0.0908	-0.552	0.1336	-0.021	149.62	0
0	1.1919	0.2662	0.1665	0.4482	0.06	-0.082	-0.079	0.0851	-0.255	-0.167	1.6127	-0.009	0.0147	2.69	0
1	-1.358	-1.34	1.7732	0.3798	-0.503	1.8005	0.7915	0.2477	-1.515	0.2076	0.6245	-0.055	-0.06	378.66	0
1	-0.966	-0.185	1.793	-0.863	-0.01	1.2472	0.2376	0.3774	-1.387	-0.055	-0.226	0.0627	0.0615	123.5	0
2	-1.158	0.8777	1.5487	0.403	-0.407	0.0959	0.5929	-0.271	0.8177	0.7531	-0.823	0.2194	0.2152	69.99	0
2	-0.426	0.9605	1.1411	-0.168	0.421	-0.03	0.4762	0.2603	-0.569	-0.371	1.3413	0.2538	0.0811	3.67	0
4	1.2297	0.141	0.0454	1.2026	0.1919	0.2727	-0.005	0.0812	0.465	-0.099	-1.417	0.0345	0.0052	4.99	0
7	-0.644	1.418	1.0744	-0.492	0.9489	0.4281	1.1206	-3.808	0.6154	1.2494	-0.619	-1.207	-1.085	40.8	0
7	-0.894	0.2862	-0.113	-0.272	2.6696	3.7218	0.3701	0.8511	-0.392	-0.41	-0.705	0.0117	0.1424	93.2	0
9	-0.338	1.1196	1.0444	-0.222	0.4994	-0.247	0.6516	0.0695	-0.737	-0.367	1.0176	0.2462	0.0831	3.68	0
10	1.449	-1.176	0.9139	-1.376	-1.971	-0.629	-1.423	0.0485	-1.72	1.6267	1.1996	0.0428	0.0163	7.8	0
10	0.385	0.6161	-0.874	-0.094	2.9246	3.317	0.4705	0.5382	-0.559	0.3098	-0.259	0.0425	-0.054	9.99	0
10	1.25	-1.222	0.3839	-1.235	-1.485	-0.753	-0.689	-0.227	-2.094	1.3237	0.2277	0.0264	0.0424	121.5	0
11	1.0694	0.2877	0.8286	2.7125	-0.178	0.3375	-0.097	0.116	-0.221	0.4602	-0.774	0.0215	0.0213	27.5	0
12	-2.792	-0.328	1.6418	1.7675	-0.137	0.8076	-0.423	-1.907	0.7557	1.1511	0.8446	-0.165	-0.03	58.8	0
12	-0.752	0.3455	2.0573	-1.469	-1.158	-0.078	-0.609	0.0036	-0.436	0.7477	-0.794	-0.181	0.1294	15.99	0
12	1.1032	-0.04	1.2673	1.2891	-0.736	0.2881	-0.586	0.1894	0.7823	-0.268	-0.45	0.0928	0.0371	12.99	0
13	-0.437	0.919	0.9246	-0.727	0.9157	-0.128	0.7076	0.088	-0.665	-0.738	0.3241	0.0797	0.131	0.89	0
14	-5.401	-5.45	1.1863	1.7362	3.0491	-1.763	-1.56	0.1608	1.2331	0.3452	0.9172	0.3921	0.9496	46.8	0
15	1.4929	-1.029	0.4548	-1.438	-1.555	-0.721	-1.081	-0.053	-1.979	1.6381	1.0775	0.0223	0.0076	5	0
16	0.6949	-1.362	1.0292	0.8342	-1.191	1.3091	-0.879	0.4453	-0.446	0.5685	1.0192	0.0866	0.0635	231.71	0
17	0.9625	0.3285	-0.171	2.1092	1.1296	1.696	0.1077	0.5215	-1.191	0.7244	1.6903	0.0164	-0.015	34.09	0
18	1.1666	0.5021	-0.067	2.2616	0.4288	0.0895	0.2411	0.1381	-0.989	0.9222	0.7448	-0.041	-0.011	2.28	0
18	0.2475	0.2777	1.1855	-0.093	-1.314	-0.15	-0.946	-1.618	1.5441	-0.83	-0.583	0.3366	0.2505	22.75	0

Figure 6.9: Credit card transaction dataset with details hidden in V-features

There is some information loss when you encode a larger dimension input vector into the smaller encoding. The idea is for the model to learn to encode so well that all the *important patterns* in data will be captured in the encoding. This concept is explained in Figure 6.10.

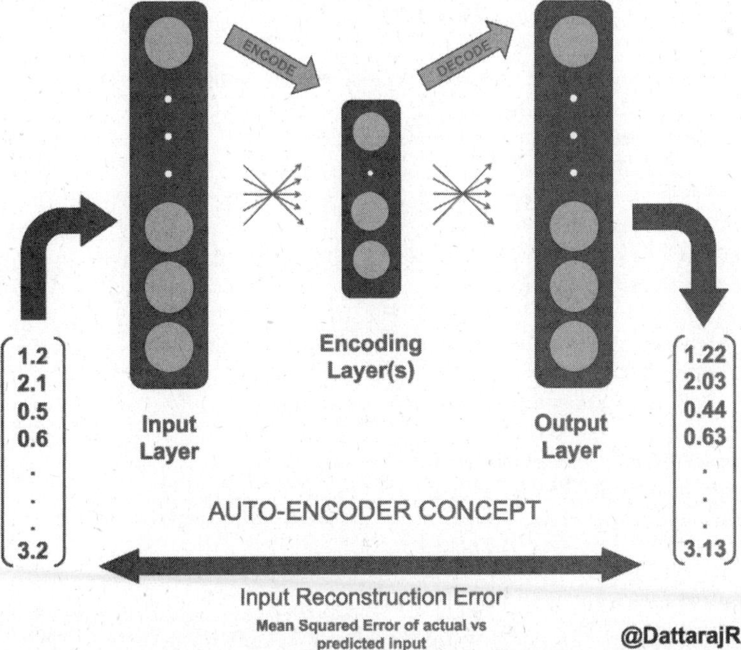

Figure 6.10: Concept of an autoencoder neural network

Let's look at the code to build the autoencoder and then use it to detect anomalies in credit card transaction data. First, we will load the CSV file and prepare the training dataset. The key thing for the autoencoder is that the input (X) and output (Y) data is the same. Hence, it will learn in an unsupervised manner and try to re-create the input fed into it. Let's prepare the training data in Listing 6.10.

Listing 6.10: Load the Credit Card Data and Prepare the Dataset

```
# import the required libraries including plotting
import pandas as pd
import numpy as np

import matplotlib.pyplot as plt
%matplotlib inline

# load the csv file with values
df = pd.read_csv('creditcard.csv')
df.head()
```

First, we will only concern ourselves with high-value transactions—say any amount above $200. We will use Scikit-Learn's built-in methods to scale the values in data frames. Then we will create a testing array with only normal transactions. Keep in mind that we only need `x_train` and `x_val` arrays since we are using unsupervised learning. Our expected Y values will be the X values themselves. You can see this code in Listing 6.11.

Listing 6.11: Prepare Training and Validations Data Arrays

```
# we will only look at transactions above value of 200
cc_data_subset = df[df.Amount > 200]

# we will scale the 'Time' and 'Amount' features to standard scale
# the V-features are already scaled
from sklearn.preprocessing import StandardScaler

cc_data_subset['Time'] = StandardScaler().fit_transform(cc_data_
subset['Time'].values.reshape(-1, 1))
cc_data_subset['Amount'] = StandardScaler().fit_transform(cc_data_
subset['Amount'].values.reshape(-1, 1))

# now we will separate normal and fraudulent transactions
cc_data_normal = cc_data_subset[cc_data_subset.Class == 0]
cc_data_fraud = cc_data_subset[cc_data_subset.Class == 1]

# list how many of each type of transactions exist
print("Normal transactions array shape = ", cc_data_normal.shape)
print("Fraud transactions array shape = ", cc_data_fraud.shape)
```

```
# get the number of fraudulent transactions present
num_of_fraud = cc_data_fraud.shape[0]
print("Number of fraud transactions = ", num_of_fraud)

# we will create a testing data frame of normal and fraudulent
transactions
df_testing = cc_data_normal[-num_of_fraud:]
df_testing = df_testing.append(cc_data_fraud)

# for training data frame we will use only normal transactions
df_training = cc_data_normal[:-num_of_fraud]

# we will split the training data into training and validation
# we will use Scikit-Learn's built0in function to do the split
from sklearn.model_selection import train_test_split

# we dont need result column in training frame
df_training = df_training.drop(['Class'], axis=1) #drop the Class column

# we will first store the testing labels in a frame and then drop the
Class column
df_testing_labels = df_testing['Class']
df_testing = df_testing.drop(['Class'], axis=1) #drop the Class column

# now we will create arrays for training the autoencoder network
x_training = df_training.values
x_train, x_val = train_test_split(x_training, test_size=0.1)

# print the shapes of arrays
print("X Training array shape = ", x_train.shape)
print("X Validation array shape = ", x_val.shape)
```

Here are the results:

```
Normal transactions array shape =  (28752, 31)
Fraud transactions array shape =  (85, 31)

Number of fraud transactions =  85

X Training array shape =  (25800, 30)
X Validation array shape =  (2867, 30)
```

Now we will build the autoencoder model. As we saw, this model will have an encoder and decoder part. The encoder takes a high-dimensional vector and generates a low-dimensional encoding. We have an input vector of size 30 and we will use an encoding size of 15. You can change this and see if you get better results. You can see this code in Listing 6.12.

Here are the results:

TIME	V1	V2	V3	V4	V5	V9	...	V25	V26	V27	V28	AMOUNT	CLASS	
0	0.0	−1.359807	−0.072781	2.536347	1.378155	0.098698	0.363787	...	0.128539	−0.189115	0.133558	−0.021053	149.62	0
1	0.0	1.191857	0.266151	0.166480	0.448154	0.085102	−0.255425	...	0.167170	0.125895	−0.008983	0.014724	2.69	0
2	1.0	−1.358354	−1.340163	1.773209	0.379780	0.247676	−1.514654	...	−0.327642	−0.139097	−0.055353	−0.059752	378.66	0
3	1.0	−0.966272	−0.185226	1.792993	−0.863291	0.377436	−1.387024	...	0.647376	−0.221929	0.062723	0.061458	123.50	0
4	2.0	−1.158233	0.877737	1.548718	0.403034	−0.270533	0.817739	...	−0.206010	0.502292	0.219422	0.215153	69.99	0

Listing 6.12: Build the Autoencoder Neural Network in Keras

```
from keras.layers import Input, Dense, Dropout
from keras.models import Model
from keras import regularizers

# dimensions of the input vector - we have 30 variables
input_dim = 30
# this is the size of our encoded representations
encoding_dim = 15

# autoencoder - neural network
# this is the input layer
input_layer = Input(shape=(input_dim,))

# encoded representation of the input
encoded_layer = Dense(encoding_dim, activation='relu')(input_layer)

# lossy reconstruction of the input
decoded_layer = Dense(input_dim, activation='relu')(encoded_layer)

# combine encoder and decoder as a single model
autoencoder = Model(input_layer, decoded_layer)

# lets compile the model using mse loss
autoencoder.compile(metrics=['accuracy'],
                    loss='mean_squared_error',
                    optimizer='adam')

# show summary of the model
autoencoder.summary()
```

Here are the results:

```
Layer (type)                 Output Shape              Param #
=================================================================
input_51 (InputLayer)        (None, 30)                0
_________________________________________________________________
dense_119 (Dense)            (None, 15)                465
_________________________________________________________________
dense_120 (Dense)            (None, 30)                480
=================================================================
Total params: 945
Trainable params: 945
Non-trainable params: 0
```

Now let's train the model on our `x_train` and `x_val` arrays. Notice that we don't have `y_train` and `y_val` arrays. We use the input as the expected output. You can see this code in Listing 6.13.

Listing 6.13: Train the Autoencoder Using Input Array Only

```
# lets train the autoencoder  for 25 epochs
history = autoencoder.fit(x_train, x_train,
                epochs=25,
                batch_size=32,
                validation_data=(x_val, x_val),
                shuffle=True)
```

Here are the results:

```
Train on 25800 samples, validate on 2867 samples
Epoch 1/25
25800/25800 [==============================] - 3s 131us/step - loss:
1.7821 - acc: 0.3620 - val_loss: 1.8113 - val_acc: 0.5225
Epoch 2/25
25800/25800 [==============================] - 1s 46us/step - loss:
1.5699 - acc: 0.5834 - val_loss: 1.7444 - val_acc: 0.6264
Epoch 3/25
25800/25800 [==============================] - 1s 48us/step - loss:
1.5282 - acc: 0.6578 - val_loss: 1.7110 - val_acc: 0.6983
Epoch 4/25
25800/25800 [==============================] - 1s 47us/step - loss:
1.5010 - acc: 0.7069 - val_loss: 1.6911 - val_acc: 0.7203
Epoch 5/25
25800/25800 [==============================] - 1s 48us/step - loss:
1.4760 - acc: 0.7460 - val_loss: 1.6697 - val_acc: 0.7719
Epoch 6/25
25800/25800 [==============================] - 1s 47us/step - loss:
1.4617 - acc: 0.7763 - val_loss: 1.6483 - val_acc: 0.7733
Epoch 7/25
25800/25800 [==============================] - 1s 47us/step - loss:
1.4521 - acc: 0.7834 - val_loss: 1.6391 - val_acc: 0.7939
Epoch 8/25
25800/25800 [==============================] - 1s 48us/step - loss:
1.4463 - acc: 0.7956 - val_loss: 1.6355 - val_acc: 0.8036
Epoch 9/25
25800/25800 [==============================] - 1s 57us/step - loss:
1.4430 - acc: 0.8025 - val_loss: 1.6298 - val_acc: 0.8033
Epoch 10/25
25800/25800 [==============================] - 1s 55us/step - loss:
1.4407 - acc: 0.8062 - val_loss: 1.6350 - val_acc: 0.8022
Epoch 11/25
25800/25800 [==============================] - 1s 49us/step - loss:
1.4398 - acc: 0.8091 - val_loss: 1.6290 - val_acc: 0.8099
Epoch 12/25
25800/25800 [==============================] - 1s 49us/step - loss:
1.4384 - acc: 0.8114 - val_loss: 1.6273 - val_acc: 0.8036
Epoch 13/25
25800/25800 [==============================] - 1s 48us/step - loss:
1.4379 - acc: 0.8126 - val_loss: 1.6258 - val_acc: 0.8183
Epoch 14/25
25800/25800 [==============================] - 1s 51us/step - loss:
1.4374 - acc: 0.8140 - val_loss: 1.6267 - val_acc: 0.8204
```

```
Epoch 15/25
25800/25800 [==============================] - 1s 49us/step - loss:
1.4368 - acc: 0.8144 - val_loss: 1.6257 - val_acc: 0.8186
Epoch 16/25
25800/25800 [==============================] - 2s 59us/step - loss:
1.4363 - acc: 0.8164 - val_loss: 1.6260 - val_acc: 0.8141
Epoch 17/25
25800/25800 [==============================] - 1s 53us/step - loss:
1.4358 - acc: 0.8174 - val_loss: 1.6253 - val_acc: 0.8190
Epoch 18/25
25800/25800 [==============================] - 1s 53us/step - loss:
1.4356 - acc: 0.8160 - val_loss: 1.6243 - val_acc: 0.8183
Epoch 19/25
25800/25800 [==============================] - 1s 50us/step - loss:
1.4353 - acc: 0.8169 - val_loss: 1.6257 - val_acc: 0.8137
Epoch 20/25
25800/25800 [==============================] - 1s 54us/step - loss:
1.4351 - acc: 0.8186 - val_loss: 1.6245 - val_acc: 0.8134: 0s - loss:
1.4152 - a
Epoch 21/25
25800/25800 [==============================] - 1s 56us/step - loss:
1.4347 - acc: 0.8198 - val_loss: 1.6237 - val_acc: 0.8116
Epoch 22/25
25800/25800 [==============================] - 1s 52us/step - loss:
1.4346 - acc: 0.8181 - val_loss: 1.6255 - val_acc: 0.8193s - loss:
1.3752 - - ETA: 0s - loss: 1.4163 - acc: 0.
Epoch 23/25
25800/25800 [==============================] - 1s 51us/step - loss:
1.4343 - acc: 0.8194 - val_loss: 1.6232 - val_acc: 0.8148
Epoch 24/25
25800/25800 [==============================] - 1s 54us/step - loss:
1.4342 - acc: 0.8189 - val_loss: 1.6230 - val_acc: 0.8155
Epoch 25/25
25800/25800 [==============================] - 1s 56us/step - loss:
1.4340 - acc: 0.8216 - val_loss: 1.6265 - val_acc: 0.8123
```

We will plot the accuracy and loss values for training and validation datasets. You can see this code in Listing 6.14.

Listing 6.14: Plot the Accuracy and Loss Values

```
# summarize history for accuracy
plt.figure(figsize=(20,10))
plt.rcParams.update({'font.size': 22})
plt.plot(history.history['acc'])
plt.plot(history.history['val_acc'])
plt.title('model accuracy')
plt.ylabel('accuracy')
plt.xlabel('epoch')
plt.legend(['train', 'test'], loc='upper left')
plt.show()
```

```
# summarize history for loss
plt.figure(figsize=(20,10))
plt.rcParams.update({'font.size': 22})
plt.plot(history.history['loss'])
plt.plot(history.history['val_loss'])
plt.title('model loss')
plt.ylabel('loss')
plt.xlabel('epoch')
plt.legend(['train', 'test'], loc='upper left')
plt.show()
```

The results are two charts, as shown in Figures 6.11 and 6.12.

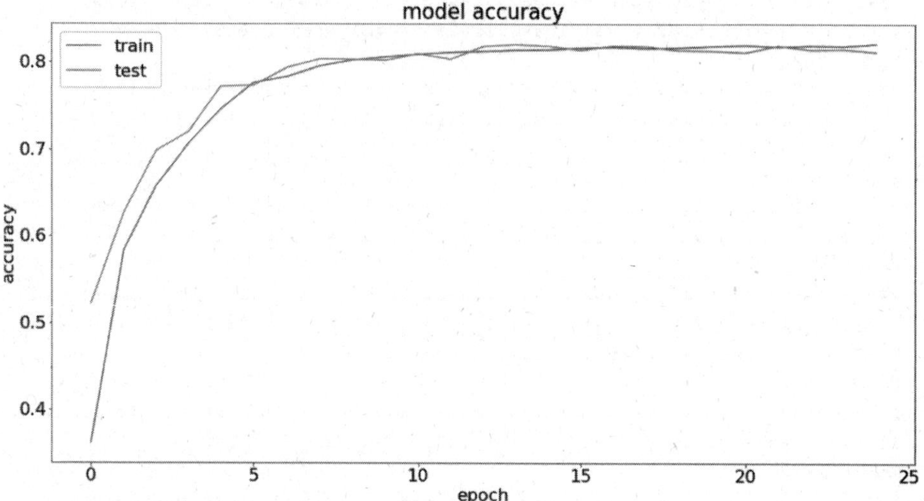

Figure 6.11: Model accuracy plot for autoencoder

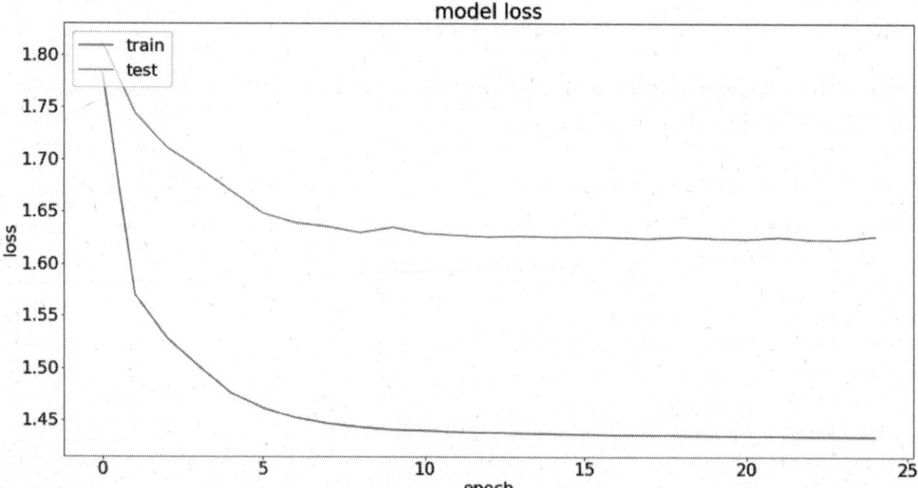

Figure 6.12: Model loss plot for autoencoder

Now we will make a prediction with the trained autoencoder on the testing dataset. We will compare the input values with predictions and calculate the *reconstruction error* for each data point. Since we trained on normal transactions, these should have a low reconstruction error. Fraudulent transactions will have different data distributions and should give us a higher reconstruction error. You can see this code in Listing 6.15.

Listing 6.15: Using Autoencoder to Make Predictions and Find Fraud Transactions

```
# set the testing array - this has 85 normal and 85 fraud transactions
x_testing = df_testing.values

# get the prediction using autoencoder network
x_predictions = autoencoder.predict(x_testing)

# calculate the reconstruction error as mean square error
reconstruction_error = np.mean(np.power(x_testing - x_predictions, 2),
axis=1)

# create new data frame with error and true class (normal/fraud)
# ideally fraud classes should have high reconstruction error
error_df = pd.DataFrame({'Reconstruction_Error': reconstruction_error,
               'True_Class': df_testing_labels.values})

# set a threshold for error
threshold_fixed = 2

# separate data in groups for plotting
groups = error_df.groupby('True_Class')

# plot the chart
fig, ax = plt.subplots(figsize=(20,10))
plt.rcParams.update({'font.size': 22})
for name, group in groups:
    ax.plot(group.index, group.Reconstruction_Error, marker='o', ms=8,
linestyle='',
      label= "Fraud" if name == 1 else "Normal")

ax.hlines(threshold_fixed, ax.get_xlim()[0], ax.get_xlim()[1],
colors="g", zorder=100, label='Threshold')
ax.legend()

plt.title("Reconstruction error for normal and fraud")
plt.ylabel("Reconstruction error")
plt.xlabel("Testing dataset")
plt.show()
```

The result is shown in Figure 6.13.

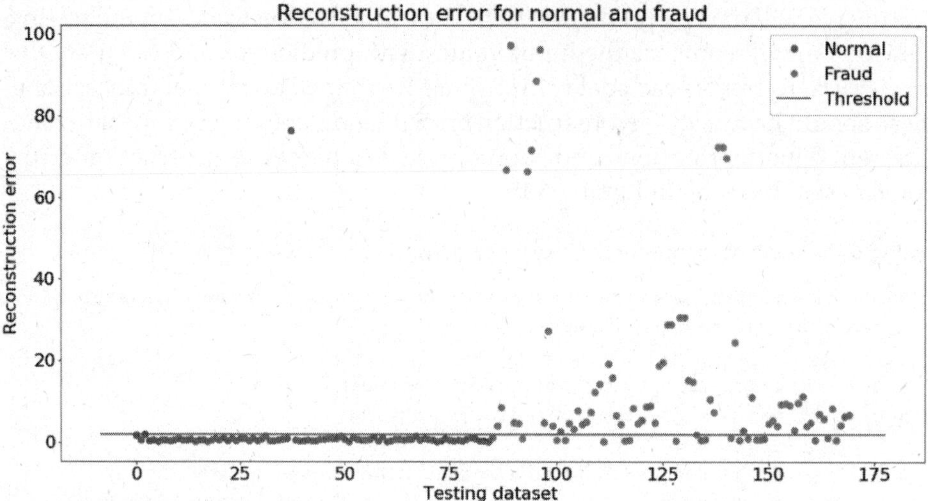

Figure 6.13: Predictions on testing data using autoencoder

This chart in Figure 6.13 tells us a good story. We see the reconstruction error as high for the fraudulent transactions, shown in orange. For the normal transactions in blue, we see most points below our defined threshold. Now we don't catch all the fraudulent transactions, but more than 75% of them, which is very good. You can explore modifying hyper-parameters like number of layers and neurons to see if you get better results. Hopefully, this code shows you the power of Deep Learning to find patterns in data and detect anomalies. Since this is unsupervised, we did not give labeled outputs. You can use this approach in pretty much any domain of data.

Summary

In this chapter, we looked at some unique applications of the Deep Learning technology. We saw how we can use the neural style transfer method to transfer the style of a painting to our own images. Then we saw generative networks and created new data points that highly resemble real data. Finally, we saw the use of a special type of network called an *autoencoder* that learns to find anomalies in data using unsupervised learning. These methods are pretty new and proposed by researchers in several publications. The Deep Learning community is truly awesome and shares valuable content with everyone. You can explore new papers as they are published on the Cornell University site (`arxiv.org`) to learn about new solutions as they are developed. Also, I highly encourage you to contribute your own papers here so everyone can benefit from your knowledge!

CHAPTER 7

AI in the Modern Software World

The first half of the book is focused on Artificial Intelligence and particularly on Deep Learning. It included examples of using Machine Learning and Deep Learning to extract patterns from data and drive outcomes like classification and regression. You saw a full example of collecting data of soft drink brand logos, augmenting the data to generate more training samples, and building a deep neural network to classify these images. You used transfer learning to take a proven architecture and customize it for a specific problem. Hopefully, with all this knowledge, you are equipped to analyze your own dataset and build models to analyze it.

In the second half of the book, we try to bridge the gap between data scientists who are the algorithm experts building models and software developers who build the code that runs into production. We see how the ML and DL models we build can be packaged with software code and deployed for real-time inference with live data from the field.

In this chapter, we take the data scientist hat off for a bit and put on the software developer's hat. We talk about how software development has evolved over the years; what kind of modern applications are being developed; and what improvements are happening in the process and tools for building software. It's important to understand these issues because this is the new domain and environment for which we need to build and deploy our ML models.

We talk about the growth of web applications, the rise of Cloud computing, SaaS versus PaaS versus CaaS, SOA versus microservices, and the latest trend of Cloud-native applications using containers. We then spend some time understanding Kubernetes and how it can help you package your code into a container for production deployment and scale it to thousands of nodes in seconds.

A Quick Look at Modern Software Needs

Software development has undergone a major transformation in recent times. Customers (who pay for software) and consumers (who end up using it) have increased demands in terms of cost, speed of delivery, faster and automated updates, and an enhanced user experience. With the rise in mobile computing, everyone has a powerful smartphone in their pockets with dedicated Internet connectivity. The expectation is that the software will take full advantage of this processing power and connectivity to get us improved outcomes. No one expects to download a binary file and plug their phone into a laptop with a USB to update to a new OS. We have started to expect over-the-air (OTA) and seamless updates that happen in the background and do not interrupt our routines.

Customers are no longer expecting large bulky and monolithic software that needs to be custom installed on racks of servers in a back office. Modern web applications are moving to public Clouds like Amazon Web Services (AWS), Google Cloud Platform (GCP), and Microsoft Azure. These Cloud vendors provide a unified ecosystem of building and deploying software very fast and take care of many infrastructure concerns for the developer. For example, with AWS, you can spin up new *virtual machines* in a matter of seconds without having to touch any hardware. All the memory, CPU, storage, and networking of the machines is done virtually. This is the age of *software-defined* hardware and networking.

We are seeing an explosion in social media apps like Facebook, Twitter, WhatsApp, and Instagram, which manage millions of users connected to each other and provide real-time updates. Customers are expecting a social media–like experience in other areas like mobile payments, movie bookings, and online shopping. A few years back I was working on software showing the status of gas turbine health. Our customer was pushing us for an interface like Twitter where, as soon as an event happened (a message by a user), the whole network was notified in milliseconds. We actually studied the Twitter architecture and ended up building a real-time notification engine.

In the previous chapters, if you used Google Colaboratory to run some of the examples, you will have noticed an extremely seamless experience and a very powerful interface. Programmers are traditionally used to desktop-based integrated development environments (IDE), which need to be installed and kept updated with the latest versions. We are now moving from desktop to web-based IDEs like Google Colaboratory, where all the cool operations that an IDE supports are done in a web browser. No installation is needed and there's no updating of code and library packages. Especially for libraries like TensorFlow that get new versions every three to four months, you can expect the web IDE to always provide the latest library version to get you going.

You can do all the coding inside the browser and run the code on specialized hardware like a GPU, all in the background. This is the level of sophistication that modern software systems have grown to expect, including a user interface that gives an almost desktop feeling to programmers when writing code, with auto-complete of code syntax. Your code runs in the background on a virtual machine with a dedicated GPU and you don't even notice it!

Another major improvement happening with software is in the user experience area. We are no longer happy with the traditional mouse and keyboard inputs for our systems. We now have to develop software that will be accessed on touchscreen phones and iPads and can listen to voice commands. We now have virtual and augmented reality devices that create an environment for the users, and our software needs to be rendered in this environment.

To meet the ever-growing needs of modern applications, the whole software development process is changing. Traditionally, we had a *waterfall* development model, where engineers spent a lot of time and money upfront capturing requirements, building a complete architecture, building a detailed design specification, and then over many months, delivering working code. The problem is that in a fast-changing world we cannot wait that long to get software. The people, environment, and requirements continuously change. Moreover, we rely heavily on the fact that we have captured all requirements perfectly, which is almost never the case. This can lead to hours of rework and extended delivery dates and missed targets.

Today, almost all organizations are moving to *agile* methods that promote smaller, self-organizing teams that build and deliver working software in short iterations or *sprints*. Many people feel that agile is building software very fast without focus on quality and documentation. That is absolutely untrue. The expectation is to deliver working production-quality code in each sprint with an acceptable level of software quality checks and documentation in these short sprints. There are formal project management techniques like *scrum* that help engineers achieve agile development practices. In order to support such an agile process, we cannot have engineers waste hours running the same unit and system tests over and over. We also cannot afford to have a manual build process to generate production code from our source repository. Our build process should be such that, as developers check in code, the tests run automatically, checking for things that are broken and helping us fix the relevant areas. Then, once the code passes all the tests, it is automatically integrated with all the right dependencies (libraries, DLLs, etc.) and deployed as a package.

To solve this exact problem, a major component of the agile process is *Continuous Integration and Continuous Delivery* (CI/CD). CI aims at integrating your source code with unit and integration testing and making sure the code is not broken. This is absolutely invaluable when you have multiple developers checking in code at the same time—sometimes across the globe. CD focuses on packaging the validated build into a binary to deploy on target computers. This is how companies manage nightly builds of their software, which can be tested immediately. For example, Google's Chrome browser has 6.7 million lines of code, and it's all managed through such a process. We can go to the website and download the latest version. Similarly, the entire Android operating system that powers smartphones has around 15 million lines of code. It's open source and you can also look at the code for free online.

How AI Fits into Modern Software Development

Now, you may ask, what does this have to do with AI? Excellent question. For AI to be effective, it needs to be part of the modern software development process. Imagine you build a very effective AI model that reads an image and if it sees a familiar face, it sets a flag to unlock the phone. A data scientist would focus on using tools like Python and Jupyter to master the face recognition algorithm. However, once this brilliant model with 98% precision is developed, how do we integrate this into the smartphone app? You have a friend who is a mobile software developer—she's an expert in C++, Java, and mobile software. This developer needs to build a wrapper app that takes the image from the smartphone camera, normalizes it, and provides it to your model. Now your model is developed in Python and stored as an H5 file. This nice mobile software developer now needs to find a way to call your Deep Learning model from inside her environment, which could be Java or C++, and run the model. Even if this is done, the model H5 file will stand out as a sore dependency that needs to be integrated in the CI/CD process.

Now imagine that a new paper is published with insights on better hyper-parameter tuning, particularly for your face recognition problem. Just to explain, hyper-parameter tuning is basically adjusting the parameters of your model that are not learned. These are configuration parameters like number of layers, neurons in each layer, etc. You are excited and integrate these changes into your data science tools and retrain a model. Now the new model has 99% precision, and you have to go back and give this new model file to the mobile developer, who has to integrate it in the code. This has the potential to happen again and again and could pretty much sour your friendship with the nice mobile developer!

As mentioned earlier, requirements keep changing in the software world and hence we need an agile process to change as requirements change. The same goes with AI. As new requirements come up, you need to modify your Deep Learning models and quickly integrate them into the software CI/CD process.

Just sending a model file across the board is not the solution. We need tools to manage the model lifecycle, evaluate models by running them in parallel, and have a seamless CI/CD process for our models. The entire Machine Learning model lifecycle needs to be considered and the right points should be automated to make the overall application development agile. This is what we cover in the second half of this book.

We will show—using the latest technologies like Cloud computing, microservices, and containerized applications—how we can modernize the model development process and make it agile, just like CI/CD does for the overall software development cycle. Modernizing the ML model development process and integrating with the software development process is an active area of study (as of 2018). The technology behind this is still being developed. I will share some of the best practices used in the industry and some top tools used. I will also show some examples of taking models developed using tools you saw in the first half of the book—like Keras and TensorFlow—and deploying these into real applications.

But before we get too far, let's talk a bit about the growth of these technologies—particularly web applications, Cloud computing, microservices, containers, and Docker. This will not be a comprehensive guide of any of these technologies. I explain them in simple language and try to relate these concepts back to the AI conversation we started with.

Simple to Fancy Web Applications

In the 1990s, as the world moved from desktop applications toward web applications, more advancements were made in making these applications dynamic and having the flexibility of desktop applications. A desktop application is something like Microsoft Word or Outlook that runs on a computer or laptop and has full access to the system's resources. Thus, we see tight control over the data and some fancy user interfaces. Web applications, on the other hand, run inside a web browser like Google Chrome, Apple Safari, or Microsoft Internet Explorer. These web applications connect to a remote computer called a web server and deliver content in a universal format, known as HyperText Markup Language (HTML). This is how the majority of web content is delivered. A user with a web browser connects to a website like Google.com. The website checks for information requested by the browser and packages a response as HTML and sends back data. HTML is the language the browser understands well. It decodes this HTML into a web page that we see. The web server does all the magic of understanding our request, getting responses from some data source, and packaging them into an HTML document that can be rendered inside the browser. See Figure 7.1.

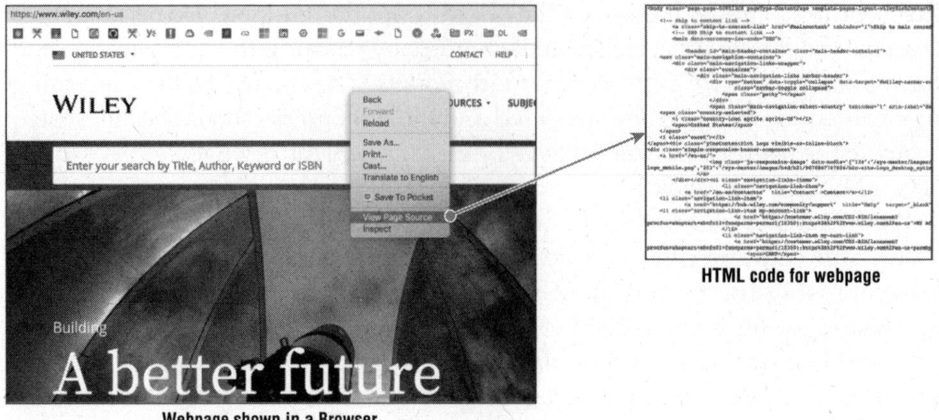

Figure 7.1: Displaying a web page and HTML code

All the underlying communication is done using a protocol called HTTP (HyperText Transfer Protocol). A protocol is basically a language that is used to transfer data on a network. The HTTP protocol defines the structure of data to be sent from the client (browser) to the server and back. Also, the verbs—like Read, Put, Delete, and Update—define the action that needs to be done at the server. For example, a browser may send a `READ HTTP` message to get back contents of a web page—the most common use case. There could be a message to `UPDATE` a value in a database like a user address or ZIP code. This is how HTTP works through messages.

In the early 1990s, web servers were pretty dumb and served just static HTML pages. So, all the logic of collecting data and building HTML was done by some person to create a static HTML page that was stored and sent back. This was not enough to keep up with the dynamic needs of web applications. Hence methods like CGI-Scripts, Java Servlets, and PHP were developed to enable server-side code to generate HTML content dynamically. So, if you needed to query a database of books for a search topic, you could do that using Java code in a servlet and the results were displayed as custom HTML.

Server-side scripting became extremely popular, but was not enough. The results still had to be sent back to the server and the client had to wait for a response, which was a full HTML document. There was advancement in scripting on the client-side with the development of JavaScript. Developers could write some amazing JavaScript code to do things like validation of data and modifying style of pages and animations. JavaScript, combined with HTML stylesheets, gave rise to a very advanced user interface for modern web applications. With the growth of Ajax, dynamic content was available for web pages without having to request an entire HTML page. Pages could only send back relevant queries and get results packaged in small packages to display on pages using Ajax.

The rise in HTML, JavaScript, and stylesheets led to something known as HTML 2.0 (see Figure 7.2), which is a modern evolving standard for building dynamic, interactive, and responsive web applications.

Figure 7.2: The HTML 2 logo
(*Source*: W3C – Wikimedia)

If you have been using a web-based email tool like Yahoo or Google Mail over the years, you have probably noticed the evolution in its user interface—from the early versions in the early 2000s, which would take a few seconds to load, to each message loading in separate tabs, to a recent (2016) more modern desktop-like user interface, letting you click and read a message in the preview pane and select and delete multiple messages.

The Rise of Cloud Computing

As web applications got sleeker and faster in the 2010s, there was also a paradigm shift starting to evolve in the backend for hosting these applications. Traditionally organizations had in-house servers tucked away at the back of their buildings in rooms with hundreds of wires and cables running along big box computers. This room generated lots of heat due to all the computers and needed dedicated cooling, with many fans. There was usually a dedicated IT admin team who knew where these wires connected and would spend hours debugging some issue. You have probably seen these server rooms in some of the '90s movies like *Office Space*. See Figure 7.3.

As applications grew in size and complexity, we soon found that the server room was not enough to maintain applications. The applications were no longer simple web pages showing reports and data entry forms. These were complex business process systems that needed high-end processing and high availability. Also, with the rise in globalization, these applications were no longer accessed from one or two regions, but there could be customers accessing these applications 24×7, from all corners of the world. These applications now needed extremely high availability with minimal downtime.

Figure 7.3: Data center with racks of blade servers
(*Source*: BalticServers.com – Wikimedia)

As our web applications grew in complexity and importance, strong metrics to track downtime started coming into play. An availability number of 95%, although initially considered good, soon started becoming undesirable—95% availability for a 24×7 website translates to a downtime of 18 days in a year. Imagine Wikipedia, Facebook, BestBuy, or your bank's website being down for 18 days of the year! So, the new availability metrics were as high as 99.99% (four nines) or 99.999% (five nines). Five nines translates to a downtime of five minutes in a year, which is becoming acceptable.

This downtime was needed because software had to be upgraded with new features or broken hardware had to be fixed or replaced. Engineers soon realized that individual servers could no longer support these global high-availability applications. This gave rise to the move of applications into dedicated *data centers* in late 2000s. The data centers had dedicated racks of blade servers with shared processing power, storage capacity, cooling, etc. There could be a dedicated IT team for the data center rather than having individual ones at sites—saving millions of dollars. Another major benefit that the data center provided was disaster recovery. If a data center was destroyed because of a natural disaster or a terrorist attack, organizations could lose years of transaction histories and valuable data. Data centers started supporting data replication at different sites in different geographic regions to avoid these scenarios. The data center was still on a private network and could only be accessed with network connectivity. It was still operating on its own intranet.

In the early 2010s, a new concept started emerging—more like a public data center or Cloud. The idea was that there would be one or more data centers with data storage and processing capability and companies would "rent" this storage and processing power. This was available on the public Internet, but everything behind the scenes was abstracted out for users; hence the term *Cloud*, since you don't really know what happens up there. You get the desired storage, memory, and processing resources and pay a monthly fee for the privilege.

The technology that enables this is called *virtualization*. The racks of servers that you see in a data center in Figure 7.3—using virtualization—can be divided into smaller virtual machines (VMs), each with a dedicated processor, memory, and storage. All communication with the data center happens over the public Internet using the HTTP protocol we discussed earlier.

A security layer is developed on top of HTTP to make sure the right users get access to their resources and unauthorized access is blocked. Many security standards like HTTPS, OAuth, and SAML have evolved to ensure exactly this. So, once you have an account established on a public Cloud provider website, you can connect to an endpoint with client software and launch a virtual machine. Based on usage, your account will be billed. This is just like using any paid subscription service like Netflix.

NOTE **Amazon was the first major Cloud provider with its Amazon Web Services (AWS) offering and as of 2018 is still leading this space. Google has GCP and Microsoft has Azure as their Cloud offerings. Anyone can sign up for these with a credit card and start creating resources in the Cloud. In fact, they all provide a free tier where you can commission certain resources for free and run them for a specific time. I highly recommend you try this to understand where the future of computing is headed and get hands-on experience with software-defined machines.**

As public Clouds gained popularity, several "as-a-Service" paradigms evolved around Cloud computing. Let me explain these with the help of Figure 7.4. There may be different versions of this block diagram available on the Internet. It's important to get the concept behind it.

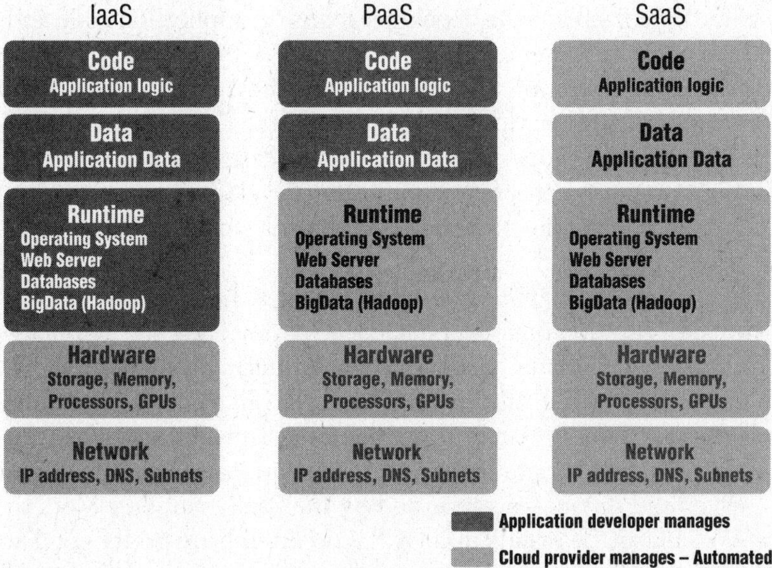

Figure 7.4: IaaS vs. PaaS vs. SaaS, explained through a block diagram

The most basic version is called *Infrastructure-as-a-Service*, or IaaS. Here you rent the hardware and network from the Cloud provider. Basically, this is logging on to AWS and commissioning a virtual machine. You specify the number and type of CPU processors, RAM, and storage capacity needed. Of course, the bigger the resources, the more you pay per hour. Then you can log in to that virtual machine with SSH (Secure Shell prompt) using a security key assigned to your account.

You can also enable Windows Remote Desktop for Windows and treat it like a regular desktop. You can install software on this machine and run dedicated processing jobs. You can install a web server like Apache Tomcat and deploy your code and have it as your web application hosted on the Internet. Then you can install a database like SQL Server on the same or different virtual machine and have your application write to this database. Many websites are hosted in this manner. This is IaaS. The Cloud vendor only takes care of the hardware and the network—the application developer handles the runtime, application data, and logic.

Application developers have to do a lot of work using the IaaS paradigm. They have to create VMs using a web admin screen, log in to the VM and then manually install the OS, drivers, web servers, databases, applications, etc. Recently, Big Data ecosystems like Hadoop have come into prominence. Hadoop allows regular Linux machines to act like an integrated cluster and distribute jobs on that cluster. This way, you get the processing power and storage of all the machines combined. If you were to set up an eight-node Hadoop cluster on your own, you would need to commission eight VMs and then configure each to be part of the Hadoop cluster. Lots of work!

To solve this problem, Cloud vendors started introducing the *Platform-as-a-Service* (PaaS) paradigm. PaaS lets the developer focus on application code and data and takes care of the runtime, as shown in Figure 7.4. Here the application developers do not explicitly commission VMs; rather, they package their code into binary files and upload them to the PaaS ecosystem. The PaaS takes care of setting up the database, the app server, and, in some cases, the Big Data ecosystem. The runtime is a major concern for application developers and installing, debugging, and managing versions can become a major workload. PaaS takes care of this for you.

Java developers package their applications into JAR files. The JAR file contains application code, configuration data, and database scripts. The PaaS automatically extracts these files and creates the environment. Internally it commissions multiple VMs to address each of the runtime concerns like server, database, etc. Developers save on deployment and maintenance time, but they have to sacrifice the fine control they would have if they used an IaaS. Also, they have to rely on the server and databases supported by the PaaS solutions. Modern PaaS tools like AWS Elastic Beanstalk and GCP App Engine are pretty good at supporting all the latest development servers and databases.

The next paradigm we will talk about is *Software-as-a-Service* (SaaS). SaaS has been used in context of the Cloud; however, SaaS solutions existed even before Cloud computing was formally defined. SaaS means you have the vendor take care of all your application concerns right from network, from the hardware to runtime to the application data and code. Most of the web-based tools like Google Docs, Gmail, Yahoo mail, etc. are SaaS tools. You don't need to install any software on your machine; you just open a compatible web browser and the entire application runs inside the browser. Companies like SalesForce.com provide extensive tools where you can build entire applications following the SaaS model. Microsoft has also embraced the SaaS model for Office-365, where you can build and manage all documents in the Cloud with an online interface.

In recent years, a new paradigm is evolving in the industry, called *Container-as-a-Service* (CaaS). Let's talk about that in the next section.

Containers and CaaS

Traditionally, web applications were packaged as binary packages like JAR files in Java or ZIP files. The development and testing teams would ensure that the package contained all the dependencies and installed fine on the app server and the platform like Java or Python. However, invariably as packages were moved from development to testing to staging platforms, there would be missing dependencies, incorrect versions, etc., causing problems. This would cause major delays in deploying software and has been a major deterring factor to agile development.

I remember once in a Java application we were developing a few years back we started getting null pointer exceptions (bad bad stuff in Java) when we moved our JAR files from the development to the staging servers. We spent two days checking versions, but all seemed fine. Finally, we discovered the charting library we used had a micro-version change on that environment and this was causing the entire chart object to be null. The problem was that we were using the chart as an external dependency, and on the new environment the expectation was that this library existed and was in the right version.

To manage problems like these, a new development pattern is evolving and getting very popular, called *containerized applications*. The idea is not just to package your application into a ZIP or JAR file, but to package the whole machine image, including the operating system, any dependent libraries, and your code as a container. A container is a lightweight virtual machine that uses shared-kernel architecture.

Normally, if you package your application as a virtual machine, the file can be a few gigabytes. To initialize it on another machine, you will need specialized software called Hypervisor, and it will take a few seconds. This is because when a VM initiates, the entire OS needs to be started, then your app server, and finally your application code.

In contrast to this, a container can get started in just a few milliseconds and the size can be a few megabytes. The reason is that containers reuse the kernel of the underlying operating system, as shown in Figure 7.5.

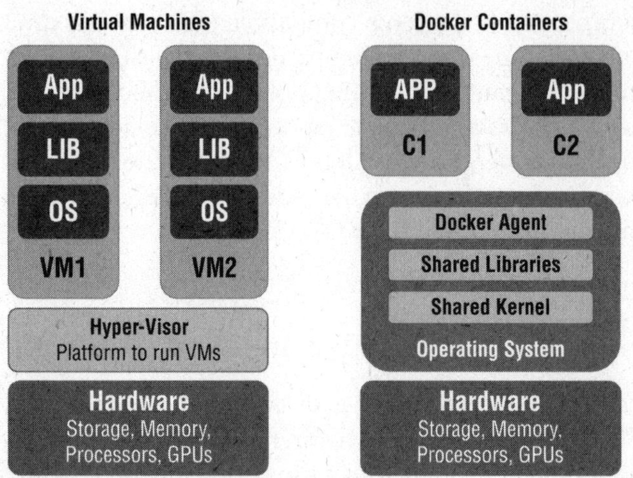

Figure 7.5: Virtual machines vs. containers

Docker is the most popular container technology today. A *container* is a standard unit of software that packages up the code and all its dependencies so the application runs quickly and reliably from one computing environment to another. A Docker container image is a lightweight, standalone, executable package of software that includes everything needed to run an application: code, runtime, system tools, system libraries, and settings.

All the host machine needs to have installed is a Docker agent. The container image is downloaded on this machine and instantiated as a container. The container reuses the Linux kernel of the underlying Docker agent. The agent also allows containers to share libraries among them, thus making the containers highly lightweight. Containers may be spun up in micro- or milliseconds and you can have thousands of containers running on a single high-end machine.

Containers run in an isolated environment with their own network stack, giving the impression of virtual machines. They use three Linux technologies to achieve this. They use namespaces to isolate specific operations. Each container has dedicated and isolated namespaces for resources, like CPU, RAM, and storage. Linux cGroups are used to assign resources to containers. These help put limits on the amount of resources consumed by containers so they can coexist on the same machine. Finally, containers use a layered operating system with every increment made to a base image. For example, we can start with a standard version of a Linux image, add a web server, add our database, and add our code. Each of these will be separate shared layers allowing the final layer to be highly lightweight with only our code. The same OS and server layers will be used on all machines.

Containers have two major advantages. One is for DevOps. DevOps is basically a new concept in agile that enables tighter integration and coordination between developers and operations teams. Instead of developers testing their code and "throwing it across the fence" for operations to do the deployment and monitoring, modern software teams have dedicated DevOps members be part of the agile teams who work on making sure the code from developers is validated and deployed correctly. Traditionally, managing dependencies of libraries in software is a nightmare for DevOps. Developers always point out the fact that "it works on my machine" and now it's up to DevOps to make it work on the staging or production machine.

Containerized applications are lifesavers for DevOps. Since along with code, we package the app server with the right version, all the dependent libraries with the right version and even the OS, we are almost guaranteed to have the code working exactly the same way it worked on the developer's machine in the staging and production environments. We don't just deploy code anymore—we deploy fully tested environments, thus making DevOps much easier and potentially fully automated. This is the major advantage of a containerized apps drive.

A second, equally important advantage of containerization is that we can quickly (in a matter of milliseconds) spin off thousands of containers in parallel without running out of resources. Resources don't get allocated in advance to containers and only get assigned when the container does some work. This shared resource model greatly helps in improving performance of applications by running them in parallel. As long as we have a good tool to schedule containers in parallel, we can run our applications at scale, talking full advantage of parallel computing.

In the last couple of years, PaaS is actively being replaced or extended by the *Container-as-a-Service* (CaaS) model. This is similar to PaaS but instead of sending a JAR file to PaaS, we point the CaaS engine to our container published to a registry like DockerHub. The CaaS engine pulls the image, deploys it, and instantiates the container in a standard runtime like Docker. The container is a fully self-contained entity with the right OS version, system libraries, web server, and all other dependencies. It can be configured to bring up your application when it starts and also to monitor if the application goes down and restart it. The entire application lifecycle is managed inside the container, which gives developers way more flexibility than with a dependency-heavy JAR file. It also gives many more insights and visibility to DevOps in terms of logging and monitoring the applications.

As CaaS is getting popular, a new complementary approach to building software applications in the Cloud is coming into prominence, called *microservices*. Using microservices architecture, a new breed of applications are being developed from the start with the Cloud in mind. These are called *Cloud-native applications*.

Microservices Architecture with Containers

Along with the move to data centers and public Clouds, architecture of software applications was also being simplified to a great extent with new styles. Software applications were traditionally developed in tiered architectures like Model-View-Controller (MVC) with strict separation of data structures, view generation logic, and controller to integrate the two. However, these applications were developed in silos, with a very limited focus on the domains that a particular application would serve. For example, a company would have a very elegantly structured maintenance management application, but it would not be able to communicate effectively to another application like inventory management. Organizations undertook huge implementations of Enterprise Resource Planning (ERP) systems to try to have different parts of the organization communicate effectively with each other.

This drive to remove monolithic applications operating in silos led to development of an architecture style or pattern called *Services Oriented Architecture* (SOA). The goal of SOA was to find data and functionality that could be shared between monolithic applications and help them integrate better.

The focus of SOA was to enable interoperability between systems. Expert software architects started identifying integration points between systems and defining *services* that enabled the sharing of data and functionality. The key challenge was to manage the lifecycle of these services and provide an easy way for them to communicate smartly. This requirement led to development of *Enterprise Service Bus* (ESB) products.

An ESB would provide a way to host services from multiple separate products and drive communication between them using common protocols like HTTP or messaging. Also, a key thing that ESB provided was the ability to store *Enterprise Integration Patterns* (EIP) in the integration layer rather than storing these in individual services. So the services could be developed generically and all the smarts in the communication was encapsulated in the ESB.

An example of such an EIP is content-based routing, where, based on the content of a message (like a mobile SMS), the request will have to be passed on to the appropriate service. This logic of processing the message and directing output to the appropriate service was managed by the ESB. An example of this is your mobile provider sending an SMS asking for feedback and you replying with 1 for positive and 2 for negative.

The goal was to minimally change the monolithic applications and capture the integration patterns and store them in the ESB. ESB has services communicating over a message broker.

With the focus on Cloud computing, there was a change in philosophy of how services would be developed and implemented. Unlike the SOA focus to integrate monolithic applications, a new architecture style started to emerge, called *microservices*. The idea of microservices is to have self-contained services that can be scaled and managed independently. Unlike SOA, there was not a focus on integrating monolithic applications, but the focus was on breaking silos and distributing functionality into smaller components. The idea was to modify applications with a focus on hosting in the Cloud and taking advantage of the distributed nature of Cloud computing.

For example, let's consider a huge shopping application that would handle all features like searching for a product, finding cost, and completing the purchase. In a microservices architecture, each functionality would be distributed to a separate microservice. The search microservice will fully own the capability of the system to provide the search UI to users, run the query, and show the results. An ideal microservice will be self-contained. So our search microservice will manage the UI shown to users and will most likely have an optimized database of products specifically for search. If a new feature needs to be added, such as a photo-based search, that would be owned and implemented by the team owning this search microservice. It will have its own codebase, test scripts, and release cycle. Also, if we saw that search was getting slow, then this search microservice could be scaled independently from 50 to 100 nodes to double its performance.

This microservice architecture leads to a highly loosely coupled architecture. Also, team structure can be customized to provide developer, tester, and DevOps resources based on specific functionalities. Many companies are starting to adopt the microservices way of developing Cloud applications. Also, we saw earlier CI/CD pipelines for software applications. We can have independent CI/CD pipelines and releases for microservices so that key functionalities can be released faster. What microservices gets us thinking about is loosely coupled applications. So if the search feature needs a quick functionality improvement, this can be implemented in that microservice without affecting others.

Earlier we saw how containers help build independent components of your software with all dependencies. As you can see, containers are tailor-made to fit the microservices model. You can package a microservice as a container and deploy it into a CaaS ecosystem, which can manage scaling and management of the independent microservice. Just as we saw it's easy and fast to scale a single container into thousands of instances, the same can be done with a microservice packaged as a container.

Revisiting the earlier search microservice of the shopping application—if we know that during Christmas or Diwali holidays, the search queries are going to double or triple, then we can scale the containers appropriately to handle this load. This independent scalability is just one of the many benefits the microservices architecture drives.

Now this brings us to the main topic of the chapter and I hope you have been waiting for it—Kubernetes. The next section explains how Kubernetes provides a CaaS framework for deploying microservices and helps take care of infrastructure concerns for the application. In the final part of this chapter, we cover some basic Kubernetes commands for configuring your own application packaged as containers.

Kubernetes: A CaaS Solution for Infrastructure Concerns

Kubernetes is basically a Container-as-a-Service platform. For one, it allows us to deploy applications packaged as containers and scale them independently. However, it does a lot more than that. The key thing that Kubernetes brings is that it takes care of many of the infrastructure concerns for applications. Before we build applications on Kubernetes, let's quickly look at the Kubernetes architecture and its key abstractions like pods, deployments, and services. I explain these concepts at a high level and show some examples. For more details, I recommend looking at the `Kubernetes.io` site, which has some excellent material, and also finding online examples you can try out. I provide some good articles on this in the "References" section at the end of the book.

Also, I will provide commands that you can run in a Kubernetes environment. To run these commands, you can either have a server-based or Cloud-hosted Kubernetes instance and connect to it. You could have a local installation on a single node on your laptop. This single-node installation is a separate product called a *Minikube*. The beauty of Kubernetes is that all the commands and containers you run on a single-node Minikube can be pretty much run on a cluster with hundreds of nodes.

This works even for the multi-node cluster you may have that is running on a server (on-premise) or on a public Cloud (hosted). Kubernetes was initially developed by Google and made open source. Hence, GCP has built-in support for Kubernetes and you can log in to GCP and quickly start a Kubernetes cluster and connect to it remotely. Internally GCP will manage the nodes, which are the virtual machine parts of the cluster—very similar to a PaaS setup. AWS and Microsoft have also recently started supporting hosted Kubernetes clusters. Kubernetes has definitely emerged as the technology of choice for managing containerized applications on a cluster.

To get familiar with it, I recommend installing Minikube on your laptop. It creates a single-node cluster where you can deploy containers. This single node acts as the master and the slave. The master controls the slave and gets jobs scheduled. Here all that is done on single machine. You can install it on Windows, Linux, or MacOS using the installation steps at the Kubernetes.io website.

Internally, this creates a virtual machine for the node, which has a dedicated IP address and network stack. You can use any virtualization engine like VMWare or VirtualBox for this. Kubernetes will connect to the virtualization engine and create a VM internally. You don't need to do anything to manage this VM. Table 7.1 lists some handy Minikube commands to make note of.

Table 7.1: Some Useful Minikube Commands

COMMAND	ACTION
`$ minikube start`	Starts the Minikube single-node cluster by initializing the VM.
`$ minikube status`	Shows the status of your Minikube cluster, if it is running.
`$ minikube stop`	Stops the cluster and shuts down the VM.
`$ minikube ip`	Gets the IP address of the virtual machine of your single-node cluster.
`$ minikube ssh`	SSHs to the single node of your minikube cluster. After SSH, you will see a big Minikube logo and then run commands like `ls`, `pwd`, and `ifconfig`. You can see with `ifconfig` that this VM has a totally separate network stack than your machine where Minikube is installed.

Kubernetes is a CaaS platform, so it lets you define containers for your application or microservice and manage the lifecycle of these. It follows a master-slave architecture pattern with slaves making their storage, memory, and CPUs available to do work and masters controlling data and jobs on slaves. The workers in Kubernetes are called *nodes*, which can be physical or virtual machines. Each node runs the container agent and can spin up containers. However, all this is hidden from the users. There are commands to see the cluster details, but typically you deal with abstractions pertaining to your application.

Once you have a local Minikube cluster or a Cloud- or server-hosted Kubernetes cluster, you can connect to resources of this cluster. One of the salient features of Kubernetes is that it exposes an extendable Application Programming Interface (API). You can connect to the Kubernetes cluster with this API and access and modify resources. This is a very uniform way of interacting with the Kubernetes system. As new resources like custom objects and data sources get added to Kubernetes, we can still access these with the same API commands.

The tool that invokes these API commands and allows us to interact with the Kubernetes cluster is called Kubectl. Kubectl can be installed on your machine and you can connect to local or remote clusters. Table 7.2 lists some essential Kubectl commands.

Table 7.2: Useful Kubectl Commands to Access Local and Remote Kubernetes Cluster Resources Through APIs

COMMAND	ACTION
`$ kubectl cluster-info`	Gets the information of the cluster, like the master node URL.
`$ kubectl get nodes`	Shows all nodes in the cluster. For Minikube, that will be a single node acting as the master and worker.
`$ kubectl get pods`	General `get` command to get Kubernetes resources, in this case pods. Here it will list all pods. We will talk about pods in this section.

Although nodes are workers in a Kubernetes cluster, we don't usually deal directly with them. Kubernetes provides a set of abstractions to run your applications on a cluster. These abstractions manage how the jobs get scheduled on nodes—saving you that effort. The key abstraction in Kubernetes is called a *pod*. A pod contains one or more containers and these share CPU, storage, and networks with each other. You will typically package your application as a single container and abstract it as a pod. Docker is the most popular container engine but Kubernetes supports others and is not tied to Docker. Each pod has an IP address associated with it. A pod is what is scheduled by Kubernetes on the different nodes. You don't have to bother with where these pods run eventually, thus freeing you from the scaling concerns.

Pods are typically not commissioned on their own. We use a higher-level abstraction called a *deployment* to create pods. A deployment is the most common type of resource in a Kubernetes cluster. It defines the pod structure, what container(s) it consists of, and the number of replicas you need. The Kubernetes scheduler creates the right number of pods and runs them on specific nodes based on resource availability. You can specify pod-creation policies; for example, create at least one instance of the pod on each node. Deployments can be created using the `kubectl run` command or by specifying a YAML file. YAML files are markup text files that specify details of the Kubernetes resource you are trying to build.

Let's look at an example of a very simple application packaged as a container and deployed on Kubernetes. I will not focus on packaging of the application right now but more on deploying on Kubernetes and scaling. In Chapter 8, titled "Deploying AI Models as Microservices," I show examples of building a web application, containerizing, and deploying at scale. For now, I will use a test web application image that I created and uploaded to a common Docker registry called DockerHub (`https://hub.docker.com`). The image is called `dattarajrao/simple-app`. It's a simple web app that displays an index page with a message in the browser. Listing 7.1 shows the deployment YAML file that creates a deployment with a Docker image.

Listing 7.1: Simple YAML File to Deploy a Web Application (simple-app.yaml)

```
apiVersion: apps/v1
kind: Deployment
metadata:
  name: simple-app-deployment
  labels:
    app: simple-app
spec:
  replicas: 1
  selector:
    matchLabels:
      app: simple-app
```

```
  template:
    metadata:
      labels:
        app: simple-app
    spec:
      containers:
      - name: simple-app
        image: dattarajrao/simple-app
        ports:
        - containerPort: 80
```

Now let's look at the steps for running this YAML file and creating a deployment. As discussed earlier, a deployment will create pods that will contain the instance of the container or our application. See Listing 7.2.

Listing 7.2: Deploy the YAML File

```
$ kubectl create -f simple-app.yaml
deployment.apps/simple-app-deployment created
```

This code creates a deployment with the YAML file. It creates a pod with a container specified by the `dattarajrao/simple-app` image:

```
$ kubectl get deployments
NAME                    DESIRED   CURRENT   UP-TO-DATE   AVAILABLE   AGE
simple-app-deployment   1         1         1            1           41s
```

The deployment is a resource you can get using the API.

```
$ kubectl get pods
NAME                                     READY    STATUS    RESTART   AGE
simple-app-deployment-98f597cdb-dtplp   1/1      Running   0           1m
```

This command gets the pod created by this deployment. In this case, it's just 1. Listing 7.3 scales the deployment resource with three replicas. Now it will create three pods.

Listing 7.3: Scale Resources

```
$ kubectl scale deployment simple-app-deployment --replicas=3
deployment.extensions/simple-app-deployment scaled
```

You can check to see if this is the case using the following command.

```
$ kubectl get pods
NAME                                     READY    STATUS    RESTART   AGE
simple-app-deployment-98f597cdb-dtplp   1/1      Running   0           2m
simple-app-deployment-98f597cdb-kch76   1/1      Running   0           7s
simple-app-deployment-98f597cdb-wgpq9   1/1      Running   0           7s
```

Now scale the deployment resource with three replicas. Now it will create three pods.

Listing 7.4 shows how to delete a pod manually. Now the deployment should re-create this pod.

Listing 7.4: Demonstration of Reliability: Bringing Up Failed Pod

```
$ kubectl delete pod simple-app-deployment-98f597cdb-dtplp

pod "simple-app-deployment-98f597cdb-dtplp" deleted
$ kubectl get pods

NAME                                   READY     STATUS    RESTART   AGE
simple-app-deployment-98f597cdb-kch76  1/1       Running   0           6m
simple-app-deployment-98f597cdb-pj7pd  1/1       Running   0           4s
simple-app-deployment-98f597cdb-wgpq9  1/1       Running   0           6m
```

The new pod is created with a new ID. Deployment takes care of restarting the needed pods when they go down:

```
$ kubectl describe pod simple-app-deployment-98f597cdb-kch76

Name:            simple-app-deployment-98f597cdb-kch76
Namespace:       default
Node:            minikube/172.17.0.7
Start Time:      Tue, 13 Nov 2018 13:22:12 +0000
Labels:          app=simple-app
                 pod-template-hash=549153786
Annotations:     <none>
Status:          Running
IP:              172.18.0.5
Controlled By:   ReplicaSet/simple-app-deployment-98f597cdb
Containers:
  simple-app:
    Container ID:
docker://e203d9037001a44e5c3b0b93945c0d06f48be29538fabe41be012e9c7757a56b
    Image:          dattarajrao/simple-app
    Image ID:       docker-pullable://dattarajrao/simple-app@sha256:e670
81c7658e7035eab97014fb00e789ddee3df48d9f92aaacf1206ab2783543
    Port:           80/TCP
    Host Port:      0/TCP
    State:          Running
      Started:      Tue, 13 Nov 2018 13:22:15 +0000
    Ready:          True
    Restart Count:  0
```

The description of the pod shows details like the image used, the IP address, and interesting log messages. We won't go through them in detail, but you can debug many problems by looking at this log and getting more logs using the `– kubectl logs <podname>` command.

In Listing 7.2, we saw an example of scaling a deployment by increasing the number of pods. Kubernetes will internally decide which nodes to run these pods on and that is totally agnostic to you. In case of Minikube, of course, all pods run on the same node. We also saw how we can manually terminate a pod and Kubernetes automatically starts it back up. This will happen if your application terminates during its run due to bad data or network issues. When the application packaged into a pod terminates, the deployment will automatically bring it back up. This is the reliability concern that is taken care of by Kubernetes. Reliability for applications deals with failure and being able to restart after a failure. If the application can be somehow restarted quickly after a failure, that will greatly improve the reliability.

You see that the pods created through deployments may get any ID, which can keep changing as pods are deleted and re-created. The IP address assigned to the pod also changes. Kubernetes manages the lifecycle of these pods. So how do we let clients call our application without specifying the absolute name or IP address of the pods? This is handled by the networking concern of the application. Networking is handled by another abstraction on top of deployment, called a *service.*

Let's look at an example of creating a service for our deployment and using this service by our clients. Listing 7.5 shows the YAML for this.

Listing 7.5: Simple YAML File with Service for Earlier App (simple-app-service.yaml)

```
kind: Service
apiVersion: v1
metadata:
  name: simple-app-service
spec:
  selector:
    app: simple-app
  ports:
  - protocol: TCP
    port: 80
    targetPort: 80
```

Now let's look at the steps for deploying this YAML file in the Kubernetes environment and creating a service. We will then use the networking features of the service to call the pods from a URL. See Listing 7.6.

Listing 7.6: Deploy the Service YAML File

```
$ kubectl create -f simple-app-service.yaml
service/simple-app-service created
```

This creates a service with YAML file. Now let's get to the details of the service:

```
$ kubectl get service
NAME                 TYPE        CLUSTER-IP     EXTERNAL-IP   PORT(S)   AGE
kubernetes           ClusterIP   10.96.0.1      <none>        443/TCP   47m
simple-app-service   ClusterIP   10.109.89.2    <none>        80/TCP    9s
```

By default, the environment has a Kubernetes service and now our `simple-app-service` has been added. It's the default type of cluster IP, meaning a unique IP address is assigned to the cluster. This service can be accessed using this IP address. Other types of services may be NodePort, where an instance is created on each node, and LoadBalancer, where a separate IP address is assigned.

Our service points to the deployment we created earlier—by the `app` field in the YAML. So, when we access the service using its URL, Kubernetes automatically directs those requests to different pods that are part of the deployment app. Multiple requests get load balanced, depending on the number of pods the application is scaled to. In this way, the load balancing concern is handled.

Finally, let's call our service. We will not use a fancy client, but just use a `CURL` command to get the HTML content. See Listing 7.7.

Listing 7.7: Calling Our Newly Created Service

```
$ curl 10.109.89.2
<html>
<title>
  Sample application by Dattaraj Rao
</title>
<body>
  <h3>Simple docker application - Hello World!</h3>
  <b>by Dattaraj Rao - for Keras 2 Kubernetes.</b>
</body>
</html>
```

We got the cluster IP of our service and call this using the `CURL` command. The `CURL` command basically gets the HTTP response from the URL. As we saw earlier, the request gets routed to the pods that are part of the deployment. This HTML looks like Figure 7.6 in a web browser.

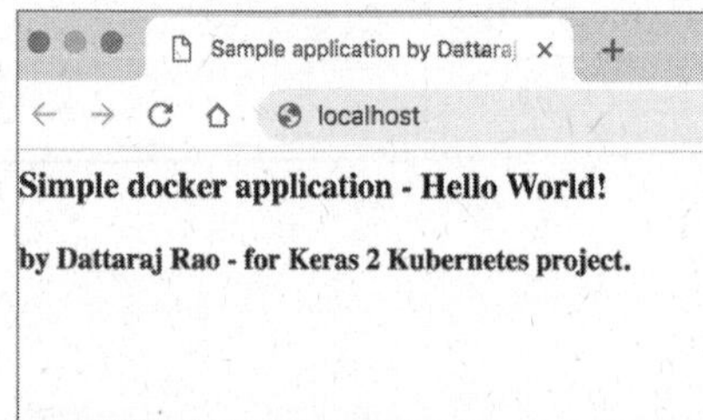

Figure 7.6: The simple application shown in a browser

Summary

In this chapter, we took a break from Machine Learning and looked at how software applications are developed. We saw the rise of Cloud computing and the rise of paradigms like IaaS, PaaS, SaaS, and the new CaaS. We saw a history of software applications with the emergence of architecture patterns like Services Oriented Architecture (SOA) and microservices. We also looked at packaging software applications into containers and building microservices.

Then we spent considerable time looking at the Kubernetes platform. We saw how Kubernetes allows deployment of applications packaged as containers at scale. We learned how Kubernetes manages infrastructure concerns like scaling, fail-over, reliability, load-balancing, and networking. We saw an example of deploying a web application on Kubernetes.

In the next chapter, we look at the Machine Learning model development cycle and how the software development architectures and practices we studied in this chapter apply there. Then we will take the Keras model we developed earlier and deploy it as a microservice on Kubernetes.

CHAPTER

8

Deploying AI Models as Microservices

In the previous chapter, we talked about Cloud computing, containers, and microservices. We saw how Kubernetes extends beyond a Container-as-as-Service (CaaS) platform into a full ecosystem for deploying software applications packaged as microservices. We also saw an example of deploying an application on Kubernetes by using abstractions like pods, deployments, and services.

In this chapter, we get into some more details of building applications using Kubernetes. We build a simple web application using Python, package it as a Docker container, and deploy to a Kubernetes cluster. Then we modify this application to actually invoke a Deep Learning model and show the results on a web page. Here we start connecting the Keras and Kubernetes worlds together. We see how to build production-quality Deep Learning applications, thus combining the best of these two technologies.

Building a Simple Microservice with Docker and Kubernetes

Let's get started by building a simple microservice application and then packaging it into a container. The idea of microservices is that the application is self-contained so it can be deployed and scaled independently as a container instance. First, our application will only show a simple message by reading a text string. We will later do some processing on that text string.

We will use Python to build this web application. Python was traditionally used more for scripting and data science applications. However, in recent years, it has gained huge popularity in developing all sorts of software, including web applications. Many web application frameworks are available that work on Python and help you quickly build the applications. Some of these are Django and Flask, which we will use.

Instead of Python, you can build web applications in languages like Java and NodeJS (JavaScript). Whatever the language, you will need some framework that will form the backbone of your application. The most popular frameworks for NodeJS and Java (as of 2018) are ExpressJS and Spring, respectively. These web app frameworks take care of a lot of the underlying details of building your application and communication over HTTP. Ultimately, you end up writing very basic and focused code specific to your application and don't have to worry about the plumbing for the whole app.

Let's look at an example in Python. You will need Python 2.7 (or above) or Python 3.3 (or above) installed. Most modern machines will have Python installed. You can download from `python.org` if not already installed. We will install the `Flask` web framework using the Python package installer—*pip*. You will also need docker engine that can be installed from `docker.com`. The commands in Listing 8.1 will enable you to check your environment for necessary installations, including Python, Flask, and Docker. We will also create a new folder with the name of your app (such as `simple-app`) and run commands to build a basic skeleton for the app. We will add details in next sections.

Listing 8.1: Commands to Get Started, Run in an Empty Folder

```
$ python --version
$ pip install -U Flask
$ docker --version
$ touch app.py requirements.txt Dockerfile
```

The `touch` command at end of Listing 8.1 creates empty files that serve as a skeleton for our web app. We create three files in this example. Let's look at what each file will contain:

- `app.py`: Main application logic in Python. Create the HTTP endpoints for the app.
- `requirements.txt`: Contains Python libraries that are dependencies for this app.
- `Dockerfile`: Contain instructions to package the app into a Docker container.

Now let's populate these three files with the logic of our app. We will start with the `app.py` file containing the application that we will develop. Our application will have some *boilerplate* code that will be needed to use the Flask framework. I will highlight it so you can just copy it directly. We will create an HTTP endpoint that will respond to incoming requests from clients. Clients will use a web browser to make HTTP GET or POST calls to our endpoint and it will respond as per the code we add. This will be the logic of our web application. Listing 8.2 shows the Python file we open in a text editor. The lines starting with # are comments.

Listing 8.2: Python Code for Web Application (app.py)

```
#### Boilerplate code - 1 #####
# import Flask library
from flask import Flask
from flask import request

# create the Flask app
app = Flask(__name__)
#### Boilerplate code - 1 #####

# build a function to act as Route / HTTP endpoint
@app.route('/hello')
def hello():
    return 'Hello, World!'

#### Boilerplate code - 2 #####
# main application run code
if __name__ == '__main__':
    app.run(debug=False,host='0.0.0.0',port=1234)
#### Boilerplate code - 2 #####
```

Listing 8.3 shows contents of the `requirements.txt` file. We have to add the libraries we need as dependencies. Here we need Flask for running our web application. We also include TensorFlow and Keras. These libraries will be used in the future when we add the DL code. We can update versions to the latest ones we use.

Listing 8.3: Contents of the requirements.txt File

```
Flask==1.0.2
tensorflow==1.9.0
Keras==2.1.6
```

Our microservice application will have a single HTTP endpoint, which will respond with a `Hello World!` message. We can test our application by running the Python interpreter on it and seeing the result in a web browser, as shown in Listing 8.4.

Listing 8.4: Running app.py and Testing It in a Browser

```
$ python app.py
* Running on http://0.0.0.0:1234/ (Press CTRL+C to quit)
```

You may be asked to allow permission to open ports on your machine. This is basically opening an HTTP protocol port and listening to messages coming in on this port. When new messages come from clients on this port, the function code is invoked and we will get a nice return message.

Figure 8.1 shows what you will see in a browser by opening `http://localhost:1234/hello`.

Figure 8.1: What you see in the browser

Now we will add a new HTTP endpoint called `process` to read a text parameter. Here is the application logic we will have. When no parameter is passed, we will show a simple HTML page with a big textbox (a `TEXTAREA` in HTML terms). We will have an HTML `SUBMIT` button so that we can submit the text back to the same `process` endpoint. Now when the form is submitted with a value for the `TEXTAREA` parameter (`text_input`), we will just display this on-screen. That's it.

Keep in mind, in real-world HTML you will use *stylesheets* to beautify this page and keep this HTML code in separate files called *templates*. Also, you will normally have multiple pages, one for showing input forms and one for submission results.

However, to keep the logic crisp and simple we have a single block of code. Let's look at the new code we add to our `app.py` file. In Listing 8.5, I show the full code for `app.py`, but the older code is grayed out so you can focus on the new code only. Listing 8.6 shows running the new `app.py` file.

Listing 8.5: Update app.py to Include New HTTP Endpoint to Process Text

```
#### Boilerplate code - 1 #####
# import Flask library
from flask import Flask
from flask import request

# create the Flask app
app = Flask(__name__)
#### Boilerplate code - 1 #####

# build a route or HTTP endpoint
@app.route('/hello')
```

```
def hello():
    return 'Hello World!'

##### New Code #####
# default HTML to show at first when no input is sent
htmlDefault = '<h4>Simple Python NLP demo</h4><form><textarea rows=10
cols=100 name=\'text_input\'></textarea><br><input type=submit></form>'

# build a route or HTTP endpoint
# this route will read text parameter and analyze it
@app.route('/process')
def process():
    # get the HTTP parameter by name 'text_input'
    in_text = request.args.get('text_input')

    # if input is provided process else show default page
    if in_text is not None:
        # just show
        return 'You typed: <b>%s</b>'%(in_text)
    else:
        return htmlDefault
##### New Code #####

#### Boilerplate code - 2 #####
# main application run code
if __name__ == '__main__':
    app.run(debug=False,host='0.0.0.0',port=1234)
#### Boilerplate code - 2 #####
```

Listing 8.6: Running the New app.py and Testing It in a Browser

```
$ python app.py
* Running on http://0.0.0.0:1234/ (Press CTRL+C to quit)
```

In your web browser, go to `http://localhost:1234/process` and you should see something similar to Figure 8.2.

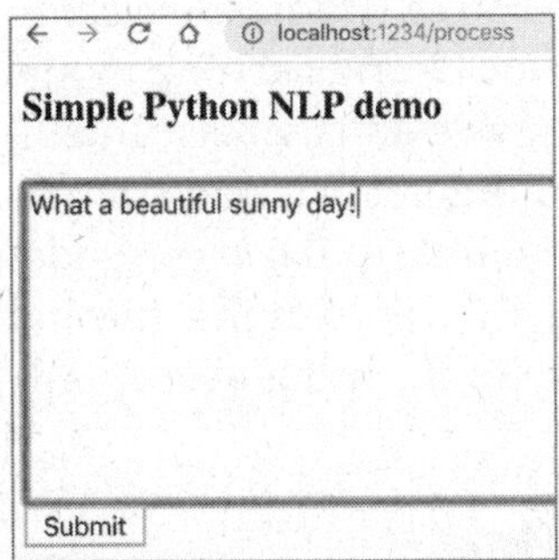

Figure 8.2: The new app.py file shown in a browser

Enter the text and press Submit. You will get the page shown in Figure 8.3.

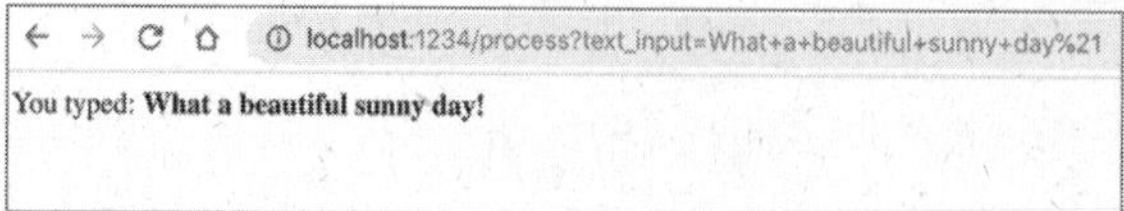

Figure 8.3: The result after pressing Submit

You can see that the text you entered was submitted to the endpoint as a parameter named `text_input` (the name you gave the HTML `TEXTAREA` field). Of course, the text is actually modified to replace spaces and commas so that it can be transmitted over HTTP properly. However, it is decoded and shown as HTML inside the bold `<B>` tag on the results page.

Adding AI Smarts to Your App

So, there we have it—we developed a new application to process text inputs. We are not yet processing any text inputs. Let's process our text using the Natural Language Processing (NLP) sentiment analysis model we created earlier in Python and Keras. If you remember from Chapter 5 ("Advanced Deep Learning"), we used Keras to build a recurrent neural network using LSTM layers. This model was trained on samples of positive and negative sentiment texts. We will now use that model in this web application.

The NLP model was saved as an H5 binary file. We will load this in Keras at the beginning when our web application loads. This instance of the model is saved in memory as long as the application is running. If we scale this application on three real or virtual machines, each machine will have an instance of the model and make predictions in its own process and memory space. That's how scaling will help Deep Learning models. We do not bog down a single node's resources but distribute our workloads to multiple machines.

Listing 8.7 shows the code to load the model and we will create a function in Python that will process the text you provide and return a 0 (a positive sentiment) or 1 (a negative sentiment). So after we apply this Deep Learning model to our text in the web application, we will be able to have an Artificial Intelligence system that can read text input and tell us if your intention is good or bad.

First, we need to place the `imdb_nlp.h5` binary model file in the same folder as our `app.py` file. The Python code shown in Listing 8.7 will load this file and create a function that we can call to get the sentiment of the input text. Again, I will highlight the new code; older code is in gray.

Listing 8.7: Update app.py to Load NLP Model and Function to Process Text

```
#### Boilerplate code - 1 #####
# import Flask library
```

```
from flask import Flask
from flask import request

# create the Flask app
app = Flask(__name__)
#### Boilerplate code - 1 #####

#### Code to load NLP Model and prepare function ####
from keras.preprocessing import sequence
from keras.models import load_model
from keras.preprocessing.text import text_to_word_sequence
from keras.datasets import imdb
import numpy as np

# maximum words in each sentence
maxlen = 10

# get the word index from imdb dataset
word_index = imdb.get_word_index()

# load the Model from file
nlp_model = load_model('imdb_nlp.h5')

# method that does the prediction - we will call this later
def predict_sentiment(my_test):
    # tokenize the sentence
    word_sequence = text_to_word_sequence(my_test)

    # create a blank sequence of integers
    int_sequence = []

    # for each word in the sentence
    for w in word_sequence:
        # get the integer from vocabulary and add to list
        int_sequence.append(word_index[w])

    # pad the sequence of numbers to input size expected by model
   sent_test = sequence.pad_sequences([int_sequence],
        maxlen=maxlen)

    # make a prediction using our Model
    y_pred = nlp_model.predict(sent_test)

    # return a predicted sentiment real value between 0 and 1
    return y_pred[0][0]

#### Code to load NLP Model and prepare function ####

# build a route or HTTP endpoint
@app.route('/hello')
def hello():
    return 'Hello World!'
```

```
##### Code #####
# default HTML to show at first when no input is sent

htmlDefault = '<h4>Simple Python NLP demo</h4><b>Type some text to 
analyze its sentiment using Deep Learning</b><br><form><textarea rows=10 
cols=100 name=\'text_input\'></textarea><br><input type=submit></form>'

# build a route or HTTP endpoint
# this route will read text parameter and analyze it
@app.route('/process')
def process():
    # define returning HTML
    retHTML = ''

    # get the HTTP parameter by name 'text_input'
    in_text = request.args.get('text_input')

    # if input is provided process else show default page
    if in_text is not None:
        # first show what was typed
        retHTML += 'TEXT: <b>%s</b>'%(in_text)
        # run the deep learning Model
        result = predict_sentiment(in_text)
        # if positive sentiment
        if result > 0.5:
        # if negative sentiment
            retHTML += '<h4>Positive Sentiment! :-)</h4><br>'
        else:
            retHTML += '<h4>Negative Sentiment! :-(</h4><br>'

        # just show
        return retHTML
    else:
        return htmlDefault

##### New Code #####

#### Boilerplate code - 2 #####
# main application run code
if __name__ == '__main__':
    app.run(debug=False,host='0.0.0.0',port=1234)
#### Boilerplate code - 2 #####
```

Take a moment to go through the code in Listing 8.7. It builds on the code we have been developing for our test web app. We take the input from the HTML form as an `in_text` variable as we saw earlier. But instead of simply writing that back, we feed that to a newly created function called `predict_sentiment`. This function calls our NLP model already loaded from a binary file. The function converts our text sequence to a sequence of integers using the same vocabulary we used for the training data.

As a reminder, the vocabulary is basically a list of all words in your domain with an integer. Typically, this integer value corresponds to how often this word appears in your list of documents. So the most common words will have a lower integer value, while less frequent words will have higher ones. The vocabulary we use is built from the IMDB dataset that Keras provides for testing our NLP models.

We have a new route called `process`, which is mapped to the HTTP endpoint with the same name. Here we take the input text passed on to our HTML form and pass that to the function. Depending on the output of our NLP model, we determine if it's a negative sentiment (output > 0.5) or a positive one (output < 0.5). Keep in mind that the model is only as good as the training data we provide. Our training data is from the IMDB movie review text database and we choose the first 10 words of the review to classify the sentiment. The accuracy will increase if you use more words or use a bigger text database. For now, Listing 8.8 shows the results.

Listing 8.8: Results of the New App in Web Browser

```
$ python app.py
* Running on http://0.0.0.0:1234/ (Press CTRL+C to quit)
```

In your web browser, go to `http://localhost:1234/process`. You should see the image shown in Figure 8.4.

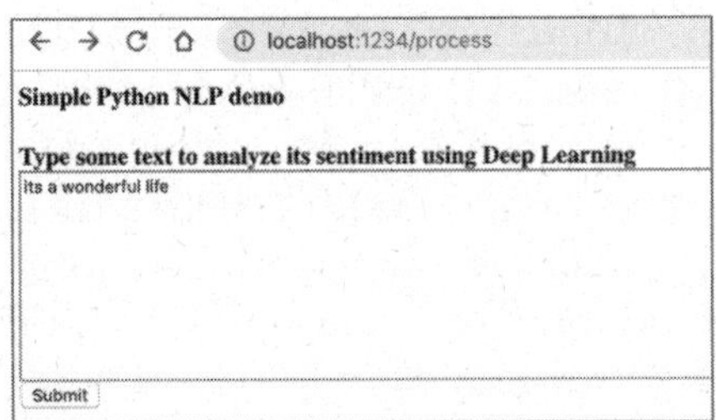

Figure 8.4: The new app demo in the browser

Type in a phrase and click Submit. Here we typed the phrase "its a wonderful life." Figure 8.5 shows the result.

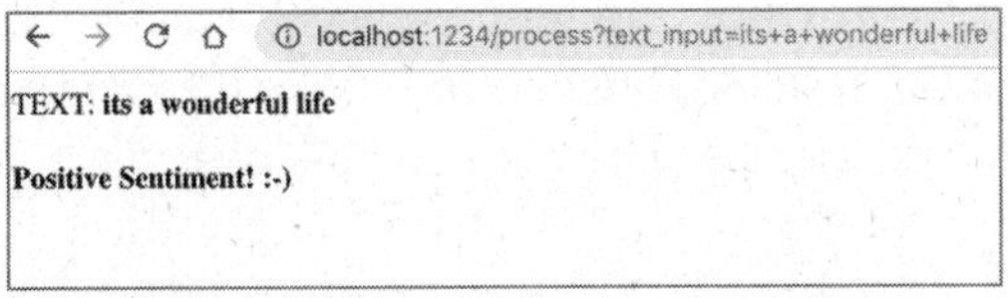

localhost:1234/process?text_input=its+a+wonderful+life

TEXT: **its a wonderful life**

Positive Sentiment! :-)

Figure 8.5: What you get after pressing Submit

That's it—this simple app reads your text and tells you what sentiment the phrase shows. Let's try another example, shown first in Figures 8.6 and 8.7.

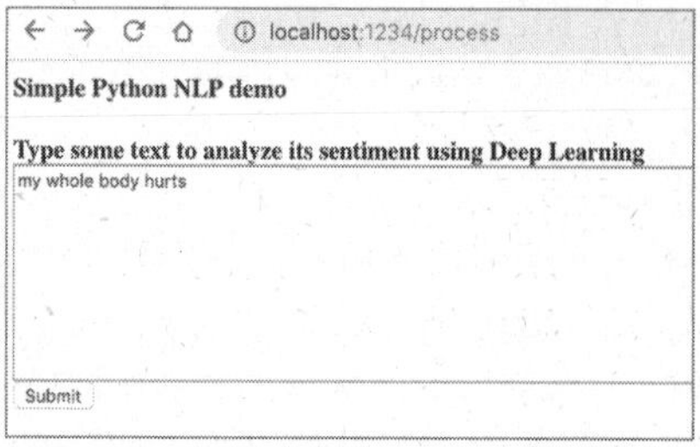

localhost:1234/process

Simple Python NLP demo

Type some text to analyze its sentiment using Deep Learning

my whole body hurts

Submit

Figure 8.6: Entering a new phrase

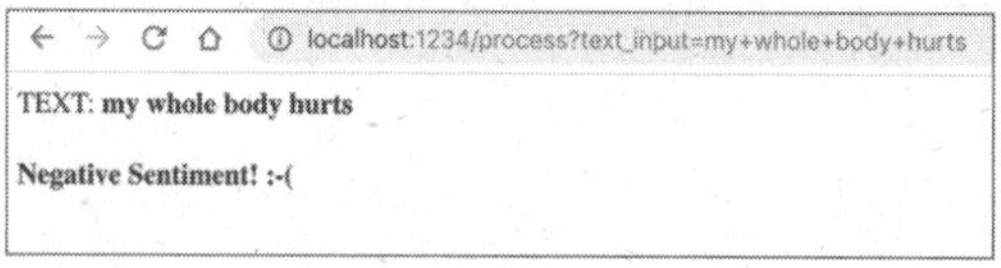

localhost:1234/process?text_input=my+whole+body+hurts

TEXT: my whole body hurts

Negative Sentiment! :-(

Figure 8.7: This one results in a negative result

You can try different phrases. The program is not guaranteed to get it right, but as you build better models, you will see the accuracy increase a great deal.

There you have it. You have developed a Natural Language Processing (NLP) model using Keras. This was a recurrent neural network model using LSTM layers. We trained this model on the publicly available IMDB movie reviews dataset for sentiment analysis. We got an accuracy of 95% on the training data and 70% on the validation set. We saved this model as an H5 file in HDF5 format.

We created a Python web application using the Flask framework. The application showed an HTML form where we could input text data and this would be sent to our application. When we get this data through our HTTP endpoint, we run the NLP model on this text and predict the sentiment. Based on the prediction, we tell the user if it's a positive or negative sentiment.

This is just a basic application. You can use the wonders of CSS and JavaScript to make this fancy, with special types of widgets for inputting and displaying data. Maybe instead of a bland text message, you want to show smileys with happy and sad emotions after submission. Maybe you want to process the text in real time as keys are entered into the textbox. As long as you have a solid Deep Learning model and a good connection established to invoke it from the HTML data, you can explore all these outcomes. The code in this chapter has hopefully given you the framework for building such awesome applications!

Packaging the App as a Container

Now let's build a Docker container with our app. If you remember, the Docker container will be holistic with the AI model, our source code, the application server, and the operating system. Of course, these will not be encapsulated into the container but referenced as individual *layers*.

First, we will fill the `requirements.txt` file with any dependencies we want to install when we build our container. In this case, we have Flask as the dependency we need to build the web application. We also need TensorFlow and Keras to run our Deep Learning model. Let's include these. You can provide a version for these libraries, or the latest version will be deployed. It is usually recommended to use the same version of libraries that you have tested on to avoid any surprises. To get the current version of the library that you have installed, you can run the following command: `pip freeze`.

Listing 8.9 shows the `requirements.txt` file.

Listing 8.9: Python Dependencies to Be Installed (requirements.txt)

```
Flask==1.0.2
tensorflow==1.9.0
Keras==2.1.6
```

Now we will populate the Dockerfile with the following instructions. You can find these instructions for other platforms like NodeJS and Java on the Internet. These are instructions we will use for Python. As we saw earlier, the Dockerfile has to be in the same folder as our `app.py` file.

The Dockerfile will have a set of commands to create your application environment from scratch. You can run this on any machine and the exact same Docker container will be created, and your app will run inside this environment. This is the power of Docker. Since you are building the whole environment from scratch you can be sure all dependencies will be taken care of. Again, in reality the whole installation does not occur, but layers are incrementally added to build the environment. Inside the Dockerfile, you will see Linux-like commands and lines starting with a hash (#), which are the comments.

Let's go through the steps for building this container—see Listing 8.10.

Listing 8.10: Script for Packaging Our App as a Container in a Dockerfile

```
# Docker file for simple NLP app
# Author: Dattaraj J Rao
# For Book: Keras2Kubernetes
```

```
# Start with latest Ubuntu image
FROM ubuntu:latest

# Install latest updates
RUN apt-get update -y

# Install Python and build libraries
RUN apt-get install -y python-pip python-dev build-essential

# Copy all files from current folder (.) to container's folder (.)
COPY . .

# Set working directory container's default folder (.)
WORKDIR .

# Install the dependencies specified in requirements file
RUN pip install -r requirements.txt

# Define which program to run when container starts
ENTRYPOINT [ "python" ]

# Pass file as parameter to the entry command to start your app
CMD [ "app.py" ]
```

Hopefully my comments are self-explanatory and you can follow each step. We start with the OS we want for our container—here we choose the latest version of Ubuntu. We run updates and install Python and some build tools. Then we copy all the files from the existing folder to the container and run `pip` to install all Python dependencies. Finally, we start our application by running the Python command with our file as the parameter.

Now, with this build script in Dockerfile, we will create our container image. This image is the template for our container and once we have it, we can spin off as many containers as needed.

Here is the command to build the image. I am calling my image `dattarajrao/simple-nlp-app`. You can give yours any name, but I prefer using the convention `<<docker account>> / <<image name>>`. That way, you can upload your images to the Docker images repository very easily. See Listing 8.11.

Listing 8.11: Building the Docker Container Image

```
$ ls
         Dockerfile
         app.py
         requirements.txt
                imdb_nlp.h5
```

First, let's see the look at the current folder. We have the application's Python file, Dockerfile, requirements file, and our NLP model binary file. If you have a more elaborate application, there will be more files like HTML, CSS, and JS files. But here we have a very simple app. Let's build the container:

```
$ docker build -t dattarajrao/simple-nlp-app
```

Here is the consolidated output of this command. We have eight steps to run defined in our Dockerfile and it will run each and show us the status. If any of the steps fails, you may want to Google the right command since these commands may change with a different version. It will take a few minutes to run depending on your Internet connection. It downloads the dependent layers needed to build the image:

```
Sending build context to Docker daemon  32.34MB
Step 1/8 : FROM ubuntu:latest

      << will take some time to download image >>

 ---> 113a43faa138

Step 2/8 : RUN apt-get update -y

      << will take some time to run command >>

 ---> a497349f5615

Step 3/8 : RUN apt-get install -y python-pip python-dev build-essential

      << will take some time to run command >>

 ---> dd4b73ae6437

Step 4/8 : COPY . .
 ---> 6cedbaa3a50a

Step 5/8 : WORKDIR .
 ---> Running in 1f83ed6e49b3
Removing intermediate container 1f83ed6e49b3
 ---> 87faae5504c6

Step 6/8 : RUN pip install -r requirements.txt
 ---> Running in e4aa8eeff06d
Collecting Flask==1.0.2 (from -r requirements.txt (line 1))
  Downloading

      << will take time to download,install dependencies >>

Removing intermediate container e4aa8eeff06d
---> 1729975b6f07
```

```
Step 7/8 : ENTRYPOINT [ "python" ]
---> Running in 24dec1c6e94b
Removing intermediate container 24dec1c6e94b
---> c1d02422f07

Step 8/8 : CMD [ "app.py" ]
---> Running in 53db54348f94
Removing intermediate container 53db54348f94
---> 9f879249c172

Successfully built 9f879249c172
Successfully tagged dattarajrao/simple-nlp-app:latest
```

Now you created a Docker image that you can see in the images list. The image is tagged by the name `dattarajrao/simple-nlp-app:latest`. This is the name we will use to refer to the image and build containers from it. We will also use this name to push this image to a central container repository, like DockerHub. Let's first see the list of images on our machine:

```
$ docker images

REPOSITORY                   TAG      IMAGE ID       CREATED          SIZE
dattarajrao/simple-nlp-app   latest   9f879249c172   25 minutes ago 1.11GB
ubuntu                       latest   113a43faa138   5 months ago    81.2MB
```

We see two images created and downloaded. One is the application image we created. It also downloaded the latest Ubuntu image and made it available on our machine. This image was used to build our application image on top.

Now we will create a container by running this image. The container will be an instance of this image and will act like a virtual machine. Only it will be created much faster (in milliseconds) and will be much smaller in size. Once created, the container will have its own IP address and will, for all practical purposes, act like a separate machine. See Listing 8.12.

Listing 8.12: Run Our Newly Created Container Image

```
$ docker run -p 1234:1234 dattarajrao/simple-nlp-app:latest
```

This command will create a container with our Docker image as a template. Since the container is a separate machine with an IP address, we need a way to access our application. So we map the port 1234 from our machine to the container port using the `-p` option. The container will start and will run the Python application that will run the Flask application. Since we are loading the NLP model initially in our application, Keras will download the IMDB dataset to get the vocabulary for feeding data to the model. Here is the typical output we will see:

```
Using TensorFlow backend.

Downloading data from https://s3.amazonaws.com/text-datasets/imdb_
word_index.json
1654784/1641221 [==============================] - 9s 5us/step

* Serving Flask app "app" (lazy loading)
* Environment: production
   WARNING: Do not use the development server in a production
environment.
   Use a production WSGI server instead.
 * Debug mode: off
 * Running on http://0.0.0.0:1234/ (Press CTRL+C to quit)
```

Don't worry about the development server warnings. Flask by itself provides an experimental web server, which is good for demos but should not be used in production. You should typically plug your application into a full web server like NGINX. You can look up how to do this in the Flask documentation.

Now since we have mapped the 1234 port from a local machine to the container, we should be able to see our application on the local host.

In your web browser, go to `http://localhost:1234/process`. You should see the screen in Figure 8.8.

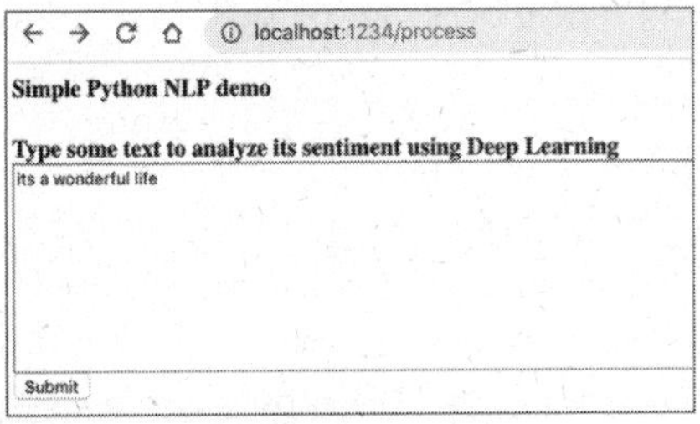

Figure 8.8: Demo on the local host

Type in a phrase and click Submit. Here, we typed the phrase "its a wonderful life." Figure 8.9 shows the result.

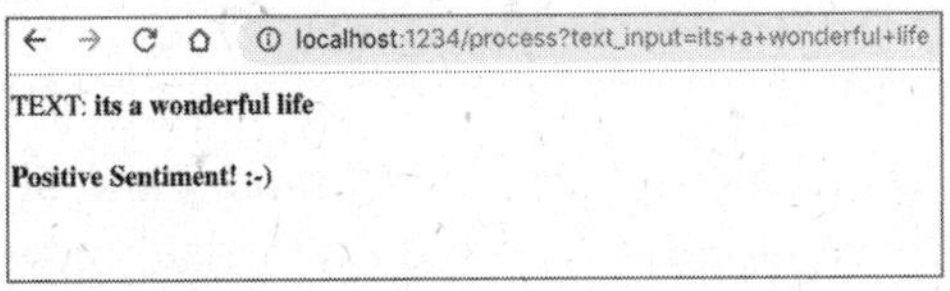

Figure 8.9: Result shown on the local host

Pushing a Docker Image to a Repository

Now we will push this container image to a common Docker image repository called *DockerHub*. Organizations may maintain their private repositories for images as needed. For our example, we will use DockerHub.

Before pushing an image, you will need an account. Log in or create an account at `https://hub.docker.com` and then use the following command to push your image. While pushing an image, the tag name of the image should match your DockerHub account. In my case, my DockerHub account name is `dattarajrao`, so I can push my image with the command shown in Listing 8.13.

Listing 8.13: Push an Image to Docker Repository, DockerHub

```
$ docker login
```

Log in with your Docker ID to push and pull images from DockerHub. If you don't have a Docker ID, head over to `https://hub.docker.com` to create one:

```
Username: dattarajrao
Password: ***********
Login Succeeded

$ docker push dattarajrao/simple-nlp-app
b0a427d5d2a8: Pushed
dcf3294d230a: Pushed
435464f9dced: Pushed
fff2973abf54: Pushed
b6f13d447e00: Mounted from library/ubuntu
a20a262b87bd: Mounted from library/ubuntu
904d60939c36: Mounted from library/ubuntu
3a89e0d8654e: Mounted from library/ubuntu
db9476e6d963: Mounted from library/ubuntu
latest: digest: sha256:5a1216dfd9489afcb1dcdc1d7780de44a28df59934da7fc3a
02cabddcaadd62c size: 2207
```

The image is now pushed onto the Docker repository and others can access it. You will notice that the push also happens layer by layer. This way, only the modified changes are overwritten instead of writing the whole image every time. We can now use this in our Kubernetes deployments.

Deploying the App on Kubernetes as a Microservice

Now that we have our application packaged along with our AI model and all dependencies as a Docker container, we can deploy it in the Kubernetes ecosystem. Just like with a regular web app we saw in the previous chapter, now we will create a deployment for this application containing an AI model.

Let's start by creating a YAML file for the deployment, as shown in Listing 8.14.

Listing 8.14: YAML File to Deploy Our Web Application (simple-nlp-app.yaml)

```
apiVersion: apps/v1
kind: Deployment
metadata:
  name: simple-nlp-app-deployment
  labels:
    app: simple-nlp-app
spec:
  replicas: 3
  selector:
    matchLabels:
      app: simple-nlp-app
  template:
    metadata:
      labels:
        app: simple-nlp-app
    spec:
      containers:
      - name: simple-nlp-app
        image: dattarajrao/simple-nlp-app
        ports:
        - containerPort: 1234
```

This YAML file looks very similar to the `simple-app.yaml` file in the previous chapter. Since all our AI logic is captured in the Docker container, our Kubernetes deployment remains very standard. The only major changes are in the name of the Docker image and the container port. We will now create a deployment using this YAML file. See Listing 8.15.

Listing 8.15: Deploy the YAML File

```
$ kubectl create -f simple-nlp-app.yaml
deployment.apps/simple-nlp-app-deployment created
```

Create a deployment with this YAML file. It creates a pod with a container specified by the image called `dattarajrao/simple-app`:

```
$ kubectl get deployments
NAME                        DESIRED   CURRENT   UP-TO-DATE   AVAILABLE   AGE
simple-nlp-app-deployment   3         3         3            3           58s
```

Depending on the size of your Keras model, the container size will increase. Thus, creating the container may take some time since it has to download the image from the repository. After some time, you will see all the pods running:

```
$ kubectl get pods
NAME                                        READY   STATUS    RESTARTS   AGE
simple-nlp-app-deployment-98d66d5b5-518x6   1/1     Running   0          1m
```

```
simple-nlp-app-deployment-98d66d5b5-95c9m   1/1     Running   0         1m
simple-nlp-app-deployment-98d66d5b5-bvnq5   1/1     Running   0         1m
```

We could use a YAML file to define a service to expose our deployment as earlier. Another way to create a service quickly to expose the deployment is by using the `expose deployment` command:

```
$ kubectl expose deployment simple-nlp-app-deployment
--type=NodePort
```

Now we will see a service with the same name as the deployment we created. If we are using Minikube, we can get the IP address of the service quickly using following command:

```
$ minikube service simple-nlp-app-deployment --url
http://192.168.99.100:32567
```

The result will be different based on your setting. If you are connecting to a Kubernetes cluster, you should be able to get an external IP address for your service. Once you have that, you can access your application using the link in the browser. See Figure 8.10.

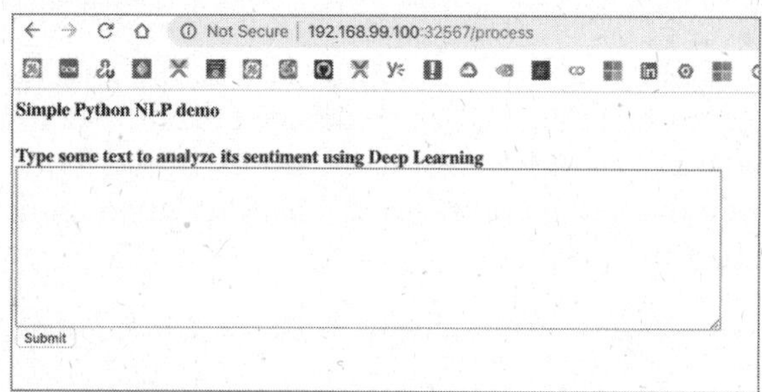

Figure 8.10: Accessing the application as a Docker app

There you have it; your NLP analytics application is now packaged as a Docker container and running inside the Kubernetes ecosystem. Now you can take advantage of all the infrastructure features that Kubernetes provides, like scaling, fail-over, load balancing, etc.

Summary

In this chapter, we developed a web application using Python and the Flask framework. We packaged it as a Docker container and deployed this to a common container registry. We updated this application to add code to invoke a Deep

Learning NLP model and display results on a web page. We moved beyond command lines and data science notebooks and learned how we can push models in the wild and have them running alongside web applications. Now we can leverage the power of the Kubernetes platform to scale and load balance these AI applications and make them secure and robust.

Getting a model deployed within a web application is just scratching the surface. We need to be able to incorporate data science steps involved in building AI models into the software development lifecycle. Using the state-of-the-art agile practices like continuous integration and delivery, we need to be able to not just integrate and deliver code, but also deliver Deep Learning models. This is what we will talk about in the next chapter. We will talk about the typical Machine Learning model lifecycle and development process. We will also explore some best practices and tools to make the deployment easier and automated.

CHAPTER

9

Machine Learning Development Lifecycle

In the previous chapter, we deployed an AI model packaged with a web application that responded to HTTP requests. We saw how we developed, trained, and validated this model with sample data. Then this model was deployed inside a web application packaged together as a Docker container. This container was then deployed on Kubernetes as a microservice with the platform, providing infrastructure features like scaling, fail-over, and load balancing. This approach is highly customized and needs tight coupling between the application code and the model. Software engineers need to know exactly how to call the model and need to manage the runtime for the model. A better approach is to deploy the model as an independent microservice and let the application call this microservice with agreed-upon lightweight protocols. This way, the application has its own development lifecycle and the model has its own. This Machine Learning development lifecycle is gaining lot of popularity in the industry.

We will talk about the steps involved in the Machine Learning development lifecycle. We will talk about some best practices used by data scientists around different steps in working on a data science problem like data collection, cleansing, and structuring. We will explore policies for selecting the best modeling technique based on the type of data and the problem being solved. Finally, we will talk about deployment of the model in production both on the Cloud and on the edge. We will understand the hardware accelerators available that can make our model training and inference much faster on edge devices.

Machine Learning Model Lifecycle

After a Machine Learning project is conceptualized and the problem domain is understood, the model-development process should kick off. Figure 9.1 shows the typical steps involved in the model development lifecycle. You may see different versions of this in other books and websites; however, the essence should be the same.

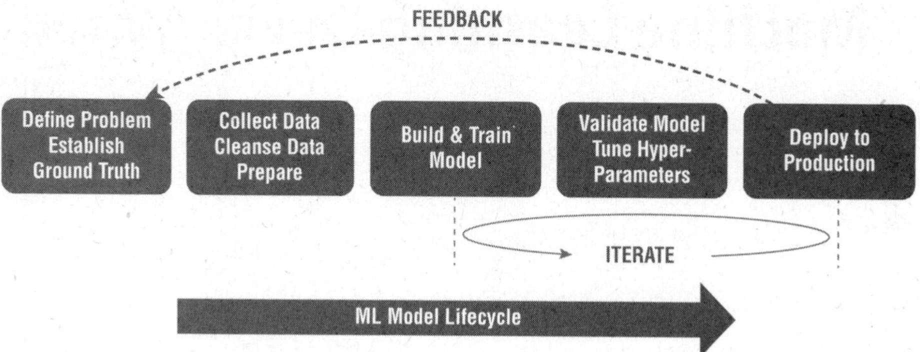

Figure 9.1: Steps in a Machine Learning development lifecycle

Data scientists typically follow these steps while building an AI-powered system. There are many time-consuming and manual activities involved in this overall ML lifecycle. We need to empower our data scientists with tools that take care of most of these manual, repetitive, and time-consuming parts of the process. These tools should help automate major portions of the entire flow of collecting data and building useful models—often referred to as the ML model *pipeline*.

In this chapter, we talk about each step of the ML lifecycle and introduce tools that can help make your life easier. The last step in this process—deployment to production—requires active collaboration between data scientists and software developers. We need tools that can automate not only the job of data scientists but also that of the developer. As you may have already figured, Kubernetes is one such tool that can help deploy software as a microservice, thus making it easier to manage and scale. Kubernetes takes care of many infrastructure concerns, like scalability, fail-over, and load balancing. Using some special *plug-ins* or *extensions*, Kubernetes can help you directly deploy ML models packaged as microservices. We will see examples of this using a special solution built on top of Kubernetes, called *Kubeflow*.

Modern software applications no longer only depend on fixed rules or logic programmed into code. We see more and more applications leveraging data-driven models that learn patterns from data and make predictions. ML models are creating major breakthroughs and modern software development often includes a step to integrate ML models with existing code. Most times, these integrations tend to be highly custom and less reusable. They need very tight coordination between the data scientist and software developer.

Today, the effort is in building tooling that can help automate these steps, not different from how continuous integration (CI) and continuous delivery (CD) tools automated the software development lifecycle (SDLC). Specific to ML, we are seeing the emergence of Machine Learning or data science platforms that are geared toward making life easy for data scientists. Examples of these platforms are Amazon Web Services (AWS) SageMaker, Einstein platform from SalesForce, FBLearner flow from Facebook, Google AutoML, and Azure ML Studio. You may have heard some of these names in news articles or even played with some of these. They provide a highly user-friendly web-based environment where data scientists can connect to data sources, work on their data, and build and train ML models ready for deployment.

In the next chapter, we look at some of the best-in-class tools in each step in the ML lifecycle and building ML pipelines on Kubernetes. Before looking at these tools, first let's talk about each step in the ML model lifecycle.

Step 1: Define the Problem, Establish the Ground Truth

The first step, as in solving any engineering problem, is to clearly define the problem that you are trying to solve. Many times, we see projects that start with a set of data that is readily available and define a problem around that. You may get away with it and the data you have will give you relevant insights. However, it is highly recommended that you take a step back before jumping into collecting and processing data. Clearly define the problem you are trying to solve and what success means to you. If you start with the data-first approach instead of the problem-first approach, you tend to get biased by the data (just like a model gets biased, as in Chapter 2).

With AI and Machine Learning becoming so popular and easily accessible in the form of libraries and Python code, it's very easy to go with the data-first approach. I see many folks get some easily available data and then try to apply AI to see what problems they solve. You may be lucky and find a good problem that has value in solving. But usually I recommend taking some time understanding your system and what problem areas exist that you can solve.

I recommend that you clearly understand the problem domain, meet with users and system experts, and ask as many questions as you can. Figure out what factors affect the problem that you are facing. Figure out what elements of the system you are studying you can measure. Determine what metrics exist and what new measurements need to be added. It may be recommended to consider this in terms of the dependent and independent variables we discussed in Chapter 2. Try to frame your problem in terms of dependent variables and find the independent variables that will affect these. Sometimes you may feel that existing data sources may not give you the full dependency of the problem you are solving. In that case, maybe you can recommend a new measurement in the system. However, for most systems, you will have to work with what data is available.

Also, once you build an AI system, you will need to measure it against something. It is highly recommended at the start to clearly define what the *ground truth* is. This is what you will measure your AI performance against.

For example, say you are building an AI system that looks at security camera video footage to monitor cars entering and leaving a parking garage. Your aim is to have a system that is as good as a human at detecting cars, maybe recording the license plate number and keeping a count of how many vehicles enter and leave the lot. Each of these actions is a problem statement on which you will build your specific ML solutions or models. Now how do you know if your system is as good or better than a human at solving these problems? For that, you need the ground truth as a reference.

You could take historical video footage of cars from the same lot and have a human sit and manually annotate when a car appears on-screen, record the license plate, and keep a count of cars moving in and out. As you can see, this is a pretty laborious activity. It is highly recommended to clearly establish the ground truth you will use as a reference for your AI problem and plan to collect information about it.

Step 2: Collect, Cleanse, and Prepare the Data

If you spend enough effort on the previous step and define the problem and establish the ground truth, you will have a pretty good idea what data sources are available in your system. These could be sensors, flat files, databases, historians, cameras, websites, etc. Your data will be used to train the model, so a Garbage-In-Garbage-Out (GIGO) principle is very much applicable. If you give it bad data, you'll have a bad model that does not generalize well on real field data.

Many times, you may feel that the current data sources will not give you a good estimation of the problem you are trying to solve. As in the earlier example of cars entering and leaving a garage, if your cameras don't face the entry and exit gates, you will not have good video that you can use to analyze and track the cars. In this case, before doing much analysis, you may need to propose the right mounting locations and angles for cameras.

Once you have the right data being collected, it is important to gauge the noise in the data and *cleanse* it. A typical step is to collect a sample from your data source and apply *descriptive statistics* to it. You may look at statistical summaries or charts in Excel or tools like MATLAB and R. If your data is unstructured like images and video, you may spend time manually checking for noise in data. Noisy data will have a major negative impact on the performance of your AI model.

Data cleansing is a very important step for getting your field data in a clean state that can be used for training your AI model. Cleansing is the removal or replacement of bad or missing data from your dataset. Bad or missing data may be due to failure in the sensing equipment in case of monitoring sensors, loss of communication when data has to be sent over a network to your analytic, human error when entering data in a database, and many more. Cleansing may involve either *deletion* of the bad/missing records or *imputation* (replacement) of those data points with new values. The third option is to raise a *fault* and not process the data when it is bad. This is usually done for mission-critical systems. This can be done with basic tools like Excel, may involve sophisticated programming in MATLAB or Python, or may even be done with dedicated cleansing tools. The level of sophistication you need in the cleansing method will depend on the impact the noisy data has on your results.

Let's say you are collecting room temperature values from a thermostat. Your data is structured as a series of values over time (a *timeseries*), with each data point representing an event in time. Now, say for certain times, you get noisy or bad data—like temperature readings of –9999 or 9999 or NULL. Depending on your data collection system, these values will indicate bad data due to sensing equipment failure. Now, you can filter these data points out and ignore them. So essentially you are not letting your model consider these events due to failure to get good data. This option of deletion is usually employed when you have lots of data points and specific points don't matter. The caveat here is that during these ignored data points, the system may be undergoing some significant change that will not be captured by the system.

Another option is to *impute* the missing data points. This is usually better when you have missing data for continuous periods. For example, say you are recording temperature from a thermostat and it gives bad data for two hours due to a dead battery. You may fill that data with the average room temperature before and after that event. Or you may fill those data points with the average room temperature for that day. Depending on your problem domain, you may choose the strategy to impute missing data.

If your problem is highly critical and the missing data may cause major issues, you might flag that as a *fault* in the system rather than attempt to do any prediction with bad data. For example, if you are measuring the heartbeat of a patient and you get bad data, it is highly recommended to flag a fault rather than try to interpolate.

Once you start collecting data and have a data cleansing strategy in place, the next step is to prepare the data for consumption by your model. This involves *feature engineering* and separating the data into training and validation sets. Feature engineering is extracting relevant features from the raw data so that these features can be used for building your model. If you have structured data like a timeseries, feature engineering involves trying to identify features of interest and possibly eliminating redundant and duplicate data. For unstructured data, feature engineering may involve many specialized techniques depending on the datatype. For example, for image data you may want to extract only the relevant features (pixel values) by converting images to grayscale, resizing, cropping, etc. These methods will reduce the size of your images and only keep relevant data that will help in your prediction model.

I see many Machine Learning projects with limited data tend to use all of it for training. Then they don't have any way to validate if their model has overfit on the training data. You need to make sure that you collect data for both training and validation and keep them separate.

We may use techniques like data augmentation to increase the volume of our data. We saw this example in our logo image-classification problem. It is usually recommended to use augmentation techniques or ways to generate non-natural data for training sets. You would be better off keeping your validation dataset as close to the real data as possible.

One way to think about this is if you were a teacher. During your normal school curriculum, you will train students on different topics. But there will be some challenging problems you will want to keep for the examination to really test if the students have learned the topic. These questions would be something out of the book so you can verify if your class actually learned the topic. In the same way, you want to keep your verification data quite challenging so that if you get a good precision score on this data you know you have a good model at hand.

Many times, the data available in the field or data stores may not be in the format you desire to train the models. You may have to do some format conversions to get the data in the format you want to do the training. For example, video data is often stored in a highly compressed H.264 format. However, for use in a computer vision or Deep Learning application, this will need to be decoded using the H.264 codec and converted to the three-dimensional pixel array for analysis. The data format is something that needs to be considered in the model development cycle.

Step 3: Build and Train the Model

Now that you have your problem defined, data sources identified, data cleansed, relevant features isolated, and your dataset separated into training and validation, we get to the fun part of building the model and training it. It is important to give considerable thought to these steps before jumping into model building in order to save on rework.

We saw in Chapters 2 and 4 different ML and DL modeling techniques. Figure 9.2 shows a high-level strategy you can follow for selecting your model. You, as a data scientist, may (and should) find your own methods for planning this strategy, but you can use this figure as a reference.

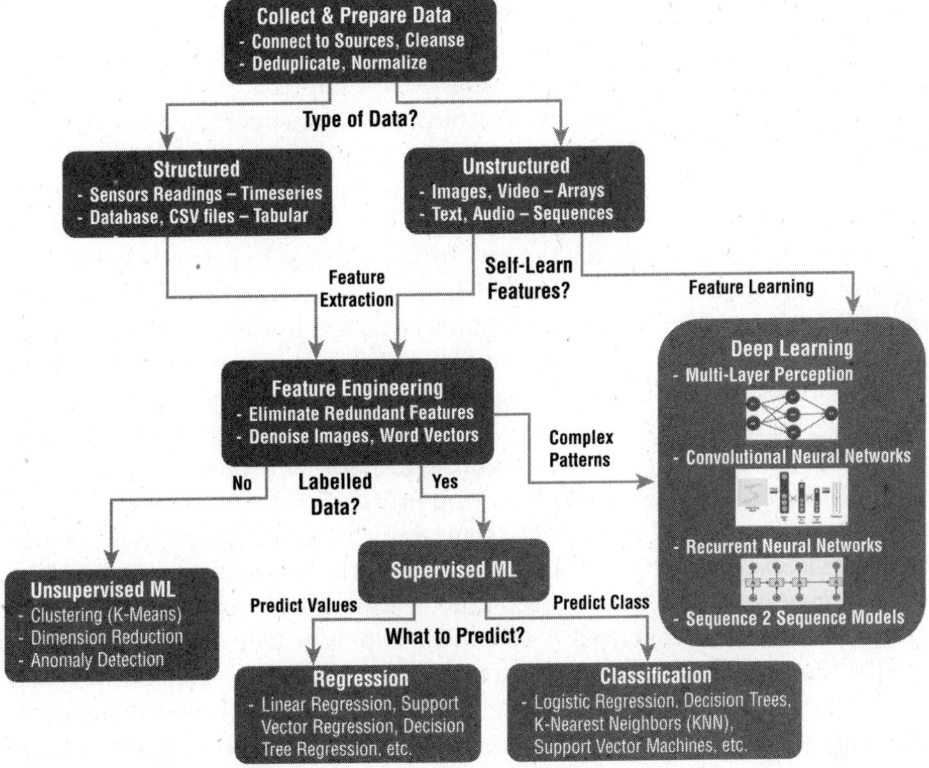

Figure 9.2: An unofficial generic guideline for model selection

The first step is to understand the type of data—structured or unstructured. With structured data, every feature or column has a significance related to our problem. This type of data will usually be in tabular format like database tables, or in timeseries format like sensor readings. Unstructured data may be images, text, audio, or video—it is represented in a computer's memory as arrays or sequence of arrays. Here each column of data does not have significance—it is usually pixel intensity values for images or word embeddings for text. These numbers only gain significance when they are seen as a whole in the image or text sequence.

For both structured and unstructured data, you can do some feature engineering. Here we try to remove features that are not significant or run some computer vision or natural language processing methods to extract valuable features. For example, in the earlier example of monitoring cars coming in and out of a parking garage, we could crop a large image into a smaller window that only shows the parking gate where a car is likely to be present. The rest of the image data is not relevant and can be eliminated. Feature engineering is particularly important with structured data.

After feature engineering, you can apply the supervised or unsupervised Machine Learning techniques we discussed in Chapter 2. Supervised is where you have labeled data to guide your training and unsupervised is where you are trying to find patterns without any knowledge of existing labels.

Now you can technically skip feature engineering and use the Deep Learning techniques we talked about in Chapter 4. Deep Learning can help us build *end-to-end models* that can take data in raw formats and automatically extract features of importance. This is of particular importance with unsupervised data. You can pass raw data in the form of images or text to Deep Learning models and, through the many layers, the model extracts important features. Starting with the lowest level of features like pixel values, at each layer you try to extract high-level features. This way you map a complex three-dimensional array of pixels to an array of 10 numbers indicating 10 classes the image may belong to.

Depending on the type of data you are processing, there are certain neural network architectures that have been standardized. For image analysis, convolutional networks are pretty much universally accepted as the chosen architecture. For a sequence of data like text or audio, the standard in the industry is the recurrent neural network (RNN)—particularly of type long short-term memory (LSTM). For converting one sequence to another, such as text from one language to another or text to speech, we have a newer architecture called sequence-to-sequence models. You may look at a popular architecture for a neural network that has been used by others to solve similar problems. For example, a particular type of Convolutional Neural Networks (CNN) architecture called VGG-16 is very popular for image recognition. If you have a similar problem, you can build your model with that particular architecture and train it on your data. Another option is to take an existing model with weights and use transfer learning to train your data. We saw examples of this in Chapter 4.

To actually build the model, you may use the common programmatic approach. Here you build the model using your preferred data science language like Python, R, or MATLAB and then store the model in a binary format for deployment. More recently many AI workbenches have come into the limelight that allow data scientists to build models by writing minimal or no code. We saw Google Colaboratory, which helps us run Python code without installing any software and on Cloud CPU and GPUs. With AI workbenches like H2O and DataRobot, even the model development can be automated. H2O.ai provides a web interface, as shown in Figure 9.3, which allows for uploading data from

CSV files and databases and helps us build Machine Learning models through configuration alone.

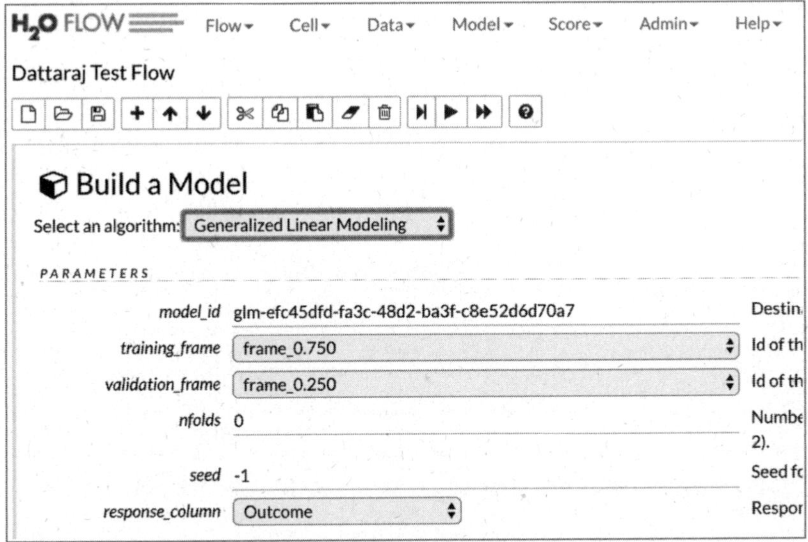

Figure 9.3: The H2O AI workbench allows codeless model development

Step 4: Validate the Model, Tune the Hyper-Parameters

After you build a model, it needs to be trained and validated against your datasets. It is very rare that you would get good precision numbers on training and validation datasets on the first attempt. You will most likely have to tune many knobs to improve these numbers. After the obvious initial decisions are made, like what ML technique to use or what deep architecture to adopt, most of the data science effort goes in tuning these hyper-parameters. By changing values of hyper-parameters like the number of layers, the neurons in a layer, the learning rate, the activation function types, etc., you can understand how to improve the precision of your model. Although most of these decisions will depend on your domain and the dataset, there are certain rules of thumb that expert data scientists use after years of practice. AI workbenches like H2O try to capture these best practices and help users modify the values accordingly.

More recently, a new technique is becoming very popular for tuning model hyper-parameters—it is called *AutoML*. AutoML is still evolving but it essentially provides an automated way of building and training your models. The idea is that to a given dataset under study, many different shallow and Deep Learning models are applied simultaneously. Each is applied with many hyper-parameters often decided by best practices followed by data scientists. Using these combinations in parallel, the best combination of model and hyper-parameters is identified for that particular problem.

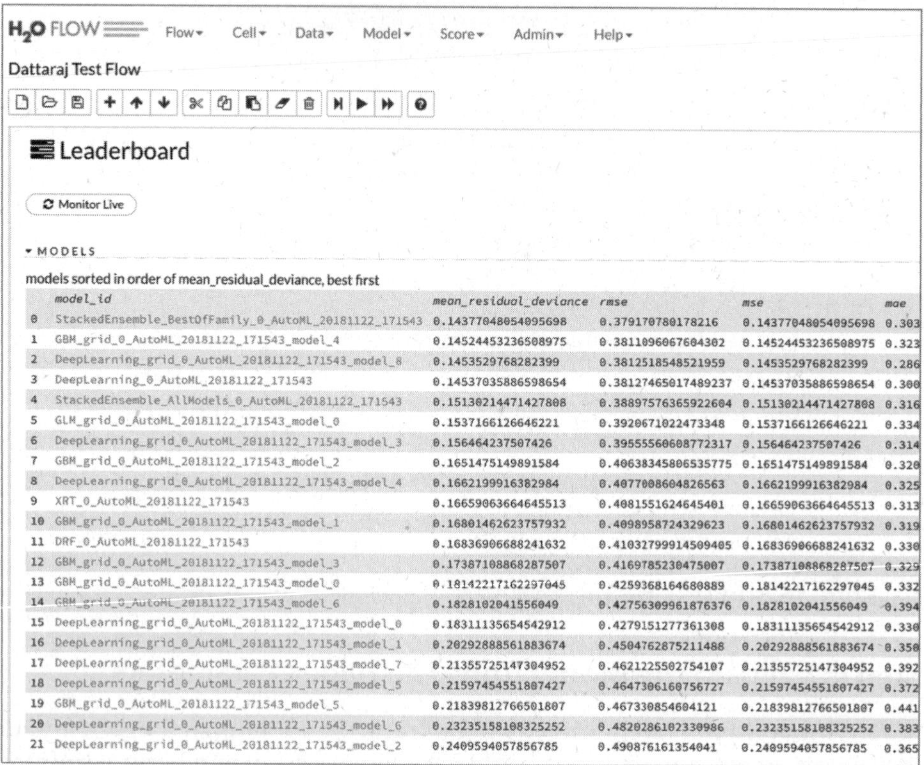

	model_id	mean_residual_deviance	rmse	mse	mae
0	StackedEnsemble_BestOfFamily_0_AutoML_20181122_171543	0.14377048054095698	0.379170780178216	0.14377048054095698	0.303
1	GBM_grid_0_AutoML_20181122_171543_model_4	0.14524453236508975	0.3811096067604302	0.14524453236508975	0.323
2	DeepLearning_grid_0_AutoML_20181122_171543_model_8	0.1453529768282399	0.3812518548521959	0.1453529768282399	0.286
3	DeepLearning_0_AutoML_20181122_171543	0.14537035886598654	0.38127465017489237	0.14537035886598654	0.300
4	StackedEnsemble_AllModels_0_AutoML_20181122_171543	0.15130214471427808	0.38897576365922604	0.15130214471427808	0.316
5	GLM_grid_0_AutoML_20181122_171543_model_0	0.1537166126646221	0.3920671022473348	0.1537166126646221	0.334
6	DeepLearning_grid_0_AutoML_20181122_171543_model_3	0.156464237507426	0.39555560608772317	0.156464237507426	0.314
7	GBM_grid_0_AutoML_20181122_171543_model_2	0.1651475149891584	0.40638345806535775	0.1651475149891584	0.320
8	DeepLearning_grid_0_AutoML_20181122_171543_model_4	0.1662199916382984	0.4077008604826563	0.1662199916382984	0.325
9	XRT_0_AutoML_20181122_171543	0.16659063664645513	0.4081551624645401	0.16659063664645513	0.313
10	GBM_grid_0_AutoML_20181122_171543_model_1	0.16801462623757932	0.4098958724329623	0.16801462623757932	0.319
11	DRF_0_AutoML_20181122_171543	0.16836906688241632	0.41032799914509405	0.16836906688241632	0.330
12	GBM_grid_0_AutoML_20181122_171543_model_3	0.17387108868287507	0.4169785230475007	0.17387108868287507	0.329
13	GBM_grid_0_AutoML_20181122_171543_model_0	0.18142217162297045	0.4259368164680889	0.18142217162297045	0.332
14	GBM_grid_0_AutoML_20181122_171543_model_6	0.1828102041556049	0.42756309961876376	0.1828102041556049	0.394
15	DeepLearning_grid_0_AutoML_20181122_171543_model_0	0.18311135654542912	0.4279151277361308	0.18311135654542912	0.330
16	DeepLearning_grid_0_AutoML_20181122_171543_model_1	0.20292888561883674	0.4504762875211488	0.20292888561883674	0.350
17	DeepLearning_grid_0_AutoML_20181122_171543_model_7	0.21355725147304952	0.4621225502754107	0.21355725147304952	0.392
18	DeepLearning_grid_0_AutoML_20181122_171543_model_5	0.21597454551807427	0.4647306160756727	0.21597454551807427	0.372
19	GBM_grid_0_AutoML_20181122_171543_model_5	0.21839812766501807	0.467330854604121	0.21839812766501807	0.441
20	DeepLearning_grid_0_AutoML_20181122_171543_model_6	0.23235158108325252	0.4820286102330986	0.23235158108325252	0.383
21	DeepLearning_grid_0_AutoML_20181122_171543_model_2	0.2409594057856785	0.490876161354041	0.2409594057856785	0.365

Figure 9.4: H2O AI example of an AutoML leaderboard

Google has been aggressively marketing AutoML as its technique where neural networks build new neural networks. The H2O workbench we saw earlier also has support for AutoML. When we run AutoML in H2O for a given problem—with training and validation data—it tries several model and parameter combinations in parallel. It then shows a leaderboard with results showing the top models and their rankings, as shown in Figure 9.4.

Step 5: Deploy to Production

After your model is trained and validated with acceptable precision numbers, you can deploy it to production. As we saw in the previous chapter, this could be done as a web application with data being fed to the model collected from a user interface. The thing to keep in mind here is that any preprocessing done to the data during training should also be done now during inference. For example, for image data we divide by 255, so that we can normalize the values between

0 and 1. The same thing has to be done in the web application before feeding to the model. The result from the model must then be evaluated.

Some environments like MATLAB and R have a way for the model to be packaged as an executable and deployed on a system. More recently, Cloud-based model deployment is getting a lot of attention. One example is the Amazon Web Services SageMaker. AWS SageMaker gives developers a Jupyter Notebook to build their model. Data can be pulled from the web or from AWS S3 (Simple Storage Service), which can store any type of file. After training and validation using code, the model can be automatically deployed in the Cloud and scaled to run on multiple machines.

In our earlier example, we packaged the model as a microservice in a Docker container and deployed it on a Kubernetes cluster. The scaling, fail-over, and load balancing is taken care of by Kubernetes. However, you have to write the application code to wrap the model file. Also, the inputs entered by the users must be formatted and fed to the model, which is invoked from the code. There is an open source solution developed by Google called *TensorFlow-Serving* that allows for automated packaging of your model files into microservices and deployment. This can now be called with a REST API using HTTP calls. TensorFlow-Serving also supports Google's high-performance Remote Procedure Calls (RPC) protocol called gRPC. We will talk about this more in the next chapter.

Feedback and Model Updates

Keep in mind that deploying the model in production is not the end of the story. A constant feedback mechanism needs to be in place to see how well the model is performing with real data. Many times, the model fails to get accurate numbers with real field data, due to several reasons. The model may need to be recalibrated and fine-tuned with new data and redeployed. The part of the ML lifecycle from building the model to deployment in production may involve several iterations. This iterative nature should be accounted for in the ML platform and we should have automated tools that can monitor performance, rebuild the model, retrain it, and deploy a new version to production.

NOTE **Each new model deployment ideally should be separated from code deployment. You *do not* want your software teams leading deployment of new ML models in production and trying to debug issues. Your ML platform should empower the data scientist to validate a new model on the data and deploy it. A good ML platform should have automation tools that auto-deploy a new version of the model with minimal manual intervention.**

It is also possible that the performance of your model will degrade over time. This could be due to changes in the environment, incorrect calibration, etc. Or it could be that the data you collected for training and validating your model is no longer valid. The system has changed and it needs retraining. Retraining is something that you should carefully consider as part of your software process. You will not be able to release a single universal model that will solve your problem forever. After a few times you will need to modify and retrain the model on new data and deploy it again. Your development process should incorporate this change management step. This way you have a defined process to collect new data, validate your model, and retrain and deploy a newer version.

Kubernetes can greatly help you in your model retraining and redeployment process. New workflow tools like Kubeflow are evolving that can help you build ML pipelines that include provisions to test models on new data, build new models, and deploy them to production. These systems integrate with existing continuous integration tools to make deployment very straightforward. We will discuss these newer tools in the next chapter.

Deployment on Edge Devices

So far, we have talked about deployment in the Cloud or on-premise servers using platforms like Kubernetes. However, many times you need to analyze data close to the source and provide results to take immediate action. Deployment at the edge on specialized hardware has its own constraints. The models are packaged as binary files and are usually invoked by embedded code written in C or C++. Another way of deploying an AI model is packaging it as a mobile app and deploying on a relatively low-powered (as compared to Cloud servers) mobile device.

These mobile and edge devices are usually limited in processing power and memory. Hence, the models need to be extremely efficient and lightweight to run on these devices. Also, these devices often use hardware acceleration to make the models run faster. These models typically are meant for real-time alerting of specific activities happening in field. For example, if you want to control the gate of the parking garage using a camera that sees cars entering, this will need a model that detects cars running on an edge device and makes a real-time call to the circuitry that opens the gate when a car approaches.

Modern edge devices are supported by hardware acceleration chips to support Deep Learning models. The most popular chip among these is NVIDIA GPU—Graphics Processing Unit. GPUs started off as specialized chips to render complex graphics on-screen very quickly. The graphics cards that are used for laptops and game consoles have embedded GPU chips. These chips could support massively parallel linear algebra calculations. They have thousands of processing cores that can do these operations in parallel and render an image on-screen.

It turns out that for advanced Deep Learning also we need massive parallel linear algebra calculations to be done. NVIDIA started extending its graphics cards for computing and they became very popular. Now NVIDIA makes dedicated GPU cards for Deep Learning. It also develops high-end systems like the DGX-1, which has multiple such GPU cards functioning as a unit and can solve complex Deep Learning problems very quickly. The idea behind GPUs is pretty straightforward. A CPU chip is a general-purpose chip that can do complex types of operations very quickly, but sequentially. Using a multi-core CPU, we could get parallelism but it would be pretty limited. GPUs extend these basic cores to thousands of cores. Thus, we get the true benefit of running calculations in parallel.

More recently (as of 2018), other companies started getting into this Deep Learning chipset space. Google launched a Tensor Processing Unit (TPU), which runs on the same principle as GPU but claims to consume less power. Microsoft is investing in a technology called FPGA (field-programmable gate array), which allows for programmatic development of processors. Microsoft claims using FPGAs gives them bigger benefits of parallel computing similar to GPUs.

This technology is evolving continuously. Though NVIDIA is the market leader with GPUs, the competition is catching up. I believe in couple of years we will be able to say for sure that a particular technology is the leader and a particular kind of chip is best for deploying Deep Learning models at the edge.

To actually show how GPU and TPU improve your Deep Learning model training times compared to a CPU, let's run the same code on different systems and analyze the performance. The easiest way to do this is to build a Jupyter Notebook in Google Colaboratory. This lets us switch the runtimes among a dual-core CPU, NVIDIA K80 GPU, and a Google TPU. This way, we can test our code separately on these three environments. Let's first see the code in Listing 9.1.

First we will determine what device is connected to our Google Colab instance—a GPU, TPU, or only a CPU. Keep in mind that both GPU and TPU are supplementary chips; the machine will still need a CPU to run the main OS.

Listing 9.1: Code to Check if GPU, TPU Is Attached

```
    # import the necessary libraries
import tensorflow as tf
import os

# Check if GPU exists
gpu_exists = (tf.test.gpu_device_name() != '')
# Check if TPU exists
tpu_exists = (os.getenv('COLAB_TPU_ADDR') is not None)

# if GPU device is attached
if gpu_exists:
```

```
    print('GPU device found: ', tf.test.gpu_device_name())
# if TPU device is attached
elif tpu_exists:
    print('TPU device found: ', os.getenv('COLAB_TPU_ADDR'))
else:
    print('No GPU or TPU. We have to reply on good old CPU!')

print ('----------------')
print ()
print ()
print('---------- CPU configuration --- START ----------')
command = 'cat /proc/cpuinfo'
print (os.popen(command).read().strip())
print('---------- CPU configuration --- END ----------')

print('---------- Memory configuration --- START ----------')
command = 'cat /proc/meminfo'
print (os.popen(command).read().strip())
print('---------- Memory configuration --- END ----------')
```

You can create a new Google Colaboratory Notebook and enter this code in the cellblock. Then, one by one, select among the three runtime options provided. After selecting each runtime, click Connect to commission a cloud virtual machine and when this machine is ready, run this code. You will know the configuration of the machine and be able to distinguish between GPU and TPU. This code is particular to Google Colaboratory, but can easily be modified for specific edge hardware you have.

Under the Runtime menu, you can select the Change Runtime Type option and then select between GPU, TPU, or None (see Figure 9.5). None means only the CPU will be available—no hardware accelerator. Then you can connect to that runtime and run this code block on different instances to see what hardware accelerator you have.

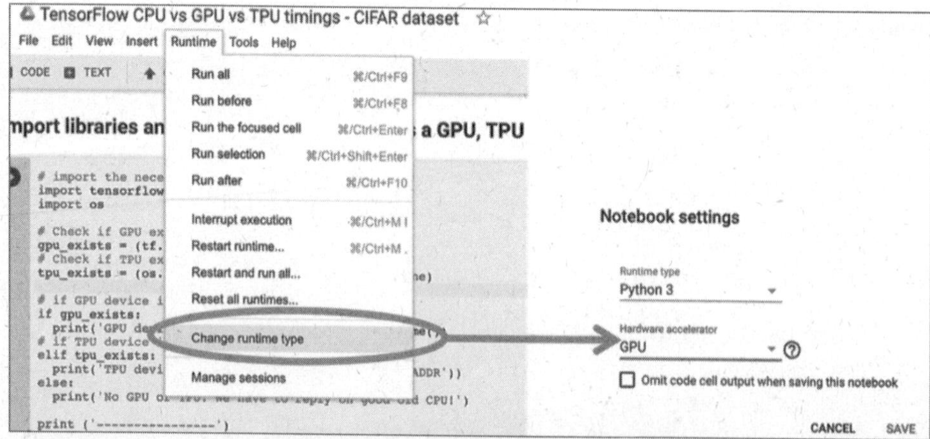

Figure 9.5: Changing from CPU to GPU runtime in Google Colaboratory

We will train a Convolutional Neural Network on the standard CIFAR dataset that comes with Keras. Then we'll change the runtime and see how the training time varies. We see that to run on GPU and pure CPU, the same code works on both. For Google's TPU, some modifications are needed. However, I feel as the TPU technology evolves, it will be able to run the same code on TPU. Ideally your hardware acceleration chip should not affect your code. The same code should be able to run on multiple environments as long as you have the right drivers configured—for GPU or TPU. After all, that's the power a platform like TensorFlow and Keras bring. See Listing 9.2.

Listing 9.2: Code to Load the Dataset, Display Some Sample Images, and Create the Model

```
    # import libraries
from tensorflow import keras
import numpy as np
# configure plotting
import matplotlib.pyplot as plt
%matplotlib inline

# import the dataset
dataset = keras.datasets.cifar10

# collect training and testing data
(train_images, train_labels), (test_images, test_labels) = dataset
.load_data()

# define the class names for CIFAR 10
class_names = ['airplane', 'automobile', 'bird', 'cat', 'deer', 'dog',
'frog', 'horse', 'ship', 'truck']

# plot some sample images
plt.figure(figsize=(8,8))
for i in range(25):
    plt.subplot(5,5,i+1)
    plt.xticks([])
    plt.yticks([])
    plt.grid(False)
    plt.imshow(train_images[i])
    plt.xlabel(class_names[train_labels[i][0]])

# preprocess the training and testing data
x_train, x_test = train_images / 255.0, test_images / 255.0
y_train, y_test = train_labels, test_labels

# build the Convolutional Neural Network Model
model = tf.keras.models.Sequential([
            tf.keras.layers.Conv2D(32, (3, 3), padding='same', input_
shape=x_train.shape[1:]),
            tf.keras.layers.Activation('relu'),
            tf.keras.layers.MaxPooling2D(pool_size=(2, 2)),
            tf.keras.layers.Dropout(0.25),
```

```
            tf.keras.layers.Conv2D(64, (3, 3), padding='same'),
            tf.keras.layers.Activation('relu'),
            tf.keras.layers.Conv2D(64, (3, 3)),
            tf.keras.layers.Activation('relu'),
            tf.keras.layers.MaxPooling2D(pool_size=(2, 2)),
            tf.keras.layers.Dropout(0.25),

            tf.keras.layers.Flatten(),
            tf.keras.layers.Dense(512, activation=tf.nn.relu),
            tf.keras.layers.Dropout(0.2),
            tf.keras.layers.Dense(10, activation=tf.nn.softmax)
            ])

model.compile(optimizer='adam',
              loss='sparse_categorical_crossentropy',
              metrics=['accuracy'])


model.summary()
```

Figure 9.6 shows the sample images.

Figure 9.6: Sample images from the CIFAR-10 dataset

Now that we have loaded the data and defined the model, we will train the model on our dataset. The model development portion of code for the GPU and TPU environments is the same. The model execution code for TPU is slightly different, so we use the `tpu_exists` flag, which tells us if TPU is attached. See Listing 9.3.

Listing 9.3: Check if TPU Is Attached and Run Code to Train Model—Capture Times

```
import datetime

# capture start time
st_time = datetime.datetime.now()

# we will train for 10 epochs
num_epochs = 10

# if not TPU then run simple train command
if not tpu_exists:
    model.fit(x_train, y_train, epochs=num_epochs)

# for TPU we have to use custom data structures
else:
         tpu_url = 'grpc://' + os.environ['COLAB_TPU_ADDR']
    tpu_model = tf.contrib.tpu.keras_to_tpu_model(
      model, strategy=tf.contrib.tpu.TPUDistributionStrategy(
              tf.contrib.cluster_resolver.TPUClusterResolver(tpu=tpu_url)
          )
      )
    tpu_model.compile(
          optimizer=tf.train.AdamOptimizer(learning_rate=1e-3, ),
          loss=tf.keras.losses.sparse_categorical_crossentropy,
          metrics=['sparse_categorical_accuracy']
      )

    # define a training function
    def train_gen(batch_size):
        while True:
            offset = np.random.randint(0, x_train.shape[0] - batch_size)
        yield x_train[offset:offset+batch_size], y_train[offset:offset +
batch_size]

    # fit the model on TPU
    tpu_model.fit_generator(
        train_gen(1024),
        epochs=num_epochs,
        steps_per_epoch=100,
        validation_data=(x_test, y_test),
        )
```

```
# record time after training
end_time = datetime.datetime.now()

print('Training time = %s'%(end_time-st_time))
```

Now let's change the runtimes from GPU to TPU to CPU and record the training times. We will see how the hardware acceleration helps in training. Training is usually the more time consuming of the Machine Learning tasks. You will most likely see the same performance improvement in inference times. See Listing 9.4 and Figure 9.7.

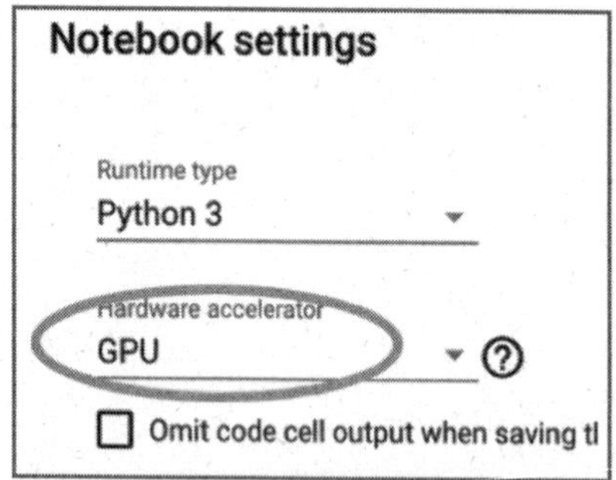

Figure 9.7: Change the setting to use GPU

Listing 9.4: Result of Running Training on GPU, TPU, and CPU

```
GPU device found:  /device:GPU:0

----------------
Epoch 1/10
50000/50000 [==============================] - 22s 430us/step - loss:
1.4497 - acc: 0.4754
Epoch 2/10
50000/50000 [==============================] - 19s 372us/step - loss:
1.0527 - acc: 0.6242
Epoch 3/10
50000/50000 [==============================] - 19s 386us/step - loss:
0.9037 - acc: 0.6807
Epoch 4/10
50000/50000 [==============================] - 19s 370us/step - loss:
0.8085 - acc: 0.7163
Epoch 5/10
50000/50000 [==============================] - 19s 376us/step - loss:
0.7259 - acc: 0.7443
Epoch 6/10
50000/50000 [==============================] - 18s 370us/step - loss:
0.6556 - acc: 0.7687
Epoch 7/10
```

```
50000/50000 [==============================] - 19s 375us/step - loss:
0.6067 - acc: 0.7864
Epoch 8/10
50000/50000 [==============================] - 19s 373us/step - loss:
0.5561 - acc: 0.8038
Epoch 9/10
50000/50000 [==============================] - 19s 375us/step - loss:
0.5156 - acc: 0.8187
Epoch 10/10
50000/50000 [==============================] - 19s 379us/step - loss:
0.4776 - acc: 0.8319
----------------

Training time = 0:03:11.096094

TPU device found:  10.12.160.114:8470

----------------
Epoch 1/10
100/100 [==============================] - 24s 243ms/step - loss: 1.6977
- sparse_categorical_accuracy: 0.3873 - val_loss: 1.4215 - val_sparse_
categorical_accuracy: 0.4956
Epoch 2/10
100/100 [==============================] - 16s 162ms/step - loss: 1.3143
- sparse_categorical_accuracy: 0.5318 - val_loss: 1.1858 - val_sparse_
categorical_accuracy: 0.5812
Epoch 3/10
100/100 [==============================] - 15s 151ms/step - loss: 1.1498
- sparse_categorical_accuracy: 0.5938 - val_loss: 1.0693 - val_sparse_
categorical_accuracy: 0.6247
Epoch 4/10
100/100 [==============================] - 16s 157ms/step - loss: 1.0443
- sparse_categorical_accuracy: 0.6324 - val_loss: 0.9734 - val_sparse_
categorical_accuracy: 0.6594
Epoch 5/10
100/100 [==============================] - 15s 152ms/step - loss: 0.9380
- sparse_categorical_accuracy: 0.6722 - val_loss: 0.9119 - val_sparse_
categorical_accuracy: 0.6779
Epoch 6/10
100/100 [==============================] - 14s 144ms/step - loss: 0.8462
- sparse_categorical_accuracy: 0.7031 - val_loss: 0.8745 - val_sparse_
categorical_accuracy: 0.6959
Epoch 7/10
100/100 [==============================] - 15s 148ms/step - loss: 0.7809
- sparse_categorical_accuracy: 0.7281 - val_loss: 0.8322 - val_sparse_
categorical_accuracy: 0.7050
Epoch 8/10
100/100 [==============================] - 15s 147ms/step - loss: 0.7181
- sparse_categorical_accuracy: 0.7507 - val_loss: 0.8213 - val_sparse_
categorical_accuracy: 0.7170
```

```
Epoch 9/10
100/100 [==============================] - 15s 148ms/step - loss: 0.6556
- sparse_categorical_accuracy: 0.7708 - val_loss: 0.7956 - val_sparse_
categorical_accuracy: 0.7236
Epoch 10/10
100/100 [==============================] - 14s 145ms/step - loss: 0.5934
- sparse_categorical_accuracy: 0.7922 - val_loss: 0.7902 - val_sparse_
categorical_accuracy: 0.7333
----------------

Training time = 0:02:58.394083

No GPU or TPU. We have to reply on good old CPU!

----------------
Epoch 1/10
50000/50000 [==============================] - 206s 4ms/step - loss:
1.4893 - acc: 0.4583
Epoch 2/10
50000/50000 [==============================] - 203s 4ms/step - loss:
1.1087 - acc: 0.6055
Epoch 3/10
50000/50000 [==============================] - 204s 4ms/step - loss:
0.9576 - acc: 0.6615
Epoch 4/10
50000/50000 [==============================] - 203s 4ms/step - loss:
0.8492 - acc: 0.7010
Epoch 5/10
50000/50000 [==============================] - 203s 4ms/step - loss:
0.7750 - acc: 0.7285
Epoch 6/10
50000/50000 [==============================] - 202s 4ms/step - loss:
0.7060 - acc: 0.7523
Epoch 7/10
50000/50000 [==============================] - 203s 4ms/step - loss:
0.6430 - acc: 0.7733
Epoch 8/10
50000/50000 [==============================] - 203s 4ms/step - loss:
0.5984 - acc: 0.7884
Epoch 9/10
50000/50000 [==============================] - 203s 4ms/step - loss:
0.5564 - acc: 0.8027
Epoch 10/10
50000/50000 [==============================] - 203s 4ms/step - loss:
0.5184 - acc: 0.8172
----------------


Training time = 0:33:54.456107
```

Now we will change the settings in colab to include a TPU and back to only CPU. Figures 9.8 and 9.9 show these settings.

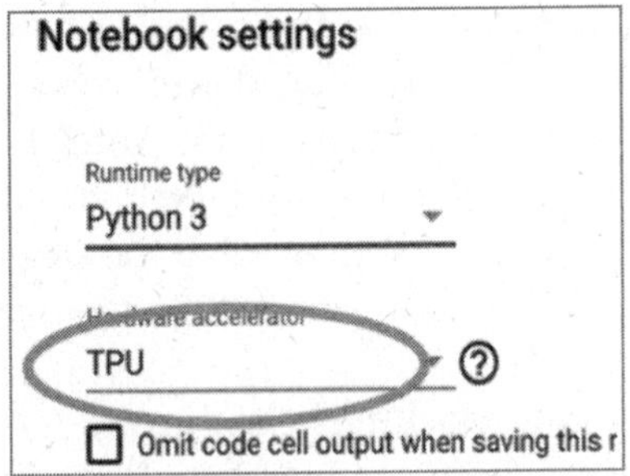

Figure 9.8: Change the setting to use TPU

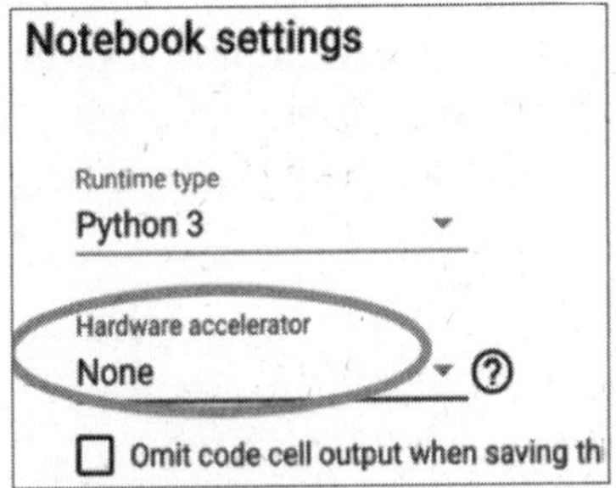

Figure 9.9: Change the setting to use CPU only

We see that GPU (time 3:11) and TPU (time 2:58) give significantly better performance for training the Deep Learning model as compared to CPU (time 33:54). We get a 10x improvement—that is, a 10X reduction in training time using a GPU or TPU. These 30 minutes for basic model training are very valuable. Especially when a data scientist has to try different scenarios and train hundreds of models, saving 30 minutes per model is extremely valuable. Hence, the GPU hardware is pretty expensive. However, if your team is involved in training many models with different configurations, you will definitely get a good return on your investment.

Between GPU and TPU, it's not really an apples-to-apples comparison, since the technology is evolving rapidly. The new NVIDIA GPUs can give better performance than K80. At the same time, Google will come up with better TPU options. You can use this code to test new devices as they become available to validate the performance.

Summary

In this chapter, we looked at the Machine Learning model development lifecycle. We saw the steps involved in procuring and cleansing the data. We saw a workflow for selecting the best model-building technique based on the type of data. We saw the hyper-parameter tuning process and upcoming AutoML technology that helps find the best hyper-parameters. Finally, we talked about model deployment to production. We also talked about deployment at the edge and using hardware accelerators, like GPUs and TPUs, to improve training and inference performance.

In the next chapter, we get specific about deploying Machine Learning models to production and talk about some of the best-in-class tools available. We will discuss examples of open source tools for different stages of the ML lifecycle and how we can combine them to form a Machine Learning pipeline using Kubernetes. We will talk about the H2O AI workbench with an example of building a regression model. We will explore TensorFlow-serving to deploy models packaged as microservices in Docker containers. We will explore Kubeflow, which helps build ML pipelines for establishing a CI process for data science.

CHAPTER

10

A Platform for Machine Learning

In the previous chapter, we talked about the Machine Learning model lifecycle. We saw how model development is a piece of the bigger puzzle that includes problem definition, data collection, cleansing, preparation, hyper-parameter tuning, and deployment. A good data science or Machine Learning platform should provide tools that can drive automation in these different phases so that the data scientist can drive the end-to-end cycle without engagement with software development. This is like the DevOps for Machine Learning. Once the models are released in production, they should be consumed by software applications without special integration.

In this chapter, we will look at some tools and technologies that are being extensively adopted for building ML platforms. We will discuss the common concerns that a data scientist has to deal with while deploying an AI solution. We will see some of the best-in-class tools that address each of the concerns. We will also see how these individual products can be tied together to form a bigger data science platform hosted on Kubernetes.

Machine Learning Platform Concerns

We saw in the last chapter how the actual algorithm selection and model development is a key activity in solving an Artificial Intelligence problem. However, it is usually not the most time-consuming. We have powerful libraries and platforms that simplify this activity and help us build and train models with a few lines of code. Some modern data science platforms actually let you select the right model and train without writing a single line of code. Model development and training with data is done purely through configuration. We see an example in this chapter of such a platform.

Data scientists typically spend more time addressing general concerns around collecting data, cleansing it, preparing it for model consumption, and distributing the training for the model and hyper-parameters. Deploying the model to production is another major activity and mostly involves lots of manual interaction and translation work between the data scientists and software developers. Data scientists state that 50% to 80% of their overall solution development time is in activities not directly related to building or training a model—activities like data preparation, cleaning, and deployment. In fact, model development today is pretty well automated with libraries in languages like Python and R. However, the rest of the data science process still remains predominantly manual.

Major efforts are underway by top analytics-consuming companies like Amazon, Google, and Microsoft in developing Machine Learning or data science platforms that can automate these different activities during the model development lifecycle. Examples of these platforms include Amazon SageMaker, Google AutoML, and Microsoft Azure Studio. These are usually tied to the respective Cloud offering of that particular provider. As long as you are okay with storing all your Big Data in the respective provider's Cloud (and paying for this), you can use their data science platform to ease up on the model development process. Depending on your specific requirements, you may find these Cloud offerings limited or may not want to store your data in a public Cloud. In that case, you can build an on-premise data science platform of your own specific to your requirements.

We talk about the pros and cons of each approach. Either way, if your company is building and consuming a great deal of analytics, it is highly recommended that you invest in a Machine Learning platform that can ease up the software activities that are done by your data scientists.

In software development, an agile framework strives to add features to the product iteratively by releasing new code faster in short development cycles. This speed is achieved using automation tools like CI/CD, which take care of concerns like code compilation, running unit tests, and integrating the dependencies. In a similar manner, a data science platform will help you collect, access, and analyze data quickly and find patterns that could be deployed in the field for monetization. There are specific data science concerns that you want the platform to take care of, so your data scientists don't waste too much time doing this manually. Let's look at some of these concerns, outlined in Figure 10.1.

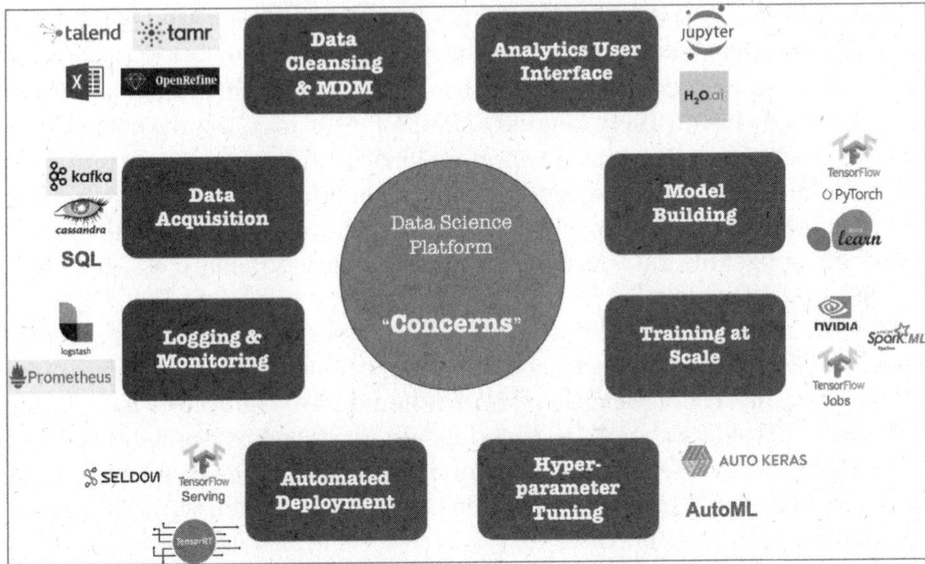

Figure 10.1: Typical data science concerns and tools that address them

Figure 10.1 shows some of the major concerns that a good data science or Machine Learning platform should address. I have been using these terms interchangeably because you will find both names used in industry. It is essentially a platform that helps data scientists address the concerns we see in Figure 10.1. Let's now look at these concerns and see how some of the leading tools address them.

Data Acquisition

Getting the right data to train your model is essential to making sure you are building a model that will work in the field. In most online tutorials or books on ML, you will see data already packaged as CSV files to be fed to the model. However, generating this neatly packaged CSV involves major effort and it will help the data scientist if the platform can take care of some of it. This involves connecting to the production data sources, querying the right data, and converting it into the desired format.

Traditional data sources used relational databases for storing large volumes of data. Structured Query Language (SQL) was the tool of choice to pull data from these databases. Relational databases store data in tabular format with tables that are linked to specific fields that are called the primary or foreign keys. Understanding the relationship between the data tables helps us build SQL queries that can pull the right data. Then we can store the results of the query in a manageable format like a CSV file.

Modern software systems often use Big Data technologies like Hadoop and Cassandra to store data. These systems form a cluster with many nodes, where the data is replicated across nodes to ensure fail-over and high availability. These systems usually have a query language similar to SQL to collect the data. Again, knowing the structure of data is important to write the right query to pull data.

Finally, an emerging trend is to have data in motion. Data events occurring continuously are pushed to a message queue and interested consumers can subscribe and get the data. Kafka is becoming a very popular message broker for high-frequency data.

A platform should be able to automatically connect to data sources and pull data. You do not need to worry about pulling data and building a CSV manually every time. A data science platform should have connectors to SQL, Big Data, and Kafka data sources so that data can be pulled as needed. This data collected from diverse data sources should be combined and given to your model for training. This should happen in the background, without manual intervention by data scientists.

One approach that is getting very popular is to use Kafka as the single source of input for all your data, from multiple sources. Kafka is a messaging system that's specifically designed for ingesting and processing data at a very high rate—in the order of thousands of messages per second. Kafka was developed by LinkedIn and then open sourced through the Apache foundation. Kafka helps us build data-processing pipelines where we publish data packaged as messages to specific topics. Client applications subscribe to these topics and get notifications whenever new messages are added. This way, you decouple the publisher and subscriber of the data through the messaging system. This loose coupling helps build powerful enterprise applications. Figure 10.2 shows this process in action.

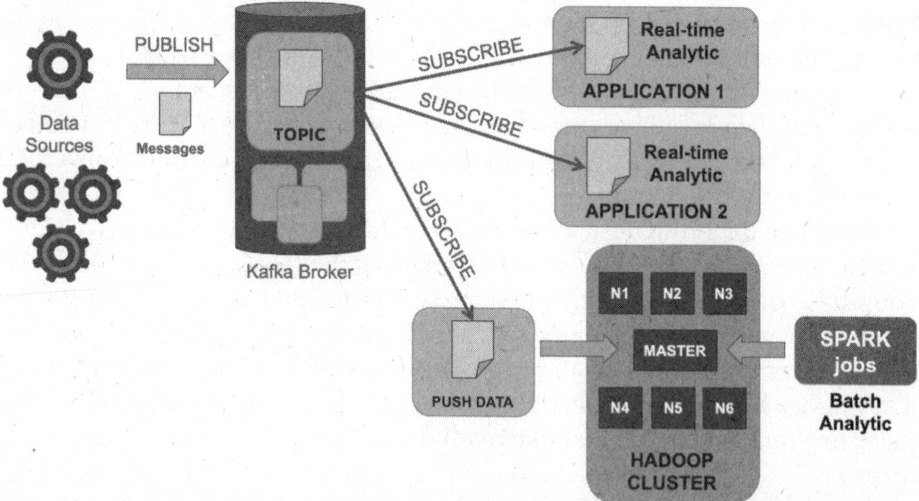

Figure 10.2: This Kafka-based system for data ingestion includes a Hadoop connector for long-term data storage

Figure 10.2 shows a Kafka broker with a topic where the data sources publish data wrapped as messages. A standardized format like JavaScript Object Notation (JSON) can be used to package your data and push this as a message. Typically, we create a topic of each data source so you can handle those messages differently. Kafka implements the publish-subscribe mechanism—one or more client or consumer applications can subscribe to a *topic* of messages, and as new messages come onto the topic, the clients that are subscribed are notified. For each new message the client can write some handling logic to describe what needs to be done with the data that comes in with the message. As new data comes in, we could do analysis on the data, such as calculate summaries, trends, and find outliers. These analytics gets triggered as new data comes in as messages and Kafka notifies the subscribers of specific topics about the new data. As you notice, we can easily add more clients to the same topic or data source, so that the same data can be shared between multiple clients. This makes this architecture highly loosely-coupled. Many modern software products follow this loosely-coupled architecture.

We also see in Figure 10.2 that there is a special client or consumer that pushes data in the Hadoop cluster. Here the messages coming in are sent to a Hadoop cluster to store data long term. Hadoop is the most popular open source data processing framework for handling batch jobs. It follows a master-slave architecture.

In Figure 10.2, we see a single master with six slave nodes. The master distributes data and processing logic across the slave nodes. In our example, along with the real-time or streaming clients, we also send our data to a Hadoop cluster where it gets stored in the Hadoop distributed filesystem. Now we can use this stored data for running batch jobs. For example, every hour, we could run a batch job on the stored data to calculate averages and key performance indicators (KPIs). Hadoop also integrates very well with another open source framework for batch processing, called *Apache Spark*. Spark can also run batch jobs on a distributed Hadoop cluster, but these jobs run in memory and are very fast and efficient. Other Big Data systems like Cassandra have ways to store data in a cluster and apply ML models to this data and extract results.

In this example, we see two scenarios for Big Data processing. We see real-time or streaming data processing using Kafka. We build subscribers for specific topics that consume the data and apply specific analytics on this data. We also see this data stored in a Hadoop cluster for long-term storage and applying ML models on this data in a batch mode.

Irrespective of the original data source, all data is converted to a common format and can be easily consumed by our analytic models. This pattern of decoupling the source of data from the consumer greatly simplifies your data science workflow and makes it highly scalable. You can quickly add new data sources by having them add data to an existing queue in an agreed-upon common format. Modern data science platforms typically support connectivity to these streaming and batch processing systems. You could have a platform like AWS SageMaker pull data from a Kafka topic and run your ML model or connect to a Hadoop data source (hosted on AWS) and read data to train your model.

Another trend that is emerging in the industry is having something called a *gold dataset*. This is a dataset that perfectly represents the kind of data the model will see in the field. Ideally it should have all the extreme cases, including any anomalies that need to be flagged. For example, say your model is looking at stock prices and making buy vs. sell decisions. If there are historical accounts of significant market rises or crashes, we will want to capture these cases and the corresponding buy or sell decisions (respectively) in our gold dataset. Any new model we develop should be able to correctly predict these patterns so that we know they function well. Typically, a gold dataset will consist of obvious cases that the model should predict for before being able to move to more complex patterns. We can also include validation against the gold dataset as a precondition for deployment into production, as part of our ML continuous integration process.

Data Cleansing

Data cleansing is all about getting rid of any noise in the data to make it ready to feed to the model. This could involve getting rid of duplicate records, imputing missing data, and changing the structure of data to fit a common format. Data cleansing may be done in Microsoft Excel by loading a CSV and applying simple search and filtering tools, although this is the most basic form and almost never done in true production environments. The volume of data in real-world systems cannot be handled in tools like Excel. We typically cleanse data using specialized streaming or batch jobs that contain rules for handling missing or bad data.

As we saw in the previous section on data collection, we could have a unified Kafka broker that serves us data from several different data sources. Now we could subscribe to these topics and write our logic to cleanse the data and write back the cleansed data to a new queue. The cleansing may be done in a batch job on data stored in Hadoop using a batch job processing framework like Spark.

There are also some dedicated tools that do data cleansing. A popular such tool is called *Tamr* and it internally uses AI to match data. It works on the *Unsupervised Learning* principle, where it tries to identify clusters of similar data and applies common cleansing strategies on this data. Another tool that has similar capabilities is called Talend. It is more deterministic and does cleansing based on predefined rules. These tools also connect to data sources like Hadoop and Kafka and provide cleansed data to build the ML model.

Another common problem with large systems with many data sources is a lack of master data. You have the same information replicated at multiple places and there is no standard identification field to relate the data. Common data fields like customer names and addresses are often stored in different ways in different systems, which causes problems while searching. Hence, large enterprises employ a Master Data Management (MDM) strategy, where data from specific data sources is considered a reference and used to represent the single source of truth. All systems use this as standard and work around it. This MDM system can serve as an excellent input for training ML models and should be considered for integration with the data science platform. Talend and Informatica are very popular MDM systems that help combine diverse data sources and establish a single source of truth to be used by downstream applications.

Analytics User Interface

The user interface for analytics should be intuitive and provide easy access to run descriptive statistics on our data. It should provide access to data sources like SQL and Kafka either programmatically or through code. It should allow us to try different ML algorithms on our data and compare the results.

Web-based user interfaces that can be opened in a browser have become the standard for building modern analytics models. Jupyter Notebooks is an open source solution that has been adopted by many data science platforms, including Google's Colaboratory (which you used earlier) and Amazon SageMaker. Jupyter provides a very intuitive programmatic interface for experimenting with data and running your code to get immediate results. Because Jupyter Notebooks is launched from Python, you can create an environment with all the necessary Python libraries and make them available from inside the Notebook. Now your Notebook can run a lot of these complex function calls without having to explicitly install these libraries. We saw an example of this in the previous chapter, when we ran custom code for running a model on a TPU in the Notebook provided by Google Colaboratory.

A couple of startups that have been working on a powerful configurable user interface for data science are H2O.ai and DataRobot. They provide very powerful user experiences that allow linking to data sources and model development without writing a line of code. These were still in the startup stage as of 2018, and we don't know how much they will grow by the time you are reading this book. Maybe one of them will become the de-facto UI tool for building ML models!

Let's now take a quick look at how H2O.ai allows us to build models without writing a single line of code. The interface may change, but I want to focus your attention on the thought process of simplifying the data science process for engineers. H2O is a distributed Machine Learning framework. It tries to address a few of the data science concerns we talked about earlier. It includes an analytics UI called H2O Flow and a Machine Learning engine that has support for some of the top supervised and unsupervised algorithms. It also provides support to store data in a cluster and distribute ML jobs on the cluster.

H2O is open source and freely available. You can download and run it on your local machine or get a Docker image from H2O.ai. Its only dependency is Java—it is basically a Java application on its own. I won't go into detail about installation and setup. I will show an example of building a model with custom data. The data I download is the wine quality dataset that is publicly available as a CSV file. The model built in H2O with this data file is shown in the next section—notice the ease of use in the user interface.

Developing an ML Regression Model in H2O Without Writing a Single Line of Code

H2O is a modern data science platform developed by the company H2O.ai. H2O allows users to fit thousands of potential models as part of discovering patterns in data. The H2O software runs can be called from the statistical package R, Python, and other environments. H2O also has an extremely intuitive web UI called H2O Flow that allows you to import data, build a model, and train it inside a web browser without writing a single line of code. All this is done using the web-based UI and its configuration. We will see an example next. To install H2O, follow the steps at this web link: `http://h2o-release.s3.amazonaws.com/h2o/rel-xu/1/index.html`.

You can install H2O as a standalone Java application or as a Docker container. After installing H2O as a standalone or Docker container, launch the web UI. You can explore different menus and help options in the web UI. For uploading your CSV file, select the Upload File option from the Data menu. H2O also supports connections to SQL databases and Hadoop Distributed File System (HDFS). The H2O web UI is shown in Figure 10.3.

Now let's use the wine quality CSV file and upload it (see Figure 10.4). Once the CSV file is uploaded, the tool will automatically parse the columns and extract the data. It will show you what fields or columns are available and what the datatype is. You can modify the datatype—for example, you can change numeric to categorical. If you have wine quality as an integer value between 0 and 10, it's better to convert it to categorical. Then by the click of a button, you can parse this CSV file and store the data in a compressed binary data structure called a *data frame*. The beauty of the data frame is that it is a distributed data structure, so if you have a five-node cluster, for example, you can store data distributed across this cluster. You don't have to worry about the distributed data storage concern—the tool takes care of that.

H2O also has an easy interface to split the data into training and validation data frames. That way, when you build the model, you can specify what data frame to use for training and which one for validation. You can specify the percentages you want to use to distribute your data into training and validation—typically this is an 80-20 or 75-25 split. See Figure 10.5.

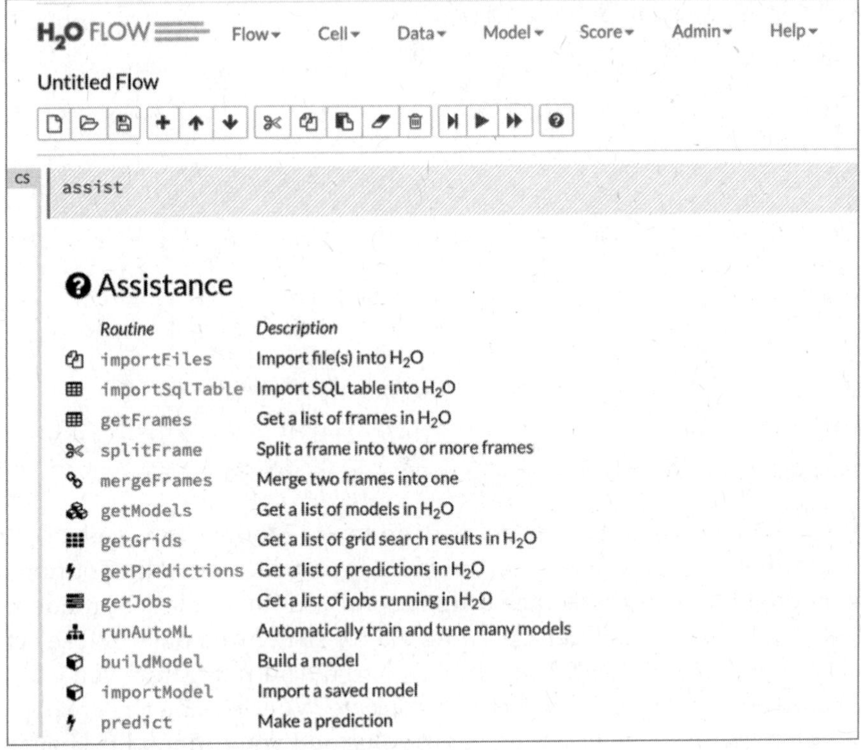

Figure 10.3: H2O web user interface (UI)—Flow

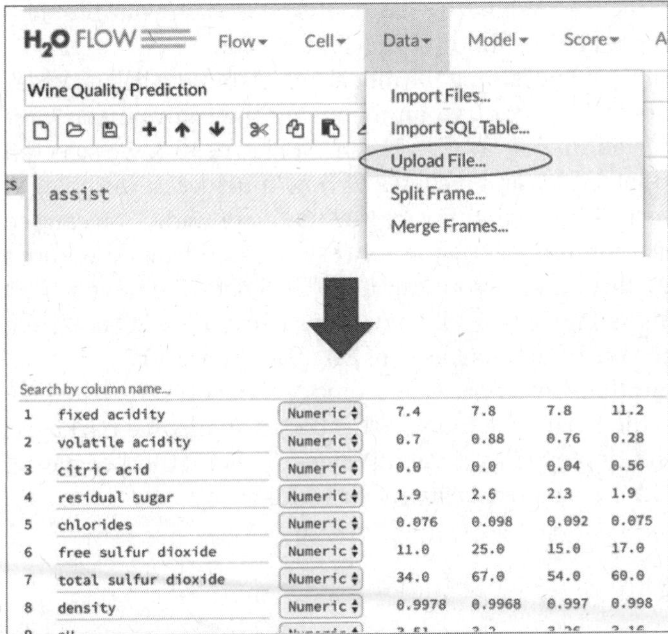

Figure 10.4: Uploading and parsing a CSV file—no code needed

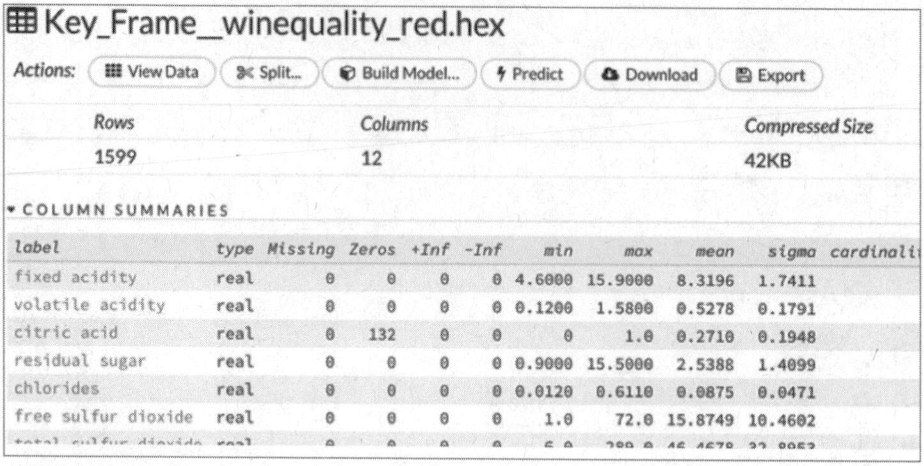

Key_Frame__winequality_red.hex

Actions: View Data | Split... | Build Model... | Predict | Download | Export

Rows	Columns	Compressed Size
1599	12	42KB

▾ COLUMN SUMMARIES

label	type	Missing	Zeros	+Inf	-Inf	min	max	mean	sigma	cardinali
fixed acidity	real	0	0	0	0	4.6000	15.9000	8.3196	1.7411	
volatile acidity	real	0	0	0	0	0.1200	1.5800	0.5278	0.1791	
citric acid	real	0	132	0	0	0	1.0	0.2710	0.1948	
residual sugar	real	0	0	0	0	0.9000	15.5000	2.5388	1.4099	
chlorides	real	0	0	0	0	0.0120	0.6110	0.0875	0.0471	
free sulfur dioxide	real	0	0	0	0	1.0	72.0	15.8749	10.4602	

Figure 10.5: Checking the parsed data frame and splitting it into training and testing sets

Once you have the data frames defined, go to the Model menu and select the algorithm you want to use. H2O (as of 2018) provides modeling options for several popular algorithms, including generalized linear models, random forests, etc. It also supports Deep Learning but for structured data. You select a model type, training and validation frames, and the output feature you want to predict. Based on selected model, the appropriate hyper-parameters are populated. Each hyper-parameter has a default value and you can modify that as needed. The selection of the correct hyper-parameters is a major concern that data scientists have to deal with. Usually, with experience, you develop some rules of thumb for selecting the right hyper-parameters based on your problem domain and the type of data being handled. See Figure 10.6.

Then you can submit the job for training the model, which builds the particular model. The tool also shows the accuracy parameters on the training and validation datasets you selected during configuration. In Figure 10.6, we selected a generalized linear model (GLM) and it shows us how much each variable (X) affects the dependent variable (Y)—in this case the quality of wine. You can see that this model was built, configured (hyper-parameters), and trained without writing any code purely through the configuration UI. That's the power H2O brings. Of course, coding will give you a lot more flexibility, but H2O is a great way to get familiar with the different aspects of ML. See Figure 10.7.

The model created can then be exported as a binary file. You can write Java code to call this binary file to run the model. This code can also be packaged as a web application and deployed as a microservice. This method of model deployment is gaining immense popularity in the industry.

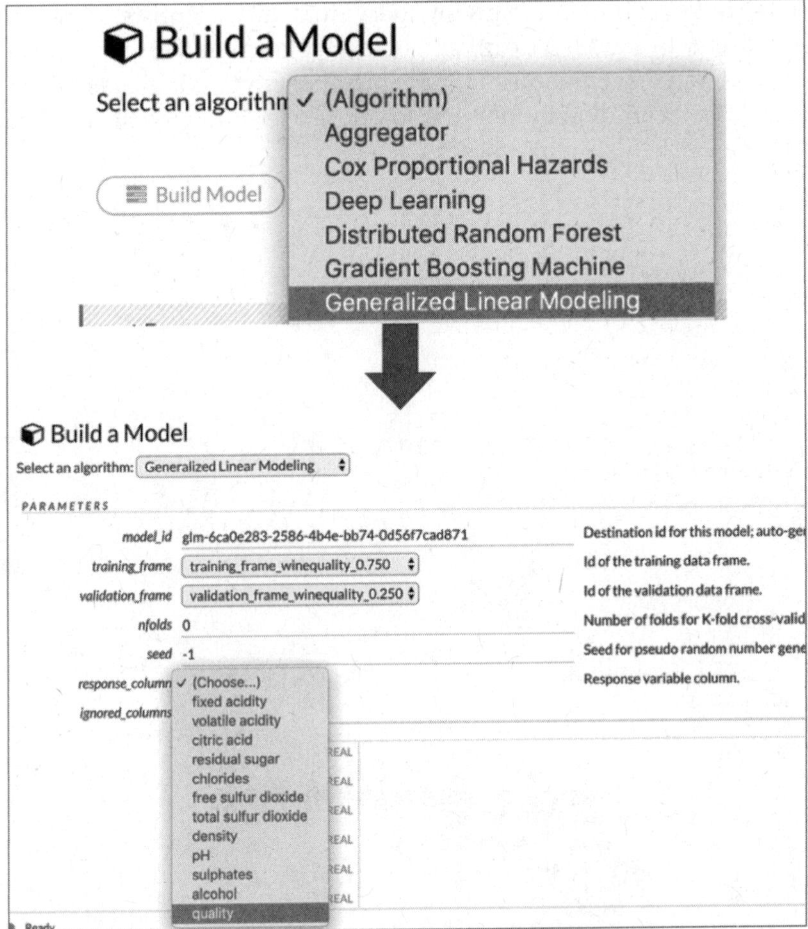

Figure 10.6: Selecting the model and defining hyper-parameters for it

That's the end of our small sidetrack to show an H2O example. Let's get back to discussing other major concerns the data scientist usually has to deal with.

Model Development

We saw how a platform like H2O takes care of the model building concerns by using an intuitive web-based UI for model development. You can host H2O or Jupyter Notebooks on a cluster of extremely powerful servers with many CPUs, memory, and storage. Then you can allow data scientists from your company, or maybe from across the world, to access the cluster and build models. This will save on the huge investment in giving individual data scientists powerful machines and licenses (like MATLAB) for model development. This is the most popular pattern today in companies that are big on analytics. It enables them to have a centralized common model development user interface that can be accessed by thin clients like web browsers.

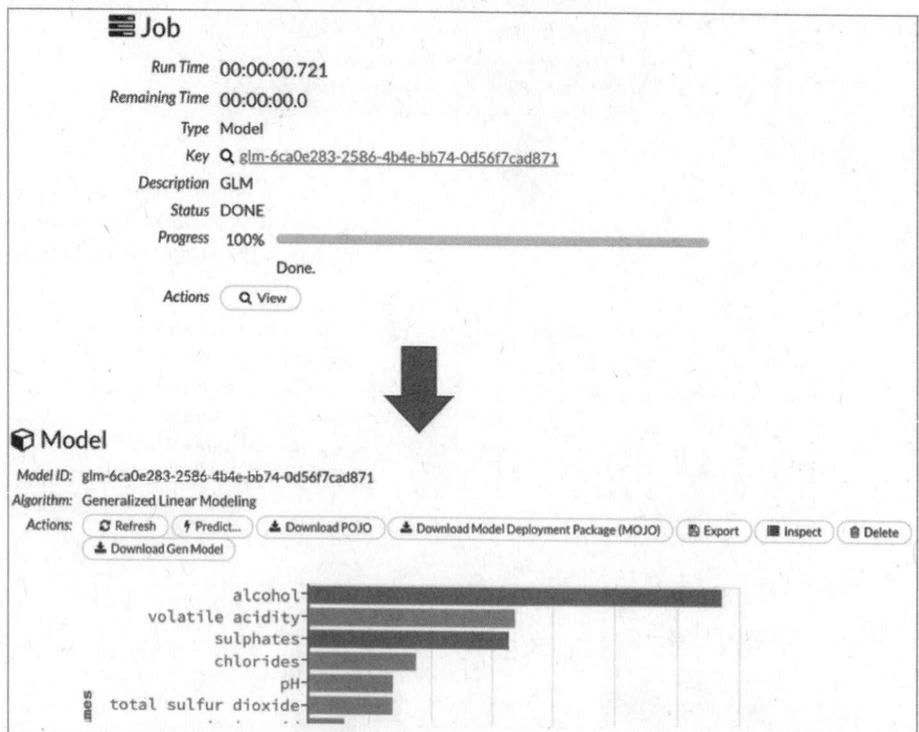

Figure 10.7: Running the training job. Evaluating the trained model. Still no code written!

If you are building models programmatically in Python, the library of choice is Scikit-Learn for shallow Machine Learning models. For Deep Learning, it's better to have a framework that allows you to build computation graphs representing the neural networks. Popular frameworks are TensorFlow by Google and PyTorch by Facebook. Both are free and open source, and can help build different feed-forward and recurrent network architectures to help you solve the problem in your domain. We typically call these frameworks because they don't just get plugged into an existing runtime, but come with a full runtime of their own. The frameworks allow developers to connect to their runtime and run training jobs using their language of choice, like Python, Java, or C++. When you build a TensorFlow model, it runs in a separate session on its own cluster, which may be composed of CPUs or GPUs.

Typically, many popular tools are available for model development with good documentation. This is the one concern that usually gets the most attention.

Training at Scale

For small demo projects and proofs of concept, you will mostly have limited data in a common format like CSV and build a quick model to see how well it fits on this data. However, the bigger the training data, the more generalized your model will be. In the real world, the data volumes will be very high and the data will often be distributed on a cluster using a framework like Hadoop. When you have large volume of data you most likely need a way to distribute your model training on a cluster to take advantage of the distributed nature of data. We saw the H2O training example earlier and it would automatically distribute your training job on the cluster. H2O captures this pattern very well but you need to be inside the H2O ecosystem to utilize it. There are other tools available that focus on addressing this concern of training at scale.

The Spark framework has an MLLib module that allows us to build distributed training pipelines. Spark has interfaces in Python, C++, and Java so you can write your logic in any language and get it running on the Spark framework. The idea behind Big Data frameworks like Spark and Hadoop is that you push the computing where the data is. For huge volumes of data distributed in a cluster, it's highly time-consuming to collect data centrally for processing. Hence the pattern here is to package your code and deploy on individual machines where the data exists and then collect the results. All this processing of data at the machines where data resides happens in background and end user has to write code just once. The Spark MLLib module usually is good for Machine Learning algorithms.

TensorFlow for Deep Learning also provides support for distributed model training. After creating a computational graph, you run this in a session, which may be run in a distributed environment. The session may also be run in a highly parallelized environment like a GPU. As we saw in the previous chapter, a GPU has thousands of parallel processing cores, each dedicated to performing linear algebra operations. Collectively, these cores help in running Deep Learning calculations in parallel and train models faster than on a CPU.

Google is also developing a TensorFlow distributed training module for Kubernetes, called *TFJob*. We will talk about this more in the last part of this chapter.

Hyper-Parameter Tuning

Typically, data scientists spend most of their time trying different hyper-parameters like the number of layers, neurons in a layer, learning rate, type of algorithm, etc. We talked about hyper-parameter tuning in the previous chapter. Usually, data scientists develop best practices for selecting hyper-parameters for a specific problem or dataset at hand. Tools like H2O capture some of these best practices and give recommendations. You can start with these recommendations and then search for better fitting hyper-parameters.

A new methodology, called *AutoML*, is evolving that automatically finds the best hyper-parameters by searching through many combinations in parallel. AutoML is still an evolving area. As it matures, this is surely going to save data scientists a lot of time.

H2O has an AutoML module in the Model menu that runs different types of models with different hyper-parameters in parallel. It shows a leaderboard with winning models. Google has a Cloud AutoML offering where you can upload your data like images and text and the system selects the right Deep Learning architecture with the right hyper-parameters. Let's quickly look at the AutoML module in H2O, discussed in the following section.

There is a new tool emerging on top of Keras called *AutoKeras*. It provides an AutoML interface for a Keras model. So now we can tune the hyper-parameters in a Deep Learning model and select the ones that give us the most accurate numbers.

H2O Example Using AutoML

We will continue with the earlier example of using the H2O web UI for regression analysis on the wine quality dataset. We will select the AutoML technique that H2O offers and see if it helps us. We first select the AutoML option and then select the training and validation data frames. See Figure 10.8.

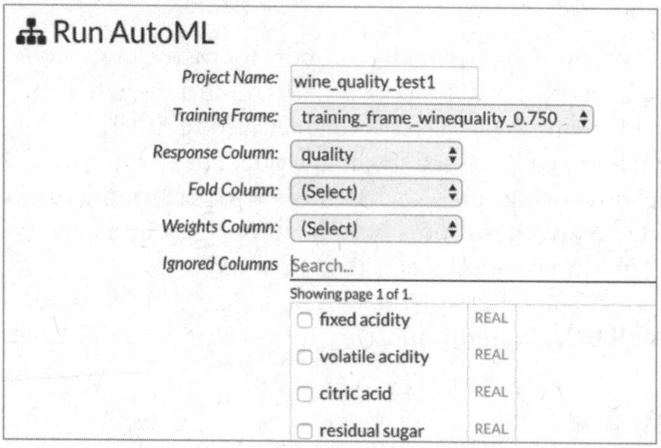

Figure 10.8: Selecting Run AutoML from the menu bar

Now we run the AutoML job. It will take a few minutes to run and show the progress on a progress bar. Once a significant number of models are run in parallel, we will get a leaderboard that compares the results. See Figure 10.9. Here we have regression, hence the `mean_residual_deviance` is used as the metric to score the model on the leaderboard. Any of the models on the leaderboard may be downloaded as binary and deployed.

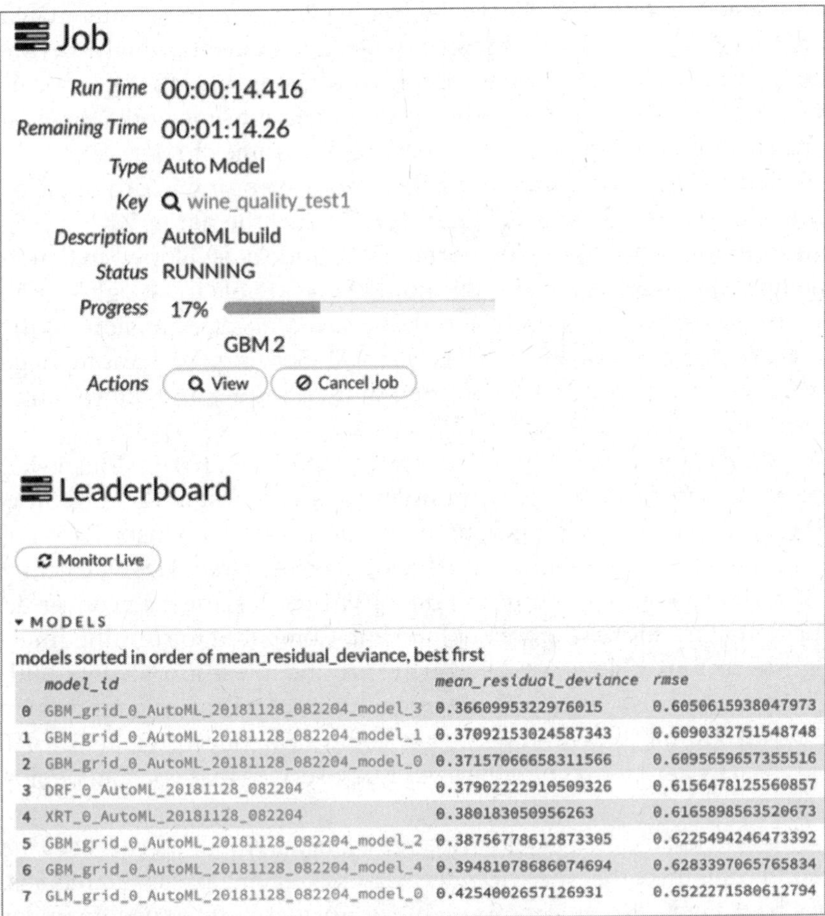

	model_id	mean_residual_deviance	rmse
0	GBM_grid_0_AutoML_20181128_082204_model_3	0.3660995322976015	0.6050615938047973
1	GBM_grid_0_AutoML_20181128_082204_model_1	0.37092153024587343	0.6090332751548748
2	GBM_grid_0_AutoML_20181128_082204_model_0	0.37157066658311566	0.6095659657355516
3	DRF_0_AutoML_20181128_082204	0.37902222910509326	0.6156478125560857
4	XRT_0_AutoML_20181128_082204	0.380183050956263	0.6165898563520673
5	GBM_grid_0_AutoML_20181128_082204_model_2	0.38756778612873305	0.6225494246473392
6	GBM_grid_0_AutoML_20181128_082204_model_4	0.39481078686074694	0.6283397065765834
7	GLM_grid_0_AutoML_20181128_082204_model_0	0.4254002657126931	0.6522271580612794

Figure 10.9: Running the AutoML job. Note the leaderboard of all different models compared for your datasets.

Automated Deployment

During model development, there are two main areas that can be automated—training the model and inference of new data. Training involves tuning the weights using the training dataset so the model can make accurate predictions. Inferencing is feeding new data to the model and making predictions. We developed a web application in the last chapter that feeds data to a trained model, makes the inferences, and shows the results in an application. This will work for a small application with basic models. However, for large applications, we need loose coupling between the software code and the model.

The most popular method of creating this loose coupling is using the microservices architecture pattern. The model gets packaged as a container and deployed as a microservice that gets called with lightweight HTTP requests. This can be done using a custom application like we did in Chapter 7 or using an automated deployment framework. Machine Learning model deployment frameworks are still evolving. Amazon SageMaker has a deployment engine that's very specific to AWS. There are a few openly available model serving frameworks that you can plug into your data science platform. Let's look at some of these.

A popular open source deployment and inference engine is provided by Google called *TensorFlow-Serving (TF-Serving)*. Despite the name, TF-Serving is pretty flexible and can also deploy normal ML models developed in Scikit-Learn. The only catch is that the model should be available in Google's open prototype buffer format. The model should be saved as an extension PB file and can then be deployed as a microservice in TF-Serving. You can manage different versions of a model and TF-Serving will load these and allow you to invoke them with separate URLs.

Another popular inference engine that is evolving is NVIDIA's Tensor-RT. This is becoming very popular for running models very fast at the edge. It is also gaining traction for server and Cloud model deployments. Tensor-RT is not related to TensorFlow—it allows models developing in different Deep Learning frameworks to be deployed and inferred upon. The models must be converted into Tensor-RT binary format before deployment. Compared to running inference using native TensorFlow, we usually get around 10x improvement with Tensor-RT. This is because Tensor-RT re-creates the Deep Learning models by applying several optimizations and with more compact architectures. Tensor-RT is available as a Docker-based containerized microservice that you can deploy in your environment.

TF-Serving is available as a Docker image in DockerHub. You can use this image to build containers that serve as microservices serving packaged models. Models are packaged into the prototype buffer format with a specific folder structure. Let's see how to do deployments. We will use a very simple example of TensorFlow code to build a basic computational graph. We will not use Keras because we don't have a deep network with many layers. We will just do basic operations to illustrate the concept.

Listing 10.1 shows the code for a simple computation graph that takes two input variables (`x2`, `x2`) and calculates an output (`y`).

Listing 10.1: TensorFlow Code to Build a Simple Model and Export It as Prototype Buffer—app.py

```
# import the TensorFlow library
import tensorflow as tf
```

```
# define path where model will be exported - with version
export_path = "/tmp/test_model/1"

# start a tensorflow session
with tf.Session() as sess:
    # define 2 constants and assign vales
    a = tf.constant(10.0)
    b = tf.constant(20.0)

    # Define 2 placeholders for x1 and x2 - fed at inference time
            # Our prediction of Y is a simple formula, y = a*x1 + b*x2
    x1 = tf.placeholder(tf.float32)
    x2 = tf.placeholder(tf.float32)
    y = tf.add(tf.multiply(a, x1), tf.multiply(b, x2))

    # initialize the variables of our graph
    tf.global_variables_initializer().run()

    # Creates the protobuf objects that encapsulate input/outputs
    tensor_info_x1 = tf.saved_model.utils.build_tensor_info(x1)
    tensor_info_x2 = tf.saved_model.utils.build_tensor_info(x2)
    tensor_info_y = tf.saved_model.utils.build_tensor_info(y)


    # Defines the signatures, uses the TF Predict API
    prediction_signature = (
        tf.saved_model.signature_def_utils.build_signature_def(
            inputs={'x1': tensor_info_x1, 'x2': tensor_info_x2 },
            outputs={'y': tensor_info_y}, method_name=tf.saved_model.
signature_constants.PREDICT_METHOD_NAME))


    # export the model to folder
    print ('Exporting trained model to', export_path)
    builder = tf.saved_model.builder.SavedModelBuilder(export_path)

    # export so that it will be called by tensorflow serving
    builder.add_meta_graph_and_variables(
          sess, [tf.saved_model.tag_constants.SERVING],
          signature_def_map={
              'predict_images':
                  prediction_signature,
              tf.saved_model.signature_constants.DEFAULT_SERVING_
SIGNATURE_DEF_KEY:
                  prediction_signature,
          },
          main_op=tf.tables_initializer())

    # save the model
    builder.save()
```

If you run this file, it will create a folder called `/tmp/test_model/1` and save the model we just created inside the folder. This was a deterministic model that will always give the same output. We could capture complex patterns and build this model.

Now we will create a container with the TensorFlow-Serving image and try to invoke our model through a REST API. The TensorFlow-Serving image is available in the open DockerHub repository and can be downloaded. We will run the Docker container from the image and pass the folder where we developed the model as a parameter. We will also map a network port from the container to our machine so that you can access the microservice by calling the host machine. The TensorFlow-Serving will wrap our model and make it available as a microservice. See Listing 10.2.

Listing 10.2: Deploying the Model as a Microservice

```
$ docker run -it --rm -p 8501:8501 -v '/tmp/test_model:/models/test_
model' -e MODEL_NAME=test_model tensorflow/serving
```

Notice that we passed the model folder and name. Also, we mapped port 8501 to our local port. The image name is `tensorflow/serving`. Now you can invoke this model directly using REST API calls, as shown here:

```
$ curl -d '{"instances": [{"x1":2.0,"x2":3.0},{"x1":0.5,"x2":0.2}]}'  -X
POST http://localhost:8501/v1/models/test_model:predict

{
    "predictions": [80.0, 9.0]
}
```

We call the URL of the model exposed by TensorFlow-Serving. We pass JSON data indicating the number of points to process—instances—and for each, the values of variables `x1` and `x2`. That's it. We can pass more data packaged as the JSON and the image will be served as a container. The result is a JSON string with the values of predictions. The same can be done for Deep Learning models with libraries like Keras.

Deployment of DL Models in Keras

The previous section was a very basic example of a computational graph in TensorFlow that we deployed as a microservice—not very impressive. Now let's take a Deep Learning model and "serve" it and invoke it using a client application. We will use the Keras model created in Chapter 5 for classifying between Pepsi and Coca-Cola logos. If you recall—we saved this model as an HDF5 file called `my _ logo _ model.h5`. We will save this file in a folder and run the code in Listing 10.3 to convert it into the prototype buffer format that TensorFlow-Serving expects.

Typically to do this sort of conversion it's better to write a generic utility file rather than custom code each time. Let's write a utility that will take the H5 file, output the model name and version as parameters, and convert your H5 file into a versioned model that we will later serve.

You can choose any language to write this utility as long as it can handle command-line parameters and call TensorFlow libraries. I will use Python for this. Listing 10.3 shows the code.

Listing 10.3: Python Code for a Command-Line Utility to Convert a Keras H5 Model File to a Versioned Prototype Buffer PB File—h5_to_serving.py

```
import os
import sys

# check if h5 file and export folder are provided as arguments
if len (sys.argv) != 4:
    print ("Usage: python h5_to_serving.py <my_file.h5>
                            <model_name> <model_version>")
    sys.exit (1)

# get the h5 file to convert and export folder
h5_file = sys.argv[1]
model_name = sys.argv[2]
model_version = sys.argv[3]
export_folder = './' + model_name + '/' + model_version

# print(export_folder)

if os.path.isdir(export_folder):
    print ("Model name, version exists - delete existing folder.")
    sys.exit (1)

import tensorflow as tf

# load the h5 file using keras on tensorflow
model = tf.keras.models.load_model(h5_file)
tf.keras.backend.set_learning_phase(0)

# Fetch the Keras session and save the model
# The signature definition is defined by the input and output tensors
with tf.keras.backend.get_session() as sess:
    tf.saved_model.simple_save(
        sess,
        export_folder,
        inputs={'input_image': model.input},
        outputs={t.name:t for t in model.outputs})

# close the session
sess.close()
```

You can use this utility and it will generate your PB file. Digging into the code, you will see that it ensures that you have passed the right parameters for the H5 file and the model name and version. Also, it verifies that the same model and version do not exist. It's a good idea when you're writing any code to check for failure modes like this. It greatly improves the reliability of your code. You never know what the user will enter for these inputs.

Then the code loads the Keras saved model from the H5 file. Since Keras runs on top of TensorFlow, this model is also automatically loaded in a TensorFlow session object. All we have to do now is save this session object and we have our prototype buffer file. That's what we do and we have the model ready for serving. TensorFlow-Serving takes the structure of `<Model _ Name>/<Version>` for the folder structure. This allows you to manage the versions of your model better.

Now let's use this utility to convert the `my_logo_model.h5` file from earlier. We put the file in the same folder where we run this Python script and then run the code shown in Listing 10.4.

Listing 10.4: Convert the H5 File to PB and Run It in a Serving Container

```
$ python h5_to_serving.py my_logo_model.h5 my_logo_model 1
```

We pass the model H5 file and output the model name and version as parameters. The result will be a new folder, called `my _ logo _ model/1`, which contains the PB file and a `variables` folder:

```
$ ls my_logo_model/1/
   saved_model.pb   variables
```

Now we will create a Docker container like we did earlier using the `tensorflow/serving` image. This container will host our model and expose an HTTP interface to call our model. We don't have to write any custom application code—all the piping for exposing the REST API is taken care by TensorFlow-Serving:

```
$ docker run -it --rm -p 8501:8501 -v '/my_folder_path/my_logo_model:/
models/logo_model' -e MODEL_NAME=logo_model tensorflow/serving

     Adding/updating models.
Successfully reserved resources to load servable  {name: logo_model
version: 1}
     ....
Successfully loaded servable version {name: logo_model version: 1}
```

We now have our logo detection model loaded in TensorFlow-Serving to serve as a microservice. In the earlier example, we used the CURL command to call our model microservice and pass parameters. In this example, we have to pass a whole 150×150 sized image to the model. For this, we use Python to load the image and call our service. Listing 10.5 builds a client that does exactly this.

Listing 10.5: Python Code for Calling Our Model Microservice

```
import requests
import json
from keras.preprocessing.image import load_img
from keras.preprocessing.image import img_to_array

# our Model Microservice URL - provide by TensorFlow Serving
MODEL_URL = 'http://localhost:8501/v1/models/logo_model:predict'

# create a function to call our Microservice and predict logo
def predict_logo(image_filename):
    # load the image and convert to array
    image = img_to_array(load_img(image_filename, target_
size=(150,150))) / 255.

    # create the payload to pass to HTTP request
    payload = {
        "instances": [{'input_image': image.tolist()}]
    }

    # make the HTTP post call
    r = requests.post(MODEL_URL, json=payload)

    # get the JSON result
    return json.loads(r.content)

# now we will call the function for different images

print('Prediction for test1.png = ', predict_logo('test1.png'))
print('Prediction for test2.png = ', predict_logo('test2.png'))
```

Figure 10.10 shows the images we used for our test (`test1.png` and `test2.png`).

'test2.png'

'test1.png'

Figure 10.10: Images used to validate the model

OUTPUT:

```
Prediction for test1.png =  {'predictions': [[1.23764e-24]]}
Prediction for test2.png =  {'predictions': [[1.0]]}
```

We see that for the Coke image (`test1.png`), when we pass the image to our model, it gives a prediction close to 0 and for the Pepsi image (`test2.png`), it gives the value of 1. That's how we trained the model and we see good results. You can also use images downloaded on the Internet and see the results.

Keep in mind that the client code we ran does not have any direct TensorFlow dependency. We take the image, normalize it (dividing by 255), convert it to a list, and pass it to our REST endpoint. The result comes back as a JSON value that can be decoded to get our result as 0 or 1. This is a binary classification; hence, we just have 1 result with 0 or 1 outcomes. Practically, you will build more complex models that will do multi-class predictions. These can also be hosted on TensorFlow-Serving.

We have seen how a major concern for data scientists—deployment of models at scale—can be handled using TensorFlow-Serving. As we saw earlier, since TensorFlow-Serving runs as a Docker container, we can easily package it as a deployment in Kubernetes and scale the deployment to multiple pods. Kubernetes will handle the scaling and fail-over to handle large client loads. You will have to create a volume for storing your model files. Kubernetes includes concepts like persistent volumes and persistent volume claims that can take care of this.

Let's return to another major concern for data scientists—logging and monitoring—and discuss how we can take care of them using this platform.

Logging and Monitoring

Finally, the two most common concerns among all types of software applications relate to logging and monitoring. You need to be able to continuously monitor your software application to catch and log errors, such as out-of-memory errors, runtime exceptions, permission errors, etc. You need to log these errors or items of interest so that the operations team can identify the health of your software or model. Your application or microservice that serves the model also needs to be monitored so that it is available for clients. If you use a platform like Kubernetes, it comes with log-collection and monitoring tools that help address these concerns. The deployment platforms like TensorFlow-Serving and Tensor-RT have logging built in and can give you quick outputs.

Monitoring and logging concerns are typically passed on to a platform like Kubernetes. If we deploy our model training and inference microservices on Kubernetes, we would use a monitoring tool like Prometheus and a logging tool like Logstash. Both of these can also be deployed as microservices on the same Kubernetes cluster.

Putting the ML Platform Together

In the previous section, we saw how tools are available to address specific data science concerns. We also saw how Kubernetes can act as a single unified platform for addressing software application concerns. By extending Kubernetes, we can also address these data science concerns. Because a lot of the tools we saw earlier can be packaged as microservices, we could host specific microservices to enable Kubernetes to handle data science requirements. This extension is done by an open source project being developed at Google, called *Kubeflow*.

Kubeflow allows easy and uniform deployment of Machine Learning workflows on a Kubernetes cluster. The same ML deployment pipeline can be done on a local MiniKube, an on-premise Kubernetes cluster, and a Cloud-hosted environment.

Kubeflow takes industry-leading solutions to address many data science concerns and deploys them together on Kubernetes. I will not talk about Kubeflow installation on a Kubernetes cluster, mainly because these instructions keep changing as the product is being stabilized. You can get the latest instructions at Kubeflow.org.

Once Kubeflow is installed in its namespace, you can list the deployments and services in that namespace to see what was installed. Kubeflow is a high-level application that is installed on Kubernetes and it installs all specific microservices. Kubeflow by itself does not solve any data science concerns but works on integrating individual components.

At a bare minimum you should see JupyterHub (Analytics UI), TF-Job (Model training), and TF-Serving (Deployment) components. You can start with the Jupyter Notebooks to build the model and submit it to the TF-Job to schedule a distributed training job. Once you have model trained you can deploy it using TF-Serving as a microservice on the Kubernetes cluster. Clients can call HTTP API to invoke the model and run inference. TF-Serving also supports Google's gRPC protocol, which is significantly faster than HTTP. gRPC packages data in binary format and takes advantage of HTTP/2 to handle unstructured data, like images.

As you see, Kubeflow is not a complete solution by itself; it's more like the glue that gives us a standard interface to integrate ML components on Kubernetes. Over time, more and more components will get added to Kubeflow and will be easily deployable on Kubernetes. If you are building your own platform for data scientists, Kubeflow on Kubernetes should definitely be on the top of your list.

Summary

In this chapter, we talked about the major common concerns affecting data scientists, like data cleansing, analytics UI, and distributed training. We looked at some industry standard tools—like TensorFlow-Serving and Jupyter—for addressing specific concerns. Then we looked at an upcoming technology called Kubeflow, which provides a standard way to deploy ML workloads on Kubernetes. We also saw an example of deploying a simple TensorFlow analytic using TF-Serving.

That's it folks, for now. We saw basic concepts of Machine Learning and Deep Learning. We learned how to handle structured and unstructured data. We developed DL models for analyzing text and image data using a popular library called Keras. We developed models to classify soda logo images and identify sentiment from text. We also saw some cool examples of making AI models create paintings and generate new images. In the second half of the book, we looked at packaging the models into microservices and managing their deployment. We looked at different data science concerns like data collection, cleansing, preparation, model building, hyper-parameter tuning, distributed training, and deployment. Finally, we learned about Kubeflow, which is an upcoming technology to deploy ML workflows on Kubernetes.

A Final Word . . .

All the code from this book is available on this GitHub link: `https://github.com/dattarajrao/keras2kubernetes`.

Hopefully this book has given you a holistic picture of building AI models and deploying these at scale in production environments. Often times we see data scientists focus on the algorithm development and don't have enough tools in their repertoire to handle other concerns like data cleansing, distributed training, and deployment. As we saw, this technology is still being developed. There is huge opportunity in this space and new solutions coming up. Hopefully this book has triggered your interest in this space and you will be able to leverage the right tools when you face these problems. Do write to me with any feedback and comments about the book. Here's wishing you all the best on your real-world Machine Learning journey!

APPENDIX A

References

In this appendix, I provide references to books, papers, and online articles that cover many topics in detail that I have mentioned in the book. I list the references by each chapter and include references that are mostly free and include code samples that you can readily use. Thanks to the absolutely amazing Deep Learning community, there are many such resources readily available to you. As long as you understand the basic concepts around ML and DL, you should be able to follow these references and the code.

Chapter 1: Big Data and Artificial Intelligence

- Dr. Andrew Ng from Stanford is one of the foremost researchers in Machine Learning and AI. I highly recommend his videos and news items that define the state of AI.

  `https://www.deeplearning.ai/the-state-of-artificial-intelligence-andrew-ng-at-mit-emtech-2017/`

- General Electric has been leading the Big Data revolution in the industrial space with the rise of the industrial Internet. Here is an excellent whitepaper on the prospect of industrial IoT from GE.

  `https://www.ge.com/docs/chapters/Industrial _ Internet.pdf`

- The industrial IoT revolution is known as Industry 4.0 especially in Europe. Here is a nice article by Bernard Marr explaining this.

  `https://www.forbes.com/sites/bernardmarr/2018/09/02/what-is-industry-4-0-heres-a-super-easy-explanation-for-anyone/#2c0bb9af9788`

- This is a nice article showing how Amazon transformed itself around Artificial Intelligence. It includes a great example of driving a platform vision to improve several products at once.

  `https://www.wired.com/story/amazon-artificial-intelligence-flywheel`

- There have been cool developments in the news about modern AI generating images of paintings and fake celebrities.

  AI-generated art sold for $432,500!

  `https://www.christies.com/features/A-collaboration-between-two-artists-one-human-one-a-machine-9332-1.aspx`

  AI generates fake celebrity photos.

  `https://www.theverge.com/2017/10/30/16569402/ai-generate-fake-faces-celebs-nvidia-gan`

- Finally, I recommend visiting the AI research pages of these top companies. They often have amazing content. Here are some pages I often visit.

  - Google `https://ai.google/`
  - Facebook `https://onnx.ai`
  - NVIDIA `https://www.nvidia.com/en-gb/deep-learning-ai/`
  - Intel `https://software.intel.com/en-us/ai-academy`
  - IBM Watson `https://www.ibm.com/watson/`
  - Salesforce Einstein `https://www.salesforce.com/products/einstein/overview/`
  - H2O: `https://www.h2o.ai/`

Chapter 2: Machine Learning

- Whenever someone asks me for a good starting place to learn ML and DL, my first reference is always the video course by Dr. Andrew Ng. This is universally accepted as the foremost resource for learning ML. It explains the different algorithms extremely well, giving you a lot of details of the basic concepts. You can join a certificate course at the following sites. The certification costs, but you can see the course videos for free.

  `https://www.coursera.org/learn/machine-learning`

  `https://www.deeplearning.ai/`

  Some parts of the course material are also available for free on YouTube.
  `https://www.youtube.com/user/StanfordUniversity`

- Google offers an online free crash course in ML that is quite good.

  https://developers.google.com/machine-learning/crash-course/ml-intro

- One of my personal favorites is the podcast on basics of ML by Tyler Renelle. I found myself hooked to this one due to Tyler's simplistic way of explaining several concepts. Highly recommended.

  http://ocdevel.com/mlg

- Here are a couple more recommended podcasts.

  https://www.thetalkingmachines.com/

  https://soundcloud.com/datahack-radio

  https://www.oreilly.com/topics/oreilly-data-show-podcast

- Another great site with awesome ML articles and sample code is Analytics Vidhya. This was founded by Kunal Jain and provides great tutorials. Here are some I found extremely helpful:

  https://www.analyticsvidhya.com/blog/2017/09/common-machine-learning-algorithms/

  https://www.analyticsvidhya.com/blog/2016/01/complete-tutorial-learn-data-science-python-scratch-2/

  https://www.analyticsvidhya.com/blog/2018/03/comprehensive-collection-deep-learning-datasets/

- Kaggle is an amazing resource for ML practitioners. It has competitions hosted by companies where they provide good datasets that you can analyze. You compete with data scientists around the world to build models with highest accuracy, scored against a predefined result. It's a great way to explore your data science skills and play with real-world data, and many of the competitions involve cash prizes. Highly recommended.

  https://www.kaggle.com/

Chapter 3: Handling Unstructured Data

- Computer vision details and tutorials are available at the OpenCV tutorials website. I prefer Python, but they have tutorials for C++ and Java also.

  https://docs.opencv.org/3.0-beta/doc/py_tutorials/py_tutorials.html

- Another fantastic resource for computer vision tutorials with some extremely well-written code is this site by Adrian Rosebrock. I particularly appreciate the sample code Adrian provides because it is highly generalized and easy to reuse.

  https://www.pyimagesearch.com/

Adrian also conducts a crash course in computer vision that is pretty good.

- For core ML algorithms, the library we use (Scikit-Learn) also provides some very good tutorials.

  `https://scikit-learn.org/stable/tutorial/index.html`

- For Natural Language Processing (NLP), there is an online tutorial by the NLP Toolkit that is pretty comprehensive.

  `https://www.nltk.org/book/`

- Also for NLP, I found this particular article straightforward and helpful.

  `https://dzone.com/articles/nlp-tutorial-using-python-nltk-simple-examples`

- Here is a nice primer on using Jupyter Notebooks.

  `https://www.dataquest.io/blog/jupyter-notebook-tutorial/`

Chapter 4: Deep Learning Using Keras

- For Deep Learning, I highly recommend the Andrew Ng video course mentioned previously. The concepts are explained beautifully and it's the best way to get started.

  `https://www.coursera.org/learn/machine-learning`

- Keras has been officially recognized as the premier frontend library to TensorFlow. The TensorFlow website now has some very good code examples that explain building deep networks using Keras.

  `https://www.tensorflow.org/tutorials/`

- For Deep Learning with Keras, I recommend the book *Deep Learning with Python* by none other than the founder of Keras, François Chollet.

  `https://www.manning.com/books/deep-learning-with-python`

- Here's a list of useful Keras resources available at François Chollet's GitHub page:

  `https://github.com/fchollet/keras-resources`

Chapter 5: Advanced Deep Learning

- Another great resource on Deep Learning is the book *TensorFlow for Deep Learning* by Reza Zadeh and Bharath Ramsundar. I particularly recommend the "Reinforcement Learning" chapter in this book.

- The website KDNuggets.com has a set of very useful Deep Learning articles using Keras. https://www.kdnuggets.com/2017/10/seven-steps-deep-learning-keras.html

Chapter 6: Cutting-Edge Deep Learning Projects

- The technical paper, "A Neural Algorithm of Artistic Style," by Leon A. Gatys, Alexander S. Ecker, and Matthias Bethge, is a great resource.

  https://arxiv.org/abs/1508.06576

- Check out the neural style transfer post with sample code by Raymond Yuan, from the TensorFlow team.

  https://medium.com/tensorflow/neural-style-transfer-creating-art-with-deep-learning-using-tf-keras-and-eager-execution-7d541ac31398

- The technical paper, "Generative Adversarial Networks," by Ian J. Goodfellow, Jean Pouget-Abadie, Mehdi Mirza, Bing Xu, David Warde-Farley, Sherjil Ozair, Aaron Courville, and Yoshua Bengio, is also a good resource.

  https://arxiv.org/abs/1406.2661

- Check out the article on generative adversarial networks with sample code from my favorite website, Analytics Vidhya.

  https://www.analyticsvidhya.com/blog/2017/06/introductory-generative-adversarial-networks-gans/

- Check out this fantastic article by Dr. David Ellison on fraud detection using auto encoders in Keras.

  https://www.datascience.com/blog/fraud-detection-with-tensorflow

Chapter 7: AI in the Modern Software World

- The Kubernetes website provides an excellent and interactive tutorial on setting up a cluster, including the basic commands. This is a great way to get familiar with the interface without doing the install on your machine.

  https://kubernetes.io/docs/tutorials/kubernetes-basics/

- Another great website that provides great interactive tutorials is Katacoda. You get the same interface that you see in a production Kubernetes install, but can safely try all the commands. It's an amazing way to teach a technology.

  https://www.katacoda.com/courses/kubernetes

Chapter 8: Deploying AI Models as Microservices

- Check out this excellent overview tutorial on microservices architecture by Martin Fowler and James Lewis. There's no code here, but it includes an amazing explanation of core concepts defining the architecture.

  `https://martinfowler.com/articles/microservices.html`

- Here's my GitHub repository, with an open source toolkit for quickly converting an image processing Keras model to a microservice hosted on Flask.

  `https://github.com/dattarajrao/keras2kubernetes`

Chapter 9: Machine Learning Development Lifecycle

- Here is a nice whitepaper by Mesosphere on building an end-to-end platform for data science. It covers several of the data science concerns and how a platform can address them.

  `https://mesosphere.com/resources/building-data-science-platform/`

- Check out "The 7 Steps of Machine Learning" video by the Google Cloud Platform team.

  `https://www.youtube.com/watch?v=nKW8Ndu7Mjw`

- Check out the blog post, "Data Scientists and Deploying Machine Learning into Production: Not a Great Match," from Algorithmia.

  `https://blog.algorithmia.com/data-scientists-and-deploying-machine-learning-into-production-not-a-great-match/`

Chapter 10: A Platform for Machine Learning

- Check out this Intel blog on training a TensorFlow model and deploying on Kubernetes.

  `https://ai.intel.com/lets-flow-within-kubeflow/`

- This is a nice article from the Google TensorFlow team called "Serving ML Quickly with TensorFlow Serving and Docker," by Gautam Vasudevan and Abhijit Karmarkar.

  `https://medium.com/tensorflow/serving-ml-quickly-with-tensorflow-serving-and-docker-7df7094aa008`

- Check out Katacoda's interactive tutorial on deploying Machine Learning workloads using Kubeflow and Kubernetes.

  `https://www.katacoda.com/kubeflow/scenarios/deploying-kubeflow`

Index

N